WITHDRAWN

Genius in France

Genius in France

AN IDEA AND ITS USES

Ann Jefferson

PRINCETON UNIVERSITY PRESS
PRINCETON AND OXFORD

Copyright © 2015 by Princeton University Press

Published by Princeton University Press, 41 William Street, Princeton, New Jersey 08540

In the United Kingdom: Princeton University Press, 6 Oxford Street, Woodstock, Oxfordshire OX20 1TW

press.princeton.edu

Jacket image: Neuroglia cells (so-called "genius" cells)

ISBN 978-0-691-16065-8

Library of Congress Control Number: 2014950433

British Library Cataloging-in-Publication Data is available

This book has been composed in Minion & Avant Garde

Printed on acid-free paper ∞

Printed in the United States of America

10 9 8 7 6 5 4 3 2 1

for Mike, again

O his breaths, his heads, his racing; the terrible
swiftness of the perfection of forms and of action.
O fecundity of the spirit and immensity of the
universe!

. . .

Let us, on this winter night, from cape to cape, from the tumultu-
ous pole to the castle, from the crowd to the beach, from glance to
glance, our strengths and feelings numb, learn to hail him and see
him, and send him back,
and under the tides and at the summit of snowy deserts, follow his
seeing, his breathing, his body, his day.

—Rimbaud, "Génie," Illuminations

Translated by John Ashbery

Contents

Illustrations

Preface

This book owes its existence to a chance conversation over dinner in Edinburgh some thirteen years ago, during the course of which I realized for the first time that "genius" is a word that it is risky to claim to understand. This discovery bothered me, and I began to read. One thing led to another, and by the time I had amassed a sizeable bibliography I had the good fortune to teach a graduate seminar in the Department of French and Romance Philology at Columbia University during the fall semester of 2006; the enthusiasm of the participants confirmed my sense that there were so many things one might mean by "genius" that it was worth writing a book about them. Let me therefore begin these preliminary remarks by recording my gratitude to Peter France and Peter Dayan for that conversation, to my colleagues at Columbia for my time as visiting professor, and to the students in the seminar for the zest and the diligence with which they entered into the spirit of the project.

I have been equally blessed by the generosity of friends and colleagues whose own interest in genius has provided me with a treasure trove of thoughts and references on which to draw. Even where I have not directly incorporated these leads, they have all nourished my reflections and contributed to my understanding of the topic. Over and above the specifics of information, reference, and quotation, the conversations I have had and the emails that followed have been a precious reassurance that my curiosity about genius is more widely shared. I hope there are no deserving names missing from this list, but I should like to place on record how much I owe to Frédérique Aït-Touati, Alain Ausoni, Claire Bazin, Terence Cave, Tim Chesters, Nicholas Cronk, Tim Farrant, Sam Ferguson, Simon Gaunt, Angelica Goodden, Mairéad Hanrahan, Nick Harrison, Wojciech Jajdelski, Andrew Kahn, Catriona Kelly, Marie-Chantal Killeen, Orsolya Kiss, Dilwyn Knox, Elisabeth Ladenson, Robin Lane Fox, Karen Leeder, Ann Lewis, Jane Lightfoot, Katherine Lunn-Rockliffe, Francesco Manzini, Toril Moi, Jonathan Morton, Adeline Mueller, Bradley Murray, Sotiris Paraschas, Thomas Pavel, Roger Pearson, Will Poole, the late Siegbert Prawer, J. C. Smith, Galin Tihanov, Kate Tunstall, Alain Viala, Caroline Warman, Wes Williams, Jenny Yee, and Andrei Zorin.

I also wish to thank the organizers and audiences of the various seminars and conferences that gave me a chance to air early versions of some chapters and to profit from responses to them. In this connection, I should like to make special mention of Brigitte Mahuzier and the students who took the seminar I shared with Elisabeth Ladenson in the summer of 2010 at the Institut d'études françaises in Avignon run by Bryn Mawr College.

The Taylorian Library at the University of Oxford—notably in the person of Nick Hearn, the French subject specialist, to whom I am particularly grateful—the Bibliothèque nationale de France, the Butler Library at Columbia University, Google, and numerous online libraries have all been indispensable in providing the material on which this book is based.

Special thanks are due to the people who devoted time and energy to reading parts of the manuscript in draft: Marine Ganofsky, Miranda Gill, Mike Holland, Jean-Alexandre Perras, and the anonymous reviewers appointed by Princeton University Press who read everything. Their comments and suggestions have been invaluable, but any errors or omissions must be laid at my door, not theirs.

It has been a joy at every stage to work with Princeton University Press, and I am particularly grateful to Ben Tate for his genial encouragement throughout.

Hannah Paul and Diane Bergman provided indispensable help in producing the illustrations.

Parts of the introduction appeared in an earlier version as "Genius and Its Others" in *Paragraph* 32 (2010), and I am grateful to the editors and to Oxford University Press for permission to use this material.

I am keen to report that this book has not been the beneficiary of any kind of award from any research funding body, but only of the sabbatical leave scheme of Oxford University. My gratitude goes to New College and to the Faculty of Medieval and Modern Languages for their trust and for the intellectual encouragement that the scheme provides. Long may it continue.

Mike Holland has put up with living with genius for a very long time, while also making his own contributions to the result. There is no one else I could conceivably dedicate the book to.

Ann Jefferson
Oxford, December 2013

Genius in France

Introduction

[W]e ought to know what "genius" is.
—Marjorie Garber, *Academic Instincts*

[L]et us not pretend to understand what genius means.
—Derrida, "L'archéologie du frivole"

Genius is a word with a long history, two etymological origins, and, according to the *Oxford English Dictionary*, seven distinct meanings, each with several subcategories. Yet since the eighteenth century the term has often been deployed in the Western world as if its sense were entirely obvious, with speakers relying on an assumption of cultural consensus to pass "genius" off as a self-explanatory notion. It was taken up by all the major European languages in response to the need for a word that would express the new sense of the value of exceptional creative originality. An accolade that defines its object as an exception in a class of its own, "genius" serves as a sort of super-superlative, possessing rather more evaluative purpose than precise semantic content. At the same time, it indicates the distinctiveness of the person to whom it is applied, the stamp of individuality being the guarantee of the originality that was increasingly associated with the term. Genius is therefore exceptional on two different counts, superior quality and distinctive character, so that to speak of "the genius of Mozart," for example, is both to place Mozart at the top of some hypothetical ranking of composers, and to allude to the particular character of his music.

If one pauses to reflect, however, "genius" is oddly hard to define, and what is odder still, this does not seem to count against its viability as a concept. Speakers continue to use the word as if they can count on listeners to understand what they mean, and the attribution of genius is often used as a clincher in discussions as if to suggest that the word is entirely self-justifying. In the early days of writing this book I attended two memorial services for people whose qualities were recalled in some detail, before the eulogist—a different one in each case—concluded with a version of the statement: "In sum, he was a genius." In the same vein, and around the same time, I overheard a student telling a friend how much he admired Dickens as a writer, and once again, after brief reflective pause, he summarized his view with the words: "Well, he was just a genius." End of story. Except that genius as a general phenomenon has regularly attracted comment and analysis, as if its lack of semantic precision were a vacuum that commentators were repeatedly drawn to fill. And often in the most interesting ways. It is with these interesting ways—in other words, with the many "uses" to which genius has been put—rather than with any attempt at definition that this book is concerned.

"Genius" is an idea that seems to answer a desire to articulate admiration for exceptional human achievement. And as a consequence of the curiosity that such achievements provoke, it invites speculation about its origins and operations, expressed in the question, "How do they do it?" This curiosity can also lead to suspicion and to a view of genius as a form of deception: apparently exceptional achievement can turn out to be not so exceptional after all, and its creators no different from anyone else. All these responses seem to me worthy of consideration, and each has produced discussions that merit closer examination. In what follows I have been guided by the inherent interest of the discussions I consider, and to that extent my approach is agnostic rather than partisan. I shall not confine myself to presenting any single view of genius, and I have no particular theory of genius of my own to advance. Instead, my aim is to present a number of different accounts of genius as they have emerged since the beginning of the eighteenth century, while restricting myself to France—for reasons that I shall explain in a moment.

The semantic imprecision of the term "genius" is due in part, as has long since been acknowledged, to its dual etymology, deriving from the two Latin words *genius* and *ingenium*. Moreover, as Jane Chance Nitzsche observes in her book *The Genius Figure in Antiquity and the Middle Ages*, the Latin word *genius* does not denote a single central concept or meaning, and its forms and associations already constitute "a bewilderingly diverse array." It referred in the ancient Roman world to a tutelary spirit that accompanied each man from his birth to his death (women had a Juno), and prior to that, it was associated with the worship of household spirits and viewed as a procreative force sustaining the family line embodied in the paterfamilias. It is in this tradition that Genius makes its return in medieval allegory as a kind of deity or spirit associated with sexual reproduction.[1] Deriving from the Latin *gignere*, this is a biological begetting and not artistic or intellectual creation.

The etymological strand that derives from *ingenium* refers to both character and aptitude. In the ancient world *ingenium* was a vital prerequisite for oratory, which is inborn but nonetheless benefits from the kind of effort that Cicero describes as "painstaking." The word was resuscitated as *ingenio* in Italian Renaissance thought, where it denoted the natural powers of mind manifested in practical or speculative pursuits.[2] French would later use the term "esprit" and the English "wit," as in the title of the 1594 translation of Juan Huarte's *Examen de ingenios*—*The Examination of Mens Wits*—which itemizes the different temperaments according to humoral principles and sets out the best way to produce talented offspring.

The two etymologies (*genius* and *ingenium*) converged around the turn of the eighteenth century to give rise to the amalgam of superiority and distinctiveness conveyed by the modern use of the word "genius" as exceptional creative capacity distinguished by originality. The other senses nevertheless remain active, with the tutelary spirit morphing occasionally into an evil genius or the (sometimes winged) personification of abstract entities, such as *Le Génie de la Liberté* on top of the Bastille Column. It merges with the *genius loci* when it embodies the spirit of a place, a nation, or other collective entity, and even a language. This kind of embodiment also tends to carry with it connotations of superiority—as the example of the "genius of the French language" has often suggested.

Any dictionary will tell you this much, and a French dictionary, such as that of Littré or the *Trésor de la langue française*, will indicate the even broader reach that the word *génie* has in the French language, since it includes the "genie" who emerges from Aladdin's lamp (and whose etymology co-opts the Arabic *Jinn*) on one side, and on the other, the engineering corps of the army and navy and their technical expertise. When qualified, as in *génie civil* or *génie chimique*, it also has the English sense of engineering (as in civil or chemical engineering). French also introduced an adjectival form, *génial*, first attested in 1838, which reflects the nineteenth-century enthusiasm for all forms genius from which it is falsely derived. Other languages restrict the sense of the word "genius," so that German, for instance, distinguishes between *Genie*, borrowed from the French and referring to exceptional creative genius, and *Genius*, reserved for genius as tutelary spirit or the genius of a nation. My point is not that French is special with regard to the way the word *génie* functions, but that its range is indicative of the remarkably labile character of the term—manifest in *all* Western languages—and contributes to what I call its semantic imprecision.

This vagueness is reflected in other ways, as genius can refer *both* to a general attribute—as in "a man of genius" or "the genius of Mozart"—*and* to the person himself or (more rarely, as we shall see in due course) herself: as in "X is, or was, a genius." "Genius" is a synecdoche that was increasingly substituted for its possessor over the course of the eighteenth century, the earliest French instance of this shift being recorded in the *Dictionnaire de Trévoux* of 1721, and confirmed in the *Dictionnaire de l'Académie* of 1740, where the word is qualified by an adjective in expressions such as *un beau génie* or *un grand génie*. The *OED* suggests that this usage existed in English as early as the mid-seventeenth century.

In similarly divided mode, the source of the exceptional quality of creative genius is imagined as coming *either* from within *or* from without, depending on the case. The genius may be viewed as *possessed* by divine inspiration or Platonic frenzy whose source lies without, or, alternatively, as *possessing* in the

form of an aptitude that lies within as innate endowment.[3] In a further ambiguity, genius is seen sometimes as an aberrant state, and at other times as the acme
of human capability, being either an index of sickness or, conversely, emblematic of health. And in the modern world, there is a certain degree of ambivalence about its status, as if we are not sure how seriously we want to take the
idea. While subscribing in all sincerity to the genius of Mozart, we allow ourselves to be seduced by advertising that facetiously tells us that Guinness is
"Pure genius," sells the French a washing powder under the label "Génie" and
Anglophones an app for their iPads that goes by the name of "Genius," or casts
its net implausibly wide as a "Genius sperm bank" provides the initial prerequisite for any woman intent on "raising a genius."

All this means that, etymologically and culturally speaking, the term is
hugely overdetermined while remaining strangely underspecified in its actual
applications.[4] Any mention of "genius" will call up all its possible meanings
whose potential relevance in a given context will hover on its fringes, and where
all will be shot through with connotations of distinctive superiority. But, rather
than being a problem, its ambiguities and the overall vagueness of its semantic
definition could, on the contrary, be a virtue. Although Marjorie Garber, in the
epigraph above, appears disconcerted to discover that we do not seem to know
what "genius" means, Derrida clearly suggests that a certain laxity in this regard
might be a positive advantage, even when he is elucidating one of the earlier
eighteenth-century discussions of the term, Condillac's *Essai sur l'origine des
connaissances humaines* (Essay on the origin of human knowledge, 1746).

Nonetheless, as I have already indicated and ambiguity notwithstanding,
European languages and cultures were broadly convergent in their use of the
term as it emerged in the early years of the eighteenth century to express exceptional creative ability. In France the *Querelle des anciens et des modernes* pre-
pared the ground for the notion of untutored genius, to which Addison gave
more coherent form in his essay on the subject (written in 1711) where he celebrated "the prodigies of mankind, who by the mere strength of natural parts,
and without any assistance of art or learning, have produced works that were
the delight of their own times and the wonder of posterity."[5] The rediscovery of
Longinus—translated into French by Boileau as the *Traité du sublime* (Treatise
on the sublime) in 1674, and into English "compar'd with the French of the
Sieur Despreaux Boileau" as *An Essay upon Sublime* (1698)—fueled thinking
on both sides of the Channel with its assertion that the sublime proceeds from
"greatness of the soul" rather than from mere technical mastery.[6] In France the
Abbé Dubos picks up the tale in his *Réflexions critiques sur la poésie et sur la
peinture* (Critical reflections on poetry and painting), whose first edition appeared in 1719. And, as we shall see in fuller detail in chapters 1 and 2, others
quickly followed.

The Germans joined in the conversation when Herder discovered Edward
Young's *Conjectures on Original Composition* (1759) and the word *Genie* en-

tered the German language courtesy of Batteux's *Les Beaux-arts réduits à un même principe* (The fine arts reduced to a single principle, 1746). Diderot read Shaftesbury, and Alexander Gerard cited Dubos in his *Essay on Genius* (1774). Shakespeare's first French translator, Le Tourneur, published a French translation of Young's *Conjectures* within a decade of its English appearance, and Kant's discussion of genius in the *Critique of Judgment* (1790) owes as much to Alexander Gerard and to his French precursors as to any foregoing German discussions.[7] French commentators regularly invoked Locke and Newton as examples of genius alongside Racine, Corneille, and Molière; Shakespeare was increasingly regarded as the embodiment of genius, even in France, where he had hitherto been regarded as a literary barbarian; and every educated person in Europe drew on the same repertoire of classical reference in support of their arguments.[8] All of which provided a common set of examples and cited authorities in the writings of the period, regardless of nationality.

This history has been extensively documented and explored in ways that lend credence to the view that genius is the topic of a single, pan-European conversation to which the French, the English, and the Germans are the major contributors over the course of the eighteenth century. Although this is indubitably true, the effect is to give piecemeal prominence to individual contributors while ignoring the nature of the disciplinary and discursive context in which those contributions were made. But by focusing on the intellectual and cultural history of a single nation, it becomes easier to acknowledge the nature of those terms and to take account of the conceptual languages and disciplines from which they derive. This is particularly true for the French contributions to the debate, which tend to be marginalized in many accounts. Logan Pearsall Smith, whose discussion of genius in his *Four Words* still carries authority, recognizes that France made its contribution to the conception of genius, but he does so in a footnote to which his only two French references—Condillac and Voltaire—are also consigned.[9]

The German tradition is better endowed with histories than the French one, with studies such as Jochen Schmidt's exemplary *Geschichte des Genie-Gedankens in der deutschen Literatur, Philosophie und Politik 1750–1945*, which has gone through two editions.[10] Otherwise, focus tends to be confined to a specific period, such as the eighteenth century, with Jonathan Bate's *Genius of Shakespeare*, which tracks the emergence of Shakespeare's status as a genius in the eighteenth century in England, Wendelin Schmidt-Dengler's history of the notion of genius in the *Goethezeit* or Herman Wolf's history of the term from Gottsched to Lessing in Germany, and, for France, Kineret Jaffe's excellent essay, "The Concept of Genius: Its Changing Role in Eighteenth-Century French Aesthetics," or Herbert Dieckmann's equally excellent account of the many uses of the term in Diderot's work.[11] At the other extreme, and closer to the present day than many of these other studies, Penelope Murray's suggestive anthology of essays, *Genius: The History of an Idea*, contains a somewhat eclectic assortment of discussions, extending from her own lucid account of the classical origins of poetic genius to current views about musical or mathematical genius, very few of which, incidentally, make any kind of reference to French discussions of the topic. In a different vein, Christine Battersby's *Gender and Genius* explores the specific issue of the implicit gendering of genius as male in the history of the idea, and draws on a wide range of sources.[12]

All these approaches, while invaluable for any understanding of the term (and I should like to record my own debt to them), are not only restricted to a single conceptual framework or to a single historical moment, but tend to position genius as any object to which any discussion might be more or less adequate, or about which a given argument might offer a particular view. Such strategies, even when they contest the notion of genius, nonetheless ignore the character of the language in which it is being discussed and so neglect to consider what investment that language and those who use it might have in the notion. It is these questions that my history of genius in France is designed to bring to light, so that, strictly speaking—and, as I am suggesting, rather more interestingly—it is less a history of the idea of genius itself, than a history of its uses and the ways in which that idea has been discussed and developed over the course of three centuries.

It may be that these ways have been more varied in France than elsewhere, or it may be that, unlike Germany, with its literary-philosophical tradition, France has had no single dominant intellectual framework to provide a consistent context for consideration of the question of genius. Added to this absence, France differs from England (which has Shakespeare), Germany (which has Goethe), Italy (which has Dante), Spain (which has Cervantes), and Russia (which has Pushkin) in that it has no single national figure around which such thinking might coalesce—although, as we shall see, Victor Hugo was happy to present himself as a candidate to remedy this lack. Discussions of genius in France have emerged in a series of very different disciplines and discourses as they themselves have emerged into intellectual life, as if—to adapt the phrase that Lévi-Strauss once used about animals—there were something about genius that made it particularly "good to think with."[13]

In the eighteenth century these new disciplines were aesthetics and sensualist philosophy. At the turn of the nineteenth century, ideas of collective and specifically national genius became the focus for thinkers in France concerned with national identity in the wake of the Revolution. Romanticism, as elsewhere, homed in on the notion of genius, but did so by giving it a strategic role in the mutual recognition of the lyric poets who established the movement in France. Psychological medicine, where the French took the lead in the nineteenth century, made genius a matter of specialist concern, while the realist novel cast genius in terms of the failure to which the genre was repeatedly drawn for its subject matter, and children's literature offered young readers a huge repertoire of youthful and morally improving examples of genius. At the end of the century the development of experimental psychology equipped future thinking about genius with a tool for its measurement in the form of the IQ test, devised by Alfred Binet before it was exported to the United States, and in the middle of the twentieth century the child prodigy, Minou Drouet, provided journalists and cultural commentators with a pretext for reevaluating genius, both for and against. Finally, in the latter part of the twentieth century, the era of French theory began and ended with reflections on the question of genius, Derrida having the last and unexpectedly positive word. The history of the idea of genius in France is therefore clearly not a continuous one, and these different approaches to the topic seem to function largely without reference to each other, further reinforcing the impression of diversity, and more especially of discontinuity.

Genius may be the object of specialist disciplinary attentions, but the idea continues to circulate freely in the wider culture—as my examples of memorial services and overheard student conversations show—although, as those examples also indicate, it does so at the cost of a certain unquestioned acceptance thanks to which it quickly reverts to cliché. So that each time it comes under scrutiny, genius must be drawn out of this banality as well as out of its constitutive imprecision to serve as an object of fresh enquiry. This challenge no doubt contributes to making it "good to think with." But there is something else as well: the connotations of originality and superiority associated with the modern meaning of the word make a genius a topic of interest to new forms of intellectual enquiry or artistic endeavor seeking their own forms of acknowledgment and legitimation. In speaking of genius, some of its supposed qualities may be thought to rub off onto those who speak of it. And in redefining genius, a reverse process of osmosis can sometimes take place, whereby genius takes on the characteristics, whether positive or negative, of the theory or discipline of which it is the object. Genius can be made in the likeness—though also in the unlikeness—of those who set out to describe it. Which means that genius is not just good, but often positively advantageous to think with.

There is no established sense of a corpus of French writings on genius, and one of the aims of this book is to outline one.[14] But since discussion of the idea of genius in France is so strikingly discontinuous, and since it is not sustained by a single tradition of intellectual reflection or enquiry, any history of French notions of genius needs some kind of rationale in order to create the corpus on which it rests. The rationale of the history I am proposing here is twofold. First, I shall make a virtue of the phenomenon of discontinuity and will argue that it is precisely the novelty of each discourse that makes genius with its associations of groundbreaking originality an attractive object of enquiry. This is a history that constantly starts afresh, very often as if unaware of the discussions that have preceded it elsewhere. The second assumption underpinning this history is less specific to France, but it is prompted by this lack of continuity in the

French tradition: namely, that the reinvention or reenergizing of genius as an idea tends to be most effective when it is brought into contact with elements that appear to be antithetical or even positively inimical to it, and which, for the sake of convenience, I shall refer to as the "others" of genius.

GENIUS AND ITS "OTHERS"

In the history of thinking about genius these others recur with remarkable regularity in the form of pathology (madness or melancholy), imposture (genius has always had its skeptics), and, finally, the spectator of genius: genius is a name conferred by those who behold it, and is very rarely claimed in the first person. Indeed, to assert "I am a genius" is almost invariably to lay oneself open to the suspicion of imposture. We take genius to be something that is instantiated in a person, but not self-proclaimed, and the category of genius depends on granting to third parties the right to determine its presence in the figures who bear a name that can be uttered only in the third, or occasionally the second person, but (almost) never convincingly in the first. Each of these "others" has its own founding text that provides points of reference in subsequent discussions: Aristotle's "On Melancholy," Plato's dialogue "Ion," and, much closer to the modern period, Kant's *Critique of Judgment*, which makes the clearest case for the place of the beholder of genius. To that extent Kant may be said to articulate a point already implicit in other discussions, but since the case is made with an exemplary combination of clarity and subtlety, I have given the *Critique* the same status as Plato's "Ion" and Aristotle's "Melancholy."

The inclusion of these external counterparts to genius might seem to go against the grain of many of the existing discussions, which have sought to arrive at some specificity of definition by contrasting genius with factors that are construed as its obverse. The emergence of genius as a key concept in the eighteenth century was frequently supported by an opposition between genius and talent: talent is the competent application of rules, whereas genius is the attribute necessary for creating original works of art, art being the sphere with which genius was predominantly (though not exclusively) associated. The following quotation from Condillac is typical of many eighteenth-century views on the subject: "[Talent] combines ideas of a known art or science in a manner that will produce the effects one would naturally expect. . . . [Genius] adds to talent the idea of a mind that is in some sense *creative*. It invents new arts, or, within the same art, new and equally valid genres. . . . A man of talent has a character that could belong to others who may be his equal or even surpass him. The character of a man of genius is *original*; it is inimitable."[15] This view of genius as the positive antithesis of talent became a commonplace, and it was widely used in conjunction with a notion of genius as unique, original, and creative.

Much was made of this in Edward Young's widely read *Conjectures on Original Composition* (1759), and his argument—or perhaps one might better say, his panegyric—includes a large number of further binaries as part of his attempt to construct an account of the creative powers of genius. The originality that is synonymous with genius is opposed to "mere" imitation: "An *Original* may be said to be of a *vegetable* nature; it rises spontaneously from the vital root of Genius; it *grows*, it is not *made*: Imitations are often a sort of *Manufacture* wrought up by those *Mechanics, Art*, and *Labour*, out of pre-existent materials not their own."[16] The supporting antitheses between the organic and the mechanical, spontaneous growth and laborious construction, the new and the secondhand are just a few of a whole series of contrasting metaphors that Young mobilizes in support of his view.

The opposition between genius and imitation evolves in turn into a further contrast between genius and learning (*mere* learning), and it too is underscored by a set of corresponding antithetical evaluations: "Learning we thank, Genius we revere; That gives us pleasure, This gives us rapture; That informs, This inspires; and is itself inspired; for Genius is from Heaven, Learning from man: *This* sets us above the low, and illiterate; *That*, above the learned, and polite. Learning is borrowed knowledge; Genius is knowledge innate, and quite our own."[17] The oppositions—afforced by the extravagant use of capitals and italics—between thanking and revering, pleasure and rapture, informing and inspiring, heaven and man, borrowed and innate are marshaled to endorse the implication that genius can be unequivocally demarcated from its lowly obverse, whether talent, imitation, or learning.

Young's text was hugely influential, particularly in the development of the idea of genius in Germany, thanks to this emphasis on originality. But unlike the *Conjectures* and other approaches that rely on an opposition between genius and its others of talent, imitation, and learning, my three founding texts on genius treat some kind of otherness as integral to a proper understanding of the topic. I shall begin with Aristotle, even though this disrupts strict chronology, since it means discussing the pupil, Aristotle (384–322 BC) before the master, Plato (424/423–348/347 BC). Moreover, when I say "Aristotle," it is safer to understand the "Pseudo-Aristotle" to whom it is conventional to attribute the *Problemata*, which contain the discussion of melancholy. For Aristotle, melancholy, or black bile, is a defining characteristic of what he calls "men who have become outstanding in philosophy, statesmanship, poetry or the arts,"[18] and his is the first text to treat what we now call genius in terms of abnormality or pathology. The idea was picked up by Marsilio Ficino in the fifteenth century with his *Three Books on Life* and by Juan Huarte in the sixteenth, before seeing its apotheosis in the new medical sciences of the nineteenth century, of which Lombroso's *L'Uomo di genio in rapporto alla psichiatria* (1888, translated into English as *The Man of Genius* in 1891), a revised version of his earlier *Genio et Follia* (1864), is a kind of summation, and which opens with a reference to Aristotle's text.[19]

The particular problem that Aristotle is seeking to explore is the association of melancholy with exceptional or outstanding figures. The two elements, melancholy and outstanding ability, are presented as being inextricably linked from the outset. Although not all melancholics are exceptional, Aristotle takes it as axiomatic that all exceptional individuals are melancholic. Melancholy is treated here in the context of the theory of the humors, and his men of exception include a broader range of figures than would normally be implied in the modern notion of genius (Hercules and Empedocles as well as Plato, Socrates, and others who have excelled in poetry and the arts), so it is not entirely straightforward to extrapolate the discussion onto modern conceptions of either pathology or genius. But the humoral principles serve to foreground the factors of admixture and instability in the account Aristotle provides of exceptional beings.

First of all, even if black bile (or melancholy) predominates in a given person, it is nevertheless just one in the compound of the four humors that are present in every individual. Moreover, says Aristotle, the "melancholic humour is [itself] already mixed in nature," since it consists of a "mixture of hot and cold."[20] This mix is to be understood as a propensity to instability between the two extremes of temperature, and hence of mood and temperament. At the naturally cold end of the scale are apoplexy, torpor, despondency, and fear; but when the humor is overheated, "it produces cheerfulness with song, and madness," and even "the breaking out of sores," this last being is one of the features of Aristotelian melancholy that cannot be straightforwardly assimilated to the manic depression that contemporary thinking tends to associate with genius. The melancholic temperament is inherently "variable," melancholics are "not equable in behaviour," and, thanks to the inherent instability of black bile, they are by nature "abnormal" in ways that those whose temperament is determined by other humors—the choleric, the phlegmatic, and the sanguine—are not.[21]

The intrinsically labile nature of black bile means that the spectrum of character produced by the humor is very wide, depending on degrees of hot and cold. Extremes of heat can produce madness and frenzy, the latter accounting for all "inspired persons." But if this sounds like an early example of modern artistic genius (and the reference to Maracus, the Syracusan, who was apparently an even better poet when he was mad, might encourage one to think so), Aristotle goes on to argue that superiority results from moderation of such excessive heat. This is the case with those melancholics who are more intelligent and less eccentric than the ones who suffer from the extremes of humoral temperature, and they are in consequence able to excel in a whole variety of domains, be it education, the arts, or statesmanship. In short, we may say that Aristotle makes mixture, variety, and instability, rather than purity, the core of his argument about the superiority of those who include the kind of figure to which later ages gave the name of genius.

Plato's dialogue, "Ion," is probably read most frequently for its discussion of enthusiasm, but it also intriguingly suggests that the phenomenon of "genius" entails an inextricable component of imposture: the poet's knowledge is shown by Socrates to be fake knowledge. This view of genius as a form of charlatanry is, for obvious reasons, unlikely to appeal to anyone other than those who are anxious to discredit the whole concept, among whom one might include the rationalists of the seventeenth and eighteenth centuries who regarded inspiration as a "dangerous word" that referred to "delusions" or an "impostures of poets." The possibility of fraudulence haunts a good many discussions of genius, and Kant specifically excludes from serious consideration those who simply choose to "speak and decide like a genius" and are in reality "charlatans" who spread "haze."[22]

Plato treats imposture as an unavoidable if regrettable element in the inspiration of the poet or rhapsode. Where Aristotle distinguishes between frenzy and the kind of superiority that interests him in exceptional beings, Plato is concerned exclusively with the frenzy of inspiration. Moreover, whereas Aristotle locates the origins of superiority in an internal humoral physiology, Plato attributes poetic frenzy to divine dispensation. This, incidentally, constitutes a further example of the instability of genius, since, as one founding text succeeds another, it slides from an external, divine source, to an internal, humoral one.[23] And while Aristotle's exceptional beings are endowed with superior intelligence and include philosophers (notably, Plato and Socrates, the author and interlocutor, respectively, of the dialogue that forms "Ion"), Socrates's quizzing of Ion casts doubt on the rhapsode's intellectual capacities by revealing that his claims to knowledge are spurious. First, it emerges that the rhapsode, who combines the role of critic-commentator with that of performer, can neither comment on nor recite the work of any poet other than Homer. Ion's knowledge is invalidated for the philosopher on the grounds that the rhapsode is unable to generalize: he knows about Homer, but not about poetry. Such specialism might be a pardonable shortcoming; however, as the discussion progresses, Socrates succeeds in demonstrating that the knowledge that poets—and the rhapsodes who are their spokesmen—pass on to their audience is without substance. Homer can describe a chariot race and quote the advice that Nestor gives his son about how to negotiate the turning post, but he or, in this instance, his representative, Ion, is unable to judge whether the advice is correct. Under further pressure from Socrates, Ion is obliged to acknowledge that "the skill of a rhapsode is different from that of a charioteer" for the obvious reason that each has knowledge of different objects.[24]

Ion has difficulty taking the point on board, but, as Socrates presents him with a series of quotations from Homer, Ion is repeatedly compelled to cede the apparent authority of the poet-rhapsode to the proven skills of various other figures—a doctor, a fisherman, and a prophet—whose expertise is cited in the poem. Worse still, when, with his back against the wall, Ion rashly lays claim to a distinctive area of professional expertise about the ways in which various classes of person speak—women, slaves, freemen, even cowherds and spinning women—Socrates disempowers him once again by refuting the assertion that the argument has led Ion to make: namely, that although a general cannot be a good rhapsode, a rhapsode would make a good general because he knows how generals speak. The imposture is patent, albeit unwitting, and Socrates ends up, in so many words, accusing Ion of deception: the rhapsode pretends to knowledge that he cannot then substantiate, and is finally quite unable to say what the objects of his expertise might be.

If Ion is ultimately exempted from the charge of fraud, this is due to the fact that poets recite "not by virtue of a skill, but in a state of inspiration and possession." A poet, says Socrates, is a "light thing, and winged and holy" who composes on the basis not of reason and knowledge, but of an inspiration that derives from the Muse.[25] Inspiration compensates to some degree for the imposture of genius, but the dialogue nonetheless makes it clear that possession is a form of *dis*possession, which keeps both poet and rhapsode vulnerable to the charge of fraudulence, since they speak without mastery of the skills and knowledge that they appear to possess. Plato bequeaths to subsequent discussions of genius an account that makes the potential for imposture inherent to the phenomenon.

The third and final instance of my "others" of genius is the Other on whom genius depends for its recognition: its reader or audience, whose human character justifies my capitalization of "Other" here. In some senses this is so obvious a factor that it scarcely seems worth the mention. But in the history of the discussion of genius, the issue of recognition becomes increasingly important. Regarded as more or less self-evident by eighteenth-century commentators, genius was evaluated largely in terms of the effects it produces on its beholders. In the case of Young's *Conjectures*, it might even be said that the very presence of genius in a work produces emotional response in its viewers, be it reverence, rapture, or the swoon of spiritual elevation. In the nineteenth century, however, the question of the recognition of genius became significant through the alleged withholding of recognition from those who supposedly deserved it most, thus requiring a new class of person able and willing to hail and defend figures who were otherwise reviled or ignored by a philistine or malevolent public.

Kant focuses primarily on the reader's perspective in the *Critique of Judgment* (1790), where genius is considered in relation to the judgment of works of art, and the *recipients* of those works—rather than their creators—provide the starting point for his argument. Genius and the fine arts are treated as more or less synonymous in Kant's discussion since for him there can be no fine art without genius. This view is present in Plato (he is discussing poets and poetry), but also in Aristotle, who suggests that *all* poets are exceptional, whereas superiority in the spheres of philosophy and statesmanship is a much rarer phenomenon. Like many of his contemporaries, Kant initially relies on a series of oppositions to circumscribe his definition: art *versus* nature, art *versus* science, skill *versus* knowledge, fine art *versus* mercenary art, agreeable art, and mechanical art. And, still in accordance with many accounts of the topic in the eighteenth century, he makes originality the chief criterion of genius: "the foremost property of genius must be *originality*."[26]

What complicates his picture of the radical autonomy and distinctiveness of genius is the way that, rather than simply asserting genius in terms of its absolute value, as Young does, Kant pursues the implications and consequences of such a view. He begins by arguing that the essential originality of genius makes redundant all existing precepts, since genius creates its own. Or, as he famously puts it, "*Genius is the innate mental predisposition (ingenium) through which* nature gives the rule to art." However, the radical originality of genius and the resistance of art to rational concepts mean that the genius-artist is incapable of formulating the rules that have produced the work, even though they are his own. If, as Kant says, natural disposition (*ingenium*) is the source of the artist's originality, his inability to explain his own rules allies genius to its origin as *daemon*—or Latin *genius*—"the guardian and guiding spirit that each person is given as his own at birth, and to whose inspiration [*Eingebung*] those original ideas are due." This is not quite the Platonic muse, but Kant's genius shares with Plato's Ion the peculiar inability to account for itself: "Genius itself cannot describe or indicate scientifically how it brings about its products, and it is rather as *nature* that it gives the rule. That is why, if an author owes a product to his genius, he himself does not know how he came by the ideas for it; nor is it in his power [*Gewalt*] to devise such products at his pleasure, or by following a plan, and to communicate [his procedure] to others in precepts that would enable them to bring about like products."[27] It is this inability that makes the artist differ so fundamentally from the scientist, who, in Kant's account, can ultimately always explain and reconstruct the procedures that led him to his new idea: "Newton could show how he took every one of the steps he had to take in order to get from the first elements of geometry to his great and profound discoveries; he could show this not only to himself but to everyone else as well, . . . allowing others to follow." By contrast, "no *Homer* . . . can show how his ideas, rich in fancy and yet also in thought, arise and meet in his mind; the reason is that he himself does not know, and hence also cannot teach it to anyone else."[28] Unlike Plato, Kant does not culpabilize the artist's inability to translate his skill into knowledge. But what follows from his peculiar incapacity is that the articulation of the rule that art seems so strongly to call for, must be given to the reader to perform.

This might seem like a way of preserving the purity of genius against the adulteration of imposture, but, as I am suggesting, it introduces and makes indispensable the presence of the Other in the identification of genius. The judgment that derives from the Other is central to Kant's understanding of genius. This is made evident on a number of counts, the first of which lies in the distinction he makes between copying and imitating. On the one hand this opposition looks like one of those that are so common in accounts of genius in the period; but on the other hand, it is curious, given Kant's insistence on the absolute originality of genius and its independence from all prior precept, that he should make the issue of imitation a central feature of his account. For him, it is precisely a mark of genius that it be imitated by subsequent artists: it may not lend itself to direct copying or what Kant calls *aping*, but the very principle of originality is, paradoxically, what must be imitated by a successor-genius if it is to exist at all. It is as if genius required an echo-chamber in the imitative response of the successor, without which it would not exist.

The second further factor that integrates reception to the otherwise autonomous genius is the requirement of taste. If Kant opposes art to mechanism, and originality to learning, he nonetheless argues that genius in its "pure" and unadulterated form is not viable, and that it requires the addition of taste (which is the province of the readers who judge) if it is to meet the fundamental character that Kant ascribes to art, namely its purposiveness. There is, he says, no fine art that does not have as its essential condition "something mechanical, which can be encompassed by rules and complied with." The work of art can never be the product of chance, and "directing the work to a purpose requires determinate rules that one is not permitted to renounce." It is only "shallow minds" who believe "that the best way to show that they are geniuses in first bloom is by renouncing all rules of academic constraint."[29] It is these shallow minds who are the charlatans in Kant's analysis, and far from undermining genius, the integration of the reader's perspective (as taste) within genius itself, seems on the contrary to be the guarantee of its full realization.

Kant concludes his discussion by outlining a kind of symbiosis whereby, in addition to the rule that genius gives to art, the work created by the genius also solicits a determinate concept by way of readerly response, even if genius then goes on to exceed that concept "so that no language can express it completely and allow us to grasp it."[30] This to and fro between genius and its beholding Other is what constitutes the fine art that Kant defines as the sole domain of genius. The reader is at once necessary to genius and invariably transcended by it in ways that subsequent discussions will continue to develop and inflect. Indeed, the modern story of genius is ultimately one of its recognition—and misrecognition—by a variety of reading, viewing, and observing "Others" whose responses form the different discourses through which the idea of genius is constantly reinvented.

In demonstrating the degree to which these three founding texts expose genius to some kind of "other," I should repeat that I am not seeking to construct any kind of theory of genius as such. Rather, my aim is to provide the basis for outlining a history through reference to the "others" that have accompanied thinking on the subject, even though the terms of reference in these founding texts have long since ceased to be part of Western thinking: humorism in Aristotle, the enthusiasm that derives from the Muses in Plato, and the taste to which Kant ascribes such an important role. In selecting the disciplines and discourses to be explored in this book, I have sought to identify moments in French intellectual and cultural life where France was in some way distinctive and not simply carrying on a francophone version of a discussion that was also happening elsewhere. And although aesthetics, national identity, Romanticism, psychological medicine, the realist novel, experimental psychology, and children's literature all have their own manifestations in other national traditions, the French version of each of these has something singular, and at times appealingly bizarre. The French contribution to the history of the idea of genius is a story worth telling in all its variety, not just because of the intrinsic interest of the discussions, but also as testimony to the fascination that constantly reinvents this semantically imprecise but strangely persistent notion in Western thinking.

PART I

Enlightenment Genius

CHAPTER 1

The Eighteenth Century

Mimesis and Effect

[G]enius is the feeling that creates.
        —D'Alembert, *Discours préliminaire de l'Encyclopédie*

The man who invents a mimetic genre is a man of genius.
The man who perfects a mimetic genre, or who excels in it is also a
        man of genius.
        —Diderot, IMITATION, *Gramm. & Philosoph.*, *Encyclopédie*

Any history of the modern idea of genius must start with the eighteenth century, when the secular values of the Enlightenment took hold of the notion in order to celebrate human achievement, advance intellectual and artistic innovation, and support the emergence of new disciplines and genres. It became a major topic of philosophical reflection, examined by authors such as Condillac, Vauvenargues, Helvétius, and Condorcet, who were concerned with what one might call philosophy of mind, and by those, like Dubos, Mercier, and Marmontel whose concerns were principally with theories of art in the new discipline of aesthetics.[1] Diderot, the Enlightenment's most famous theorist of genius, contributed to both types of debate. For most of the eighteenth century genius referred to an attribute rather than to an individual, to "genius" in general rather than "*a* genius" in particular. Although it was possible to refer to *l'homme de génie* (the man of genius) and even to speak of him as *un beau génie* (a fine genius) or *un grand génie* (a great genius), the man *as* genius does not become common currency until the end of the century. Women rarely figure in these debates where the masculine third-person pronoun is the norm, and I shall return to this issue in part IV.

The century is characterized above all by a huge appetite for knowledge, and it is in this context that genius began to take its modern form. It became the object of new enquiry, but was also regarded as its privileged source. In the words of D'Alembert in the "Preliminary Discourse" to the *Encyclopédie*, genius "[opens] unknown routes, and [advances] onward to new discoveries." The products of genius benefit humanity in general, as humanity becomes the collective "Other" of genius to which it responds with admiration and grateful recognition. The *Encyclopédie* itself, whose twenty-eight volumes were published between 1751 and 1772, is the most visible manifestation of the new epistemological zeal, and its stated aim—still in D'Alembert's words—was to examine "the genealogy and the filiation of the parts of our knowledge, the causes that have brought the various branches of our knowledge into being, and the characteristics that distinguish them."[2]

Genius had a vital role in this ambitious project. Knowledge for the Philosophes is democratized and is of two kinds. The first is "direct," entering the human mind through the senses "without resistance and without effort" on our part, and it finds "all the doors of our souls open." The second, "reflective" type of knowledge results from the mind's operations on this initial material. But although access to information about the world may be universal as a consequence of its spontaneous passage through the senses, history suggests that in reality, enlightenment has been spread by a "small number of great geniuses" and that it is they who have had the privileged part to play in making it available to the rest of humanity.[3] Novelty was the watchword, and genius its guarantee.

Invention

"Invention" is the defining characteristic of such genius and is the principal means whereby it makes its enlightening discoveries. As defined by the *Dictionnaire de l'Académie française* of 1762, invention designates the capacity to "find something new through the power of the mind or the imagination," and its objects may include entities as extensive as an entire art, a science, a system, or a machine.[4] In his *Essai sur l'origine des connaissances humaines* (1746) the philosopher Condillac specifically credits invention with the capacity of genius to bring new knowledge about the world to light: "It considers things from perspectives unique to it; it gives birth to a new science, or carves out a path through those that are already cultivated, leading to truths that no one thought could be reached." In his book *De l'esprit* (On mind, 1758), Helvétius also associates invention with the productive capacity of genius when he goes back to the etymological origins of the word—"*gignere, gigno; I give birth, I produce*"—in support of the claim that "[genius] always presupposes *invention*," and that invention is the attribute common to all types of genius. Condorcet, writing in 1794, adduces the same correlation between genius and invention when he describes invention as "the primary faculty of the human intelligence that has been given the name *genius*." Genius is portrayed in his euphoric account as the driving force behind progress in human knowledge, whether scientific or artistic, from the ancient Greeks to the present day.[5]

Invention is repeatedly celebrated as proof of genius, even if there were differences of perspective when it came to the detail of its functioning. For some, it designated a capacity for the association of ideas, and Condillac argues that new ideas are a higher-order form of knowledge whereby "we combine, through a process of composition and decomposition, the ideas that we receive through the senses." This was also the view of Helvétius, who furthermore argued that such associations—and thus genius itself—were the product of chance circumstance, a thesis Diderot took issue with in his refutation of Helvétius's essay *De l'homme* (On man). In the entry for "Génie" in a supplement to his *Dictionnaire philosophique* (written in 1771), Voltaire acknowledges that "the term *genius* appears necessarily to designate talents that include invention, rather than great talents indiscriminately."[6] Although he himself had reservations about this assumption and preferred perfection in a work of art to the invention of new forms, his comment acknowledges once more that the name the eighteenth century most frequently gives to the source of the superior knowledge supplied by genius is "invention."

Genius in general was viewed by many as an association of different qualities or attributes, albeit with invention as their dominant. For Condillac it is a combination of "*good sense, intelligence, judgment, discernment, reason, conception, sagacity, depth,* and *taste*," and he credits the combination with creative powers. The *moraliste* Vauvenargues suggests that it depends to a large extent on our "passions," but adds that "it is created by a combination of many different qualities," the precise nature of which varies according to the particular sphere in which genius is applied. Ultimately, however, whatever the particular amalgam of qualities that constitute genius, they are seen as the means whereby information may enter the doors of the soul and the world be imprinted upon the mind in ways not hitherto registered by others: "the first advantage of genius is to feel and conceive the objects it is concerned with more keenly than the same objects are felt and perceived by other men."[7] Invention is the end product of an unusual receptivity that provides the mind with new knowledge about the world it inhabits.

This exceptional keenness of perception is understood chiefly in terms of the mental qualities that support it—observation and sensibility. Conceptions of the physiological basis of genius had evolved since earlier periods, though some of its legacy survives in glancing reference: Charles Bonnet ascribes the aptitude of genius for attention to "the strength of the *fibers* on which attention is deployed." Abbé Dubos suggests that genius is due to "a happy arrangement of the organs of the brain" as well as to the quality of the blood. Heat is recurrently associated with genius in accordance with the Aristotelian discussion of the humors, although it also carries an increasingly metaphorical charge, as for example, when Vauvenargues speaks of "that heat of genius and that love of its object, which allow it to imagine and invent around the object itself." More idiosyncratically, Diderot invokes the "diaphragm" as the bodily seat of genius;

and, while acknowledging that it doubtless owes much to "a certain structure of the head and the intestines [and] a certain constitution of the humors," he concedes that a precise notion of these things is impossible to come by, and that it is mental attributes, such as the power of observation, that offer the greatest explanatory potential.[8]

These physiological comments about the location and constitution of genius bear the trace of early modern discussions such as those of Ficino and Huarte, but in an Enlightenment context they serve above all to ground an understanding of genius in the terms of sensualist philosophy that makes the mind the seat of the knowledge that derives from the impressions that the world makes upon the senses. As the "Article Génie" in the *Encyclopédie* puts it,

> Breadth of mind, strength of imagination and activity of the soul, these are *genius*. . . . Most men experience keen sensations only through the impression made by objects that have a direct relation to their needs, their tastes, etc. . . . The man of genius is someone whose vaster soul is struck by sensations coming from all beings, is interested in everything found in nature, and does not receive an idea without it awaking a feeling; everything animates him, everything is stored within him.[9]

Genius is an enhanced capacity to register the world as sensation, to respond to beings and objects in all their variety, and to serve as a respository for knowledge about the world that is beyond the reach of more limited mortals. It is this aptitude that also distinguishes genius in the realm of the arts where mimesis is the principal aesthetic criterion.

Mimesis and the Arts

D'Alembert places the fine arts and philosophy alongside each other as parallel examples of reflective knowledge. Both philosopher and artist are conceived in terms of their capacity to portray the world in which they find themselves, and to do so for the benefit of others in the form of insights about its real nature. The arts differ from other forms of knowledge in that they replicate this experience for their recipients through mimetic representation—or what D'Alembert calls "imitation": "This is what we call the imitation of Nature. . . . Since the direct ideas that strike us most vividly are those we remember most easily, these are also the ones that we try most to reawaken in ourselves by the imitation of their objects." It is in the plastic arts that "imitation best approximates the objects represented and speaks most directly to the senses," painting and sculpture being the most immediate forms of "the knowledge that consists of imitation." Poetry (the generic term for literature) comes next in the order of mimesis: it represents to the imagination—as opposed to the senses—"the objects that make up this universe" and does so "in a touching and vivid manner." Music is the least mimetic of the arts, but has the merit of being the medium that acts most directly on the senses. Works of art re-create the sensory being's experience of the world, and mimesis is conceived principally in terms of the effects it produces on its audience: "The mind creates and imagines objects only insofar as they are similar to those it knows already through direct ideas and sensations."[10] And, whether in painting, poetry, or music, genius is the attribute that most successfully replicates knowledge of the world as an experience for its spectators, readers, and listeners.

Genius in eighteenth-century aesthetics is not primarily a capacity to create a beautiful work of art, as it could be said to have been for Boileau, or even for Perrault, whose epistle to Fontenelle on the subject of genius was a precursor to the discussions in the following century. Boileau's *Art poétique* (1674) treated genius as the essential requirement for successful application of the rules of art, while nevertheless warning the would-be poet against mistaking a simple "love of rhyming" for true genius. As his translation of Longinus, the *Traité du sublime* (Treatise on the sublime), maintained, "greatness of soul" is the indispensable requirement for good writing. Perrault, whose *Epître* dates from 1688 and was written in the heat of the *Querelle des anciens et des modernes*, presents genius as a form of inspiration that allows the poet to produce forms of language that will rouse the passions of his readers: "Heat must be spread through the soul / to raise it and move it to external action, / to provide it with a language which, whether willingly or by force finds approval in each listener, . . . and which through the beauty of its expression, / kindles every passion within the heart."[11] It speaks volumes that in the original French, Perrault rhymes *passions* with the beauty of *expressions*. For his eighteenth-century successors, by contrast, the work of art becomes a vehicle for mimesis, and genius consists in the ability to create a touching likeness. It is this likeness, rather than any stylistic beauty, that will ignite the passions of the eighteenth-century human heart.

Genius in its Enlightenment guise works according to what M. H. Abrams calls a poetics of the mirror, which gave way only later to a Romantic aesthetic of the lamp.[12] The mirror was fundamental to the way in which genius was conceived, and the mimetic capacity ascribed to genius was viewed first and foremost in terms of its effect upon its reading or viewing "Other." It was no coincidence that the issue of the reader's perspective proved to be so integral to Kant's understanding of genius, though the "others" of imposture and madness will make a brief appearance before the century is out.

As in other branches of knowledge, the man of artistic genius is endowed with qualities that allow him either to penetrate the world through his observational powers, or else, on the basis of his sensibility, to take up its imprint and make it legible in turn to his readers and viewers. He sees things in the world that have not previously been seen, or realities that have hitherto been overlooked, and he creates a likeness that makes it possible for others to share his discoveries. It is a two-stage process whereby the relation between nature and the man of genius is replicated in the relation between the work and the reader-spectator, the difference being that where the man of genius is alone in what he discovers, his artistic representations are universally available to the many who constitute his public.

There are, to be sure, differences of emphasis and concern, but the twin linchpins of the discussion of genius across the century, from Dubos to Diderot, are mimesis and readerly effect. It is for this reason, no doubt, that the art forms most thoroughly explored in this context are the most overtly representational: painting and literature, especially in the forms of tragedy and the classical epic—though not the lowly form of the novel. Dubos's *Réflexions critiques* are devoted to "poetry" (i.e., to literature) and to painting; Batteux's analysis of "the fine arts" principally addresses the same fields, while making an occasional nod in the direction of music; and Diderot's discussion of genius either is so general as not to require reference to any particular art form, or else arises as part of his writing on painting (viz., the *Salons*), literature (the *Éloge de Richardson* would be a prime example, and incidentally constitutes an exception to the exclusion of the novel from the purview of genius), or else the theater (the *Entretiens sur le Fils naturel* [Conversations on "Le Fils naturel"] and *Le Paradoxe sur le comédien* [Paradox of acting]). Music, despite its importance in the eighteenth century, provides little pretext for extensive discussion of genius, except, briefly, in Rousseau's entry on genius in the *Dictionnaire de musique* (1768) and in Diderot's *Neveu de Rameau* (Rameau's nephew), which I shall be discussing in the next chapter.[13]

OBSERVATION

Even where the nature depicted in the work of art is an idealized version of reality—*la belle nature*, for which Batteux makes a strong case—it still relies on the artist's powers of observation for its existence. When constructing the figure of the misanthropist in *Le Misanthrope* (a work much cited in the eighteenth century for its genius), Batteux argues that Molière did not set out to find a living example he could then copy. Instead, he based his portrait on his observation of "the features of black bile" in a variety of different figures that he synthesized into a composite character who provided more insight into misanthropy than could any more slavish depiction of particular individuals. He dismisses Platonic frenzy as the source of genius in favor of this capacity for attention to natural phenomena: "It is active reason, which is exercised with art upon an object, industriously seeks out all the real aspects of the object, all its possible aspects, methodically dissects its most delicate parts, and measures its most remote connections: it is an enlightened instrument, which explores thoroughly, digs deep and quietly penetrates. Its function consists, not in imagining what cannot exist, but in *discovering what does exist*."[14] His defense of *le vraisem-*

blable against *le vrai* may carry with it the rider that imitation should not be literal, but Batteux still makes the principle of insightful observation central to the workings of genius.

Equally, although Diderot takes different views at different times about the importance of inspiration, the value he places on observation never varies. The *Éloge de Richardson* (In praise of Richardson), published in 1762, describes the art of the painter and the poet as being that of revealing "a fleeting circumstance that had escaped you." Diderot goes on to applaud Richardson for his "astonishing knowledge of the laws, customs, habits and practices of the human heart and of life," knowledge that presupposes on the part of the novelist an "inexhaustible store of morality, experience and *observations*." At a later stage in his career, when pondering the one indispensable factor required for genius, he rules out a number of possible contenders, including imagination, judgment, wit, fire (*fougue*), sensibility, and taste, and retains only what he calls "an observant outlook" (*l'esprit observateur*). True, it is a more spontaneous form of observation than the one described by Batteux—for Diderot "[it] is exerted without effort, without contention; it does not look, but sees, learns, and expands without the aid of study"—but it is the single mental attribute on which genius, whether literary, philosophical, painterly, or musical, most consistently depends in its drive to portray the world and construct likenesses that will convey this new knowledge to its listeners, viewers, and readers.[15]

ORIGINALITY

Just as genius "industriously seeks out all the real aspects of the object" and "methodically dissects its most delicate parts," so genius itself is dissected into its component features by its eighteenth-century analysts. Observation is the first of these features, but originality, sensibility, and imagination are also examined as necessary prerequisites for perceiving and portraying a reality that went by the catchall name of "nature." Originality has a key role to play in artistic genius, although it is sometimes viewed with a degree of ambivalence, as Diderot's *Neveu de Rameau* will illustrate.[16] Its positive qualities are foregrounded when it functions as an adjunct to observation, supporting genius in its mimetic intent. There is none of the Romantic sense of originality as having a value in its own right or being the mark of freedom from inherited convention. Rather, it provides a perspective from which reality—even the most familiar kinds of reality—will be revealed as containing something previously unremarked. Originality supports genius in its ability to bring novelty and difference to light in what otherwise appears as uniformity. This is an attribute whose importance is stressed by Dubos: "A man born with genius sees the nature that his art imitates with other eyes than people who do not have genius. He discovers endless difference between objects which to the eyes of other men look the same, and he succeeds so well in making this difference felt in his imitation, that the most hackneyed subject becomes a new one beneath his pen or his paintbrush." The observing gaze that the man of genius turns on the world is powered by a "penetration" that serves as the "inseparable companion of the genius [that] allows him to discover new aspects in subjects that are commonly believed to be the most exhausted."[17]

The path genius takes toward reality is always individual, so when Racine and Corneille treat the same subject (the story of Bérénice, for instance) there is a world of difference between the two results: "the poets, each guided by an individual genius, so rarely see things the same way that one may say that, as a general rule, they never see things the same way." This divergence is guaranteed by the fact that genius spontaneously chooses nature, rather than existing models, for its subject matter: "nature is even richer in different subjects than the genius of artisans is varied." The capacity of genius to reveal the variousness of the natural world applies equally to the inner world of the human heart, as Marmontel asserts in his *Éléments de littérature* (Elements of literature), published over seventy years after the first edition of Dubos's *Réflexions critiques*: "the man of *genius* . . . has a way of seeing, feeling and thinking that is particular to him . . . ; he penetrates farther into our hearts than we ourselves were able to do before he enlightened us; he allows us to discover new phenomena both inside and outside ourselves."[18] Genius brings its audience new knowledge about every aspect of their own world, whether inward or outward.

Imagination

The revelatory power of originality is further supported by the imagination that enables the artist, as it were, to get inside his subject and to flesh it out from within. If, as Dubos asserts, imitation consists in endowing with being objects that are liable to please and touch, then imagination plays a large part in producing this depiction of natural phenomena: "One merits the name of poet by making the action in question capable of moving an audience, and this is done by imagining which feelings are appropriate to the presumed characters in a given situation and by extracting from one's own genius the features that are best suited to expressing those feelings." It requires more imagination, Dubos continues, to portray Caesar's response to the death of Pompey than to invent any number of allegorical figures: "One needs a more fertile and more accurate imagination to picture and to match the features that nature employs in the expression of passion, than to invent emblematic figures."[19] Imagination distinguishes poetry from history by making poetic representations more like life than that those of the historian, and it serves to enhance mimesis by matching the features that nature itself employs, rather than seeking to invent alternatives to it.

The relation of genius to the world in the attributes of observation, originality, and imagination tends, as many of the above examples imply, to be figured as a form of penetration. Batteux and Dubos both make explicit use of the term. Genius is projected into the phenomena that it represents in order to open them up for subsequent scrutiny by a wider public, which is portrayed as a passive recipient of the knowledge that genius has actively gone out to retrieve.

Sensibility

In the case of sensibility, however, genius and public are allied in a much greater similarity of stance: the public is touched and moved by the work that genius creates in much the same way as genius itself is touched and moved by the objects it encounters. The "Article Génie" in the *Encyclopédie* places considerable emphasis on this attribute: "The man of *genius* is he whose vaster soul . . . , interested by everything found in nature, never receives an idea without it awakening a feeling." And, the entry continues, "he does not restrict himself to seeing, he is moved." This receptiveness to effects from without has in common with the other attributes of genius the ability to bring to light ever greater variety within the world: "[genius] has its source in an extreme sensitivity, which makes it susceptible to a host of new impressions."[20] It brings us news of the world by virtue of its exceptional sensitivity, as it picks up impressions that would be lost on less sentient beings, and transmits them to the public by means of the likenesses that it produces.

This quality may not be one that helps the philosopher whose work, as the article comments, requires a scrupulousness of attention and habits of reflection that do not sit well with emotion: "it requires exploration, discussion, slowness; and these qualities are not to be had either in the tumult of passion, nor with the fiery bursts of the imagination."[21] Although philosophy and the fine arts share the aim of passing on new knowledge, they differ in the use they make of sensibility, both in their relation to the world they portray and in the response they seek to elicit from their public. Admiration may accompany the learning that the public acquires from the pursuit of philosophy, but emotional response actively determines the forms of knowledge that the reading and spectating public derives from the arts.

Response

It is Dubos who introduces most clearly the principle whereby the arts are evaluated in terms of their capacity to elicit emotional response in their public. He begins his discussion of genius in the *Réflexions critiques* by declaring that "[t]he sublime character of poetry and painting is to touch and to please." Genius produces this effect through its ability to "grant being to objects that are able to move and to please us in their own right," and the reader's response to the representation of those objects becomes its measure: "I acknowledge the artisan who plays upon my heart in this way, to be a man capable of doing something divine."[22]

The feelings that art ignites are evidence of the human soul's inveterate desire to be occupied: "the natural tendency of our soul is to give itself up to everything that occupies it," feeling being the name for what happens when "the soul gives itself over to the impressions that external objects make upon it." Aesthetic responses may differ from those in real life, since we derive pleasure from situations that, if actually experienced, would cause pain and distress. But the aesthetic response is triggered only if a work of art provides a convincing likeness of objects:

> Painters and poets excite artificial passions in us, by presenting us with imitations of objects capable of exciting real passions within us. As the impression that these imitations make on us are of the same type as the impression that the object imitated by the painter or poet would make on us; and as the impression that the imitated object would make [differs] only in being less strong, it is bound to excite in our soul a passion that resembles the one that the imitated object might have excited. The copy of the object is bound, so to speak, to excite within us a copy of the passion that the object itself would have excited.[23]

Mimesis is always geared to the effects it produces.

Dubos suggests here that the second-order character of both mimesis and response means that they necessarily exist in an attenuated form, but the rhetoric of other commentators in describing response is far less restrained. In his *Éloge de Richardson*—where he repeatedly praises Richardson for his genius, and places him in the same class as Homer, Euripides, and Sophocles—Diderot establishes a precise equation between the mimetic accuracy of Richardson's novels and the intensity of the reader's emotional reaction to them. Reader response was of course the informing principle of the novel of sensibility, and Richardson's *Clarissa* was a prime example of the genre. But if the impact of Richardson's novel is more than superficial and ephemeral, this, says Diderot, is precisely because he depicts a world so recognizably the one the reader himself inhabits, populated by characters who have "all possible reality," and containing passions that readers will know from their own experience. The effects produced by such mimetic prowess are conveyed in the picture Diderot paints of his friend as he observes him retire to a quiet corner with *Clarissa* and begin to read: "I examined him: first I see tears flow, he breaks off, he sobs; suddenly he rises, he walks without knowing where he is going, he utters cries like a man in despair, and he addresses the bitterest reproaches to the entire Harlove [sic] family."[24] The tears and cries of this distracted reader are testimony to the exactness of the representation that is the mark of the novelist's genius.

They are also, by extension, testimony to genius itself. Imprecations against the Harlowe family are not so far from being admiration for the genius of the novelist who created them. For Marmontel—a former playwright and fellow *Encyclopédiste*—these two forms of response are indistinguishable. Writing about genius in his *Éléments de littérature*, he makes this point by saying that whether it is the character of Dido in the *Iliad*, the recognition scene between Oedipus and Jocasta in Racine's *Oedipe*, or the confrontation between Molière's miser who refuses to lend and the son who wishes to borrow, the effect of each of these instances is to "astonish the understanding, penetrate the soul, or subjugate the will." The precise words of the text will eventually fade from the reader-spectator's memory, and what he is left with is an overall impression that evolves from these immediate emotional reactions (astonished understanding, penetrated soul, subjugated will) to a longer-lasting admiration for the genius that is their origin: "it is the conception that strikes us, it is the thought that remains with us and the confused memory of which is, if I can put it like this, a long shock of admiration."[25] The felt presence of genius itself is responsible for this more durable legacy, which remains within the reader or spectator as an index of its mimetic power.

SELF-EVIDENCE

All this suggests that before any defining and explaining can begin, genius is quite simply felt. There is, in other words, something astonishingly self-evident about genius as it is presented in most eighteenth-century accounts, and this contrasts with later periods when genius is increasingly misrecognized, is derided, or acquires problematic status of one kind or another. None of the eighteenth-century commentators appears to hesitate in proclaiming that a given figure is endowed with genius. The author of the "Article Génie" may be cautious about definitions of genius, but he has no doubts about its recognition: "It is better felt than known by the man who wishes to define it." And Voltaire, who takes a broadly pragmatic view of genius as "superior talent," asserts quite categorically that "Poussin, who was already a great painter before he saw good pictures, had the genius of painting. Lulli, who saw not a single good musician in France, had the genius of music."[26] This feeling for genius—you know it when you see it—is illustrated in the many oppositions that commentators construct in their efforts to define it. The topic of genius, as shown by the examples from Condillac and Edward Young quoted in my introduction, has a tendency to spawn negative definitions, opposing it variously to talent, intellect (*esprit*), imitation (in the sense of mimicry rather than mimesis), learning, convention, and the "rules." (The opposition between genius and taste is less straightforward than the rest and will require separate discussion.)

Talent

The opposition between genius and talent is a particularly recurrent topos, Voltaire's views about genius as superior talent notwithstanding. Condillac distinguishes between the two by describing talent as an ability whose results are entirely predictable, and genius as an attribute that adds to talent a creative cast of mind conducive to originality. Genius invents new art forms, new genres, and new sciences, and approaches the world from a perspective that is unique to its possessor: "A man endowed with talent has a character that could belong to others: he may be equaled, and sometimes even surpassed. A man of genius has an original character, he is inimitable."[27] Talent simply replicates existing forms and practices, whereas genius surprises with the novelty and ambition of its inventions.

Marmontel bases his entire account of genius around the opposition between the two terms, talent being an aptitude for producing work that will be correct, "a form that art approves and by which taste is satisfied," and genius being quite simply "the ability to create." The creative and original character of genius is contrasted with the technical competence of talent: "The productions of talent consist in giving form; and the creations of *genius*, in giving being; the merit of the one lies in industry; that of the other in invention." Echoing Condillac's comment, Marmontel claims that the man of genius owes his creative power to the individuality of his character and "a way of seeing, feeling and thinking that is particular to him." Talent functions with a restricted horizon, its appeal lying at the level of detail, whereas genius operates on a much grander scale and it is the whole that impresses. The difference between the two is unmistakable. Who, when confronted with mere technical competence, could possibly confuse it with the glories of original invention? And who, when offered a choice between manipulation of minor detail and the wholesale invention of a new art, would hesitate to ascribe the one to talent and the other to genius? Indeed, as Marmontel goes on to say, the distinction between genius and talent is so self-evident that "the great number of cultivated men are in a position to feel it."[28]

Rules

The antithesis between genius and talent is supported by the accounts of genius that present it as being largely independent of learning and rules. Dubos is the first to establish genius in these terms. Genius, he argues, is innate and not taught: "What a man born with genius does best, is that which no one has shown him how to do." Dubos does not pretend that genius can dispense altogether with poetic or painterly protocols, but, he says, a poet of genius would need no more than a couple of months to master the entirety of the rules of French poetry. From this it is only a short step to the view advanced by Marmontel that genius can afford quite simply to neglect the rules; and when it does have recourse to them it infuses them with new life, imparting "a heat that revivifies them and makes them germinate." The "Article Génie" is even more extreme and presents the rules as positively inimical to genius: "Rules and the laws of taste would shackle *genius*; it breaks them so as to be able to rise to the heights of sublimity, pathos, greatness." The decorum of the rules (here the rules of taste) is contrasted with "strength and abundance, and I know not what roughness, irregularity, sublimity, pathos," which characterize genius in the works it produces.[29] Genius is known by the abrasive power with which it stamps its creations, and which is quite different from the polish required by the norms of taste whose labor should remain invisible.

INTELLECT

A further contrast commonly adduced in these discussions is that between genius and intellect (*esprit*). In his *Salon of 1765* Diderot writes, "Beware of people whose pockets are filled with intellect, and who scatter it about at every pretext. They have no daemon [*démon*]. They are not sad, gloomy, melancholic or silent. They are never clumsy or foolish."[30] Intellect is rather like the rules of taste: its harmless chatter fails to make any impact, unlike the awkward, ill-behaved example of genius, which, when night has fallen and the prattling wits are asleep, will fill the woods with its song. Vauvenargues, whose primary interest is in the mind, and who has a fairly complex model of its workings, draws a similar distinction, arguing that intellect alone does not make for genius, which requires the support of other qualities such as passion, originality, sensibility, and the capacity to focus on a single object. While this is not as extreme as Diderot's antithesis, Vauvenargues establishes a clear difference between intellectual ability and the more complex and inventive character of genius.

The playwright Louis-Sébastien Mercier turns this distinction between the two into wholesale antagonism and his narrative poem, *Le Génie, le goût et l'esprit: poëme, en quatre chants* (Genius, taste and intellect: a poem in four cantos), is a brief history of mankind in which *Génie* is pitched against an implacable *Esprit*, to which it tragically succumbs. Genius is portrayed as a creative deity: "he will be the father of everything. / He comes to create, and without him life is only death."[31] Taste in this instance is brother and mentor to Genius, and though weaker, provides him with the necessary gift of embellishment. *Esprit*, their odious rival, is the child of *Envy* and *Caprice*, its mode is fury and fanaticism, it foments strife and seeks to dominate the world from its base in the Schools where systems reign. The hostility between the forces of genius and intellect is extreme in Mercier's narrative, but it shares with all the other antitheses by which genius is defined the underlying opposition between life and its obverse: without genius there is only living death.

In their lexicological commentary on "genius" in the eighteenth century, Georges Matoré and A.-J. Greimas note that the opposition between *l'homme de génie* and *l'homme d'esprit* is established relatively early in the century, and they suggest that its significance lies in the fact that genius is associated with the soul, which was regarded as the seat of life, and with a sensibility that was contrasted with the intellect.[32] The association of genius with life is a recurrent feature of its portrayal, whether the life is associated with the soul, as Matoré and Greimas argue, with its spontaneous emergence as a gift of nature (as Dubos is the first to say), with its energy (emphasized by the "Article Génie"), its heat (as described by Vauvenargues), or the creative force, specifically described by Marmontel as the capacity to endow objects with "being." The living character of genius that emerges with such recurrence from the antitheses favored by commentators of the period is ultimately the factor that makes the presence of genius something to be *felt*.

In his essay *De la poésie dramatique* (On dramatic poetry), Diderot explicitly observes that "Genius is felt; but it cannot be imitated," and this introduces a further antithesis—though it is implied in most of the others—namely, the one between genius and the kind of imitation that Kant refers to as "aping." Genius neither imitates nor can be imitated. (The coincidence of the two senses of the word "imitation" is unfortunate, since mimetic representation has proved to be such vital feature of genius, but the insertion of the adjective "mere," following eighteenth-century practice, should serve to distinguish between the two senses of the word.) The entry on "Pastiche" in the *Encyclopédie* makes this point by observing that while the technique of an artist may be imitated, his individual genius cannot: "It is impossible . . . to mimic the genius of great men, but people sometimes succeed in mimicking their hand."[33] In sum, the work of genius and the work of imitative talent are informed by two entirely different principles, which it is hard to imagine the large number of cultivated men mentioned by Marmontel failing to distinguish.

TASTE

In practice, however, things are more complex, though not in any way that will significantly alter the passive positioning of the reader-spectator as he registers the presence of genius. Genius, as we have seen, is almost always presented as unmistakable and it is always to be preferred to the various alternatives with which it is regularly contrasted. However, there are occasions when genius needs to be either supplemented or modified by other factors, most notably taste. Taste takes account of the sensibilities of readers and constitutes a repertoire of acceptable practice. To that extent, it would seem to represent the reverse of all that is most commonly celebrated in genius, its originality in particular. Indeed, taste is presented by the "Article Génie" as positively antithetical to genius, genius being "a pure gift of nature" and taste the result of learning; the products of the former are the work of an instant whereas those of the latter are the outcome of laborious effort.

In general, however, taste is commonly attached to genius throughout the century as its necessary counterpart. Mercier makes Taste the indispensable companion to Genius. In the introduction to his poem Mercier writes, "I have given him [i.e., Genius] Taste for a brother; & it is this God who reveals all the secrets of Genius to me, and initiates me into his mysteries." As well as providing a decorative adjunct to Genius, Taste acts as an intermediary between Genius and its public, ensuring its intelligibility. Taste is furthermore a source of wisdom, and the first admirers of the "miracles" produced by Genius also treasure the "oracles" of Taste.[34] The creative force of genius makes it liable occasionally to step outside the bounds of what the public can accept, and Taste is there to contain its excesses. This is an argument later picked up by Kant, but its strongest exponent is Batteux.

Batteux, who is one of the more conservative commentators on genius in the eighteenth century, accords an important place to taste. The emphasis of his argument shifts between a version where taste is on the side of the public, and a version where taste is inseparable from genius itself. In one role it is a kind of censor or arbiter, defending the interests of the public, which has the last word in determining the validity of the work of art: "taste, for which the arts are made, and which is their judge, will be satisfied when nature has been well chosen and well imitated by the arts." In its other guise, taste appears as something rather more like the fraternal Mentor from Mercier's poem: "Genius and taste are so intimately related in the arts, that there are cases where it is impossible to combine them without them appearing to merge, nor separate them without stripping them of their specific functions."[35] Taste, in other words, is much an enabler of genius as its regulator.

There seems to be something like a conflict at work here: for genius to be intelligible it needs to collaborate with taste. But at the same time, as the "Article Génie" points out, the recognition of genius relies on an opposition to all that is nongenius, taste included. In other words, the reader, whose function in both cases is to acknowledge the presence of genius, fulfills that function in two rather different ways: the one by vouching for the absolute originality of genius, and the other by ensuring that the productions of genius do not exceed the bounds of what its audience is able or willing to recognize as valid mimesis. Such contradictions notwithstanding, and with or without the accompaniment of taste, genius will always register with readers who need take no active steps to discover it.

The self-evidence of genius continues unchallenged. This is in part due to the function of mimesis that allows the reader-spectator to compare a representation with its object, and so ratify the likeness that only genius is capable of producing. In fact, Batteux describes this comparison as being one of the pleasures of reading or viewing: "The mind is exerted in comparing the model with its portrait; and the judgment it derives makes an impression upon it that is all the more agreeable for being proof of its penetration and intelligence."[36] It is because the reader-spectator has his own sensibility and powers of observation that he can, as it were, endorse the work of genius.

Aesthetic issues would seem therefore to be best understood by exploring what goes on inside the reader, not the artist, and this is precisely what Dubos claims when he says that his purpose in the *Réflexions critiques* is to "make the reader aware . . . of what goes on within himself."[37] The reader-spectator's response is the key to insight into genius. Or indeed to its very survival, as Mercier's narrative poem suggests when, after Genius has been vanquished by its enemy *Esprit*, it is the devotion of the public that calls it back to life from beyond the grave. However, as time goes on, their paths will diverge.

CHAPTER 2

Genius Obscured

Diderot

> I agree that it is only men of genius who feel and mark these
> differences; but I say, however, that it is only by observing them,
> and others like them, that we are able to produce the illusion.
> —Rousseau, *Dictionnaire de musique*

Rousseau is one of the first to articulate a view of genius that dispenses with its public when, in his entry on Genius in his *Dictionnaire de musique*, he suggests that the qualities required for its recognition can only be those of genius itself: "its marvels are scarcely felt by anyone who is incapable of imitating them," *imitating* being understood here in the positive sense that Kant later gave to the term. He concludes the entry with an admonishment to the third-party spectator when he writes, "Vulgar man, do not profane this sublime name. What use would it be to you to know it? you would not be able to feel it." The public—now deemed "vulgar"—lacks the requisite sensibility to respond to genius, and is bracketed out of a relation that now goes exclusively from genius to genius. As Rousseau says in addressing the "young Artist," "If you have it, you will feel it inside. If you do not have it, you will never know it."[1] Genius remains self-evident, but only to the man who is already endowed with it: he alone is equipped to recognize it, whether in himself or another.

Rousseau is not the only person to establish a link between genius and genius in a manner that sidelines the public. Voltaire comments in his entry on Genius that the "Article Génie" in the *Encyclopédie* has the advantage of having been written by "men who possessed it," thus making it hard for him to add anything further. A footnote names Diderot, who himself made a similar point, albeit in negative terms, about Helvétius's discussion of genius, when he suggests that the analysis is seriously undermined by the total absence of the quality its author claims to be elucidating: "Helvétius's system is that of a man with considerable intellect [*esprit*], who demonstrates in every line that the tyrannical impulse of genius is foreign to him and who talks about it like a blind man about color."[2] As the burden of recognition is shifted from reader-spectator to genius itself, the continuity between reader-spectator and genius is broken, and the self-evidence of genius begins to wane.

Insensibility

This loss of self-evidence is not simply a result of the view that only genius is capable of recognizing genius. It also follows from Diderot's demonstration in the *Paradoxe sur le comédien* (whose first version dates from 1769) that genius is not necessarily what it might seem. The genius of the great actor derives not, as his audience likes to believe, from a superior sensibility, but rather from a willfully insensate capacity for observation and mime. The actor-genius and his audience operate according to quite different criteria, the one of affectless observation, the other of reactive sensation: "We [the audience] feel; they [the actors] observe, study and portray." The actor imitates passion, but the audience is moved by it, and, at the end of the performance "[t]he actor is weary, and you are sad; because he has had exertion without feeling, and you have had feeling without exertion."[3]

The mismatch is patent; but Diderot argues that the actor who lets himself be guided by the sensibility that the audience attributes to him, will only ever be a mediocre performer. The tears shed in the auditorium should never be allowed on stage, and the less the actor shares the responses he elicits, the better his performance will be. Diderot describes the genius of the performer as that "of being thoroughly acquainted with the external symptoms of the soul he has borrowed, of targeting the sensations of those who are listening and looking at us, and of *deceiving* them with the imitation of those symptoms and an imitation that will magnify everything inside their heads and provide the rule for their judgments."[4] The actor manipulates the sensibility of the public through an act of calculated deception. His skill consists in an ability to observe the outward signs of inward passion and to replicate them on the magnified scale that the stage requires, thus further dividing performer from an audience that continues to believe that the criteria and proportions of everyday reality are those that govern the representation on the stage.

Mimesis remains the basis of the art of theater, and Diderot describes the actor as "a mirror always positioned so as to display objects and to do so with the same accuracy, the same force and the same truth." But the *Paradoxe* repeatedly draws attention to the gap between the drama that the actor portrays on stage and his own private preoccupations. As the actor Lekain emerges in Voltaire's *Sémiramis* from the tomb of his father having just killed his mother, hands red with matricidal blood, eyes wild with horror at the act he has just committed, the audience trembles with him and experiences his apparent terror. Meanwhile he, having noticed an earring on the floor, kicks it into the wings before leaving the stage. And, as the actress Mlle Gaussin lies dying in the arms of her stage partner Pillot in Rameau's *Castor et Pollux*, she whispers to him, "*Ah! Pillot, you stink!*"[5] These anecdotes illustrate the disparity between the respective experiences of the actor-genius and his audience, highlighting the distance between the two, which is not just that between observation and sentiment, but that of outward appearance and inner reality. The audience weeps and trembles while the actor steers a lost earring back toward its owner or protests about her partner's body odor. This is a very far cry from Dubos or Condillac, whose focus on the response of the reader-spectator provided a reliable means of insight into the workings of the genius that was the source of those effects.

For now the audience continues in blissful ignorance as it basks in its own sensations, but with Diderot's *Neveu de Rameau*, the gap between spectator and genius grows deeper and wider as genius is turned into an object of active curiosity, ambivalence, debate, and ultimately envy.

LE NEVEU DE RAMEAU—INDETERMINATE GENIUS

In the early 1760s Diderot used an imagined encounter between his alter ego and the nephew of the composer Rameau, to open up the issue of genius to a new kind of scrutiny. This scrutiny is less a celebration in the manner of the *Éloge de Richardson*, than an exploration that breaks genius down into the constituent parts already identified in the existing literature before proceeding to observe those parts at work within a single human individual through the medium of a reported dialogue. On this occasion genius is examined in terms of differences that are not those of the conceptual binaries that structure other discussions of the topic, but those of character and cast of mind, of philosophy and performance, of Moi and Lui. The result is to make genius harder to define and considerably less self-evident, and although it continues to fascinate its beholders, the relation between genius and its audience is decisively altered.

Diderot's writings on genius are many and varied, and he is probably the best known eighteenth-century French commentator on the topic. I say commentator because, unlike Dubos or Batteux, he is not in any strict sense of the word a theorist of genius. He may, or may not, have been the author of the entry on the subject in the *Encyclopédie*—the scholarly consensus is that the text was almost certainly penned by Saint-Lambert, but that it reflected many of Diderot's own ideas on the topic.[6] And even if one were to read the "Article Génie" (1757) along with the unpublished little essay "Sur le génie" (On genius), which dates from the early 1770s and has been more confidently attributed to Diderot, the thoughts expressed in these texts are very far from representing the full range of his reflections on the subject, which were as contradictory as they were recurrent in his work. Diderot's discussion tends to be glancing, or incidental, as if genius were a topic that arose as an offshoot from other considerations rather than as the principal object of a sustained analysis.

An anthology of his comments would consist of odd pages and paragraphs taken from different parts of his œuvre, and from which it would be almost impossible to construct a consistent overarching view. It would, however, confirm the depth and permanence of his interest. In addition to the *Éloge de Richardson* (1762) and the two articles I have just mentioned, it would include extracts from the *Entretiens sur le Fils naturel* (1757), the *Salons* of 1765 and 1767, the *Réfutation d'Helvétius* (1775), the *Paradoxe sur le comédien* (written between 1769 and 1779), and, notably, but problematically, the *Neveu de Rameau*, which Diderot began in the early 1760s and continued to write and revise until 1782. The composition of this last text (which, like many of Diderot's writings, was never published during his lifetime) covers the period in which his other multifarious discussions of genius were written.

My listing of these discussions is not exhaustive; and if I suggest that the *Neveu de Rameau* takes a problematic view of genius, this is not so much because it lacks anything approaching a theory, but rather because, as I have already said, it confronts the topic in two very different idioms, each grounded in the particular character and circumstances of the two participants in the dialogue. Moi adopts a predominantly philosophical outlook and approaches the issue with a strong ethical bent. For Lui (the Neveu) the primary task is to instantiate, one after the other, a good many of the attributes commonly ascribed to genius. Genius is reworked here by being instantiated (rather than treated as an abstraction), by being examined through its constituent parts (rather than as a single entity), by being debated (rather than celebrated or theorized), and by constructing a new relation with its observing other. Diderot's contribution to the literature on genius consists above all in the resulting change of perspective that he brings to bear. Genius shades into imposture as the Neveu mimes enthusiasm, and the same enthusiasm takes him briefly into the realms of madness. But more than anything else, genius loses its self-evidence in a process that continues nonetheless to affirm its importance as an object of critical and philosophical enquiry.

The starting point for this enquiry is the underlying assumption that "genius" is one of those words—like "*law, taste, beautiful, good, true, usage customs, vice, virtue instinct, intellect* [esprit], *matter, grace, beauty, or ugliness*"— that, as Diderot says in one of his *Salons*, are at once "the most general, the most sacred, and the most used," but invariably with the most baffling vagueness or inconsistency or meaning. Moi endorses this view in *Le Neveu de Rameau* when he says, "Our memories contain only words which, from the frequent and even the appropriate use we make of them, we believe we understand, but of which our minds contain only vague notions."[7] The text duly subjects the word "genius" to a scrutiny that reveals just how vague the mind's grasp of the notion really is.

Genius Parsed

In the course of the discussion between Moi and Lui, most of the attributes commonly ascribed to genius are rehearsed and inspected by means of the text's combination of illustration and debate: a gift for mimesis, sensibility, originality, imagination, inspiration, indifference to laws and convention, exclusive focus on a single preoccupation, ethical merit, a tendency toward extremes, an aversion to mediocrity, an association with insanity, and a basis in innate character. Each receive their due. Diderot is adding nothing new to the mix, only sifting its contents in a particular context that will fundamentally alter the frame in which they appear.

To begin with mimesis, the sphere in which genius principally excels for eighteenth-century commentators. Lui's greatest talent is for the mimetic domain that is pantomime, and he graphically conjures up the scenes he describes, such as his pimping of an imaginary young "Miss," the performances on the violin and the harpsichord, and the operas of Duni and Jomelli where he acts the parts of the orchestra as well as the singers and brings to life a whole gamut of states and entities: "he was a woman swooning with grief; a wretch overcome with despair; a temple rising up from the ground; birds falling silent at sunset; rivers murmuring their way through cool solitudes or cascading down from high mountains; a storm; a tempest, the moans of the dying mingling with the whistling of the wind and the crashing of the thunder; night, with its darkness; shadows and silence." Pantomime may have been low in the contemporary hierarchy of genres, but in the *Entretiens sur le Fils naturel* Diderot has Dorval defend pantomime as the means whereby genius might best succeed in renewing an ailing theatrical tradition: the world of theater awaits "a man of genius who knows how to combine pantomime with speech, and intersperse a spoken scene with a silent one."[8] According to the *Entretiens*, pantomime is the ultimate manifestation of the mimetic ability of genius on the stage.

As if to corroborate this point, the effect of Lui's performance on his spectators—namely, Moi and the chess players who abandon their game to watch his impromptu performance—is to take hold of their souls and to suspend them "in the most extraordinary state of being." Moi describes his own response as offering the tribute of admiration and emotion which normally signals success: "Was I filled with admiration? Yes, I was. Was I moved to pity? Yes, I was." But these feelings come mixed with "a tinge of ridicule" which undermines their force.[9] Mimesis as the mark of genius is energetically demonstrated but fails in some unspecified way quite to carry full conviction.

In describing the prelude to his attempts at composition, Lui also lays claim to the sensibility that earlier discussions had portrayed as the basis of the mimetic power of genius. "I can feel, yes I can feel," he claims, and by way of proof "he mimicked a man growing angry, indignant, emotional, then a man commanding, then entreating; he began declaiming impromptu speeches full of rage, or commiseration, or loathing, or love; his sketches of the nature of the passions were astonishingly delicate and true." This is a convincing exhibition of the emotional susceptibility that is the supposed origin of mimesis. But when it moves him to take up his pen and produce a verbal representation, he falls to chewing his fingers and scratching his head, before conceding finally that the genius he was convinced he possessed is absent, and that he is merely "a fool."[10]

Lui is also described as being endowed with "an exceptionally vivid imagination," and his strategy throughout the encounter with Moi is always to replace intangibles with concrete example, whether anecdote or pantomime, or a combination of the two. In his essay *De la poésie dramatique* Diderot defines imagination as "the ability to recall images," and asserts that it is an essential component, not just of creative production, but of human existence in general. Without this faculty, says Diderot, the human mind would be reduced to mechanically repeating words and notions learned in childhood, a gross form of the repetition that it is the mark of genius to dispense with. The faculty of imagination makes it possible to move from abstraction and generality to physical instantiation, to pass from "abstract and general sounds to less abstract and less general ones, until it arrives at a concrete representation." It is just this principle that Lui upholds when, in one of his many ripostes to Moi, he claims not to understand one of Moi's comments since it "sounds like philosophy," and this he definitely does not "dabble in."[11]

Lui deals only in specifics and concrete entities, and accordingly reduces philosophical concepts—such as happiness or virtue—from universals to simple matters of individual taste. Not everyone, he argues, has an aptitude for virtue or a penchant for philosophy, and these preferences are nothing more than "oddities" whose origins lie in the quirks of individual character: "If you have them, good luck to you."[12] Imagination gets the better of philosophy in this encounter by reducing abstraction to concrete representations. In the process, *Le Neveu* implicitly confirms the acknowledgment in the "Article Génie" that the requirements of philosophy (patience, logic, persistence) are the obverse of the "eruptions [*fougues*] of the imagination" that are the index of genius.

Lui is described by Moi as an unusually curious character, distinguished by what Diderot calls his "singularity" (*originalité*). This quirky form of originality may be the mark of his own character, but as deployed by the Neveu it is also infectious, drawing out the distinctiveness of others and restoring to each person he encounters a portion "of his natural individuality." In this resistance to the universals of philosophical discourse, it is as if Ion had found a way of turning the tables on Socrates, and confounding the philosopher's superior, generalizing insight into his talents. Moi affects to condemn this trait in the Neveu ("I hold such eccentrics [*originaux*] in low esteem"), but singularity as a feature of genius does appear to be endorsed elsewhere in Diderot's thinking where genius is intimately bound up with the individual in whom it is manifest. As many commentators have already observed, it is with Diderot that genius becomes particularized, seen less as a general quality that certain individuals exemplify than as the manifestation of an individuality on which the resistance to rules and convention depends.[13]

Indeed, Moi himself concedes that "men of genius are usually singular," and the discussion of genius in Le Neveu de Rameau is principally a discussion of individual examples: Rameau (the Neveu's composer uncle), Racine, Greuze, Voltaire, Buffon, Montesquieu, Leonardo da Vinci, Pergolesi, Duni, the Renegade of Avignon, and so on. Genius is innate and, as such, a feature of the person before being that of any work of art or science. This is how the Renegade of Avignon can qualify for the title, and why it is possible to consider chess players, orators, and women as potential candidates for genius, despite the absence of any work to illustrate the attribute. And when Moi asks Lui why, with all his gifts, he too has no work to show for them, Lui himself seems less concerned by the absence of any masterpiece than by the lack of a certain something inside his own head, which he beats with his fists as if to rouse his missing creativity: "It seems to me that there is something in there, but however hard I knock it and shake it, nothing comes out. . . . Either nobody's home, or they don't want to answer."[14]

Genius here is personal. Rameau and Racine are considered for the kind of individuals that they were: Rameau brutal, tightfisted, a bad father, husband, and uncle, and Racine "a swindler, a traitor, ambitious, jealous, and spiteful," albeit also the author of Andromaque.[15] Greuze is mentioned for his vanity and Voltaire for his touchiness, but these human failings are deemed to be inseparable from the ability of the painter and the writer to move their readers and viewers.

Envy and the Experience of Genius

This ability to move an audience is, as we have seen from the work of Dubos, the principal achievement of genius as it is understood in the eighteenth century. Moi seems to subscribe to this criterion when he tests his own responses to Lui's performance—admiring, pitying, but remaining ultimately unconvinced. Lui, however, sticks entirely to the personal. The focus of his interest is the experience of the man of genius, but this preoccupation is grounded more in envy for the man than in admiration for the work. A performance of the overture to his uncle's Indes galantes prompts rage and regret that he did not compose the piece himself. The younger Rameau wants—quite simply—to be a man of genius: "I'd love to be someone else, even at the risk of being a man of genius, a great man."[16] He covets the praise that is lavished on the great man, longs to share the composer's confidence in his own greatness, and is jealous of the material benefits of fame. The "Other" of genius here is not the spectator whose heart is touched, but the one who simply envies or is intrigued by what it is to *be* a man of genius.

The relation to genius is radically altered here, and Lui is not alone in this shift. Diderot himself may not admit to envy, but he too displays as much interest in the experience of the man of genius as in the experience of the effects of his work. The portrait in the *Éloge de Richardson* of the reader moved by Clarissa Harlowe is matched by the portrait in the *Entretiens sur le Fils naturel* of Dorval in the throes of enthusiasm. The Moi of the *Entretiens* describes the playwright standing in the shade of an oak and contemplating the view of nature before him. This, says, Moi, is "the sacred abode of enthusiasm," and he proceeds to observe inspiration at work in his friend. On this occasion, inspiration does not carry with it the element of the ridiculous that leaves the Neveu's interlocutor so uneasy at the end of his performance. The sound of Dorval's voice is altered, his imagination heats up, and passion rises to take him through a sequence of emotions where he is first astonished, then moved, indignant and finally angry: "The poet feels the moment of enthusiasm; it comes after he has meditated. It is heralded inside him by a quivering which starts in the chest and moves rapidly and deliciously to his extremities. Soon it is no longer a quivering; it is a powerful and persistent heat which sets him aflame, makes him pant, consumes and destroys him; but which imparts soul and life to everything he touches."[17] The physical experience of heat and of the shiver that runs through his body constitutes an ordeal that culminates in a torrent of ideas that eventually bursts forth from him—and which notably fails to erupt from the Neveu. Dorval goes on to affirm that without inspiration of this kind, the poet cannot create.

It has been said that Diderot is writing here from his own experience, and this may well be true. But what is significant is that he chooses to ascribe the experience to a third party—Dorval—and to report it as viewed by an external observer, Moi. When Dorval emerges from his trance he has no memory of having spoken the words that Moi has noted down: inspiration is an experience of which, as Condillac had already noted, its subject has no conscious knowledge or recall, and which can be observed only from without. In this state he is not "master of his reflections," but, as Condillac asks, "how can one analyze it when one is no longer experiencing it?" The only solution is to extrapolate from its effects upon those who witness it.[18] For Diderot, the moment of enthusiasm is the object of active curiosity on the part of the person witnessing the occasion, who is led to wonder what genius *feels like* for its possessor, or, in the case of the Neveu, to *envy* him the experience. The *Entretiens* are a narrated dialogue similar to that of *Le Neveu de Rameau* where the Moi figure is both participant in the reported dialogue and narrator of an encounter—or series of encounters—with an interlocutor who is a creator (Dorval, the fictional author of *Le Fils naturel*) or who would dearly love to be (the Neveu).

In the case of *Le Neveu de Rameau* the relation to genius is duplicated. Lui envies the man of genius in general and his uncle in particular, and his antics may be viewed as an attempt to appropriate the experience whose principal features are then exhibited in his performance. In a second relation, Moi observes Lui and his illustration of these traits of genius. This doubled relation foregrounds curiosity about the personal life of the man of genius and helps to make sense of the apparent volte-face in Diderot's view of genius as he portrays it in the *Paradoxe sur le comédien*. Here, as we have already seen, the genius of the stage actor consists in suppressing the turmoil that for Dorval accompanies inspiration. But in both cases, the observer has his attention directed to the *experience* of the man of genius, and it is that experience—whether of shivers and heat or of cool control—which becomes the object of enquiry and constitutes the focus of analytical interest.

The mediating figures provided by the two Mois of the *Entretiens* and *Le Neveu de Rameau* and by the two interlocutors in *Le Paradoxe sur le comédien* are the pivot on which the changed relation to genius turns, stimulating the reader's own curiosity and offering privileged insight into the inner life of the *man* of genius, which is not necessarily visible to the admirer of the *works* of genius. This mediation will become all the more necessary for the understanding of genius in the following century, when it will take on a number of different guises—critical, female, and medical by turns.

PART II

Nineteenth-Century Genius

The Idiom of the Age

CHAPTER 3

Language, Religion, Nation

In judging the genius of a people, the true philosopher does not
limit himself to seeking out a few great men here and there.
—Chateaubriand, *Génie du christianisme*

In 1798 Jean-François de La Harpe introduced his eighteen-volume history of
literature, the *Lycée, ou Cours de littérature ancienne et moderne*, with a discussion of genius in which he deplores what he sees as the current misuse of the
term. His principal objection is that genius has come to be routinely opposed
to taste, talent, and the rules of art. This opposition has fostered what he regards as a complacent and self-congratulatory assumption among the younger
generation that their disdain for matters of taste is a sure sign of their own
genius. Moreover, he continues, the words "genius" and "taste" have been endowed with a regrettable arbitrariness since "the person employing them gives
them the value he chooses." Semantic instability has led to disagreement: "at
the word *genius*, disputes erupt, and people can no longer agree," and because
of this misuse of words, "people manage to deny genius to the greatest writers
and grant it to the worst." The problem has arisen, says La Harpe, as a result of
the underlying shift in the meaning of the word since the days of Boileau,
when it referred simply to "natural aptitude" (*ingenium*) and had none of the
connotations of preeminence or superior ability that it has acquired since Voltaire's time (La Harpe's dating) when it began to be used in its recent "absolute"
sense.[1]

SEMANTIC PROFLIGACY AND THE LITERARY CONNOISSEUR

Despite his apparent traditionalism on semantic matters, La Harpe recognizes
that this new sense of the word "genius" is here to stay: "This way of talking . . .
belongs to our times," and since this usage is now "universal," "we must speak
the language that everyone speaks." But the imprecision of its terms has made
it all the more necessary to introduce some rigor into their application. For La

Harpe, this means treating taste and talent as inseparable from genius, rather than its converse, and he calls for a new semantic vigilance to be exercised by "real connoisseurs" whose knowledge will either correct or confirm the uninformed "impressions of the multitude."[2]

The public is no longer a reliable guide to the presence of genius, whose recognition will henceforth depend increasingly on specialist knowledge. According to La Harpe, it is the philosopher who must now act as the self-appointed guardian of its meaning; and when it comes to individual writers, their particular genius is a "secret" that the critic alone knows how to uncover. The genius of Racine or of Voltaire, for instance, can be brought to light only through the most "attentive study," since the applause offered by the crowd will reveal none of the "precious features" or the "details of perfection" that "a few connoisseurs enjoy alone and in secret."[3] At the turn of the century, the critic asserts himself as a necessary mediator between the writer of genius and the mass of his allegedly ignorant readers. In doing so, he paves the way for the career of Sainte-Beuve whose development of literary criticism for popular consumption in the press was based on broadly the same premise.[4]

La Harpe was born in 1739 and died the year before the final volume of his *Lycée* was published in 1804. A literary critic, playwright, and one-time friend of Voltaire, he abandoned his former radical views after the experience of imprisonment under the Terror, and his introduction may well be a reflection of his disenchantment. At any rate, he comments in his preface to the same enterprise that the French Revolution, and the Terror in particular, were hostile to literature, science, and "all kinds of instruction and morality."[5] The *Lycée* itself is based on the series of lectures he began delivering in 1786 at the recently established institution that lends its name to La Harpe's title. The book is an extraordinary attempt to construct a complete history of literature from the ancients to the present day. Even more extraordinary is the fact that the introduction to such an ambitious historical project should be concerned almost exclusively with genius and its definition. For all the conservative brake that La Harpe sought to apply to its usage, his discussion speaks volumes about the importance that the notion had acquired, and consciously or not, the terms in which he presents it announce the agenda for its future life in the nineteenth century. Genius was indeed the idiom of the age.

If genius no longer has the self-evidence that was attributed to it in the eighteenth century, this is due in part to the profligacy—noted by La Harpe—with which the word had come to be used. While the term is widely invoked—in fact, ever more widely so—it is rarely the subject of sustained theoretical scrutiny of the type established by aesthetics and philosophy in the previous century. This dearth of conceptual discussion marks France out from other countries, where genius continues to be the object of philosophical and aesthetic theorization and debate. In Germany, Schelling and Jean-Paul pursue the philosophical discussion established by their eighteenth-century predecessors, and Schopenhauer returns repeatedly to the topic in the various editions and revisions of *The World as Will and Representation*.[6] In England genius is the topic of influential essays and lectures by Coleridge and Hazlitt; and in America, Ralph Waldo Emerson's essay "Self-Reliance," from 1841, is largely devoted to the topic.[7]

The relative scarcity of focused philosophical discussion in France combined with the widespread use of the term may, paradoxically perhaps, be one of the reasons for the degree of importance that the notion acquired as it was picked up by a whole range of new disciplines and discourses that emerged over the course of the century: literary criticism, Romantic poetry, psychological medicine, realist fiction, children's literature, and experimental psychology. For most of these disciplines genius arises incidentally, making a strategic appearance in their evolution, rather than constituting the central focus of their concerns. But the very novelty of these emergent discourses has an invigorating effect on the ways in which genius is conceived, and the notion develops out of its immersion in these discussions in renewed and repeatedly revitalized form.

With the profligate use of the term condemned by La Harpe continuing unchecked by the theoretical rigor of any single discursive system, the word "genius" is everywhere. There were poems and odes to genius, especially in the early decades of the century as genius becomes a collective entity taking many different forms which often inspire a celebratory mode of portrayal. There were numerous descriptions of national genius and character—Italian, Polish, Spanish, Serbian, Roman, Greek, and so on, but most of all French. There was a genius of Revolution, and a genius of peace, celebrated in a pantomime performed at the wedding of Emperor Napoleon to Marie Louise of Austria in 1810. The July column in the Place de la Bastille was topped with the gilded *Génie de la Liberté* cast by the sculptor Auguste Dumont in 1835 (Figure 1). There were books celebrating the genius of women and extolling their civilizing influence, and others devoted to a "financial genius," a genius of labor, and an "industrial genius," a genius of history and of tragedy as well as a genius of architecture, French literature, and the painting of the Italian Renaissance.

The Genius of the French

This was an era sustained by a belief in progress that was often attributed to genius, both collective and individual, and promoted under titles such as *Le Génie de la France à l'exposition universelle de 1855* (The genius of France in the universal exhibition of 1855), which detailed "the most remarkable products of French industry" with a view to showcasing the nation's achievements. "Modern genius" was demonstrated in "Agriculture, aerostation, and astronomy," while "rural genius" also received its due. Genius was offered in many how-to forms, with publications on the "genius of opposition" for the benefit of voters, but also of grocery in 1827 (*Le Génie de l'épicerie et ses branches accessoires* [The

Figure 1. *Le Génie de la Liberté*, on the July Column, Place de la Bastille. Photo by Marie-Lan Nguyen/Wikimedia Commons (Public Domain)

genius of grocery and its ancillary branches]) and of tailoring in 1879 (*Simplicité, rapidité, précision. Le Génie du tailleur, innovation d'une méthode de coupe facile à apprendre seul* [Simplicity, speed and accuracy. The genius of tailoring, an innovation in cutting method that is easily learned alone]). There was a genius of whist, and a genius of fashion celebrated in the title of a periodical that ran from 1862 until the last year of the century. The ubiquity of genius attracted its own form of piety, as when the author of a novel titled *Naissance et génie* (Birth and genius) promises to depict "the poetry of duty," and, in a six-volume account of the "rights of genius," the failure to pay homage to genius is portrayed as an unpatriotic betrayal of industrial progress.[8]

The genius celebrated in this popular usage was, more often than not, a collective phenomenon linking success or supremacy with the individual character of institutional or abstract entities in a way that combined genius as *ingenium* with genius as the form of superlative excellence. The genius of the French (and other) languages had been promoted and discussed since the sixteenth century, and many nineteenth-century translations of classical and other foreign texts are described as being "in accordance with the genius of the French language." National genius was a well-established notion that linked it as a near synonym for "character" to both language and mores. Voltaire specifically mentions national identity as one sense of the word "genius" in his entry for the word in the *Dictionnaire philosophique*, noting that "[w]e call the character, the customs, the principal talents, and even the vices that distinguish one people from another the *genius of a nation*. One has only to look at the French, the Spanish and the English to feel this difference."[9]

This view is reflected in a number of publications in the latter part of the eighteenth century, such as the *Dictionnaire classique de Géographie Ancienne* (Classical dictionary of ancient geography), dating from 1768, which claims in its subtitle to provide "a succinct idea of the Genius, the Practices, the Religion, the Customs, the Commerce of the Peoples of the earth under the different Rule of the Persians, the Assyrians, the Greeks & the Romans," or the two-volume *Description historique de l'Italie, en forme de dictionnaire* (Historical description of Italy, in dictionary form), published in 1790, whose contents include "The genius and the customs of [the country's] inhabitants."[10]

All this is relatively neutral, but with the increasing anthropomorphization of nation-states, national genius—especially French national genius—began to acquire more of the overtones of preeminence associated with exceptional individuals, and to raise questions about the ways in which those exceptional individuals might relate to the collective whole. Alongside all this, the Revolution and its aftermath turned the whole issue of French national identity and "French genius" into a source of national anxiety, lending a degree of urgency to the question that became a frequent topic of discussion in the early years of the century.

THE GENIUS OF THE LANGUAGE

The idea of a "genius of the language" had for some time provided a means of thinking about national identity and its place in an imaginary pecking order of nation-states. National languages were related to national character and commentators posited an analogy between the differences that distinguish individuals from each other and those that mark out one nation from another. In the late seventeenth century Dominique Bouhours had treated linguistic expression as an effect of character, both individual and collective, on the basis of his claim that "language usually follows the cast of mind; & every nation has always talked in accordance with its genius." Just as individual painters adopt different styles, he says, so too do nations. But French is not just different from other comparable languages, it is also implicitly superior—"marvelous" (*merveilleux*)—thanks to its capacity to combine nobility and majesty with simplicity and candor.[11] It is distinctive, too, for supposedly being the only language that follows the natural order of thought as it arises in the human mind. The "genius" of the French language may initially be little more than a synonym for character, but it begins to accrue connotations of preeminence that increasingly suggest a continuity between the ways in which individual and collective forms of genius are conceived.

At any rate, "the genius of the (French) language" had become a commonly used in expression by the eighteenth century. Condillac devotes a chapter of his *Essai sur l'origine des connaissances humaines* to the topic, where he relates national character not just to language but also to government, and by extension all three to each other. These are not static entities but they develop over time, and he argues that national languages have to reach a certain stage of development before literature is able to make use it them. The genius of the language equips the individual poet of genius with tools that allow him to produce a language of his own, and this individual literary idiom is subsequently absorbed back into the national idiom, further contributing to its collective genius. The model for this harmonious series of mutually enhancing relations among government, national character, language, and individual genius is the era of Louis XIV, which, as Condillac observes, saw an exceptional flourishing of individual talent that in turn significantly benefited the collective linguistic whole.

These arguments were picked up and presented with considerable bravura by Antoine Rivarol—satirist, *homme de lettres* and wit—in his prize-winning essay *De l'universalité de la langue française* (The universality of the French language), published in 1784, just five years before the Revolution, after which questions about national character and appropriate forms of government could no longer command the sort of consensus anticipated by Rivarol's exposition. His equation of French linguistic genius with universality was to some extent dictated by the topic that was set by the Berlin Academy in 1782 for its annual essay competition, in which candidates were invited to consider whether the French language deserved the "prerogative" of its universality and to comment on the likelihood that this status would last.[12]

The prize for the best essay was awarded jointly in 1783 to Rivarol and to one Professor Schwab from the University of Stuttgart. Founded by the Francophile Frederick the Great, the Berlin Academy had a cosmopolitan membership that included both Voltaire and Maupertuis, the French mathematician, who served as its president from 1746 to 1759. The official language of the academy was French, which was also spoken at court. Under these circumstances the universality of French might seem to be an established fact, but Rivarol sets out to demonstrate exactly what it is about the French language that justifies the presumption of universality and, by implication, its superiority over the linguistic alternatives.

He compares French to the other main European languages, all of which, on closer examination, prove to have features that disqualify them from claims to universal status. One of these features is excessive internal diversity: German is "too rich," Spain is undermined by having two quite separate languages—Castilian and Catalan—and Italian has too many *patois*. France, by contrast, while physically straddling the North and the South of Europe, is represented by a single language, so that geographical variation is transcended by linguistic unity. This unified French language is no formal or genealogical accident, but the manifestation of national character. The analogy between individuals and nations allows Rivarol, following previous discussions, to define language as the expression of thought at a collective as well an individual level, and to invoke "the eternal alliance of speech and thought" in individuals as a means of explaining "the union of the character of a people with the genius of its language."[13]

FRENCH WRITERS AND THE FRENCH LANGUAGE

In a further analogy, individuals contribute to the construction of the national linguistic whole because, "if languages are like nations, words are like men." This relation of lexical part to linguistic whole applies, as it did for Condillac, to the relation of the writer to the national language. Rivarol follows Condillac, too, in arguing that French achieved its linguistic preeminence in the seventeenth century when "a host of geniuses took hold of the French language and rapidly put it through all its periods." But he takes Condillac's argument about government one stage further when he claims that this absorption of individual talent into collective national genius was made possible by Louis XIV, "the veritable Apollo of a French Parnassus," whose qualities meant that "poems, paintings and marble lived only for him." A single individual—Louis XIV—had the power to draw together the energies of the various writers and artists of his day so as to create the global entity of French national character, which is reflected across its politics, its culture, and its language because "everything was done in the name of France."[14] Rivarol even goes so far as to suggest that France owes its international prestige to its culture and its language, rather than to its military achievements, and that the success of the treaties drawn up by Louis XIV was due more to the style in which they were composed than to the political content of their terms.

In Rivarol's account, individual differences are repeatedly subsumed into a single national genius, so that, for example, one of the chief characteristics of the French language is its ability to connect individuals through the practice of conversation. Rivarol himself had a reputation for being an exceptional conversationalist, and he was described by his memorialist Chênedollé as "the king of conversation."[15] Personal proclivities aside, Rivarol cites Leibniz's view that linguistic diversity is antithetical to genius, and the whole thrust of his argument binds individual literary talent to a composite national genius, whether as its reflection or as one of many contributory parts. The sense of "genius" in Rivarol's definition of French national and linguistic genius is much more than "character," and the universalism that he claims for the French language gives it the kind of exceptional status that is elsewhere associated with genius as increasingly applied to individuals.

Chateaubriand and the Genius of Christianity

Chateaubriand's *Génie du christianisme* (Genius of Christianity), published in 1802, was one of the first books to place collective genius on the cultural map of nineteenth-century France and to continue the exploration of the relation between collective and individual genius. The book was conceived as an apology for Christianity following Chateaubriand's conversion, which he describes in the preface to the first edition. After his mother died, his sister Julie wrote to him to inform him of their mother's death and of her dying wish that he return to the Christian faith to make amends for the "impiety" of his *Essai sur les révolutions* (Essay on revolutions), published in 1797. By the time the letter reached Chateaubriand in London, where he had been living in exile since 1793, Julie too was dead: "I was struck by these two voices emerging from the grave . . . . I became a Christian."[16]

Chateaubriand's account of the genius of Christianity is inseparable from the issue of French national genius, which the Revolution had thrown into question, and was the pretext for the *Essai historique, politique et moral sur les révolutions anciennes et modernes considérées dans leurs rapports avec la Révolution française* (Historical, political, and moral essay on ancient and modern revolutions examined in their relations with the French Revolution), which had so distressed his mother. In this earlier text, begun in the aftermath of the Terror, Chateaubriand describes the Revolution as "this astonishing tragedy," and while he acknowledges that he was himself an "actor, and a suffering actor, an unhappy Frenchman [who] had seen [his] fortune and [his] friends disappear into the abyss of the revolution," this tragedy is less personal than general.[17] Whence the world-historical rather than the autobiographical approach.

The French Revolution had put the French nation out of joint with its times, and split it into two factions, one of which had run ahead of itself toward "imaginary perfections," and the other of which still clung to values that harked back to the fourteenth century. Chateaubriand depicts the two groups as stranded on either side of the river of the age on whose current the unified destiny of the nation should have been borne onward to the future. Rather than participate in the mutual recriminations of the two parties, Chateaubriand's purpose is to explore a number of general questions about revolution and its relation to national character. He maps out a history of revolutions in a number of other societies in order to establish whether any of them can be compared to recent events in France. A comparative study of the genius of different nations at various points in history from the ancient world to the present is designed as a means of casting light on the underlying causes of the French Revolution and of addressing the fundamental question that could be crudely summarized as "Was the Revolution French?"

The *Génie du christianisme* adopts a rather different idiom, being an apology rather than enquiry, but its starting point is the same. It was begun while Chateaubriand was still living in England, where an early version was published in August 1799. He returned to France in May 1800, shortly after Napoleon had been elected First Consul, and the first complete edition of the book had a well-timed appearance in Holy Week of 1802, one year on from the introduction of the Concordat, whereby the French government recognized Catholicism as the majority religion in France. Political as well as personal circumstances justified Chateaubriand's presentation of the preeminence of Christianity that is signaled in his choice of the word "génie" for the title. The genius of Christianity is not neutral in the way that the genius of the ancient peoples in the eighteenth-century *Dictionnaire classique de Géographie Ancienne* or that of the inhabitants of Italy in the *Description historique de l'Italie* were clearly understood to be.

Or rather, it is not only neutral. Chateaubriand never pauses to define or theorize the term, and his use of it seems to place it between the two senses of character and preeminence. It is with the latter sense that his originality lies, for his principal defense of Christianity is contained in the secular-sounding and decidedly tautological claim that its (collective) genius consists in an ability to nurture (individual) genius. Christianity, he says, is a poetic religion, and one that therefore fosters poetry: "of all the religions that have ever existed, the Christian religion is the most poetic, the most human and the one most favorable to freedom, the arts and letters." It is responsible for the greatest human achievements, such as "the temples built by Michelangelo and adorned by Raphael." And although Christianity has undoubted moral benefits, Chateaubriand has much more to say about its literary effects: "it should be said that [Christianity] favors genius, purifies taste, fosters virtuous passions, imparts vigor to thought, proposes noble forms to the writer and perfect molds to the artist [and suggests] that there is no shame in believing along with Newton and Bossuet, Pascal and Racine."[18] The advantages that Christianity offers to individual genius are stated in so many words, and they are further underscored by the mention of Newton, Pascal, and Racine, who had been regularly cited in the literature as paradigmatic examples of genius.

God is frequently referred to as "the Creator," and the analogy between God and the creative artist is made on more than one occasion: the superiority of

Genesis over other cosmogonies is compared to the way that an original painting stands out from copies because it bears the stamp of "the master's genius."
Chateaubriand goes on to summarize the story told in the book of Genesis as
that of "the Creator descending into the ancient dark, to create light with his
words." Any poet would aspire to use language with comparable effects. Indeed,
over the course of four chapters, Chateaubriand proceeds to demonstrate that
"the Bible has more beauty than Homer," which supports his view that the
greatness of poets is in direct proportion to their religion. According to this
logic Homer would have been an even better poet had he been a Christian. The
beauties of the "bizarre production" that is Dante's *Divine Comedy* derive entirely from Christianity, while its faults are those of his times and of Dante
himself. Similarly, the "superior beauties" of Milton's *Paradise Lost* are due "essentially to our religion." Milton is said to be sublime in his depiction of Adam's
wakening to the world, and this prompts Chateaubriand to ask, rhetorically,
"but would he have raised himself to the level of these thoughts if he had not
known the religion of Jesus Christ?"[19] The answer is clearly no, as the case of
Voltaire demonstrates by inverse example.

In Chateaubriand's view, Voltaire is not as great as writer as he might have
been because he allowed his anticlerical philosophical system to freeze his poetic genius, thus illustrating the principle whereby "[i]t is possible to have wit
[*esprit*] without religion; but it is difficult to have genius."[20] Chateaubriand's
assertion is made with reference to Voltaire's historical writings, for like poetry,
the disciplines of history, philosophy, eloquence, and the plastic arts are also at
their best only when informed by Christianity. This is why, when set alongside
the Christian poetry of Racine or Milton, even Homer and Virgil prove to have
their limits. Whatever angle of approach Chateaubriand adopts on his subject,
tautology is everywhere affirmed: Christianity is poetic, and the best poetry is
Christian. All of which suggests very powerfully that the genius of Christianity
is to be understood in terms of the genius celebrated in poetry and the other
arts: as creative, individual, and preeminent.

POLYSEMANTIC GENIUS

Chateaubriand is also remarkably profligate in his use of the word "genius," and
it appears with other senses and in other connections, as if the enthusiasm with
which he advances the case for the genius of Christianity had released a whole
range of other energies and associations contained in the word. The core sense
repeatedly relates it to the sublime, the word that Chateaubriand uses to describe Milton's portrayal of Adam. It is characterized by simplicity and magnifi-
cence; but its power can also take negative forms, as in the case of the serpent
whose "genius" inspires both horror and adoration and before which men will
willingly fall. Atheism too is described as "the genius of evil."

In a different register, genius is treated as just one among several other human attributes, though all of the nobler kind. It is frequently paired with wisdom, but also with virtue and the soul. The qualities of genius, feeling, and imagination are distributed respectively between Homer, Virgil, and Tasso, and the French are said to be Roman in "genius" and Greek in "character," as if feeling, imagination, and character were attributes on a par with genius itself. Elsewhere, recalling the earlier *Essai*, genius seems more or less synonymous with national or collective character as Chateaubriand speaks of the genius of Orientals, the Moors, the Greeks, and the Italians. He mentions a genius of antiquity and a genius of mothers. The genius of the language of nature is said to lie in its barbarisms, though this is clearly not to be understood as a virtue, and, in a different discussion, Chateaubriand compares the genius of the Greek and Hebrew languages to the detriment of the former.

In the main, however, the sense of genius as preeminence is inseparable from its sense as "character," especially when it comes to individuals. Just as the genius of Bernardin de Saint-Pierre was nurtured by his reading of the Scriptures, so the genius of Montesquieu is exemplified in his command of all periods of history, which he owes to the single religion of Christianity. The genius of individuals is radically individual: it neither imitates nor can be imitated by others. It is a personal expression of the artist's own experience: "We are convinced that great writers put their own story into their works. The only thing that can be painted well is one's own heart, ascribed to another, and the best part of genius consists of memories."[21] Chateaubriand claims that Milton's portrayal of the reconciliation between Adam and Eve in *Paradise Lost* owes its greatness to the fact that he was inspired by memories of his first wife.

This emphasis on the unique as a necessary dimension of genius leads Chateaubriand to speak of individuals as *being* geniuses, as well as *having* genius. He refers, for instance, to Plato as "that genius so amorously devoted to the higher sciences," and describes Pascal, the precocious inventor of mathematics and modern physics, as "this terrifying genius." But if Pascal succeeded in solving one of the biggest problems in geometry, the thoughts he put down on paper "owe as much to God as to the man."[22] The greatest individual genius depends on the collective genius of the Christian religion, which—tautologically—is illustrated in turn by the individual. Individual genius and institutional genius mutually confirm each other through this complementarity.

NATIONAL GENIUS: MADAME DE STAËL

Even before Chateaubriand published the *Génie du christianisme* and made his claims about the beneficial effects of Christianity on genius, Mme de Staël was outlining a view of the relations between the individual and collective in *De la littérature* (1799) where she explores the dependence of genius on its political, cultural, and historical context. She was writing explicitly in the aftermath of the Revolution, and her aim is to remind "enlightened minds" about the "delights of philosophical meditation" and to revive the intellectual fortunes of France. Individual genius in her account never loses its connection with its larger social and cultural context: "the most remarkable genius never rises by more than a few degrees above the learning of its time." Even the rarest genius will have some relation to the thinking of its contemporaries, and, to be fully appreciated, must be evaluated with regard to the state of knowledge of its own times. Equally, it depends on the accumulated insights that precede it, and this allows Montesquieu, Pascal, or Machiavelli to achieve the brilliance of genius with a single touch, where Tacitus, who had many fewer centuries of writing behind him, was condemned to a much more laborious elaboration of what Mme de Staël calls "the eloquence of thought."[23]

The most powerful determination is, however, geographical: the North with its mists, its melancholy, and its Christian traditions favors genius far more than the South, so that, although Petrarch may have been as much in love as the creator of Werther, or the English writers Pope, Thompson, and Otway, theirs is the greater genius. Had these Northern poets lived in Italy rather than Germany or England, they would not have written as well about the passions they felt. The example that ranks the minor poet James Thompson (who was in fact Scottish) and the minor dramatist Thomas Otway higher than Petrarch is perhaps unfortunate, if sincere on Mme de Staël's part; but the importance ascribed to national context in the development of individual genius becomes central to thinking in the nineteenth century and is fully established in Mme de Staël's *De l'Allemagne* (On Germany).

Written in exile ten years after *De la littérature*, the book was banned on the eve of its publication in September 1810 at the behest of Napoleon who was outraged by the book's unpatriotic praise of his enemies England and Germany, as well as by its failure to include any mention of him. Mme de Staël was ordered to leave France within twenty-four hours, and when she objected, she received a letter from the chief of police that stated baldly, "Your latest book is not French."[24] The discussion of national genius had material as well as intellectual consequences.

The intellectual ones are, however, those that concern us here. Mme de Staël's thinking about genius, both national and individual, is not entirely coherent—which is another way of saying that it benefits from a productive inconsistency.[25] At times she appears to be arguing that the social institutions and the decentered political organization of Germany are conducive to genius in general, as if genius were always and everywhere the same. In this vein she refers on a number of occasions to "true" or "real" genius, claiming that the genius of Charles-Quint was too great to confine him exclusively to any one nation and that "there is always something universal in genius."[26]

She also makes several comments about the general characteristics of individual genius, most of which repeat the views she had inherited from the eighteenth century and are not inflected with national character. Genius is associated with imagination, instinct, feeling, and sensibility; it is bold and original, and sets itself no bounds; it is powered by enthusiasm and its own internal *élan*; it is bestowed by nature and is itself natural; it is intrinsically inclined to goodness and is fundamentally creative. The discussion even echoes some of Chateaubriand's thinking in maintaining that genius is intimately bound up with religion, and with Christianity in particular.[27]

German Genius

Elsewhere, however, Mme de Staël refers abundantly to the specific character of German genius, even if she does not always give it a particular content. She speaks variously of "German genius," "the genius that is natural to German writers," "the genius of the Germans," and so on. This national genius is more often affirmed than defined, but where it is characterized, its features are those of profundity and a comparative lack of sociability, which lead Germans to study books in preference to people, as the French so inveterately do. The genius of German writers is portrayed in somewhat greater detail when Mme de Staël states that "[t]heir imagination delights in ancient towers and battlements, amid warriors, witches and ghosts; and the mysteries of an entrancing and solitary nature constitute the principal charm of their poetry." In her discussion of Goethe, she claims that he exemplifies to a preeminent degree the main characteristics of German national genius, which she defines as: "great profundity of ideas, a grace born of imagination, which is a more original grace than the one created by wit in society; in sum, a sensibility that is sometimes fantastical, but which for that very reason is better suited to interest readers who read books in search of a means to vary the monotony of their existence, and who require poetry to provide them with a substitute for real events."[28]

These characteristics of German national genius are reflected in the national language, which has its own additional genius. Unlike Rivarol's definition of the genius of the French language, German linguistic genius is marked by its intrinsic diversity. The German language is special, since the political decentralization of Germany is matched linguistically by a range of different dialects, each of which nonetheless draws on a single "mother tongue" (*langue mère*), a common origin that "renews and multiplies expression in a manner that always matches the genius of a nation."[29] The central, maternal core of the German language serves paradoxically to sustain its continuing variety, and in poetry the multiplicity of these dialects has the special merit, in Mme de Staël's estimation, of introducing beauty and diversity in the use of epithets.

What Mme de Staël seems to admire most in German national genius, over and above its qualities of profundity, imagination, and so on, is this multiplicity, whether linguistic or cultural. While Goethe may be said to embody the national genius, the number and variety of other individual men of genius, each with his own distinguishing features, is in and of itself a tribute to a collective German genius. Mme de Staël devotes detailed discussion to Klopstock, Lessing, Schiller, Herder, and Leibniz, for example, carefully drawing out the special character of each. National genius is not automatically reduced to national character, and Jean Paul is clearly regarded as being too German for his own good.[30]

When it comes to genius, individual difference is a virtue that far outweighs strict conformity with national character. Lessing's genius was supposedly nurtured by his knowledge of both French and English dramatists (particularly the latter), and the entire thrust of De l'Allemagne is an invitation to the French to emerge from the insularity of their own culture by acquainting themselves with the cultural achievements of another nation. Mme de Staël is reputed to have said, "From now on we must have a European outlook,"[31] an ambition that was not intended as the snub to national honor that Napoleon took De l'Allemagne to be. As we shall see in chapter 10, her own Corinne illustrates the unhappy consequences of the failure on the part of one nation to recognize the qualities of a genius born in another.

In this promotion of diversity the term "genius" itself appears with semantic variants that hark back to earlier uses of the word. The Rhine is described as Germany's "tutelary genius"; on more than one occasion Mme de Staël mentions good or evil geniuses being at work; and Faust is described as calling up a spirit that in French is un génie and in English a genie. The word has an energy, which, informed by the value placed on diversity in Mme de Staël's thinking, sees it spinning off into these secondary meanings of the term, and away from a central core that might otherwise be susceptible to theorization. The elaboration of a view of national genius simultaneously consolidates the notion for further development over the course of the century and fosters a multiplication of the sense of the word "genius" itself.

A brief caveat at this point will return us momentarily to the issue of the recognition of genius. While Mme de Staël's hope is clearly that her French readers will adopt the European spirit that she is urging upon them and will direct their attention to the examples of Germany and England, she also suggests that genius can be recognized only by those who are themselves endowed with its qualities. Genius is able to transcend national boundaries because "persons of genius are always compatriots amongst themselves," and men of genius of all nations are geared to understand and admire each other's qualities (she speaks of genius here with reference only to men). The ability to identify genius is itself a lesser form of genius: "after genius, the thing that is most similar to it, is the power to know and admire it."[32] This issue of the recognizability of genius will return to haunt its solitary exemplars.

CHAPTER 4

Individual versus Collective Genius

Vassal of Heaven, Pontiff and King of Nature.
—Chênedollé, *Le Génie de l'homme*

[H]e belonged to the race forever cursed by earthly powers.
—Vigny, *Stello*

Chateaubriand and Mme de Staël each construct a view of collective genius that relates to individual genius in relatively complex ways. For Chateaubriand, the genius of Christianity goes hand in hand with the most extreme individuality, and for Mme de Staël German national genius is demonstrated by the variety of individuals of genius as well as by the variety of forms of the German language. But as time goes on, and especially when it takes the form of encomium rather than analysis, this relation is apt to lose all complexity: the individual is either a microcosmic replica of the national macrocosm, or else finds himself at odds with a national or social whole that rejects the creative contributions he seeks to offer to its glory and for which he is denied recognition.

To begin with the first category, Chênedollé, a member of Mme de Staël's circle as well as a friend of both Rivarol (whose memoir he authored) and Chateaubriand (whose sister he fell in love with), wrote a long didactic "hymn" to the genius of man, *Le Génie de l'homme*, published in 1807. It records and celebrates a range of individual men of genius across a number of intellectual disciplines from astronomy (Copernicus, Kepler, Newton) and natural philosophy (Pliny, Buffon) to poetry (Racine, Tasso) and social thought (Montesquieu). Each of these figures exemplifies a single "genius of mankind," which is repeatedly portrayed as the means whereby nature can be revealed as evidence of God's creative power. Human genius is at once a reflection and a revelation of the divine. At the end of the poem, the new century is placed under the sign of Napoleon, who, under divine aegis and "covered by the wings of genius," has saved the nation from ruin and strife to open the way toward a glorious future.[1]

THE NINETEENTH-CENTURY NATION

This view is confirmed and described in considerably more detail by Édouard Alletz, who, some thirty-five years later, implicitly picks up Chênedollé's narra-tive in his *Génie du dix-neuvième siècle, ou esquisse des progrès de l'esprit humain depuis 1800 jusqu'à nos jours* (Genius of the nineteenth century, or outline of the progress of the human mind from 1800 to the present), whose wordy title clearly indicates the author's approach. Alletz wrote a number of books offering a commentary on the times (he was born in 1798), and in his introduction to the *Génie du dix-neuvième siècle* he confidently defines the features that have determined the genius of the century as being generalized war, the decline of the aristocracy, and the invention of the steam engine.

A diplomat who served as French consul in Genoa and Barcelona, Alletz had the broadly European overview urged by Mme de Staël, and his examples of the genius of the nineteenth century include figures from England, Germany, and Italy as well as France. France, however, constitutes the core of his account of the century whose characteristics—as identified by Alletz—are more rele-vant to French national identity than to any other. The wars of the empire, says Alletz, are worthy of a Homeric epic, and "[t]he name of Napoleon will travel across the vast spaces of different eras, like those distant meteors whose light traverses incommensurable distances to bring us illumination."[2] This is not a view that anyone other than a Frenchman is likely to have taken.

Similarly, the decline of the nobility and the aspiration to equality were ex-perienced with a particular acuity in France as a result of the Revolution. And if the steam engine was not a French invention, the enthusiasm with which Alletz extols its benefits for a steam-powered printing industry reflects the huge expansion of the French press that had begun in the previous decade. The ide-ology of Alletz's nineteenth century is also decidedly Gallic in its combination of egalitarianism, progress, and Catholicism, and he concludes his fifty-page introduction with a patriotic invitation to writers and thinkers to add to the glory of the nation: "Do you wish to contribute to the greatness of France? then act so that your genius will be an honor to her."[3]

The collective genius that Alletz is setting out to present and applaud—acclaim is once again the dominant mode of exposition—is thus predominantly French. From his invitation to individual writers to contribute to that genius, it is also clear that he is envisaging the relation of individual to national genius in terms which by the 1840s had become an accepted commonplace. His prosely-tizing stance is both religious and pedagogical, and in fact the *Génie du dix-neuvième siècle* is an expanded version of the introduction he wrote for the eighteen-volume *Encyclopédie catholique: répertoire universel et raisonné des sciences, des lettres, des arts et des métiers, formant une bibliothèque universelle* (Catholic encyclopedia: A universal and systematic catalogue of the sciences, literature, arts and crafts, constituting a universal library), whose first volume had appeared in 1839. Religion and pedagogy combine to promote the tone of encomium.

Celebration—whether religious, national, or a mixture of the two—would seem to presume legibility, and the qualities required for the role of celebrant are those of fervor and conviction rather than of specialist insight. The accounts of collective genius favored by the nineteenth century were almost all forms of such homage. The genius they pay tribute to is relatively unproblematic, and as a result, inclines fatally toward blandness, as the opening lines of Alexandre Bardenet's *La France et son génie. Union, fédération des peuples, civilisation universelle* (France and its genius. A union and federation of peoples, a universal civilization, 1867) would seem to confirm: "O France! O my country! Yes since my sweet childhood / I have felt the power of your sacred love." And so it goes on.

It is when the relation between individual and collective includes consideration of the individual that interest returns, and this happens in Michelet's *Le Peuple* (The people). Its first edition was published in 1846, three years after Alletz's *Génie du dix-neuvième siècle*, and two years before the Revolution of 1848. A fourth edition appeared during the Second Empire in 1866, and a fifth in 1877. Like Chateaubriand in his *Essai sur les révolutions*, Michelet claims that France has lost sight of its distinctive identity, which his book aims to restore. It does so by means of its appeal to the qualities of *le peuple*—simplicity, warmth, life—and Michelet asserts that "the Revolution was the belated, but just and necessary manifestation of the genius of this people" through which France had "finally discovered its right."[4]

In addition to identifying national genius with the Revolution, Michelet supports his argument with a discussion of the individual man of genius who, in his simplicity and creativity, has significant affinities with "the people" where France's salvation lies. But rather than the individual passively reflecting the collective, the traffic goes in both directions, and the attributes of the individual genius also exist in the collective, with whom he has a "secret kinship." In an even more striking formulation, the soul of the man of genius is described as containing the blueprint for an ideal form of society: "The soul of the man of genius, which is visibly divine since it creates like God, is the inner dwelling place [*cité*] upon which we should plan the outer dwelling place, so that it too becomes divine."[5] The future of France depends in equal measure on the man of genius and the people.

CHATTERTON: THE POET AND NATIONAL POLITICS

Nevertheless, whatever claims Michelet makes for the individual as a template for collective genius, and however much individuals themselves may have aspired to this status, literary accounts of the question suggest that public recognition was rarely granted to them. This is despite the fact that, as Alfred de Vigny asserts in the preface to his play *Chatterton* (first performed in 1835), the individual man of genius brings honor to his nation, which is lucky if it can number two of his kind in a thousand years. Chatterton himself, while driven to suicide for lack of recognition by the state, describes himself as wanting nothing more than to contribute to the nation's glory by adding "another pearl to the English crown," and as being willing to plunge "into many seas and rivers to seek it."[6] But for all the poet's good intentions, the play demonstrates that the representatives of national power do not see his ambitions in the same light, and, as so often happens in nineteenth-century literature, individual genius is obliged to confront this absence of public recognition as one of its commonest and more painful experiences.

The return to a preoccupation with the experience of the man of genius, and the concomitant retreat of individual genius from recognition in the public sphere, are also exemplified in Vigny's *Stello*, which includes a shorter prose version of *Chatterton*. Published in 1832—three years before the stage play and two years after the disappointment of the July Revolution—*Stello* tells the tales of three unfortunate men of genius at the hands of an indifferent society: the poet Gilbert who lost his reason and died in the last years of the ancien régime; the English poet Chatterton who committed suicide in the bourgeois society that supported the English constitutional monarchy; and the poet André Chénier who was guillotined under the Terror. These stories are narrated by a fictional Dr. Noir, who supposedly knew each of the poets personally and who also happened to witness their deaths, and they are told to an equally fictional poet, Stello, as a means of curing the "blue devils" that have him laid up with a combination of migraine and spleen. (The cure, incidentally, works.)

Although Stello and Dr. Noir are Vigny's inventions, the poets in the three stories actually existed and had already acquired reputations as examples of the figure of *le poète malheureux*. Gilbert, who died in 1780 at the age of thirty, set the tone in his own autobiographical poem, *Le Génie aux prises avec l'infortune, ou le Poëte malheureux* (Genius grappling with misfortune, or the unhappy Poet), written in 1772. Nodier's edition of Gilbert's works, published in 1817 with the *Le Poëte malheureux* in first position, contained a sympathetic biographical portrait by way of a preface, which endorsed Gilbert's gloomy view of "society's destructive systems."[7]

Chatterton, who died aged eighteen in 1770, was already known from a number of English accounts. Keats later bemoaned Chatterton's fate in a sonnet dedicated to him: "Oh Chatterton! How very sad thy fate! / Dear child of sorrow—son of misery! / How soon the film of death obscur'd that eye, / Whence Genius mildly flash'd, and high debate." And Wordsworth famously described him in the poem "Resolution and Independence" as "the marvelous Boy" whose life illustrated the truth that "We Poets in our youth begin in gladness; / But thereof come in the end despondency and madness." This motif was picked up in the *Génie du christianisme* when Chateaubriand mentions both Gilbert and Chénier as examples of glorious talents lost by France at the moment of their emergence. Finally, in February 1832, two months before the book publication of *Stello*, the literary world was shaken by the deaths of two teenagers, Victor Escousse and Auguste Lebras, who committed suicide at the respective ages of nineteen and sixteen after the failure of the play that they had written together.[8] The unhappiness of the poet may have had causes beyond those of society's incomprehension, but misrecognition becomes an integral part of the image of individual genius in the nineteenth century.

In Vigny's analysis, the cause of this misrecognition lies in the fact that— contrary to the spirit of Rivarol's account of Louis XIV—political power of any type and any nation is inherently incapable of appreciating the work of the poet, and will dismiss him as a nuisance, a threat, or an irrelevance. Vigny's Louis XV complains that poets merely dress up a few philosophical and political approximations in fancy rhetoric and then insist on their right to preach. His Saint-Just regards writers as "the nation's most dangerous enemies" who must be treated as counterrevolutionaries unless they agree to support the cause by accepting commissions for hymns to the republic and poems for special occasions.[9] Equally devastating, if less overtly hostile, is the view of Vigny's Beckford, the Mayor of London, who derides poetry as nothing more than a trivial occupation which almost everyone dabbles in during their youth—especially as it pleases "les *young ladies*"—but which must be abandoned with the arrival of the economic responsibilities of adulthood. The vision and the imagination of the man of genius—or Vigny's "Poète," with a capital P—do not register in a society whose only values are those of productive labor and financial return.

Chatterton's suicide is brought about because he can neither write to order and "open up his heart for display on a shop counter," as he puts it, nor accept the demeaning position of *valet de chambre* which the Mayor has offered him as a means of earning his keep. The poet's labor, Chatterton declares, comes from his mind and not from his body. Moreover, the products of his mind are not those of numbers or calculation: one hour of his *rêverie* will yield more than do twenty days of the type of work performed by others. When Chatterton compares the nation to a ship on which everyone fulfills an essential function, Beckford responds by asking what the devil the poet does. To which Chatterton replies in turn, "The poet looks to the stars in search of the path shown to us by the Lord's finger."[10] This is a vision on which the Mayor immediately pours scorn as an anachronistic fantasy that belongs in ancient Greece with its sandal-wearing seers. Only Dr. Noir, who witnesses the scene, is moved by the remark and he leaps up in sympathy to shake the poet by the hand.

In his preface to *Chatterton*, the "Dernière nuit de travail" (Last night of labor), Vigny contrasts the *Poète* to two lesser categories of writer: the "Man of letters," for whom literature is just a profitable business, and the "Great Writer," whose pragmatic approach to writing commands the support of public opinion but offers nothing more. *Le Poète* is a much rarer creature, and he is invariably met by the incomprehension of the "multitude": "his chosen language is understood only by a small number of men he himself has chosen."[11] Neither society en masse, nor its political leaders—whether they be kings, revolutionaries, or mayors—are willing to give time to the visions of the *Poète*.

It would seem in the case of Chatterton that the only people capable of appreciating the visionary and imaginative qualities of his genius are Dr. Noir, Stello, and Kitty Bell, who tries to protect him against the capitalist accounting of her husband and is secretly in love with him—in other words: a poet, a woman, and a doctor who is, moreover, the kind that practices a medicine of the soul. Vigny's tales of his unfortunate poets may be read as a fable from which these three figures emerge as the only ones capable of recognizing genius. By a telling coincidence they represent the three major groups through which the notion of genius evolved over the remainder of century: fellow poets, the medical profession, and women.

CHAPTER 5

The Romantic Poet and the Brotherhood of Genius

> [P]ersons of genius are always compatriots
> amongst themselves.
>
> —Mme de Staël, *De l'Allemagne*

For the poet in the first decades of the century genius is conceived as a distinctly solitary affair. The cases in Vigny's *Stello* are emblematic of an entire generation where poets go unheeded by the wider world, and genius is confined to private recognition. Even Moïse in Vigny's poem of that name, who can justifiably claim to be a "Prophète centenaire, environné d'honneur" (Centenarian poet, surrounded by honor), becomes the pretext for a portrait of genius abandoned and alone.[1] The one-time leader of his people is now regarded as a stranger and he addresses God from the top of Mount Nebo with repeated versions of a question where he asks: "Je vivrai donc toujours puissant et solitaire?" (Shall I always live powerful and alone?). The power of the man of genius is not in doubt, but it condemns him to absolute solitude. As Vigny explained in a letter to his English translator, Moses stands for "the man of genius, weary of his eternal widowerhood and in despair at seeing his solitude grow ever vaster and more arid as he himself grows greater."[2]

The poem was written in 1822, the year in which Lamartine's *Méditations poétiques* (Poetic meditations) appeared in their ninth edition (the first dates from 1820) and Victor Hugo began what would later prove to be a monumental career with his *Odes et poésies diverses* (Odes and diverse poems). These two collections marked the emergence of a new poetry that presents its credentials as lying not with any preexisting literary or national tradition, but with the genius of the individual poet. Despite the real success of these volumes, both of which rapidly went through several editions, the poet is portrayed, like Moses abandoned by his people, as having no public. The collective "other" that might afford him recognition is absent, and in the words of the epigraphs of the first two Books of Hugo's *Odes*, his was a voice crying in the wilderness, and singing to the deaf.[3] The new poets enter the literary field announcing in advance that they will go unheard by a world that is fundamentally hostile.

Rejected Genius

Hugo hailed Lamartine's *Méditations* on their first publication with the words "Here at last are poems by a poet, poems that are poetry!" but he went on to warn the "young poet" (who was actually Hugo's senior by twelve years) that banishment would be his only reward: "[Y]ou are one of those whom Plato wished to shower with honors and to banish from his republic. You should expect to see yourself banished from our land of anarchy and ignorance, and your exile will be without the triumph that Plato did at least grant to the poet, the palms, the fanfares and the crown of flowers."[4] In the 1824 preface to the *Odes*, Hugo asserts that this lack of public recognition is not a natural state of affairs for the poet of genius. Each of David (the psalmist), Homer, Virgil, Tasso, Milton, and Corneille was representative of his respective national literature, and the genius that was the sole quality they had in common was precisely what allowed each of them to "express and . . . enrich public thought in his country and his times."[5]

The poet-genius fulfills his true function when he leads his people "like a light" and "shows them the way."[6] Or, as Hugo puts it in "Fin" (End, which dates from 1828), "Le Génie a besoin d'un peuple que sa flamme / Anime, éclaire, échauffe, embrase comme une âme" (Genius needs a people that his flame / Enlivens, illuminates, warms and ignites like a soul). Meanwhile, in the modern era, an abyss separates the poet from the collectivity whose spirit, unbeknownst to them, he expresses and for whom, although they are blind to it, he is a leader. However much he longs to be the expression of national genius, the continuities between collective and individual genius, which in their various ways Rivarol, Chateaubriand, Mme de Staël, Chênedollé, Alletz, and Michelet all take for granted, are starkly absent for the poet of the 1820s.

This perceived lack of fit between what the new poetry has to offer and the public's alleged lack of appreciation has several causes. Lamartine's assertion that "tout génie est martyre" (every genius is a martyr) and Hugo's claim that "Ses plus chers favoris sont toujours des victimes" (His best loved favorites are always victims) originate in the late eighteenth-century figure of the *poète malheureux* whose misfortunes Vigny revisited in *Stello* a decade later. But in the 1820s, other circumstances exacerbated the poet's sense of isolation and rejection. The very novelty of the new poetry is an obvious obstacle to its reception by a public schooled in the culturally conservative tradition of the time. The emergence of what Hugo called the "deep and vast movement . . . at work within the literature of this century" had produced two opposing literary "camps" each speaking a different literary language, and warring just as furiously as the two political parties of the day.[7]

In his preface to the 1849 edition of the *Méditations*, Lamartine recalls the false and trivial notion of poetry inculcated by the education system of his youth, and, though the first *Méditations* were in reality very successful, he deplores the denigration and mockery accorded to his poetry by a press that represented the "the old, classical *literati* who felt ousted by this novelty." The classical tradition sustained by the liberal press and the education system was in large part a Revolutionary tradition, and Lamartine and Hugo share a view of the literature of the Revolution as "hideous and inept." For reasons of their respective family backgrounds, both poets were fiercely royalist in their youth (though both subsequently evolved toward more radical positions), and they regarded the post-Revolutionary French public of the 1820s as philistine and incapable of appreciating true art. The newspapers Lamartine mentions as having attacked his poetry were the liberal *Constitutionnel* and *La Minerve*. More precisely, but in more extreme terms, he saw the cultural ideology bequeathed by the Revolution as one where "[le] souffle aride / De notre âge a séché les fleurs" ([the] arid breath / Of our times has dried up the flowers), and where "le lourd compas d'Euclide / Étouffe nos arts enchanteurs" (Euclid's heavy compass / Is stifling our entrancing arts). The "transports of the soul and of genius" had been replaced by "cold obsession with calculation," and the icy finger of bourgeois society had frozen all of nature in its desire to record the measurements of the natural world rather than appreciate its beauties.[8]

In the case of Hugo, his early monarchist sympathies encouraged a preoccupation with images of deposed kings, rejected and reviled by the people they once ruled. He celebrates the installation on the Pont-Neuf of the statue of Henri IV whose remains had been exhumed when the royal tombs in the chapel of Saint-Denis were desecrated under the Terror. He devotes a poem to the exiled king of Sweden reduced to living as an ordinary citizen under the name of Colonel G.-A. Gustaffson, and he dedicates "Le Repas libre" (The free repast) to "the Kings of Europe" who are compared to early Christian martyrs thrown to the lions. The king bereft of his people provides the poet with an analogy that is spelled out in "L'âme" (The soul), where Hugo has the poet say, "Je suis le roi banni, superbe et solitaire" (I am the banished king, splendid and solitary), and he quotes Lamennais in the epigraph to his poem "Le Génie" to refer to "the royalty of Genius" and "[t]hose kings who do not bear the name."[9] As Hugo's political sympathies evolved toward the republican cause and a retrospective allegiance to Napoleon, it is this same image of a dethroned ruler that informs his celebration of the one-time emperor in poems such as "À la Colonne de la place Vendôme" (To the column on the Place Vendôme). The deposed and exiled leader—whether monarch or emperor—is an alter ego for the poet-genius who alone is able to appreciate his true stature.

The prefaces Hugo wrote for the successive editions of the *Odes* repeatedly stress the unprecedented character of the new poetry. For both Hugo and Lamartine the individual becomes the source of a poetry whose fundamentals have been completely transformed. Lamartine's *Méditations poétiques* open with the lonely figure of the poet in "L'isolement" (Isolation), and he later claimed to have been the first to bring poetry down from the classical heights of Parnassus and to compose it, not on the conventional strings of the lyre, but on "the very fibers of the human heart, touched and moved by the countless vibrations of the soul and of nature."[10] Taste no longer constitutes a viable basis for literature, and instead, as Hugo puts it, literature "must be invigorated by poetry and enriched by genius." Genius is the source of literary originality because it is creative rather than imitative, it takes its cue from nature rather than from prescription, and inspiration is proof of its presence. Lamartine portrays this inspiration in "L'enthousiasme" (Enthusiasm) as an all-consuming flame:

> Étonné du feu qui me brûle,
> Je l'irrite en le combattant,
> Et la lave de mon génie
> Déborde en torrents d'harmonie,
> Et me consume en s'échappant.

> (Astonished by the fire that burns me,
> I exacerbate it by combating it,
> And the lava of my genius
> Spills over in torrents of harmony,
> And consumes me as it escapes.)[11]

Hugo's "Mazeppa," which was written in 1828 (though included not in the 1828 edition of *Odes et ballades*, but in *Les Orientales* of 1829), portrays—and addresses—genius in a similar spirit as a "fiery charger" with wings of flame. Describing the helpless rider but addressing the unstoppable mount, the poet continues,

> En vain il lutte, hélas! tu bondis, tu l'emportes
> Hors du monde réel, dont tu brises les portes
>   Avec tes pieds d'acier!

> (In vain he struggles, alas! you leap, you carry him away
> Out of the real world whose gates you break open
>   With your feet of steel!)

The poem ends with the vindication of genius as the rider emerges triumphant from the ordeal of inspiration: "[il] se relève roi!" ([he] rises a king).[12]

Addressing Genius: Lamartine

The centrality of genius to the new poetry makes it one of poetry's chief and most explicit topics. Genius is described and defined by the poetry that it implicitly inspires. But, more importantly, it is repeatedly *addressed* as the recipient of the poems, and poetry is constituted as the recognizing "other" of genius in place of the painfully absent collective "other" of the public. This address to genius serves at once to delineate the field of the new poetry and to provide the new poets with an entry into it.[13] To speak *of* but also *to* genius is the means by which a new poetry is affirmed, so that the importance of genius lies less in its theorization than in its function as a means of literary legitimation. Over the head of a deaf and uncomprehending crowd—*le vulgaire*—the poet asserts his right to poetic utterance by positing the poet and genius as the sole recipients of his address. Paradigmatically, both Lamartine and Hugo wrote poems with the title "Le Génie," each describing and addressing the genius who is its subject matter—Bonald in the case of Lamartine, Chateaubriand in the case of Hugo. Genius becomes the object of direct and individual address because the only person capable of recognizing genius is another poet, and this exclusive recognition of individual genius against the horizon of an indifferent or hostile crowd results in a triangulation of poetic utterance that characterizes the poetry of the 1820s and determines its self-definition.

Hugo has Mazeppa's wild ride on the steed of genius result in his triumph, but Lamartine takes a more ambivalent approach. But although his celebration of genius is qualified, and although genius is shown on a number of occasions to be a less than an entirely reliable or desirable quantity, the poet is uniquely empowered to make these judgments. Only the poet can vouch for the way genius is visited upon him in an experience that may not always be welcome and whose outcome depends on the moral character of the individual concerned. By demonstrating that the effects of genius can be destructive and that it can be put to morally dubious use by the individual, Lamartine turns the presence of genius into a drama whose focus rests on the individual's response. It is his own experience of genius that gives him insight into its workings, and he uses the mode of direct address to make his point.

Where genius is not equally balanced by feeling and personal merit, the results can be catastrophic. The poem "L'Homme" (Man) is an address to Byron in which the speaker castigates the English poet for allowing his genius to be directed toward infernal ends. Genius is not automatically beneficial; it can be "bon ou fatal" (good or disastrous), and in the case of Byron, as the speaker says to him,

> Le mal est ton spectacle, et l'homme est ta victime.
> . . .
> Ton génie invincible éclate en chants funèbres;
> Il triomphe, et ta voix, sur un mode infernal,
> Chante l'hymne de gloire au sombre dieu du mal.
>
> (Evil is a spectacle, and man your victim.
> . . .
> Your invincible genius bursts out in funerary song;

It triumphs, and your voice, in infernal mode,
Sings a hymn of praise to the dark god of evil.)

Rather than Prometheus, who was a common figure for genius in this period, Byron is portrayed as the eagle that devours human remains. Later in the poem he becomes the fallen angel who has forgotten his divine origins, which the speaker urges him to rediscover: "C'est pour la vérité que Dieu fit le génie. / Jette un cri vers le ciel, ô chantre des enfers!" (It is for truth that God made genius. / Cast a cry toward heaven, O bard of Hell!). Commenting on the poem in the notes included in the 1849 edition of his complete works, Lamartine makes it clear that Byron's misappropriation of his gift was due to his failings as an individual, not to a lack of poetic talent: "in him the poet was immense, but the man incomplete, puerile, and filled with ambition for vacuities."[14]

Much the same is suggested about Napoleon, who provides another example of misdirected genius in a poem with the anti-Napoleonic title of "Bonaparte," written a few months after the former emperor's death in 1821. A lack of humanity is alleged as the source of Napoleon's "crimes," and once again the point is made in the form of direct address to its subject: "Rien d'humain ne battait sous ton épaisse armure" (Nothing human beat beneath your heavy armor), says the speaker. As Lamartine observes in his later gloss on the poem: "In itself genius is . . . simply a gift, a faculty, an instrument: it expiates nothing, it aggravates everything. Genius badly employed is a more illustrious crime: this is the prosaic truth."[15] Genius pure and unadulterated is a guarantee of nothing, and whether for poets or for emperors, it is worthless without a complementary humanity that it is up to the individual to provide.

The relation between individual and genius is maintained in Lamartine's account of his own experience of genius as inspiration or poetic gift. The arrival of "enthusiasm" in the poem of that title turns the poet into its victim: "Muse, contemple ta victime!" (Muse, contemplate your victim!). It "consumes" him as he becomes the medium for harmonies that demand the sacrifice of his last breath which he would prefer to devote to love: "Tu veux que je lui [la gloire] sacrifie / Ce dernier souffle de ma vie! / Je veux le garder pour aimer" (You want me to sacrifice / The last breath of life [to fame]! / I want to keep it for love). In the poem titled "Les Préludes" (Preludes), published in the *Nouvelles méditations* and dedicated to Hugo in the second edition, Lamartine sets up the same either/or opposition between the harmonies of genius and the experience of love:

Un seul soupir du cœur que le cœur nous renvoie,
Un œil demi-voilé par des larmes de joie,
Un regard, un silence, un accent de sa voix,
Un mot toujours le même et répété cent fois,
O lyre! en disent plus que ta vaine harmonie,
L'amour est à l'amour, le reste est au génie.

(A single sigh from the heart, which the heart returns,
An eye half veiled by tears of joy,
A look, a silence, a tone in her voice,
A word ever the same and repeated a hundred times,
Say more, O lyre! than your vain harmony,
Love belongs to love, and the rest to genius.)

Like humanity, the love felt by the poet is the necessary complement to genius, and without it the harmonies of poetry are "vain." At the end of the poem, the poet bids farewell to "divine Genius," urging it to return to heaven and the "abode of pure harmony" while he himself gladly pursues his earthly and human existence. This is a choice that ultimately validates the individual in his confrontation with genius.

This ambivalence about genius certainly complicates the notion, but none-theless makes individuality its measure in the establishment of the new poetry. Lamartine's address to genius in "Le Génie" written in 1817 describes its mani-fest presence in its addressee, Bonald. In his later note on the poem, Lamartine claimed that at the time of writing he had not read any of the counterrevolution-ary Bonald's work, and that he was moved to write the poem out of love for the pseudonymous "Elvire" whose salon Bonald patronized. Be that as it may, the portrait of genius that emerges from the poem sets up very clearly a three-cornered scenario where the speaker and his addressee, "que le génie / . . . ravit si loin de nos yeux" (whom genius / . . . ravishes so far from our eyes), are posi-tioned against a backdrop consisting of "les flots de l'adversité" (the torrents of adversity) and "Les lâches clameurs de l'envie" (Base clamors of envy). The vul-gar crowd constitutes the third term which the speaker enjoins a wounded but ultimately victorious Bonald to despise: "le mépris du vulgaire / Est l'apanage des grands cœurs" (the scorn of the vulgar crowd / Is the privilege of great hearts).

"Le Génie" is not one of Lamartine's best poems. It is decidedly grandilo-quent and its polarities are very simple. But it is exemplary of the speech situa-tion so often associated with genius where it is both anatomized and directly addressed by the poet over the heads of an ignorant and hostile herd: "Tu tires du sein des ténèbres / D'éblouissantes vérités"; "Tu vois d'un œil inaltérable / Les phases de l'humanité," or "Tu ris des terreurs où nous sommes" (You draw dazzling truths / From the depths of gloom; You see with a steadfast eye / The different phases of humanity; You laugh at the terrors in which we exist). The poet allows himself to instruct the man of genius to remain true to his calling: "Poursuis ta sublime carrière, / Poursuis," "Retrempe ton mâle courage," or "Va! dédaigne d'autres armures" (Pursue your sublime course, / Pursue; Steel your masculine courage once more; Go! spurn all other armor), and so on. In this case the mode of address was more than just a rhetorical strategy, and Lamar-tine actually sent the poem to Bonald, who responded with the gift of an edi-tion of his complete works.

This type of exchange between the poet and an addressee is a feature of a large number of Lamartine's poems whose titles or dedications identify a specific recipient. "À Elvire" is the title of the third poem and "La Providence à l'homme" (Providence to man) defines what follows as a form of address. Many of the poems are presented with a combination of title and dedicatee, key instances being "L'homme. *À Lord Byron*" and "Le Génie. *À M. de Bonald.*" Others include "La Retraite (Retreat). *À M. de C***,*" "La Gloire. *À un poète exilé*" (Glory. To an exiled poet), "Philosophie (Philosophy). *Au Marquis de L.M.F,*" and so on. What is interesting about so many of these examples is that the name of the dedicatee is not immediately recognizable to anyone positioned outside the particular channel of communication that the poem establishes. The poem consequently appears as a private exchange between poet and dedicatee from which the philistine public is excluded, and where the reader is implicitly cast as eavesdropper.

This is certainly how Lamartine's later notes on the poems portray the circumstances of the composition of many of them, so that the poems read as a response to a private visit or a personal encounter. As he says, for example, of the dedicatee of "Philosophie": "The Marquis de La Maisonfort [a friend of Rivarol, as Lamartine records] was a poet: he welcomed me like a father, and opened more portfolios of poetry than portfolios of dispatches." Lamartine recalls the effects of reading "Le Poète mourant" (The dying poet) (from the *Nouvelles méditations*) to his friend M. de Virieu who was ill at the time: "I read him these stanzas, which are sad but serene echoes of two lives coming to an end. I could see from my friend's tears that the poem had come from the heart, since it produced such a vivid impression within his own. I left the poem with Virieu to be printed, and he returned it some months later."[16] Virieu's tears are proof of the communicative power of the poem as it passes between two individuals, and if it eventually appeared in published form, this was the result of the strength of the impression it made in private.

Genius is not the sole interlocutor of the poems, but Lamartine's poetry is broadly constituted by this interlocutory mode where genius is a privileged, if also occasionally ambivalent, figure in a colloquy between individuals. Lamartine's preferred conception of poetry was as a version of prayer, a tête-à-tête between the speaker and God, of which Vigny's "Moïse" is itself an example. Or, as Lamartine put it in his note on the poem titled "La Prière" (Prayer), "I have always thought that poetry was above all the language of prayers. . . . When a man is speaking to the supreme Interlocutor, he must necessarily employ the most complete and perfect form of the language that God has placed within him. That relatively perfect and complete form is obviously poetic form."[17] The perfection of the language of poetry is determined by the perfection of its interlocutor, and viewed from this perspective, one can see why genius might be a privileged figure for poetry's address.

Hugo and the Martyr's Palm

The interlocutory mode predominates in Hugo's *Odes*, and although he uses it to apostrophize a whole range of figures from the infant Duc de Bourgogne to the ghosts of the Virgins of Verdun, Liberty, the Vendôme Column, the ruined Château de Montfort-Lamaury, his father, his future wife, and many others, one particular group stands out as the regular recipient of his poetic utterance: poets. Some of these poets are anonymously generic, as in the opening poem "Le Poète dans les révolutions" (The poet in revolutions) or "Le Poète." But several are also named, as they are in the odes to "M. Alphonse de L." (Lamartine), "Mon ami S.B." (My friend S.B.) (a barely concealed Sainte-Beuve), and "M. de Chateaubriand," who is also the dedicatee and evident addressee of "Le Génie." These names are not mere ciphers, and, unlike the poems addressed to public figures or other entities, the odes addressed to poets presuppose the larger dialogue that is taking place between poets in this period. The solitary genius of the Romantic poet cannot exist in isolation: it needs to be recognized by someone qualified to do so—and to offer recognition in return.

The mutuality of this recognition matters. Hugo's first attempt at the age of fifteen to establish himself as a poet was through competition. The *Victor Hugo raconté par un témoin de sa vie* (Victor Hugo recounted by a witness of his life—the witness being his wife Adèle, who composed it under her husband's guidance) recounts his submission of a poem to the annual poetry competition organized by the Académie française. Its members were duly astonished to discover the age of the author whose poem earned him a "mention" from the judges and a certain amount of publicity in the press. Hugo was also an assiduous competitor in the Académie des Jeux Floraux (founded in 1694 by Louis XIV and nearly as old as the Académie française), to which he addresses one of his odes and of which he became one of the "maîtres" at the precocious age of eighteen. But open competition and consecration by the "learned body"[18] of a venerable gerontocracy meant that success was dependent on conforming to the established conception of poetry represented by these academies. This was clearly not the best way to stake out the literary principles of an entirely new conception of poetry.

Hugo's recognition of Lamartine in his 1820 review of the *Méditations poétiques* is an important moment in this process. When he describes the poems as those of a poet that are "at long last poetry," the statement comes after the claim made at the beginning of the article where he says of "people in society, men of letters, [and his] contemporaries," that not one of them knows "what a poet is."[19] To hail Lamartine as a poet is to single him out for a particularly important role in establishing the new poetic idiom. The dialogue between the two continued as Lamartine responded to Hugo's praise by dedicating "Les Préludes" to him in the second edition of the *Nouvelles méditations poétiques* published in 1824. And Hugo returned the favor in October 1825 with the ode addressed to "M. Alphonse de L." Poetry was a form exchange in its own right that contributed with other written and human means to consolidate its new identity.

Sainte-Beuve's review of the 1826 edition of the *Odes et ballades* instigated a similar process. Writing in *Le Globe* in January 1827, Sainte-Beuve acknowledged the existence of "a poetry that was for a time striking in its air of novelty, its brilliant promise of talent and a sort of daring." It constituted "a complete poetic system" that had settled finally into being the product quite simply of the soul of its poets. This brief—and largely positive—summary was a way of granting semiofficial endorsement to the Romantic poetry of the 1820s. Sainte-Beuve identifies Hugo as the most independent and the most inspired, as well as the youngest, of the poets associated with this new "system," and he captures its spirit when he says of Hugo's work that "the thought that lives and breathes at the heart of all his compositions is eminently poetic."[20]

Although Sainte-Beuve was writing here as a well-informed and clearly very competent literary critic, Hugo reciprocated later in the same year with a poem that portrays him exclusively as the poet he also was, and hails him already in the first line as *le génie*.[21] One generous accolade deserves another. The dialogue established between the two men through the review and the answering poem was continued in other poems, but the primary result of the meeting was the creation of the literary circle, Le Cénacle, and a group identity under the leadership of Hugo, which soon supplanted the model of exchange between equal and isolated individuals.

The most important of these individual exchanges was, however, the first in which Chateaubriand was the poet's interlocutor. The ode to "La Vendée," written in 1819, was dedicated to "M. le Vicomte de Chateaubriand" at a time when, according to the *Victor Hugo raconté*, it was more common to make fun of the author of *Atala*, irreverently parodied as *Ah! la, la!* According to Hugo, mockery of this kind is the response on the part of "the vulgar crowd" to originality, and in taking Chateaubriand seriously, Hugo is crediting himself with the ability to recognize such originality against the grain of popular misrecognition. For his part, Chateaubriand had apparently been favorably impressed by Hugo's ode on the death of the Duc de Berry written in 1820. He had described its author as "a *sublime child*," a remark that the right-wing deputy Agier duly recorded in an article on the ode. Good manners required that Hugo acknowledge this compliment by paying a visit to Chateaubriand, on which occasion the great man compounded his praise for the young poet by observing that his recent work contained "things that no [other] poet of our times could have written." On a second visit, Chateaubriand favored Hugo with yet another endorsement by urging him to continue writing poetry, not just because he had a gift for it, but because "it is literature from on high." He underscores the point by adding, "The true writer is the poet," which means, as he says in so many words to Hugo, that "[y]ou are on a more elevated plateau than mine."[22]

Chateaubriand claims to regret having stopped writing poetry and mistakenly believes that his own youthful verse was better than his prose, a view that Hugo pointedly corrects when, in the first preface to the *Odes*, he refers to "the fine works of poetry in all genres, whether verse or prose, by which this century has been honored." It is the author of the *Génie du christianisme* whom Hugo admires and from whom he is glad to receive admiration in return. Hugo can see this better than can the "illustrious writer" himself who, after making his comment about the superiority of poetry, proceeds with "with pomp and conviction" to read to the young poet extracts from his *Moïse*, a lackluster tragedy in verse, and finally honors him with the informality of taking a bath in his presence.[23]

These exchanges, which date from 1820, have the important effect of licensing Hugo's poetry and his own posture as a poet, and this is certainly how the narrative of *Victor Hugo raconté* presents them some thirty years after the event. Appropriately, Hugo's response to Chateaubriand's commendation is, as he himself records, to compose an ode titled "Le Génie," explicitly dedicated to "M. de Chateaubriand." The poem was written in June 1820, and was followed up with a second ode to "Monsieur de Chateaubriand" in June 1824, when, in a small-scale version of the deposing of monarchs, Chateaubriand was stripped of his position as minister for foreign affairs. In both poems genius is once again both their topic and their addressee, with the poet's address staged in a context of universal hostility. This is the first stanza of "Le Génie":

Malheur à l'enfant de la terre,
Qui, dans ce monde injuste et vain,
Porte en son âme solitaire
Un rayon de l'Esprit divin!
Malheur à lui! l'impure Envie
S'acharne sur sa noble vie,
Semblable au Vautour éternel;
Et, de son triomphe irritée,
Punit ce nouveau Prométhée
D'avoir ravi le feu du ciel!

(Woe to the child of earth,
Who in this vain and unjust world,
Bears in his solitary soul
A ray of the divine Spirit!
Woe to him! impure Envy
Is bent on destroying his noble life,
Like the eternal Vulture;

And, exasperated by his triumph,
Punishes this new Prometheus
For having ravished fire from heaven!)

The solitary soul of the man of genius is the victim of an unjust world whose hostility is fuelled by envy of his gifts. In addition to such "impure envy," genius encounters "injustice," "grief," and "L'erreur, l'ignorance hautaine, / L'injure impunie et la haine" (Error, haughty ignorance, / Unpunished insults and hatred). The poet places himself to one side of "a people of dwarves" in order to speak directly to the "giant" who towers above them: "Chateaubriand, je t'en atteste, / . . . Tout doit un tribut au génie" (Chateaubriand, I can vouch that / . . . Everything owes a tribute to genius). He recounts Chateaubriand's life to him in the second person, adopting a majestic "tu" form, and commands him in a series of bold imperatives to hold fast to his mission: "Brave la haine empoisonnée!," "Sois fier d'avoir tant combattu," "Poursuis, remplis notre espérance; / Sers ton prince, éclaire la France" (Brave poisonous hatred; Be proud to have fought so hard; Pursue and fulfill our hopes; / Serve your prince, enlighten France), and so on.

The poem is obviously intended as the poet's own tribute to genius, and although Hugo was an eighteen-year-old "child" in relation to his fifty-two-year-old interlocutor, the poet nonetheless speaks on an equal footing. He even offers his elder a larger picture of his condition than he himself appears to have, and is able, for example, to see better than Chateaubriand supposedly can that genius is a gift to be accepted with joy, even at the price of the suffering it brings. Genius is a martyrdom that earns its own consecration: Chateaubriand is "*Honoré du double martyre / Du génie et de la vertu*" (*Honored* by the dual martyrdom / Of genius and virtue), or, as Hugo writes in "Le Nuage" (The cloud), "Le génie est plus grand d'envieux *couronné*" (Genius is greater when *crowned* with the envious).[24]

The banishing of the "impious horde" from the causerie between poet and addressee in "La lyre et la harpe" (The lyre and the harp) is repeated in many of the other poems, and it underscores the exclusiveness of the communication between the two figures. Sainte-Beuve somewhat sardonically comments that if the French public was irked at being disdained by a poetry that claimed to be the literature of the century, the poets themselves manifestly had not the least desire to understand society, and seemed far keener to acquire the martyr's palm than the poet's laurels.[25] In the ode to Lamartine, the nature of the bond between two poets is spelled out when Hugo describes Lamartine's muse as his "accomplice," and announces to his fellow poet that "nous combattrons en frères" (we shall fight as brothers):

Montés au même char, comme un couple homérique,
Nous tiendrons, pour lutter dans l'arène lyrique,
Toi ta lance, moi les coursiers.

(Mounted in the same chariot, like a Homeric pair,
To fight in the lyric arena, we shall hold
A lance for you, and the chargers for me.

The collaboration in poetic combat against the world follows from the reciprocity written into the exchanges that structure and define the poetry itself.

GENIUS RISING

Although Hugo borrows a number of features from Lamartine's muse—and the figure of a martyred genius despised by *le vulgaire* is certainly one such feature—the language and imagery in which Hugo presents genius are his own. The interlocutory model is replicated in Hugo's imagery: hostility is figured in the form of stormy elements through which genius rises toward an encounter with the sky or the sun, or, in another scenario, where it joins the ocean. Chateaubriand, as we saw, is a giant, and the genius in "Fin" is also "a capricious giant," whose height allows him to take wing and ride the storm with one foot standing in what Keats at the same time called "a dread waterspout,"[26] while his arm holds the heavens aloft. The mountaintop above the clouds is an appropriate home for genius or, as in "À mes odes" (To my odes), a simile for the inspired poet who is likened to

> . . . ces grands monts que la nouvelle aurore
> Dore avant tous à son réveil.
> Et qui, long-temps vainqueurs de l'ombre,
> Gardent jusque dans la nuit sombre
> Le dernier rayon du soleil.

> (. . . those great mountains that the new dawn
> Gilds before all others else at its wakening.
> And which, long triumphing over the shadows
> Retains until gloomy night
> The last ray of the sun.)

The sun answers the appeal that genius seems to make through its very elevation.

Since genius invariably views the world from a height, wings are one of its more recurrent attributes and it is frequently portrayed as an eagle. "À mon ami S.B." opens with the words "L'Aigle, c'est le génie!" (The Eagle is genius). It is "[l']oiseau de la tempête" ([the] bird of the storm), or as "Le Poète dans les révolutions" has it, "pour l'aiglon, fils des orages, / Ce n'est qu'à travers les nuages / Qu'il prend son vol vers le soleil" (for the eaglet, child of the thunderstorm, / It is only through the clouds / That he can take wing toward the sun). In its guise as eagle, genius rises through cloud and storm toward the sun whose light is its destination and reward. It is credited with eyes of flame whose flashes answer the sun: "[son] œil flamboyant incessamment *échange* / Des éclairs avec le soleil" ([his] eye of flame unceasingly *exchanges* / Flashes with the sun).[27]

This mutuality, raised above base indifference, defines the new poetry as the literature of the nineteenth century. Once again, a new language—this time the language of poetry—is drafting in genius as a necessary adjunct to its emergence. But it is also a language that—at least in the case of Hugo—makes speaking both of and to genius the means of making genius itself speak. Or to put it more bluntly, it makes the speaker a genius. This may not be said in quite as many words, but if, to quote Balzac, "[p]etty souls are always mistaken when assessing great ones," it follows that those who do give proper due to great souls must themselves be so endowed.[28] And, to put the matter more bluntly still, it takes one to know one.

CHAPTER 6

Victor Hugo, William Shakespeare, and the Dynasty of Genius

> To be great is to be misunderstood.
> —Ralph Waldo Emerson, "Self-Reliance"

In 1864, while Hugo was in exile, he returned to the topic of genius in an essay originally conceived as an introduction to the translation of the complete works of Shakespeare by his son, François-Victor. Shakespeare as a "supreme genius" is the pretext both for a lengthy discussion of genius in general and for a barely concealed statement of Hugo's own candidacy for the title. The mode of direct address is no longer used, but like the *Odes* in the 1820s, Hugo's account is presented as offering insights that he is uniquely equipped to provide. The image repertoire associated with genius also remains more or less unchanged: the genius is a giant, his place is on the mountaintop above the clouds, he is an ocean, he climbs, he is a sun, he is the infinite, his creations are divine, he is a visionary, he is a leader of his people. And he is persecuted: "A genius is a man accused."[1]

The term "genius" is now fully established as referring to individuals—the genius, *tout court*—and it has many synonyms: *seer, priest, pontiff, prophet, magus, thinker, dreamer, apostle, redeemer, liberator,* etc.—and *poëte* with that distinctive dieresis over the "e." This *poëte* is no longer identified exclusively with poetic form, and the genius-poet is now above all, in Paul Bénichou's words, the "man of spiritual quest" and the acme of a secular sainthood.[2] To speak of genius is no longer simply a means of entry into literature for the novice poet, but a justification for his acceptance as the leader of his people: "poets are the first educators of the people."[3] This mission has yet to be realized, but Hugo's claims *about* genius once again become the means of making a claim *to* genius.

PERSECUTION

In taking Shakespeare as his pretext for discussing genius, and setting him alongside the likes of Homer, Aeschylus, Job, Juvenal, Dante, Michelangelo,

Rabelais, and Cervantes, Hugo can hardly be said to be pleading the cause of unrecognized genius. But the oppression of genius is presented as an established fact: "Shakespeare's life was thoroughly embittered. He lived with perpetual insult . . . and was persecuted like Molière later on." Likewise, "the reproaches unanimously addressed to Shakespeare" by his public are pretty comprehensive: "—Conceits, wordplay, puns.—Improbability, extravagance, absurdity.—Obscenity.—Puerility.—Bombast, emphasis, exaggeration.—False glitter, pathos.—Far-fetched ideas, affected style.—Abuse of contrast and metaphor.—Subtilty.—Immorality.—Writing for the mob.—Pandering to the rabble.—Delighting in the horrible.—Want of grace.—Want of charm.—Overreaching his aim.—Having too much wit.—Having no wit.—Overdoing his work."[4] Any excuse will do for the world to find fault with genius, and in this Shakespeare was not alone. During his lifetime Aeschylus was the public butt of "every hatred." Genius is imprisoned, as was Cervantes; or else it is exiled, as were Aeschylus, Juvenal, Dante, Voltaire—and Hugo himself.

In the opening section of *William Shakespeare* Hugo paints a picture of his family, huddled against the winter storms in Marine Terrace on the island of Jersey where they had recently sought refuge. "These were outcasts," he explains. He goes on to draw the ironic, if somewhat hyperbolic, inference from their plight: "To have written is to provide a motive for bolted doors. Where might thought lead if not to the prison cell?"[5] Exiled after Napoleon III's coup d'état in 1851, which prompted Hugo to declare him a traitor and subsequently to denounce him in two published tracts, Hugo could justifiably claim to have shared the experience of many of the geniuses he writes about, and to do so as a publicly recognized poet. His literary reputation was in the ascendancy and the previous decade had seen the publication of three major volumes of poetry—*Les Châtiments* (1853), *Les Contemplations* (1856), and *La Légende des siècles* (1859)—as well as the hugely successful novel *Les Misérables* (1862).

If accusation is the lot of genius, then persecution becomes a badge of honor, a perverse form of recognition: "It is very fine to be attackable," writes Hugo. All the more so as it is the greatest minds that are the most contested. Inspiration is "suspect on the grounds of freedom," poetry is assumed to be "extralegal," and geniuses, by definition, "disconcert." They are "excessive," and their inability to comply with any rules or restraint makes it impossible for most social institutions to accommodate them:

> [M]en of genius . . . are imperious, tumultuous, violent, passionate beings, hard riders of winged steeds, transgressors of limits, "overleaping all boundaries," having their own goal, which itself is "beyond the mark," flying abruptly from one idea to another, and from the North Pole to the South Pole, crossing the heavens in three strides, making little allowance for the scant of breath, shaken by all the winds of space, and at the same time full of some unaccountable equestrian confidence amidst their bounds across the abyss, intractable to the "Aristarchs," refractory to official

rhetoric, not amiable to asthmatic *literati*, unsubdued to academic hygiene, preferring the foam of Pegasus to ass's-milk.[6]

For Vigny, the mismatch between the nature of the poet on one hand and the requirements of the state and its social organization on the other was reason to condemn the social and political order. For Hugo, it is the pretext for an irrepressible celebration of genius.

In the main, says Hugo, it is sheer pusillanimity that lies behind society's condemnation of genius: the pedantry of artistic schools, officially sanctioned literary criticism, "official and unofficial rhetoric," the "academic hygiene" that governs the universities, and the "bourgeois men of letters" who live by the cautious virtues of common sense, moderation, and temperance. Mediocrity inevitably feels envy when confronted with the superiority of genius; and, occasionally, even genius can fail to give genius its due: "bizarrely, the inspired can misrecognize inspiration."[7] The list of those who found grounds for criticizing Homer includes sixteen individuals from Pythagoras to Erasmus and Voltaire, as well as an assortment of anonymous Church Fathers and families of philosophers. But as a rule, the contrast between those who accuse, insult, or persecute genius and those to whom this treatment is meted out, redounds entirely to the credit of the latter.

ADMIRATION

Hugo's main contribution to the discussion of genius in *William Shakespeare* is his conception of a "dynasty" of geniuses. Insofar as Hugo has a theory of genius in general, it emerges from his account of a series of individual geniuses in whom, like water boiling at one hundred degrees, human thought achieves its maximum intensity. Hugo's roll call of genius includes Aeschylus, Job, Phidias, Isaiah, St. Paul, Juvenal, Dante, Michelangelo, Rabelais, Cervantes, Shakespeare, Rembrandt, Beethoven, "and a few others," with Homer as the first example to be discussed in detail. There is no hierarchy in this order, and each is equal to the others. But each is also *different* from the others. "Every genius has his own invention or discovery," and the implied task of the commentator is to capture what is distinctive about each and every one of them. Isaiah is like "a grumbling of continuous thunder," Ezekiel is "the wild soothsayer. A genius of the cavern," St. John the Divine is "the virginal elder," and so on. Between them they constitute a kind of composite in which they are connected less by genealogy than by a sort of transhistorical "conversation." Each genius may be unique and distinct, yet they communicate among each other by means of "effluvia"— like the stars.[8]

The form of this communication is, in the first instance, one of complementarity: many of these figures are explicitly described as complementing the qualities of a previous one. Aeschylus—albeit unwittingly—"completes" the resignation of Job with the revolt of his Prometheus. If Job embodies a notion of duty, and Aeschylus a notion of rights, Ezekiel brings a third term that combines the first two, in the form of the idea of progress. Juvenal has "everything Lucretius lacks," the one being the "universe" and the other "place," so that "between them they have the dual voice that speaks to the land and the city." Of course, it takes the grandeur of Hugo's own vision to make these connections, and to see that "[t]he entire Bible is contained between two visionaries: Moses and John," or that "Shakespeare is brother to Dante," and that here too "[o]ne completes the other."[9]

What begins as a description of this conversation gradually becomes a bid on Hugo's part to contribute to it in his own right. For genius is not just a dynasty, it is also a brotherhood. Its mode of relation is fraternal: "They receive you in their home with the *brotherliness* of archangels." The welcome offered by genius is made possible by the admiration that is Hugo's answer to the problem of misrecognition. Moreover, admiration provides access to genius in a way that criticism does not. The objections that have been made to Shakespeare are those of critics ("implausible," "obscene," "puerile," "exaggerated," etc., etc.), and Hugo quite explicitly rejects criticism—in both senses of the word—as a mode of discourse about genius. Genius is like nature, to be taken on its own terms: "Admiration. Enthusiasm. It seemed to me that in our times this example of foolishness was a good one to set."[10] Admiration is foolish only in appearance for it shrinks the distance between the admirer and the figure he admires.

As Hugo states in an essay on genius written in 1863, "[I]t is impossible to admire a masterpiece without at the same time feeling a certain self-esteem. One is grateful that one can understand. There is something fortifying in admiration, which enhances and adds dignity to intelligence." The admirer acquires some of the qualities of genius itself: "Understanding brings one closer."[11] The enthusiasm that Hugo urges upon himself in his own response to genius is another name for the inspiration that produces the greatest works of art. Indeed, there seems to be nothing quite as splendid as the spectacle of one genius granting recognition to another. This is the case of Aeschylus's lost work of homage to Orpheus, *The Apotheosis of Orpheus*, where one "god" interpreted another and each was a full match for the other: "[I]t is between equals, from one genius to another, from one sovereign to another, that these acts of homage appear as magnificent. Aeschylus raises a temple to Orpheus in which he himself could occupy the altar: this is a grand sight."[12] If Hugo's admiration is designed to raise his own altars to the supreme geniuses he marshals here, it follows that there is a barely concealed ambition to join them.

Admiration may not take the discursive form of direct address, but it is a relation to the "other" of genius that invites the reciprocity of fraternizing. Genius constitutes a dynasty, not because genius begets genius in genealogical sequence, but because it forms an open series that encourages further additions.

Genius is essentially generous: "These supreme geniuses are not a closed series. The author of All will add a name when the needs of progress require it."[13] It is here that Hugo's candidacy begins to take a more perceptible shape, and it does so with particular reference to the needs of his own time and place.

A GENIUS FOR THE PEOPLE

In one sense genius transcends its historical moment, and Homer is as close to the present as Shakespeare or Beethoven, while simultaneously being untimely—"beyond the limits of temporality," as Henri Meschonnic aptly puts it.[14] Yet one of the prime functions of genius according to Hugo is to be *of* its time by signaling the passage from one epoch to another. The openness of the series formed by genius does not preclude a historical dimension: "The two geniuses that are Homer and Shakespeare closed the two first gates of the barbarian era, the doors of the ancients and the Gothic doors. This was their mission, and they fulfilled it." But there is a third era—the era of monarchy—which still needs to be brought to an end so that the era of revolution can be fully inaugurated by a genius for the times: "The third great human crisis is the French Revolution; it is the third huge gate of barbarianism, the gate of monarchy, which is closing at the moment. The nineteenth century can hear it rolling on its hinges. Hence, for poetry, drama and art, the current era is as independent of Shakespeare as of Homer." Hugo maps out a new historical moment—the present—which awaits its consecration. Thanks to the French Revolution, the "caravan of humanity" has reached a new plateau and requires an even greater contribution from a man of genius who will both clinch and direct the "forward march of the human race."[15] For the time being this space remains empty, but it is hard not to infer that Hugo is making a bid to fill it.

This unfilled space is partly temporal and partly geographical, which is to say partly that of the century and partly that of France. It is here that Hugo's discussion connects with the issues raised by the accounts of collective genius that I have already explored. Just as Alletz had declared, the nineteenth century is deemed to be the era of genius, or, as Hugo himself puts it, "Being genius itself, it fraternizes with geniuses." And it owes its genius to the Revolution: "The Revolution forged the trumpet; the nineteenth century is sounding it." In an echo of Michelet, who was soon to publish a fourth edition of *Le Peuple*, the mission of genius is the "transformation of the crowd into a people." This has still to be accomplished, and it can be achieved only by the geniuses who emerge from the people and dedicate themselves to it: "To whom do geniuses belong, if not you, the people?" asks Hugo.[16]

The vulgar crowd over whose heads genius once spoke in Hugo's earlier writing has now become its direct addressee and beneficiary. Genius relates not only to other geniuses, but to the people of his own time and place. Shakespeare's treatment of the "rabble"—allegedly condemned by the critics—is an exemplary instance of a theater of the people, with whom the poet demonstrably has a natural connection. What Hugo envisages now is a "fraternal" exchange in which the poet-genius speaks to the people in response to their need for him. The brief is becoming very clear: the nineteenth century requires its own man of genius to embody the revolutionary era and dedicate himself to the people by means of his poetry.

In Hugo's account France is the country where the nineteenth century has been most fully realized (as Alletz had also maintained). If the nineteenth is a century of revolution, then its home is France, France having exported revolution to America and offered a model for the rest of the world to follow: "France has borne this century, and the century bears Europe." The people Hugo describes as being in want of a genius to lead and educate it is not explicitly defined in national terms. But, in a book written in the French language by a French writer fifteen years after the revolution of 1848, the word *peuple* must perforce have a French resonance, consecrated by Delacroix's *Liberty Leading the People*, which celebrated the July Revolution of 1830, or by Michelet, who attributes the inspiration of *Le Peuple* to national feeling and "the idea of the Fatherland."[17] The people in need of a poet can only be French.

Genius may transcend its place and time, but to do so it needs to be grounded in both. Shakespeare is English—even too English, says Hugo—but in his (totally counterfactual) view it took the French to recognize the genius to which England owes its greatness. Genius both embodies and transcends national character, and Hugo lists the geniuses who have represented their nations: "The great Pelasgian is Homer; the great Hellene is Aeschylus; the great Hebrew is Isaiah; the great Roman is Juvenal; the great Italian is Dante, the great Englishman is Shakespeare; the great German is Beethoven."[18] And there it stops, with France pointedly absent from the inventory. Once again, Hugo has carved out an empty space for genius with the unmistakable implication that he would be the man to fill it.

In this way he comes full circle back to the claim he made in the 1824 preface to the *Odes* about the mission of genius being to express the thought of its place and time and to lead its people "like a light." The difference is that forty years previously the claim was general and abstract, whereas now, in the 1860s, it has acquired a barely concealed personal reference to Hugo himself, to France, and to the present of the nineteenth century. The people who abandoned Vigny's Moïse to his solitude are now equipped to understand their own need for him, and Hugo is poised to respond. The one-time *pair de France* and indecisive participant in the 1848 Revolution had found himself a far greater political role in exile as the opponent of Napoleon III's Second Empire, denounced in *Napoleon-le-Petit* (1852) and in grander poetic vein in *Les Châtiments*. His genius may by then have become a widely recognized fact: Dickens claims to have been "much struck by Hugo himself, who looks a Genius, as he certainly is," and the Goncourt brothers described *Les Misérables* as "[t]he most magnificent failure . . . ever produced by a man of genius."[19] But the honorary national leadership that Hugo ascribes to genius adds a whole new dimension to its significance. For the poet, to speak *of* genius is once again a bid to speak *as* a genius, but to do so as a means of finally transforming individual genius into the embodiment of the genius of the nation.

PART III

Genius in the Clinic

CHAPTER 7

Genius under Observation

Lélut

that mental illness called genius
—Émile Lauvrière, *Edgar Poe, sa vie et son œuvre*

When Vigny's Stello is laid low by an attack of the "blue devils" he is cured by a remarkably effective "physician of the soul," Dr. Noir, who is blessed with an ability to "see to the heart of everything" and has insight that distinguishes him from the rest of humanity as well as from physicians of the body who can see no further than the surface of things. His diagnosis and cure—stories of unhappy poets—may appear unorthodox, but insight into diseases of the soul had been the basis for the recent emergence of a new medicine of the mind in France. Philippe Pinel, whose influential *Traité médico-philosophique sur l'aliénation mentale* was published in 1800, laid the foundations for a fresh understanding—and innovative treatments—of mental illness. These were further developed by his pupil Jean-Étienne Esquirol, and France remained at the forefront of the new discipline of mental medicine throughout the nineteenth century. The specialty went by many names—*aliénisme, médecine morale* or *mentale, psychologie physiologique, psychologie morbide, médecine psychologique*—before the term *psychiatry* was finally established at the end of the nineteenth century and the torch passed to Germany.[1] Unlike Dr. Noir, however, not all the practitioners of the new medicine were the friends of genius as it increasingly became the object of their new medical expertise.

The philosophical component of the new medicine, alluded to in the title of Pinel's treatise, was based in large part on the principles of eighteenth-century sensualist philosophy, with Condillac its most cited example. This tradition held out to the practitioners of mental medicine the presumption of a connection between the body and the mind, which had particular importance for their growing interest in genius. The broad consensus that had existed in the eighteenth century between aesthetics and a philosophy of the mind is mostly lost in the nineteenth century as two opposing models of mental functioning emerge. The powers of observation widely attributed to genius in the eighteenth century were now claimed as the prerogative of (medical) science, and contrasted with imagination, which was predominantly associated with genius and the arts. More important, imagination itself came to be conceived rather differently, and was no longer understood as the adjunct to mimesis that it was for Dubos or in the *Encyclopédie*'s "Article Génie."

IMAGINATION

Imagination was now viewed as a feature of subjective expression, located in the mind, rather than as a means to enhance the representation of external reality. For writers and poets, this move is a positive one, but for the medical profession, it made imagination the source of mental malfunctioning. As early as 1796, Mme de Staël condemns the emergent medical view of the perils of the imagination when she writes, "Much has been said about the dangers of the imagination, and it would be pointless to search out the things that the impotence of mediocrity, or the severity of reason have repeated on this subject." Against medical judgment of the matter, she argues that "[t]here is no faculty more precious to man than the imagination," and in *De l'Allemagne* she urges French writers to become "conquerors of the empire of the imagination" by following the example of their German counterparts and turning their focus inward.[2]

Vigny identifies imagination as the attribute that distinguishes the rarity that is the "Poète," from the mere "Man of letters," or the worthy but dull "Great Writer." It is the imagination of the poet that "[irresistibly] transports his faculties toward the heavens" and leads him to discover "unknown worlds." And when in the *Salon of 1859* Baudelaire declared the imagination to be, quite simply, "the queen of the faculties," he did so specifically in protest against the realist aesthetic of his day.[3] In the spheres of poetry, painting, and literature more generally, this redefined imagination continues to be a characteristic of genius, while the emergent sciences gradually abandon any claims to genius of their own and make a virtue of their developing protocols of observation.

There are references here and there to "medical genius" in the early years of the century. Esquirol called Pinel's program "the fruit of observation and genius," and Pinel was praised for his genius in an unsigned note published in the *Journal général de médecine* in 1818: "Although the *Traité* of Monsieur Pinel has been translated into every language [and] is the manual of every physician who treats lunatics, the celebrated professor, with that candor that belongs only to genius, never ceases to invite his students to improve upon what he has already begun."[4] The entry for "Génie" in the *Dictionnaire des sciences médicales* envisages the possibility of a specifically medical form of genius by distinguishing three separate classes: one based in inspiration and associated with the liberal arts; one based in reflection and instanced by the sciences of mathematics and physics; and a mixed variety, characteristic of politics, the military arts, and practical medicine.[5] In other words genius is perceived in the early years of the century as having a value that medicine briefly, if somewhat ambivalently, aspires to, before abandoning the attribute to the creative artist and an association with insanity in order to establish its own authority on a quite different basis.

For the medical profession, the genius associated with the creative artist was located in the brain—with the gut drafted in from time to time to provide corroborative evidence, as noted by one commentator when he writes that "[n]owadays, it is even claimed that genius can be evaluated according to the state of the stomach."[6] This embodiment—as brain or gut—is the means whereby genius becomes a potentially pathological object. Mental medicine revives the view of genius as pathology, calling up echoes of a history that goes back to (Pseudo-)Aristotle's discussion of melancholy, quoted on the first page of Lombroso's *The Man of Genius*, and to Plato's idea that inspiration is a form of madness. Melancholy has left a well-documented record in poetry and painting from the Middle Ages onward, with genius offering exemplary illustrations of its effects.[7] Medicine also reverts to a physiological basis for genius first elaborated by Aristotle, but maintained in later writers such as Marsilio Ficino, whose *Book of Life* (1489) had argued that intellectual health depends to a considerable degree on physical health, which depends in turn on climate, diet, and daily regimen.

In the eighteenth century Dubos alludes to the notion that genius derives from a particular organization of the brain, the stomach, and the blood, and Diderot suggests that genius may have a physical basis in the "the structure of the head and the intestines, and a certain constitution of the humors"—as well as in the diaphragm. At the same time the life of the mind was increasingly being associated with physical and mental suffering of various kinds, thanks to which the body of the artist and the writer was progressively pathologized. Rousseau is mentioned in Samuel Auguste Tissot's *De la santé des gens de lettres* (On the health of men of letters, 1758) as a source of wisdom about the deleterious physical effects of "work in the study," but he was more often mentioned as a classic example of those effects, and was still being cited in the nineteenth century as having suffered from "a sick and hallucinated imagination."[8]

With the advance of medicine in the nineteenth century, genius is even more closely associated with physical attributes as it becomes the object of specialized knowledge about insanity and the preserve of a medically informed expertise. Understanding of brain anatomy and function progressed exponentially, from Gall and phrenology at beginning of the century to a model of neuroanatomy that is recognizable to neuroscientists working today. With this knowledge to underpin it, genius could then be regarded *either* as an instance of optimal performance of brain, *or* as an effect of its malfunctioning, and both views will be discussed in the following chapters. Whichever the case, the issue for medical science is not so much the identification of genius, as its explanation. Even where cases are already familiar from the existing literature on genius (Socrates, Pascal) mental medicine presents itself as being uniquely equipped to provide insights into its nature, as no other discipline—let alone genius itself—can. Medical science now speaks in the place of genius as genius ceases to be considered as the *source* of knowledge, and instead becomes its *object*.

THE ANATOMY OF GENIUS

This shift is made possible by the polarization of mental faculties into imagination associated predominantly with creative genius, and observation associated predominantly with medical science.[9] This division presupposes an observing doctor on whom a proper understanding of genius is made to depend, since the mind of the genius is now assumed to be grounded in the body. There was a widespread view (inherited from the eighteenth century) that men of letters were unusually prone to physical illness thanks to their nervous temperament, which inclined them to overwork. They were susceptible to a variety of ailments, including digestive upset, constipation, hemorrhoids, poor posture, headaches, apoplexy, melancholy, and an excessive sensitivity, which, as Réveillé-Parise reports in his *Physiologie et hygiène des hommes livrés aux travaux de l'esprit* (physiology and hygiene of men devoted to mental labor), could lead to insanity or even death.

However vaguely formulated, such medical accounts all presupposed the existence of some ultimately physical basis for the mind, as implied by terms such as the "*lesions* of the functions of the understanding" mentioned by Pinel, or Moreau de Tours's notions of "excitement"—for which he preferred the more physiologically suggestive terms of "éréthisme" (*erethism*) or "diathèse" (*diathesis*). Heredity—also according to Moreau—revealed genius in telling association with a whole variety of physical disorders and debilities. In his medical account of Pascal's pathological genius, Louis-Francisque Lélut describes ideas as "daughters of the soul, but born of the impressions of the body," and he adds that "they bear the ineradicable imprint of that fatality of matter which rebounds on the mind itself."[10] Mental activity is to be studied by the medical experts as an entirely physiological phenomenon, subject to this "fatality of matter."

Despite the rapid development of anatomical knowledge, and despite its own claims, mental medicine remains surprisingly vague about the specificities of the physiological basis for the pathologies it claims to describe. But rhetoric and terminology compensate for this imprecision through a reliance on powerfully physical imagery, which supports the basic principle that, to quote Lélut again, "the greatest man . . . is bound to the earth, through his body, which is itself earth . . . he has a double nature, *homo duplex*." It is through this alleged attachment to his earthly body, that the great man becomes available for observation and the object of medical knowledge:

> the man who wishes to know man and to share this knowledge, must study him in his mind and his organs, in their connections and their mutual dependence. He needs to know, and to make it known that this dependence is greater, or at least more evident, in sickness, when such dependence is increasingly to the advantage of the organs; that especially in those diseases known as diseases of the mind, the supremacy of the body is practically absolute; whence the woeful degradation, which, in this kind of morbid condition, reduces . . . the greatest personages to the level of the smallest.[11]

In sum, whatever physiological model is invoked, mental functioning—even that of the greatest minds, such as those of Socrates and Pascal, anatomized by Lélut—is always described as conjoined with, or more often, pathologically compromised by the body.

The medical profession had a considerable investment in constructing genius in terms of pathology. As Lélut says, the mind's dependence on the body is more visible in sickness than in health, and that dependence applies very particularly to genius. Medicine was not alone in creating this association between genius and insanity, which had become something of a commonplace. Dryden's comment that "Great wits are sure to madness near allied, / And thin partitions do their bounds divide" is one of the most quoted sayings about genius in general. Schopenhauer wrote that "genius and madness have a side where they touch and even pass over into each other," citing Seneca's gloss on (Pseudo-) Aristotle to the effect that "[t]here has been no great mind without an admixture of *madness*." One could also mention the speed with which artists and writers adopted this view in the nineteenth century, as they internalized medical knowledge and presented an increasingly sick and suffering bodily image of the artist in their work. Balzac's Louis Lambert, the Goncourts' Charles Demailly, and Zola's Claude Lantier are prime instances of this phenomenon, and I shall return to them in later chapters.[12] But for now the focus is on the discipline that sought to provide an expert scientific account of this pathology over the course of its development in the nineteenth century.

INTELLECT VERSUS HALLUCINATION

The medical approach was most effectively directed at figures from the past whose reputations for genius were already established, but whose pathologies are retrospectively brought to light by medical analysis. It would clearly have been inappropriate for doctors to publicize cases of insanity among supposed geniuses currently in their care, although they frequently hinted at their ability to do so, and they were perfectly willing to generalize on the basis of their own professional experience. Pinel mentions in his *Traité médico-philosophique sur l'aliénation mentale* that he is treating a "former *littérateur*," and he suggests that this was not an isolated case:

> It is well known, that certain professions conduce more than others to insanity, which are chiefly those in which the imagination is unceasingly or ardently engaged, and not moderated in its excitement by the exercise of those functions of the understanding which are more susceptible of satiety and fatigue. In consulting the registers at *Bicêtre*, we find many priests and monks, as well as country people, terrified into this condition by the anticipation of hell torments: many artists, painters, sculptors and musicians: some poets extatized by their own productions: a great number of advocates and attorneys.

He goes on to mention specifically that medical men do not feature among these inmates: "there are no instances of persons whose professions require the habitual exercise of the judging faculty; not one naturalist, nor a physician, nor a chemist, and for the best reason in the world, not one geometrician."[13]

The implication of all this is that there is a categorical difference in the kinds of mental faculty used by different professions, which, crudely summarized, contrasts imagination with an "intellect" consisting of observation, judgment, and, given the immunity of the geometrician to madness, one should add calculation. This distinction places the artist and the poet alongside the credulous and the insane under the banner of imagination, and the scientifically informed medical man under the banner of an empirically grounded intellect alongside the naturalist, the physicist, and that geometrician. It also established a set of power relations whereby the madman and the artist were laid open to the gaze of the physician as passive objects of an observation that was strictly a one-way process. This relation is central to the pathologizing account of genius to be found in Lélut's studies of Socrates and Pascal, *Le Génie, la raison et la folie* (Genius, reason, and madness), first published in 1836 under the title *Du démon de Socrate* (Socrates' demon) and *L'Amulette de Pascal pour servir à l'histoire des hallucinations* (Pascal's amulet, a contribution to the history of hallucinations, 1846), of which a preliminary edition appeared in the previous year under the title *De l'amulette de Pascal, étude sur les rapports de la santé de ce grand homme à son genie* (Pascal's amulet, a study of the relations between the health of this great man and his genius). These are the first examples of the genre that has subsequently come to be known as pathography, and they are also among the first fully documented medical accounts of genius as a form of insanity.[14]

There are three factors involved in Lélut's pathologizing of genius, the first and the most important of these being imagination. Hallucinations were viewed as the symptom of a malfunctioning of the imagination, which was widely regarded as inherently vulnerable to pathology. Pinel implies this in the comment quoted above, but he made a number of other remarks where its pathological character is more explicit, as when he says, "Of all the faculties of the under-standing, the imagination appears to be the one most liable to profound le-sions." This view is inherited from the eighteenth century, when, in addition to its role in revealing reality, imagination had also figured in discussions that saw it as the pathogenic cause of melancholy, and when madness in general was considered to be "an error of the imagination." In his *Essai sur l'origine des con-naissances humaines*, Condillac defines insanity as "an imagination, that with-out one noticing it, associates ideas in a thoroughly disorderly fashion, and at times influences our judgments or our behavior."[15] It is this kind of attitude that Mme de Staël has in her sights when she defends the imagination against those who warn against its supposed "dangers."

Its literary defenders notwithstanding, Lélut incriminates the imagination in general as much as Rousseau in particular when he describes Rousseau as having "a sick and hallucinated imagination."[16] He portrays the imagination as a form of mental functioning where the mind generates ideas from within in a process that he contrasts with the norms of the sensualist model of the mind, where ideas derive from without as information about the external world is transmitted by the senses. It is thanks to this generative or projective model of the mind that it was possible for figures such as Socrates and Pascal to be pathologized in preference to the more predictable examples, such as that of Tasso whose melancholy madness was part of his popular image in the early years of the nineteenth century.

The introduction to *L'Amulette de Pascal* sets all this out very clearly, and Lélut is quite explicit about his allegiance to the key notions of sensualist phi-losophy. In line with many alienists of his time, he places himself in the tradition of Locke and Hobbes, and he specifically cites Condillac as "the great sensualist philosopher." From this perspective the artist and the madman—albeit to differ-ing degrees—are both aberrant in their reliance on the imagination, whose workings are contrasted to the empiricist model of the mind, which sensualist philosophers treated as the norm: "Ideas that draw their direct origin from sen-sations are those whose nature makes them most worthy of the name." If the best ideas are those that derive from a necessary and direct relation with the impression made by external objects on the senses, the ideas that derive from the sense of sight are "ideas *par excellence*," a view that further endorses the privileging of medical observation over literary or philosophical imagination.[17]

Lélut contrasts these sense-based ideas with those that emerge autono-mously and spontaneously from within. They are generated by the mind, which attaches sensory form to them only secondarily. They exist in a range of differ-ent types on a continuum that goes from the fruits of inspiration and the cre-ations of genius at one end, to the hallucinations of the insane at other. In the case of the first, which Lélut calls "image-ideas" (*idées-images*), ideas are con-verted into images that portray nature on the basis of an innate model of an ideal informed by a natural preference for "beauty and greatness." The creativity that is at once the mark and the condition of genius allows the artist to produce images endowed with such "vivacity" that they are "the equivalent to the reality of things." True geniuses—and here Lélut quotes Leonardo da Vinci—"work . . . with an inner concentration, pursuing invention, and creating these conceptions in their minds, those *perfect ideas*, which they then translate with their hands."[18] The sources of artistic creativity may lie within, but the potentially pathological and hallucinatory tendencies of the imagination are offset by the artist's inborn sense of beauty and by the skill with which he endows them with physical form. Importantly, the artist is also assumed to be aware that the source of his creations lies within himself.

At the next point along the spectrum, ideas are falsely concretized and the "image-idea" is replaced by the "sensation-idea" (*idée-sensation*) where the idea is objectified as a sensory experience whose source the imagining subject erroneously attributes to external reality. There are varying degrees in the intensity of this phenomenon, which extends from the dreams of the sleeper and the somnambulist, to illusions where the subject misinterprets the nature of an external object that actually exists: seeing a pyramid in place of a rock, or parents as executioners, to quote two of Lélut's own examples. The far end of this continuum of false sensations is occupied by the phenomenon of outright hallucinations. These are a form of sensation-idea that has no basis at all in external reality, although for the hallucinating subject external reality is exactly where he locates what he thinks he sees or hears. The hallucination is "a false sensation that is taken to be a real sensation."[19] The hallucinator is entirely cut off from the outside world and constructs an alternative reality that is nothing more than a projection of his own inner imaginings. The difference between creative genius and insanity is that whereas the artist is aware that his projections have come from within himself, the madman attributes them unequivocally to the world without.

For Lélut, imagination is a deeply ambivalent entity. In positive mode it will "place a compass in the hands of Archimedes and a lyre in those of Homer, and make Plato at once a poet, a philosopher and [tellingly, in light of Pinel's remarks] a geometrician." It is imagination too, which, "under the name of genius . . . reveals to élite intelligence facts previously concealed in ordinary experience, and truths that for the rest of mankind are still only paradoxes." But, it is also imagination "whose disorderly action can, under fatal circumstances, transform their conceptions and ideas or the images through which they represent them, into false sensations, which these ardent minds will have as much faith in as in their more usual sensations."[20] Imagination and creation are thus opposed to perception and observation, the artist and the madman illustrating the first, and the empirical sciences—with mental medicine to the fore—once again representing the latter. For the medical profession, observation will trump imagination every time.

LEVELING

If, despite their similarities, Lélut's account implies a hierarchy that places the imaginings of genius above the hallucinations of the insane, insanity itself is presented as a great leveler, and it is through this leveling that the insane, whatever their other qualities, such as the genius that distinguishes Socrates or Pascal, become available to the diagnostic scrutiny of the alienist. While the madman lives in a world entirely of his own imagining, cut off from the physical realities that surround him, he is reduced by his insanity to a predominantly physical condition. He lives in his mind, but it is his physiology that determines the functioning of this mind. The imagination itself had a physiological basis and was regarded as the most corporeal of the mental functions, located precisely at the intersection of the physical and the moral between which it was thought to act as an intermediary. It was for this reason that—at least in Condillac's view—even animals were considered to be endowed with imagination.[21]

In mental illness, the mind is reduced to the body and creative genius to unfettered hallucination. Social differences are also erased by insanity, and Lélut stresses that all classes are equally prey to the demons of their hallucinations, with the result that there are "demons of every shape, every color, every stripe, but, most importantly for us here, demons in elevated positions, with elevated titles, elevated merit and elevated renown: baron and baroness demons, marquis and marchioness demons, duke and duchess demons, prince and princess demons, minister and diplomat demons, composer and great composer demons, poet and great poet demons, warrior and great warrior demons."[22] Insanity is no respecter of rank or talent, and it turns the artist, the poet, the scholar, or the philosopher who was once the "glory of the world" into "a mad wretch," the object of pity rather than of admiration.[23]

The leveling that results from the medical pathologizing of imagination is the exact reverse of the way imagination is portrayed by the poets for whom it is the elevated "queen of faculties." The Socrates who is the founder and the greatest representative of European philosophy proves, on informed medical examination, to be no different from the lunatics encountered by Lélut in the course of his clinical practice, and he includes a number of case histories in his appendix for illuminating comparison. So, when Socrates speaks of being able to control others through a power of influence that needs neither word nor gesture and can be exerted through solid walls, Lélut comments that such "extravagant" claims are entirely characteristic of insanity and that "hallucinators, who before [his] very eyes, claim to be sending or receiving remote influences of a physical, magnetic or Free-Masonic kind, talk no differently than Socrates, and their insanity is no greater than was his."[24] When insanity takes hold, great minds become malfunctioning bodies, and great artists no more than deluded "wretches."

Equally, barons and ministers of state have nothing to distinguish them from the anonymous cobbler admitted to Bicêtre in May 1828, persecuted by figures whose taunts keep him awake at night, disturb and threaten him. As the lunatics fill their imaginary world with the voices of demons, robbers, murderers, and, in the case of one hallucinating baroness, an entire cavalry regiment that enters her room through a keyhole each night, the medical man sees a mind subjected to the workings of a body that override both rank and talent.

PATHOGRAPHICAL PERSPECTIVES

It is this inclusion of the body that allows the doctor to claim that the medical view provides the only comprehensive view. Lélut makes this point in the preface to his study of Pascal where he asserts that the exaggerated estimation of certain figures derives from the very partial picture that posterity has created after their deaths. The picture is partial, he claims, because, for all its luster, it leaves out the "humanity" of those it claims to celebrate. A true estimation can be provided only by evaluating genius according to "the common rules of a philosophy of man that considers man as a whole, and never separates . . . his reason from his instincts, his will from his desires, and finally his mind from his organs, the organs being the indispensable and frequently fatal condition for the exercise of thought."[25] In affirming the link between body and mind, physiology and imagination, instinct and reason, the medical perspective also positions the past alongside the present. Lélut's studies of genius draw on the past for their subjects, notably Socrates and Pascal, who are then compared to cases of insanity in the modern world in order to highlight the similarities between the two groups. By setting the temple of Minerva alongside "Charenton and its gloomy hillside," Socrates alongside the hallucinating cobbler in the asylum at Bicêtre, Lélut claims to be providing a fuller picture of the man than the one that will see in him only "the father of all philosophy and . . . all philosophers." The man considered to be "an exceptional man amongst all men" turns out, when seen in the physiological round, to be a lunatic like any other.[26]

Lélut's portrait of Socrates focuses principally on his daemon, the source of the voice that he claimed dictated his actions. Lélut was not the first to do so, and the issue had received more than incidental mention in the classical sources. For example, Plutarch's essay, translated in French as "Le démon de Socrate," consists in large part of a discussion between various personages about the nature and significance of the daemon. Continuing interest in the issue is evident in the edition of Lélut's Démon de Socrate held in Queen's College Library in Oxford, which has bound into it a copy of Robert Nares's An Essay on the Demon or Divination of Socrates from 1782. But whereas Plutarch's essay praises Socrates for ridding philosophy of superstition and treats the daemon as a mark of his superiority, Lélut ignores all this and diagnoses the daemon as pure hallucination. He translates the Greek *daemon* as *démon* in French, but he also frequently uses the word *génie*, which offers scope for a convenient ambiguity between the *genius* that is the Latin translation of the Greek daemon and the genius that marks Socrates out as an exceptional figure: "Socrates could have remained a singular or extraordinary man throughout his life if, however, from his childhood onwards, being acted on by his genius [*son génie*], he had not been disposed to take the inspiration of his consciousness for the voice of a supernatural agent."[27] The original title of Lélut's case study of Socrates is *Du démon de Socrate*, but the second edition continues to exploit the potential for ambiguity by making this the subtitle of a book whose main title then becomes *Le Génie, la raison et la folie*: Socrates's genius is merely a demon of the kind that torment the inmates of Bicêtre, whispering in his ear, and proof of "irrefutable insanity."

There is a further confusion in Lélut's argument which is more than just verbal, and he seems to veer between two views of this irrefutable insanity: one where it undermines the status that Socrates has as the founder of Western philosophy, and the other where his ability to function philosophically, despite the mental impairment represented by his hallucinations, actually becomes an index of his mental superiority: "It is only the best constituted individuals [*les grandes organisations*], such as Socrates, who can bear such a burden, bear it for a long time, occasionally conquer it, and when they succumb to it, leave the world uncertain as to whether the principle behind their efforts should be called genius or something very different."[28] He makes the point in slightly different terms when he suggests elsewhere that other exceptional figures, such as Muhammad, Joan of Arc, Ignatius of Loyola, and Luther, would now be diagnosed as insane, but were able to occupy a powerful national and political role in the past precisely because their condition was not recognized for what it actually was. In both these comments, it is possible to read an implication that the component of insanity in genius is also proof of the presence of a genius capable of withstanding it. But this is just an excursus in an argument that otherwise treats genius as pure pathology.

If the ancients failed to perceive the hallucinations for what they were, this is to be explained, says Lélut, by the undeveloped state of human knowledge: "At the time Socrates lived, knowledge about the boundaries that separate reason from madness, and especially knowledge about the very curious phenomenon of hallucinations, was far from being sufficiently advanced, either amongst philosophers or amongst physicians, for it to have been possible to see Socrates and the other great men who lived with the same condition for what they were." Indeed, he continues, "This is so true, that even now, at a distance of more than two thousand years, there is only a small number of men capable of seeing clearly on this issue." Greek culture was dominated to such a degree by superstition and polytheistic religious belief that it was perfectly possible not to think

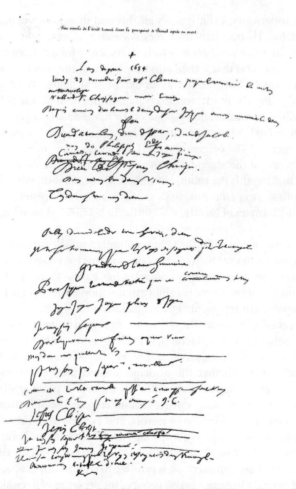

Figure 2. Facsimile of Pascal's "amulet." From Lélut's *L'Amulette de Pascal* (1846).

that there was anything remarkable in Socrates's invocation of his daemon. Lélut nevertheless expresses surprise that the pathologies he describes had not been noticed sooner: "It is simply extraordinary that so little attention was paid to this general state, or that its significance was not better appreciated."[29] The suggestion seems to be both that the pathology is in principle self-evident, and that it requires the professional expertise of the modern medical man to recognize it for what it is.

In compiling the case studies of both Socrates and Pascal, Lélut starts with the existing version or versions of his subject's life, and then rewrites them in his own, medical terms. His principal sources on Pascal are Gilberte's narrative of her brother's life, the memoir left by his niece, and the strange document known as the "amulette," which records the so-called night of fire and was found after Pascal's death sewn—apparently by his own hand—into the pocket of his doublet. For Socrates, Lélut draws extensively on the testimony of Plutarch, Diogenes Laertius, Plato, Xenophon, and a number of other ancient sources. Lélut had a classical education, which he drew on to summarize the established version of Socrates's life before proceeding to denounce it as false by contrasting the explanations for Socrates's daemon given in the literature of the ancient world and what he calls the "truth of the matter." This, quite simply, is that Socrates was subject to hallucinations, which, if they were reported by a philosopher in the modern world, would have him incarcerated in a cell at Charenton rather than offered a chair in the Faculty of Letters at the university. The daemon is recast in contemporary medical terms as the product of false sensations, reason as madness, and the voice of deities as auditory hallucination. Even melancholy is renamed "by science" to become *hypocondrie*.[30]

The genius of Socrates is pathologized as a result of being modernized: think of Socrates as a candidate for a chair at the Sorbonne talking about his daemon and his insanity becomes obvious. Both studies include a large amount of documentary material as appendices, including a facsimile of Pascal's record of his night of fire in the *Amulette de Pascal* (see Figure 2). Readers are thus invited to consider the evidence for themselves and are positioned to arrive at the same "objective" and empirical diagnosis as the medical author, according to which the man of genius will be judged—quite incontrovertibly—to be insane.

CHAPTER 8

Genius, Neurosis, and Family Trees

Moreau de Tours

Poetry is a disease of the brain.

—Vigny, *Chatterton*

The pathologizing of genius continued in the work of Jacques-Joseph Moreau—known as "Moreau de Tours"—who adopted the eloquent term "morbid psychology" for his particular branch of mental medicine and defined genius as a form of neurosis. His book on the subject, *Psychologie morbide: dans ses rapports avec la philosophie de l'histoire, ou de l'influence des névropathies sur le dynamisme intellectuel* (Morbid psychology: In its relations to the philosophy of history or the influence of neuropathy on intellectual dynamism), published in 1859, examines the general phenomenon of "neuropathy" rather than confining itself to the study of individual cases as Lélut had done. But the underlying assumptions and approach remain the same, and Moreau follows Lélut in asserting the physiological basis of mental malfunction when he insists that "it is essential . . . to explore man in his entrails and to abandon visions of pure reason in the regions of the absolute."[1] The mind exists in inseparable conjunction with the body, and genius is inherently pathological, placed within a configuration of mental debility that extends from imbecility to delirium. Moreau also develops the principles of medical observation outlined by Lélut, where the neutral, observing medical mind is constructed in opposition to the excitable and involuntarily productive mind, which, according to Moreau, is found as commonly in genius as in other forms of insanity.

HEREDITARY PATHOLOGY

Moreau's pathologizing of genius extends beyond the single phenomenon of hallucinations as he establishes a "consanguinuity" between all types of disturbances of the mind that can be attributed to a single "primordial lesion." While this lesion is never given a precise anatomical location, Moreau presents disruption of the nervous system as the consequence of a "predisposition" that many carry within themselves. It can manifest in a variety of forms that include rickets and scrofula as well as delirium and imbecility: "By virtue of their common origin, and certain physical and moral characteristics, people afflicted with *insanity, idiocy, scrofula* or *rickets*, should be regarded as children belonging to the same family, and different branches on the same tree trunk." Moreover, each condition contains the others in latent form, so that "organic causes or dispositions are, most often, concealed beneath very misleading appearances." This means that "insanity and idiocy, which is to say the expression of the gravest disturbances of moral life, contain the potential for the most transcendent intellectual qualities and for genius, just as the womb contains the embryo, and vice versa."[2] Insanity may have the potential for genius, but the reverse is equally true.

Moreau's reference to a tree is no rhetorical coincidence, and on the last page of his book he includes a diagram representing a kind of family tree of pathologies, with a "Hereditary idiosyncratic nervous condition" forming the base of its trunk, off which there grow various branches such as "Rickets," "Spontaneous phrenopathy due to intoxication," and "Exceptional intelligence," each of them adorned in turn with leaves bearing the names of conditions such as the "Otitis" or the "Hyperesthesia," which are attached to the branch named "Disturbances of general and particular sensitivity" (see Figure 3). The notion of a family tree is relevant here, not just because it graphically supports the principle of organic links between the various conditions it maps, but more importantly because the interconnection between these conditions is presented by Moreau as the consequence of heredity. If there are "lesions" within a single individual that predispose to various forms of morbidity, families also distribute such pathological conditions around their members and across the generations. Readers of Zola will be familiar with these ideas that derive from Prosper Lucas's *Traité philosophique et physiologique de l'hérédité naturelle* (Philosophical and physiological treatise on natural heredity, 1847) and Bénédict-Auguste Morel's *Traité des dégénérescences physiques, intellectuelles et morales de l'espèce humaine* (Treatise on the physical, intellectual and moral degeneracy of the human race, 1857), which dominated much thinking in the latter part of the nineteenth century.

Lombroso picked up this strand with considerable enthusiasm and followed Moreau in providing thumbnail family pathologies to back up his claims in *The Man of Genius*. Part III of Moreau's *Psychologie morbide* is entirely devoted to "Biographical Facts" and contains an eclectic list of figures going from Socrates and Pausanius, via Charlemagne and Frederick the Great, to the artist David and the sculptor François Rude, with anecdotes illustrating their own pathologies or those of family members. Hegel's sister was insane and believed she was a parcel who would be sealed and sent away; she trembled at the sight of strangers, and finally drowned herself. Auguste Comte, who was without doubt "one

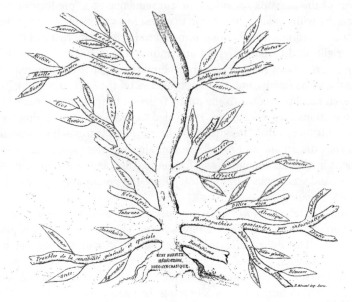

Figure 3. Moreau de Tours's tree of pathologies. From his *Psychologie morbide* (1859).

of the most vigorous and remarkable geniuses of our time," suffered from an attack of mental illness (*aliénation mentale*) for a year in 1826.[3] And there are many more examples in the same vein.

While the alienist can confidently distinguish between, say, "idiopathic" and "symptomatic" versions of acute delirium (two conditions that figure in the tree diagram), the pathologies themselves are alarmingly labile and take very different forms as they travel between brother and sister or from parent to child. Furthermore, as the case of Comte suggests, they can also metamorphose within a single individual who could go from being a genius to an imbecile within a single lifetime—or even, as Moreau says, from one moment to the next. Being dependent upon the material substratum that is "a semi-morbid state of the brain," the man of genius is always potentially a mixed being, as liable to produce unequivocally pathological thoughts as he is to come up with the most "sublime conceptions." And it is on this basis that Moreau concludes by making his provocative claim that genius, "which is to say the highest expression, the *nec plus ultra* of intellectual activity is merely a neurosis."[4] Predispositions, heredity, and this semi-morbid condition of the brain all contribute to Moreau's picture of genius as congenitally compromised, inextricably connected to pathology or poised to revert to it.

EXCITEMENT AND PRODUCTIVITY

There is one particular factor that genius and mental illness have in common and that makes for the almost inevitable exchange between the two: excitement. This phenomenon deserves separate attention because of the importance Moreau gives it in his discussion of the activities and products of the mind of the artist and the mentally ill. It is a commonplace of nineteenth-century medical thinking that artists, writers, and intellectuals have a nervous temperament. (The English expression "highly strung" captures the condition very well.) Some accounts are more essentialist than others and treat this nervousness as the defining attribute of the man of letters, whereas, according to other approaches, it is an effect of the manner in which the man of letters lives his life. But either way, there is broad consensus about the nervous and oversensitive character of intellectuals and artists that applies a fortiori to genius.

Moreau differs from other commentators in both the scope and the intensity he attributes to this sensitivity, and he presents it as a hyperactivation of the nervous system that predisposes equally to insanity as to genius. It goes by many names in his study, most of them graphically physiological: "a state of *erethism* and general *orgasm* of the nervous system . . . which tends to be concentrated in the encephalos." Some terms are even more scientific in character, such as "neurotic diathesis" (*diathèse névrosique*), and the condition that is described variously as "an excess of life," "mental over-activity," or "a state of intellectual over-excitement" is also more technically termed "the state of intellectual hyperesthesia that accompanies all mental illness at its onset."[5] The exuberance of the overexcited nervous system is matched in Moreau's description by a proliferation of the terms he finds to name it, and their quasi-physiological and scientific flavor may be read as an index of the significance that excitement has in his thinking.

Many of the examples of this excessive mental activity are associated with directly pathological conditions: acute and chronic delirium, imbecility, rickets, scrofula, epilepsy, hysteria, raving madness (*folie furieuse*), or stupor, but "intellectual hyperesthesia" also characterizes the operation of the superior mind. In his description of "the working methods of most men of genius" Moreau portrays the mind of the man of genius as abnormally overactive, and his working practices as being "most often strange, peculiar, beyond the habits of the common run of men, habits in which one may discover the original imprint and something like the vestiges of a prior morbid condition (*vestigia ruris*)."[6]

This morbidity is spelled out in so many words, but its features are those of the sort of mental excesses that Moreau ascribes to the insane: "work in the case of superior men . . . is the result of impulse, an instinctive need, a sort of appetite of the intellect" in which "the head is in a manifest state of *oestuation*, and one can sense that it is in labor and about to give birth to powerful and elevated ideas; an impetuous current of arterial blood, saturated with oxygen, calories and electricity, supplies it with extraordinary heat."[7] According to the *Oxford English Dictionary*, "estuation" is a (rare) term derived from the Latin *aestuare* whose figurative meaning is feverish disturbance but whose literal sense is boiling or overheating. Moreau seems to have confused its etymology with the frenzy of reproductive estrus (etym. *oestrus*), but the conflation of the two ideas vividly conveys the pitch of excitement reached by creative genius.

The estuating heat associated with the rush of arterial blood recalls the temperature of Aristotle's black bile that characterizes the man of exception, but the key features of Moreau's excitement are not heat as such, so much as the excess and the agitation that genius shares with insanity. The exaggerated sensitivity generated by excitement will overflow at the least pretext, and needs only "the slightest spark to create an explosion and break out into all types of functional disturbance of thought and movement." This comes from a description of the effects of excitement in insanity, but genius manifests in a strikingly similar way, its nature being to "catch fire at the least encounter, the most trivial-seeming pretext, such as a falling apple or a lamp swinging to and fro, etc."[8]

In addition to this proclivity to excess and overflow, insanity and genius share a disorderly, erratic mode of operation. Moreau cites Julien-Joseph Virey (one of the contributing authors to the *Dictionnaire des sciences médicales*, from which I have already quoted) to assert that "the fragile, delicate, vulnerable bodies of hypochondriacs, hysterical women and *all those who are subject to irregular nervous emotions*, live entirely in bursts and jolts." He ascribes a similar condition to literary genius, which suffers "sublime surges, abrupt transitions, monstrous juxtapositions, the most eloquent disorder of furious and raving passions." The source of this disorder is the "maniacal excitement" whose unpredictability affects genius of all kinds:

> those audacious minds given over to the whims of an active and powerful imagination, and filled with conviction, enthusiasm and persistence, [are] precisely those to which we owe the most curious discoveries, the most original and novel thoughts; those that, in their haphazard trajectory through the domains of philosophy, science and letters, encounter the largest number of those great truths or startling paradoxes which, through the floods of light with which they suddenly illuminated things, or through the false glimmers that they spread, abruptly change the course of general ideas, undermine and shake human institutions right down to their centuries-old foundations.

Extreme in all things, minds of this kind proceed only by fits and starts; their disorderly activity is revealed only through blinding flashes, which are immediately followed by deep darkness.[9] There are echoes of Lélut here in the mention of an imagination whose activity is liable to produce false illumination, but Moreau's argument is concerned less with imagination as such than with excitement and its wayward operations, since it is on this ground that genius and insanity are conflated.

The mind of the man of genius is also overwhelmingly—if intermittently—productive, in ways that once again are shared with the insane. The image of this productivity has echoes of Plato's model of inspiration, and the man of genius is portrayed by Moreau as utterly lacking in control or self-possession when in its grip. The illuminations of Newton and Galileo may have been the products of genius, but it took the accident of a falling apple or a swinging lamp to bring them about. Inspiration, says Moreau, is spontaneous and unwilled, it is "an appreciation of truth *without the intervention of the will or of the personality.*" The man of genius is a passive vehicle for thoughts that take form in him without his active involvement and of which he is most often unaware: "thoughts are never bolder or more energetic, intellectual combinations never vaster and more rapid than when the faculties are more independent of the *self,* and when they are more inclined to escape inner consciousness."[10] Insanity is visited in a similar manner upon its victims, who in any case may well be future or one-time men of genius. The madman is at the mercy of his heredity and of the predisposition that he can neither choose nor reject.

Artistic masterpieces are spontaneous products that emerge when the artist is in a state of "intellectual rapture transmitted by means of material symbols." Exactly the same mechanism is shown to be at work in the case of a young woman in Moreau's cave, and whose condition is characterized by a state of poetic frenzy. Although genius for Moreau is implicitly gendered male, not all his lunatics are men, and although some mental diseases were frequently gendered—most notably the hysteria associated exclusively with women—such "graphomania," originally identified by Esquirol, was found in patients of both sexes. Following a disappointment in love, Mademoiselle X*** had developed the habit of writing verse on a variety of topics. Like a poet in the grip of the muse, she was prolific and her pen could barely keep pace with her thoughts: "*Mademoiselle* seemed to write more at the dictation of some mysterious being than at her own instigation; as she said herself, she was barely conscious of what she was doing."[11] The writing was not, in the judgment of Dr. Moreau, devoid of literary qualities, but these qualities do no more than tally with the compulsive, barely conscious condition that supposedly drives many recognized poetic geniuses. When deprived of paper, "Mademoiselle" would use any substitute she could lay her hands on, and when even these were not to be had, she took to answering the doctor's questions in verse before she eventually collapsed into a state of complete mental and physical apathy. The difference between insanity and genius hangs by a hair, both being equally subject to spontaneous impulse and equally lacking in conscious control.

MEDICAL SELF-SCRUTINY

Whereas spontaneity and uncontrolled productivity are the chief characteristics of both genius and insanity in Moreau's account, the medical man is portrayed as being as self-possessed as he is observant. Pinel had already claimed that "the lunatic [is] incapable of any self-awareness," a limitation that was the counterpart of the hallucinator's lack of relation to the external world. Commenting on Moreau de Tours's ideas, the writer and critic Émile Deschanel describes the madman as "a stranger to himself" and the Latin gloss that he adds—*alienatus a se*—underscores the implications of the French term "aliéné" (*lunatic*). Likewise, as Moreau himself says, for the man of genius, "work is never better than when it is the least free, and when it is executed without the direct involvement of the will, and almost without the self being aware of it."[12] In both genius and insanity, then, the subject is at odds with or, rather, at some remove from himself.

In combination the results are disastrous, as Lélut had already indicated when he maintains that Socrates, "the greatest mind of antiquity," was incapable of seeing "what he was in reality and allowed himself to become insane without sensing that this was happening to him."[13] Moreau suggests that the self-coincidence that is self-scrutiny is hard for anyone to achieve, even for those who are sound of mind, and that the wisdom and penetration we bring to bear on the external world often prove to be lacking when we turn our attention to ourselves. He himself, however, claims to possess just this attribute that, he argues, he owes to his medical expertise and that endows him with superior insight into mental disturbance.

His experience of hashish was the occasion for this self-scrutiny. He first encountered the drug in the Near East where as a young doctor he accompanied a patient for therapeutic purposes. Later, between 1844 and 1849, as a founder member of the Club des Hashischins, he participated alongside Baudelaire, Gautier, Nerval, and others in the *fantasias* that were held in the Hôtel Pimodan on the Île Saint-Louis in Paris. Hashish gave Moreau the opportunity to experience madness—albeit what he calls an artificial madness—firsthand. Hashish leads the mind to clothe sensations in material form and to project them onto external reality in ways that parallel the hallucinations of delirium. Moreau was thus "initiated into the mysteries of insanity" and allowed to discover the otherwise hidden source of the many disorders that go under the name of madness. But whereas the genuinely insane have no self-awareness, and whereas the observing medical man is normally obliged to rely on the potentially misleading procedures of reasoning and induction, Moreau was able to apply the professional habit of medical observation to himself. His account of the relation between hashish and insanity consists of "simple and obvious facts established by inner observation" of his own sensations and perceptions under the influence of temporary and artificially induced insanity. Moreau's boast at the start of *Du hachisch et de l'aliénation mentale* (On hashish and insanity) is that "[p]ersonal experience is the *criterium* of truth here."[14]

This unique medical authority is based on "reflection," which he defines as "the power that the mind has to turn in on itself, so to speak, that mirror of sorts in which it can contemplate itself at will, and which provides it with a faithful account of its innermost movements." Such self-scrutiny is no Romantic pretext for self-absorption but a guarantee of the accuracy of the observations of the insane. Where his colleagues can only surmise, Moreau knows from his own experience what his patients are undergoing, and, on the basis of the physical symptoms they present, he is able to make informed judgments about their underlying causes. This requires professional expertise as well as firsthand experience, since the physician is confronted by "mysteries of the intelligence . . . that morbid psychology alone can penetrate."[15] The aim of Moreau's study is as much as anything else to establish the epistemological credentials of the discipline of morbid psychology, in whose eyes those of genius appear merely as a variant of the pathologies of mental functioning.

The Medical Daguerreotype

Accurate observation provides the diagnostician with the information he needs and is the principal index of professional expertise. Moreau notes the importance of "what we learn from the close, accurate and we might call *truly medical* observation of insanity." In this connection he describes at some length the case of a young man in the grip of extreme mental disturbance where what is reported is not just the agitation, the volubility, and the physical distress of the patient as he leaps about the furniture or collapses into apathy, but Moreau's own presence on the scene. This is discreetly alluded to as he records his attendance, one day at a time: September 1855, 20 December, and, as the crisis mounts, 1, 3, 4, 6, and 7 March, when "[the patient] has several scares in my presence."[16]

Mostly, however, Moreau's part in the picture has to be inferred from the impersonal forms he seems to favor: "several terrors that it was possible to abort [*qu'on peut faire avorter*], and finally another that it was not possible to halt [*qu'on ne peut arrêter*]." More common still are formulations that exclude all agency except those of the symptoms themselves, so that the entry for 6 March reads simply, "Spasmodic and painful contraction of the toes on both feet, and occlusion of the left eye, which is intermittently very painful. Several terrors." Moreau sums all this up by saying, "These phenomena are observed [*s'observent*] more or less constantly," cumulatively yielding a proof "perfectly designed to open the least perspicacious eyes."[17] It is as if the scenes played out before the observing physician provided their own self-evident truth about their underlying basis in a single "morbid cause."

In the conclusion to the second part of the book Moreau reiterates the argument for seeing the "intellectual supremacy" of genius as part of a spectrum of mental disorder. He contrasts the scientific evidence with the idealized view of genius that bears no relation to reality, and he argues for the need to "record the moral and intellectual physiognomy of these great individuals as if in a daguerreotype."[18] The connotations of the daguerreotype are telling: medical observation is a matter of registering with impartial objectivity and total accuracy the facts of the pathology that the doctor has before him. This contrasts with the overflowing productivity of both insanity and genius. The doctor unobtrusively registers and records, whereas the lunatic and the genius uncontrollably produce.

But there is more to this opposition, since a different temporality is associated with each mode: if the productivity of insanity and genius is discontinuous and erratic, the comparison with the daguerreotype and its long exposure times defines medical practice in terms of constancy and sustained duration. The flashes and explosions, the abrupt shifts and leaps of the pathological or creative mind are the reverse of the steady progress of medical knowledge as Moreau describes it in the rest of the passage: "If we wish to remain in the domain of truth and concrete evidence . . . , we need as a first priority to base our assessment on the scientific data that we have just outlined, following up the hereditary facts, weighing their influence on the physical and moral constitution of individuals, not losing sight of the organic origins of their good or bad qualities, or of the countless particularities that reveal this supra-nervous origin: then, and only then, shall we have before our eyes the complete man, natural and not fictional, a man who is truly man."[19] The scientific data accrue in what is evidently a continuous process as the doctor traces the etiology back to its origins, and refuses to be distracted from his attention to organic conditions. The thoroughness and the persistence with which the doctor pursues his enquiry will eventually have their reward in the form of a total picture of its object. The time of medical science brings greater gains than the fireworks that genius shares with insanity.

Moreover, medical knowledge is itself a cumulative and collective enterprise, and for this reason too, the time of medical science can be only continuous and progressive. The practitioners of mental medicine were very conscious of belonging to a developing profession that—despite some ups and downs—was acquiring ever greater status and recognition over the course of the century.[20] Whereas the genius is a lone operator, the medical psychologist acknowledges his place in a scientific discipline on which he draws and to which he hopes to contribute. Moreau may seek to distinguish himself from his colleagues through his claims to self-scrutiny, but he nonetheless gives ample due to predecessors in the specialty that goes by the name of "morbid psychology."

He refers on several occasions to Lélut (footnoting his own review of *Le Démon de Socrate*), as he does to Esquirol, he mentions Pinel and Réveillé-

Parise, cites authorities such as Broussais's *De l'irritation et de la folie* (1839), and is particularly fulsome in his acknowledgment of the "most remarkable book" by Prosper Lucas. In addition, he refers copiously to recent medical literature on heredity and a range of conditions such as epilepsy, suicide, rickets, and so on. The footnotes testify to the extent of Moreau's acquaintance with work in his area of medical expertise, which is noteworthy in view of his statement that he has written his book as much for the general public as for his specialist colleagues. In other words, Moreau is presenting himself as a participant in an evolving professional enterprise. Medical time is a continuously progressing time, and its difference from the disrupted, chaotic time of insanity or genius plays a large part in the way in which medical knowledge is constituted, and positively distinguished, even from works of genius.

CHAPTER 9

Genius Restored to Health

Artistic genius is no longer a monster or a miracle.
—Séailles, *Le Génie dans l'art*

The pathologizing of genius reached a pitch with Cesare Lombroso's *Genio e follia*, first published in 1864. Subsequently revised and expanded under the title *L'Uomo di genio* in 1877, it was translated into French in 1879 as *L'Homme de génie*. In Lombroso's account, genius becomes a mark of degeneracy and is associated with epilepsy and "moral insanity." These claims are supported with numerous examples from the past, and with references to French precursors in this line of thinking, notably Lélut, Réveillé-Parise, and Moreau de Tours. The French commentators who came after Lombroso also took these authors, along with Lombroso himself, as the key proponents of the theories that link genius with insanity. However, they did so mostly in order to refute this association, and to argue instead for a model of genius defined as the optimal expression of the human mind. This view dominated discussion in the last twenty years of the century, when the medical profession mounted a challenge to its previous pathologizing of genius, and devoted its energies and insights to bringing it back within the bounds of normal mental functioning.

Readers of Lombroso were not the first to baulk at the medical association of genius and insanity. Moreau de Tours mentions the outcry caused by Lélut's work on Socrates and Pascal—as indeed does Lélut himself in his preface to the second edition of *Le Démon de Socrate*. In the early 1860s Pierre Flourens, the founder of experimental neurophysiology in France, used his book, *De la raison, du génie, et de la folie* (On reason, genius, and madness) to argue against Moreau de Tours's view of genius as neurosis and to make the case for genius as "superior reason."[1] This view was repeated three years later by Deschanel, a self-styled practitioner of "physiological criticism," who devotes an entire chapter of his *Physiologie des écrivains et des artistes* (Physiology of writers and artitsts) to a critique of Moreau de Tours. Although he is clearly intrigued by Moreau's view of genius, Deschanel insists that it applies to only a small sample of a category whose greatest representatives, by contrast, "possess health in body and soul."[2]

Superior Intellect and the Normalizing of Genius: Séailles

The theme was taken up by the philosopher Gabriel Séailles in his *Essai sur le génie dans l'art* (An essay on genius in art, 1883), his doctoral thesis, which established his academic career and led to a position at the Sorbonne, where Proust later attended his lectures. Drawing partly on the new discipline of experimental psychology and the work of Hippolyte Taine (whose *De l'intelligence* I shall be discussing in chapter 14) as well as on that of the British psychiatrist Henry Maudsley, Séailles argues for a view of genius as a manifestation of the healthy human mind: "Genius is not, as some have maintained, a sort of mental illness, an abortive insanity; genius is health of the mind." Moreover, it is viewed as a feature of *all* minds, not just the exceptional few. The mind—any mind, including that of the genius—spontaneously seeks to make conceptual sense of what it encounters by organizing perceptions into harmonious unity, and the universality of this response means that genius is "present everywhere: from the humblest to the greatest."[3]

Séailles distinguishes between scientific and artistic types of mental operation, but, unlike his pathologizing precursors, it is to the detriment of neither. The unity toward which the mind aspires is intellectual in the domain of science, where the mind attempts to conceptualize the natural phenomena it confronts. In the case of the artist (with whom genius is largely synonymous in this account), the mental synthesis operates on sensation rather than perception, and transforms its multiplicity into a single, harmonious image. The resulting poetry is not just the stuff of high art but an everyday phenomenon: "it is the very law of inner life," and each of us contains a hidden poet.[4]

There are, however, degrees of genius, and what distinguishes the greatest genius is, first, the completeness of the mental synthesis he achieves and, second, its spontaneity. The more complete, and the more spontaneous the genius, the less he is aware of the workings of his own mind, which means that it takes a third party—the critic or the psychologically informed philosopher—to spell these out. Genius may be "the unity of the living mind, . . . the combining of all its powers in a single act," or even "the mind reaching its apogee in the moment when it moves beyond reflection and becomes nature once more," but this insight depends on the critic whose own art "consists in following these regular laws as they are transformed by individual genius, and in using analysis to elaborate all the thought that a picturesque work of art contains in concentrated form and which is grasped in a single glance."[5] Genius and its interpretation are henceforth placed on a continuum of normal—as opposed to pathological—mental behavior.

This normalizing of genius was in the air, and was further supported by the revision and republication in 1881 of Réveillé-Parise's *Physiologie et hygiène des hommes livrés aux travaux de l'esprit* (Physiology and hygiene of men devoted to labors of the mind). Updated "in accordance with scientific progress" by one Dr. Édouard Carrière from the Académie des sciences, it was now read as evidence of the basic health of those engaged in intellectual work, whose ailments were purely the product of their occupation and not of their nature. In 1896, Édouard Toulouse, chief medical officer in the asylum at Villejuif and director of the experimental psychology laboratory at the École des hautes études in Paris, published a detailed study of Émile Zola, subtitled *Enquête médico-psychologique sur les rapports de la supériorité intellectuelle avec la névropathie* (Psychomedical enquiry into the relations between intellectual superiority and neuropathy), whose approach and findings were largely endorsed a year later by Maurice de Fleury's *Introduction à la médecine de l'esprit* (Introduction to medicine of the mind), which won prizes from the Académie française, the Académie des sciences, and the Académie de médecine. Fleury's study went through several editions in the following years: the copy I have consulted is a well-thumbed tenth edition dating from 1918 with many pencil markings from its former owner (or owners).

Physiology remains the focus of medical attention, and if anything, genius becomes even more embodied than in previous accounts. Where Lélut and Moreau held off from identifying any precise anatomical basis for the pathologies they described, the workings of the body of the man of genius are now examined in elaborate detail. Toulouse's medical investigation of Zola is nothing if not exhaustive, extending, as we shall see, from analyses of his urine to a mapping of his visual field. Medical attention is directed almost exclusively at literary examples (although Toulouse followed up his study of Zola with an account of the mathematician Henri Poincaré), and the literary text is read as an imprint of its author's physiology. Or as Deschanel had already argued, "the physical organization of the writer or artist leaves its trace, so to speak," adding that "the critic must be able to decipher it."[6] Critic and doctor now work with the same material.

The healthy genius is as much the concern of medical science as was the hallucinating or neurotic genius. However, although the same (medical) expertise is brought to bear on the man of genius, the shift of emphasis from pathology to health alters the field in two important ways. First, in losing its link with the other of insanity, genius seems also to lose a good deal of its distinction. And, second, in ceasing to be the "other" of the observing medical diagnostician, the man of genius finds himself making common cause with the neurologists who are simultaneously seeking to lay claim to his literary territory.

THE MEDICAL COMPANION

The term "genius" does not vanish entirely from medical currency, but there are signs of a certain diffidence about its use. Flourens and Deschanel had already chosen to refer to "superior reason." Toulouse tries to avoid the word "genius" and speaks instead of "intellectual superiority" (as his title has it) or the "highest psychological faculties." The man of genius is simply more intelligent than most, and he uses his intelligence with greater efficiency. In the case of Zola, "superior forms of intelligence, everything that constitutes judgment, imagination and will, is in a state of perfect health and equilibrium."[7] Antoine Rémond and Paul Voivenel (a neurologist and a neuropsychiatrist, respectively) echo this emphasis on the equilibrium and harmony of the qualities of the phenomenon, which they are still happy, in a book of that title published in 1912, to call *Le Génie littéraire*.

Since genius is considered to be a matter of degrees of intelligence, the man of genius belongs to the general class of "men devoted to mental labor" whose various ailments may now be considered as relevant to the centuries-old question that Toulouse formulates as that of "the relations between intellectual superiority and neuropathy."[8] Just as "genius" is downgraded to "superior intelligence," so the insanity it was formerly associated with is moderated to "neuropathy" or "neurasthenia," which is nothing more disturbing than a professionally incurred "nervous exhaustion" that presents as weakness and irritability. The man of superior intelligence may, but equally may not, suffer from the symptoms of neuropathy, and the writer is no longer viewed as a potential inmate of the asylum.

Toulouse and Fleury follow Réveillé-Parise in regarding the ailments of those who work with their minds as the consequence, and not the cause or the necessary condition of their activity. Deschanel had already warned his readers not to assume that "genius is necessarily as frenzied as a prophetess; or that its hair is always as windswept as the portrait of Chateaubriand by Guérin" (Figure 4).[9] Instead, the man of genius is likely to be a fundamentally balanced individual whose work, according to Fleury, makes him prone to a set of relatively trivial ailments: "peculiarities, *idées fixes*, prejudices, obsessions" and, on occasion, "moral perversity, lapses in reasoning." These problems are due to nothing more serious than "ticklish pride, vibrant sensitivity, extreme irritability, a fear of failing," which, in Fleury's estimation, go with the territory. The physical manifestation of this touchiness is most likely to be found in the digestion, and Fleury graphically informs his female reader: "Your favorite novelist, Madame, has a deplorable digestion. After each meal, he turns red, he is sleepy, he feels weighed down; his stomach swells and his waistcoat is too tight for him: you may be sure that he unbuttons it if he is dining with his family. . . . Lastly, the greatest pity is that he has put on weight prematurely and aged beyond his years."[10] The doctor's role is not merely spot this condition. His chief task is to provide medical advice and to propose a healthier regime: regular mealtimes, no fatty foods such as oily fish or cheese; no soup or spicy sauces; no pastries or sweets; no beer or apéritifs, no red wine, and just the occasional glass of white wine diluted with water; in any case, no liquids at mealtimes; and so on. Toulouse suggests that the seven hours of sleep Zola has each night are not quite

Figure 4. Portrait of Chateaubriand, backdrop of mountain scenery. Attributed to Pierre-Narcisse Guérin.

enough, but he praises the novelist for the determination with which he has stuck to a diet after managing to lose weight.

The doctor becomes a friend to the man of superior intellect, and, as Réveillé-Parise recommends, he helps to restore equilibrium in a body destabilized by the excesses of the mind. There is, however, an art to the treatment of the illnesses of the man of genius, and it needs to be learned. The medical friend must never lose sight of the overactive nervous system of the thinker who is liable to be knocked sideways by "the preferment of a rival, the criticism of a book, an article in a newspaper, an animated discussion, a letter, or a single word." With the right patient (the blind Milton is cited as an example) the role of the doctor could even become "sublime," and, "an illustrious poet, who *gives you a temple in his poems*, does more for you than fortune ever will."[11] Medicine now collaborates with poetry and the doctor becomes the indispensable companion to the man of genius.

Genius in the Laboratory: Édouard Toulouse

The collaboration is indeed a two-way affair, as is demonstrated by Zola's own contribution to Toulouse's *Enquête médico-psychologique*. Toulouse found in Zola the nearest thing he was willing to acknowledge as genius—the greatest writer of the age. But Zola was also a writer who knew more about medical psychology than any of his contemporaries, he had learned much from reading Moreau de Tours and had drawn extensively on Lombroso's work for his portrait of Jacques Lantier in *La Bête humaine*. Toulouse's aim was to undertake a properly scientific investigation of his subject—the relations between superior intellect and neuropathy. This meant replacing the unscientific reliance on anecdote in the work of Moreau de Tours and Lombroso with expert analyses of a living organism. Over the course of a year, some seventeen different specialists

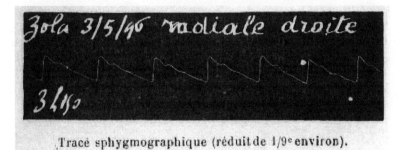

Tracé sphygmographique (réduit de 1/9ᵉ environ).

Figure 5. Results of Zola's sphygmometer test. Included in Édouard Toulouse, *Emile Zola: Enquête médico-psychologique* (1896).

were brought in to examine Zola, to record his weight and waist measurement, the size and shape of his hands and feet, the circumference of his skull, his fingerprints (the Englishman Francis Galton was called upon for this), his heartbeat, his hand pressure, his skin sensitivity, his hearing, his sight, his verbal and visual memory, and so on. Dr. A. M. Bloch used his new achromatometer to measure the capillary circulation in Zola's fingers, and a sphygmometer recorded his pulse (Figure 5).

Toulouse himself quizzed Zola about his heredity, his daily habits, and, very discreetly, about his sex life.[12] The study amounted to a kind of living autopsy, and in the letter of authorization which forms the Preface to the book, Zola presents himself as having donated his body to science and offered his brain as if his skull were made of glass. A fair proportion of the results of the investigation are, on Toulouse's own admission, without immediately obvious significance for his project, but he is confident that one day the information he has assembled will be found to have made an invaluable contribution to scientific knowledge.

Both writer and doctor portray themselves as equally devoted to the higher cause of truth, and they are described as having an identical approach to this goal. Zola follows medical advice about his diet and has also given up smoking. His daily regime is presented by Fleury as a model. More significantly, Toulouse makes much of the accuracy of Zola's sense perceptions, his nose in particular being "famous" after his description in *Le Ventre de Paris* (The belly of Paris) of the cheeses in Les Halles: "M. Zola's perceptions are characterized above all by their accuracy (Touch, Vision, Time), and also by their subtlety (Touch, Smell). . . . His perceptions are connected to physical sensations." Which is to tantamount to saying that as "a piece of machinery, Zola could be compared to a racehorse."[13] Or that Zola's own physiology functions rather like the instruments whose results are included in the text, supported by photographs of his hands (left and right, dorsal and anterior views), a full set of fingerprints, the

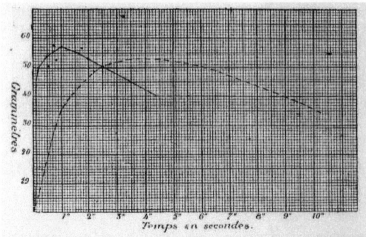

Courbe des travaux de la main de M. Zola avec le dynamo-
mètre de M. Charles Henry (Il faut multiplier les nombres
de grammètres par 36 pour avoir les travaux qu'exécuteraient
normalement ces muscles fléchisseurs) ¹.

Figure 6. The strength of Zola's hand grip as recorded by Charles Henry's dynamome-
ter. Included in Édouard Toulouse, *Emile Zola: Enquête médico-psychologique* (1896).

pneumographic record of his breathing, the dynamometric record of his hand-
grip, and so on (Figure 6).

In summing up the results of the tests of Zola's sensory functions, Toulouse
advances the view that Zola's realism derives from the precision of his percep-
tual apparatus and that it has all the virtues of the kind of scientific investigation to which he has himself been subjected: "His realism, his need for truth . . .
could be explained in part by the accuracy of his perceptions; the same goes for
his desire for clarity."[14] The accuracy of his perceptions is matched by the clarity
of his concepts, the sureness of his judgment, the orderliness of his working
habits, and the tenacity with which he pursues his goals. In other words, the
very qualities that had previously been the preserve of the medical diagnostician now become the hallmark of the greatest writer of the age. Added to this is
Toulouse's comment that Zola lacks imagination; but rather than being a flaw—
literary or psychological—this deficiency preserves him from the distractions
that make for "dilettantism." Imagination is no longer predisposes to insanity,
but is simply a feature of inferior literature.

Toulouse nevertheless allows the writer a margin of neuropathy. While reporting that Zola shows no sign of major pathology, and while arguing too that
neuropathy is nothing more than a coincidental accompaniment to intellectual
superiority, Toulouse notes a series of mild abnormalities in his subject: sexual

timidity, imaginary chest and stomach pains, frequent urination, a shaking hand, an obsessive need to touch certain objects before going to bed, a tic in one eye, and so on. He excludes any connection with epilepsy or hysteria, and suggests instead that minor irregularities of this kind can be a positive advantage to the writer, since they enhance sensitivity and brain function, which are necessary for all intellectual work. Whereas insanity risks totally disqualifying the work of a writer, a dash of neuropathy will work in his favor.

This is certainly how Zola responds to the diagnosis, and he comments in his prefatory letter that Toulouse's portrait of him has demonstrated that his public image as "a boor, a workhorse, with a thick skin and coarse senses, laboriously executing his task out of the sole and squalid need for lucre" is false. Instead, Toulouse has shown him to be "the poor tormented creature" that he truly was, "trembling and suffering at the least breath of air, only ever sitting down to his daily task each morning in a state of anxiety, only ever managing to produce his *œuvre* in a continuous struggle between his willpower and his doubts!"[15] The collaboration between the medical psychologist and the naturalist novelist has clearly worked to the advantage of both parties.

The Doctor as Literary Critic: Maurice de Fleury

Over and above this mutually beneficial arrangement, medicine and art share the same aims and the same values. This is not just because the medical profession can help the artist to reach the top of his form. Nor is it due to the fact that sculptors and painters learn anatomy from the doctors, that philosophers can allegedly no longer write about language, human passions, or the will without consulting neurologists, and that, according to Fleury, an entire school of novelists owes as much to Claude Bernard as to Balzac. Medical knowledge can illuminate every aspect of the literary field. If, as Deschanel had already argued, the literary text bears the imprint of its author's physiology, it is now the doctor who is best qualified to provide a proper understanding of that text. In writing about Zola, Toulouse produced a model of mental functioning that both writer and doctor could subscribe to, but the medical practitioner's dream, as Fleury announces, was to place literary criticism itself on a medical footing and to demonstrate that "literary criticism and art criticism belong to the man of science and to him alone."[16]

Criticism has two tasks in Fleury's view: to explain the work with reference to the individual who created it, and to assess its aesthetic worth. As regards the first of these, Toulouse himself had already claimed that the study of the work's genesis can be carried out only by the psychologist or the physiologist, since what is at stake is the relation between the work and the physical and mental constitution of its author. As regards the second task, Fleury maintains that since it concerns the aesthetic emotions generated by the work of art, the psychologist is once again the person best equipped to determine this.

Toulouse confines himself simply to setting out the case for a medical criticism of literature, but Fleury takes it upon himself to make a number of practical gestures in that direction. He does this largely by correlating literary and medical health. A survey of the smoking habits of writers leads him to declare that the quality of their writing can be directly linked to their use of tobacco— or rather to its absence: the greatest writers of the century, Hugo, Balzac, Michelet, and Dumas, never smoked, and some explicitly condemned the habit. By contrast, "Musset smoked; and so his reputation lost its great luster." Similarly, "George Sand smoked . . . to the point where she ceased to be intelligent, the moment she no longer had a cigarette between her lips."[17] Quotations from Hugo and Balzac are adduced to suggest that literary and medical wisdom coincide on the issue of tobacco, but medicine alone can provide the systematic knowledge that allows a reliable correlation between the two to be made.

Fleury extends this approach to the phenomenon of neurasthenia, which he regards as a further negative index of literary worth. He attributes what he sees as the rise of mysticism—philosophical, Christian, Buddhist—to degeneracy and neuropathic heredity: in sum, "we are in the midst of mental pathology."[18] He claims that the current literary field is a chaos of different tendencies, as a result of which the public is confused, and the critics unable to tell good from bad. However, on the basis of his diagnostic competence, the medical man is qualified to discriminate in ways that no one else can, and he is the only person—or so Fleury asserts—capable of identifying the true direction in which the literature of the present is currently developing.

Literature and psychological medicine have reached a point of convergence whereby writer and doctor subscribe to the same principles, share the same mental functions, live in the same world, and endorse each other's work. Insanity is no more of a threat to the artist than to a stockbroker, a businessman, or a placid bourgeois. The physiologist and the medical psychologist take over from the literary critic in identifying literary distinction or intellectual superiority, and psychiatric expertise has substituted these attributes for genius. Over a century later, many of these claims may seem more than faintly ridiculous, but the arguments are telling. For they suggest that as medicine and literature converged, and as genius was normalized to intellectual superiority, and its association with insanity reduced to the occupational hazard of neurasthenia, it gradually vanished as a concept liable to excite the curiosity of the French medical establishment. Without the "other" of pathology, genius was now embarked on a long decline.

PART IV

Failure, Femininity, and the Realist Novel

CHAPTER 10

A Novel of Female Genius

Mme de Staël's Corinne

> Minerva, the goddess of genius, was a virgin; her name . . . means without breasts, or, according to the energy of the terms, *not effeminate.*
> —Julien-Joseph Virey, "Génie," *Dictionnaire des sciences médicales*

Genius is a masculine noun and is generally gendered male. In the ancient world it was a tutelary spirit reserved for men since women were provided with a Juno. It was associated with the *paterfamilias*, and its begetting has invariably been viewed as a masculine rather than a feminine affair. For long enough this went without saying. But with increasing interest in the physiological basis of the mind and with the greater cultural prominence of women, there was a corresponding increase toward the end of the eighteenth century in the active assertion of the incompatibility of genius with the female sex. Women were not just the "other" of genius, but its very antithesis.

Rousseau is blunt in his exclusion of women from genius when he asserts that women are constitutionally unsuited its demands: "Women in general possess no artistic sensibility . . . nor genius." They can acquire knowledge through a certain diligence, but, he continues, "the celestial fire that emblazons and ignites the soul, the inspiration that consumes and devours, . . . these sublime ecstasies that reside in the depths of the heart are always lacking in women's writings." The characteristics that made learning and talent the laborious obverse of genius are also those of women. Christine Battersby, who cites Rousseau's remarks in her book *Gender and Genius*, makes it clear that such attitudes were common currency at the time.[1]

Diderot stands out from most other commentators by taking the possibility of female genius seriously, and in an essay on women written in 1772 as a riposte to a recently published *Essai sur le caractère, les mœurs et l'esprit des femmes dans les différens siècles* (An essay on the character, habits and mind of women in different ages) by one Antoine-Léonard Thomas, he suggests that genius in women has its distinctive—and distinctively positive—modes: "When they possess genius, I believe that it makes a more original impression than in us." This, he says, is because "[w]omen carry inside them an organ that is subject to terrible spasms, over which they have no control, and which creates phantoms of every kind in their imaginations. . . . It is from this origin, which is particular to their sex, that their extraordinary ideas arise."[2] But such views were rare.

When the question of the character of women was set as the topic for the essay competition run by the Société des Sciences, Lettres et Arts de Mâcon in 1809, the more commonplace negation of female genius is given an aura of medical endorsement by Julien-Joseph Virey in his prize-winning entry when he writes that women combine tenderness, seduction, and charm, but that—in an echo of Rousseau's claim—men alone are capable of the "fiery transports of genius." Women are physically unsuited to the creativity of invention, being both delicate and inconsistent; their domain is feeling, while that of men is "thought"; they are designed to be subjugated, while men aspire to an "immortality" that would be incompatible with the expectation of "modesty" in women. Virey backs up these claims with references to further medical authority in the form of one Doctor Roussel, author of a *Système pratique et moral de la femme* (Practical and moral system concerning women), published in 1775, as well as to Rousseau's discussion of women in *Émile*. In Virey's account women are not just unsuited to genius, they are its active negation, for as the representatives of "taste" in society, they pose an active threat to "the strength of genius," which succumbs all too easily to the "brilliant games of elegant wits" favored by taste.[3] In sum, whether it is women's association with diligence, wit, or taste, which the eighteenth century opposed to genius, or whether it is the physical, moral, and intellectual nature attributed to them in philosophical and medical discourse, there would seem to be no place for women in genius or for genius in women.

WOMEN AND THE RISE OF THE NOVEL

At the same time, the novel, which was traditionally associated with a female readership, was gaining status as a literary genre. In her *Essai sur les fictions* (Essay on fictions) Mme de Staël asserts that "a novel as we conceive it, and which we have a few examples of, is one of the finest creations of the human mind." She makes the point again in *De la littérature*, where she describes novels as "those varied creations of the mind of the moderns," and this insistence on the modernity of fiction anticipates the importance the genre went on to acquire in the nineteenth century. A large part of this modernity is due, in Mme de Staël's argument, to qualities associated with women. Citing the excellence of English novelists, she claims that the "host of subtle nuances and touching situations" that provide fiction with its subject matter and inspire the creativity of its authors is the direct result of the influence of women in English society.[4] This comes very close to saying that Richardson owes the genius celebrated by Diderot to the female sex, whose sensibility is responsible for bringing the subtleties of his fiction into being.

Fiction also offers scope to genius, which for Mme de Staël consists in the fidelity of its depiction of the real: "It is in truth that the divine stamp is found: we attach the word invention to genius, and yet it is only by tracing, connecting and discovering what is, that it has earned its creative renown." This is not yet, and not quite the realism of Balzac's *Comédie humaine*, and it is still part of the aesthetic of effects that belongs to the eighteenth century, but those effects and their incitement to virtue are directly dependent on the grounding of action in "present circumstances." The intimate knowledge of the human heart, which novels provide and women facilitate, requires the depiction of "all the situations of private life, and the impressions that they give rise to."[5] There is, in other words, something specifically gendered female—if only by association—in fiction, which makes a virtue, not just of virtue, but also of its realism.

The realist tradition of the nineteenth-century novel is, as critics have remarked, a largely masculine one, but it also has a feminine streak. Balzac prided himself in his "Avant-propos" to the *Comédie humaine* on writing a form of fiction that was faithful to social realities, and this included the fact that in society—as distinct from nature—women are not always "the female of the male."[6] Realist fiction may be written by men, but it has been made possible by women, it needs to be (in part) about women—and it will continue, as it always has, to be read by women.

As the status of the genre rose, one might expect it to be associated with the same sort of ambition toward genius that poetry exhibited, and Balzac's cry on thinking up the scheme for the *Comédie humaine*—"Congratulate me because I'm well and truly becoming a genius"—confirms that the novel was seen as an arena for inventive prowess.[7] But in the main, the novel's role seems to have been to provide a forum in which genius could be examined by writers whose own relation to the phenomenon was, more often than not, distinctly ambivalent. Whereas genius in poetry suffers and goes unheeded until it is recognized by its fellows, in the novel it almost always fails.

Nineteenth-century French fiction—France's "great tradition"—is not so much a pretext for the demonstration of authorial genius, as the means of portraying the failure of genius in a fictional character. The latter does not totally exclude the former—Mme de Staël and Balzac being cases in point—but genius becomes an uncertain value. Some of this is no doubt due to the novel's rivalry with science. Balzac sets himself up as the equal of Cuvier and Geoffroy Saint-Hilaire, and Zola's fictional alter ego is the physician and geneticist Doctor Pascal. As Zola's encounter with Dr. Toulouse indicated, the language of medicine rubbed off on the novel, and with it a certain detached approach to genius and a certain set of quantificational protocols for its observation. In sum, realist fiction is less a means for the direct affirmation of genius than for its scrutiny—and predominantly in the mode of failure.

This fictional scrutiny is very often carried out by placing genius in conjunction with a female character in a variety of permutations. In Mme de Staël's *Corinne*, the genius—for once—is herself a woman. In Balzac's *Louis Lambert*, Lambert is a (possibly) mentally ill genius who retreats into a world to which only his erstwhile fiancée has access. And in Zola's *L'Œuvre*, Claude Lantier is the failed genius whose art is both inspired and destroyed by a female muse. Genius is put to the test by means of these associations with women—tested and mostly found wanting, but in ways that make it both more ambiguous and more interesting than a simple summary of its failures might suggest.

CORINNE: THE CROWNING OF A WOMAN OF GENIUS

Mme de Staël was, as we have already seen, one of the rare women commentators on genius, but in those comments, she made no explicit attempt to counter the arguments of those who denied genius to her sex. Indeed, she echoes many of their assumptions—albeit in less virulent mode—as when she writes that "[w]omen have not composed truly superior works but they have eminently served the progress of literature by all the thoughts inspired in men through their relations with these mobile, delicate creatures."[8] They have facilitated genius in men but never achieved it themselves. It is perhaps all the more extraordinary, then, that Mme de Staël should portray the heroine of her second novel, *Corinne* (1807), as an unambiguous incarnation of female genius. If *Corinne* is a novel of failed genius, it is not because its heroine, Corinne, is prevented from realizing her genius, but because, having had it, and moreover having been lavishly and publicly acknowledged as having it, she then loses it. The pathos of the novel derives from the narration of the circumstances that lead to this loss, and though it is significantly enhanced by the fact that Corinne is a woman, the question of whether the failure of her genius can be ascribed to her sex is not a straightforward one.

Corinne is not just a women of genius, but a national genius too. She makes a triumphant entry into the novel aboard a chariot drawn by four white horses that takes her to the Capitol in Rome for her laureation, where she is hailed as Italy's greatest living genius. Her talents are multiple, and she is eulogized for her skills as a tragedienne, a dancer, a painter, and a conversationalist, as well as for her ability to improvise in verse, which she goes on to demonstrate in the ceremony itself. She is described as the most famous woman in Italy, and the crowd on Capitol Hill greets her with cries of "*Long live Corinne! Long live genius! Long live beauty!*" Her genius is a matter of patriotic pride for the Italians who regard her as "the image of our beautiful Italy."[9]

There is no equivocation in the public recognition of her genius, and no one holds it against her that she is a woman. In the "song" that she writes for her last public appearance before her death, Corinne thanks Italy, a "liberal nation," for not banishing women from the temple of "glory"; and the odes composed by her fellow poets for the laureation ceremony praise her in terms that also speak generously of a whole tradition of women of genius. This goes back as far as Sappho and includes Corinna the great rival of Pindar, whose name Mme de Staël's heroine has taken.[10]

The accolade "*genius*" is bestowed unstintingly, but mostly in conformity with the norms of the day whereby genius is an attribute or a quality and not a person: whence "a man," or in the case of Corinne, "a woman of genius." This formulation is elaborated in the description of Corinne during her performance in the laureation ceremony where she is presented as "an inspired priestess joyfully dedicating herself to the worship of genius."[11] This image of a priestess evolves later on in the novel into the figure of the Sybil: Corinne's house is built opposite the temple of the Sybil, and toward the end of the novel when her former lover, Lord Nelvil, is visiting Italy with his new wife Lucile, he is stopped in his tracks by Domenichino's "Sybil," in which he evidently sees a likeness of Corinne. Despite the difficulties of imagining a woman genius in the period, the image of the priestess in the temple of genius or the prophetess in the grip of divine inspiration is one means whereby it becomes possible for such a figure to take plausible form.

The Comte d'Erfeuil pays Corinne a rather backhanded compliment when he comments that she is a person of such superior intellect, depth of learning, and delicacy of feeling that the rules by which women are ordinarily judged cannot be applied to her. But Erfeuil is French, and the Italians take a more enlightened view of female genius than do their fellow Europeans. In short, Mme de Staël could hardly have imagined a more propitious configuration of talents and circumstances for her heroine, and Corinne certainly fares much better than the male geniuses that her contemporaries were soon to portray, whether Vigny's Chatterton, the other poets who appear in *Stello*, Hugo's Chateaubriand, Lamartine's Bonald, or Balzac's fictional Louis Lambert, all of whom encounter a hostile world in which even male genius finds it hard to flourish.

RECOGNITION: *GLOIRE* AS LOVE

If Corinne's genius fails, this is not because genius in itself poses a problem for women in the idealized Italian world of the novel, but because there are aspects inherent to genius that eventually succeed in undermining it. The first of these is *gloire*, or what the *OED* calls "honourable fame." This is the indispensable form taken by the recognition of genius, but its effects insidiously work to destroy the phenomenon it celebrates. Corinne herself acknowledges the extent to which she depends on her audience for her improvisatory skills: she describes her improvisations as a "lively conversation" in which, as she explains, "I go along with the impression that my listeners' interest makes on me, and it is to my friends that I owe the greatest part of my talent in this field."[12] For Corinne, the audience plays an integral part in her own artistic creations, which are almost all performances of one kind or another.

But there is more to *gloire* than this, for, as Corinne herself affirms, "Genius inspires the need for fame," and "she admitted unaffectedly that admiration was very attractive to her." The real problem is not the desire for *gloire* as such, but the fact that the recognition provided by *gloire* has a variant in the form of love. Corinne has a tendency to conflate the two with what turn out to be disastrous consequences: "Love and fame [*gloire*] had always been mingled in her mind." It is here that the gendering of genius begins to open up the possibility of its own destruction, since this conflation—or so Corinne herself suggests—is one that women are especially prone to make: "in seeking fame, I always hoped that it would make me loved. What use would it be, at least to women, without that hope?"[13] All this notwithstanding, Corinne is initially as blessed in her search for love as she is in the genius with which she is endowed by her creator: the laureation ceremony rewards her not just with the crown of laurels but also with a lover, Oswald (Lord Nelvil).

He sees Corinne for the first time in the ceremony, which offers him the first chance he has ever had to witness a woman of genius being publicly rewarded. An exchange of glances between himself and Corinne reveals another aspect of the exceptional woman, an aspect that, complicatedly, makes her like all women: "[I]n the midst of all this splendour and success it seemed to him that Corinne's eyes had sought the protection of a man friend, a protection no woman, however superior she may be, can ever dispense with. And he thought it would be pleasing to be the support of a woman who would feel the need for such support only because of her sensitivity." If Corinne comes over here as a woman in search of love, love is immediately defined as a superior version of the recognition that is granted by *gloire*. As Oswald listens to the poets singing her praises, he hears nothing in their eulogies of Corinne that could not equally well be applied to any of the talented women to whom she is compared. The lover, in contrast to the public speaker, can offer a type of recognition that is an infinitely more precise response to the specific qualities of the woman who is nevertheless so generously celebrated: "Lord Nelvil was already suffering from this way of praising Corinne. He felt already that, just by looking at her, he could there and then have produced a truer, more accurate, and detailed portrait, a portrait which would have fitted no one but Corinne." This is not just the wishful thinking of the would-be lover. Prince Castel-Forte, who delivers the eulogy, makes a similar point when he says that though Corinne is the most famous woman in the land, only her friends will be able to paint an accurate portrait of her, because "the soul's qualities, when they are genuine, always require other people to sense them."[14]

Love appears at this stage to be a more responsive and therefore superior form of recognition than *gloire*. But the two eventually prove impossible to combine, and these apparently complementary forms of response to genius become opposed, to the ultimate detriment of genius itself. The lovers are gradually torn apart by their differences over the relative values of *gloire* and love and whereas Oswald begins by rejoicing at the prospect of all Corinne's gifts being bestowed on him in the private domain, Corinne comes to realize that "[t]alent needs an independence that true love never allows." The difference between the lovers on this issue becomes decisive with Oswald's provocative reply to her: "If that is the case, . . . may your genius be silent, and your heart be all mine."[15]

It doesn't help that Corinne has the misfortune to find in Oswald a lover whose cultural assumptions are very different from her own, and who, as an Englishman reared in Scotland, places the highest values on duty and self-sacrifice in women, and can imagine love only in the guise of conjugal domesticity. It is these factors (along with his guilty desire to comply with his late father's wishes on the matter of a suitable wife) that draw him to Lucile, who is in every way the opposite of Corinne, despite being, as is later revealed, her half sister.

SENSIBILITY AND SUFFERING

And yet these polarities are not as simple as they might appear. Even if Corinne had found a lover with cultural assumptions closer to her own, the tension between love and *gloire*, intimacy and the public domain, is written into genius from the outset. This is because genius itself is defined as having its source in the personal characteristics of its possessor: if genius is "essentially creative," this is because "it bears the stamp of the individual who possesses it." It is a matter of individual qualities, rather than a particular aptitude in a given artistic sphere, and in Corinne these qualities are described as "liveliness of mind," "freshness of imagination," and "passionate sensibility," which enable her to "understand the affective links between the beauties of nature and the most deep-seated impressions of the soul." Her originality—through which her genius is manifested—is attributable to her character and above all to her "way of feeling."[16] This *manière de sentir* proves to be the second major element whereby genius is, as it were, undone from within.

There is nothing exceptional for its time in the definition of genius as deriving from imagination and sensibility. Equally, if Corinne possesses an unusually wide range of talents, these are portrayed as a symptom of her reluctance to be bound by any set of rules and conventions, and as so many languages that

collectively enable her to express a single imaginative power. Her verse improvisations are the greatest of these talents, but in the course of the novel she also
dances, acts in Shakespeare's *Romeo and Juliet*, takes a role in a comedy, and
paints a portrait of Oswald's late father that bears an astonishing resemblance
to him. However, the qualities that lie behind these multiple forms of artistic
expression exact their own toll: "Corinne's ardent imagination was the source of
her talent, but unfortunately for her, her imagination was linked to her natural
sensitivity and often caused her great pain."[17] Imagination and sensitivity are at
once the source of her genius and the cause of the suffering that brings about its
destruction. It is this conundrum that the novel brings to light.

Corinne's love for a man is the specific origin of her misery, but this aptitude
for unhappiness is not specifically gendered. Corinne may conclude at the end
of her life that of all the "faculties of the soul [she] has received from nature,
that of suffering is the only one [she] has fully put into practice," but in this,
according to Mme de Staël, she is doing no more than exemplify the finest of
human qualities as they exist in the modern world regardless of gender. Dis-
coursing to Oswald on the history of the arts during a visit to the Vatican Mu-
seum, Corinne herself comments, "In our modern times, in our cold, oppres-
sive society, grief is our noblest emotion, and in our day, he who has not suffered
will have neither felt nor thought." Whereas in the ancient world nobility was
expressed as a "heroic calm" and a "sense of power," the modern world turns
individuals in upon themselves to feed upon their inner feelings—and genius is
no exception to this historically determined rule.[18]

The truth of this phenomenon is borne out by the example of Tasso (to
whom Corinne is specifically compared), which prompts the conclusion that it
is the very condition of genius to multiply the causes of its own suffering:
"When persons of genius are endowed with real sensitivity, their sorrows are
multiplied by those same gifts . . . , and as the heart's unhappiness is inexhaustible, the more ideas they have, the more they feel it."[19] Corinne's unhappy experience illustrates a universal truth about genius. Loving and suffering are not
the unique preserve of the woman genius, but are the inevitable consequence of
the combination of imagination and sensibility that characterizes all genius in
the modern world.

The drama of the novel comes from the paradoxical results of this principle,
which demonstrates that genius is destroyed by its own virtues. Corinne's suffering is caused in part by a man who, in loving the personal qualities of which
her genius is made, also wishes to remove them from the public stage on which
they exist. Her suffering is further exacerbated by his subsequent preference for
a woman—Lucile—who is not encumbered by genius, though she makes him
no happier than Corinne. The focus of the narrative is Corinne's gradual loss of
her own genius, as she slides from a voluntary relinquishing of her talents to a
painful endurance of their absence. In deciding to follow her lover, she acknowledges that she knows what price she will be paying: "I shall be following

Oswald without knowing what fate he has in store for me, the man whom I prefer to the independent destiny thanks to which I have passed such happy days! I shall perhaps return, but with a wounded heart and a withered soul, and even you, fine arts and ancient monuments . . . , will no longer be able to do anything for me." Her prediction is confirmed in due course and, as she finally lies dying in Florence, she laments the fact that Oswald stifled the gifts that were designed to "arouse enthusiasm in hearts in harmony with mine."[20] Her genius is gone, wasted on a love that is ultimately denied her.

The gendering of genius in Mme de Staël's novel serves to highlight a certain paradoxical truth about genius, which applies as much to men as to any woman. As a woman, Corinne may be more vulnerable to suffering because of a woman's supposed desire for protection and the consequent confusion between love and *gloire*, but suffering has many causes, and is not confined to female experience. Genius contains the seeds of its own undoing, and this is the truth that Mme de Staël depicts in *Corinne*.

Author or Protagonist?

In view of all this, one might wonder about Mme de Staël's own investment in her creation of the first female genius in French literature. *Corinne* was a huge success, not just in France but across Europe too. Despite the fate of Mme de Staël's genius-heroine, readers saw in the novel proof of the genius of its author: Maria Edgeworth hailed *Corinne* as "a work of splendid genius," and later in the century, George Eliot would ensure that Maggie Tulliver owned a copy of the novel in *Mill on the Floss*. One of the paradoxical effects of the novel's success was that Mme de Staël was popularly imagined as Corinne herself. Her own response to this blurring of her identity with that of her heroine was to say, "I am not Corinne, but if you like I shall be."[21]

A few months after the publication of the novel, the painter Elisabeth Vigée Le Brun portrayed Mme de Staël as Corinne, an association that Mme de Staël herself seems to have encouraged and that she was happy to underscore by commissioning a (slightly more flattering) copy of the portrait from a local Genevan painter. Certainly posterity saw her in this light, and the painting commissioned from François Gérard after her death depicts her in the role of Corinne at Cape Miseno, with the same lyre and heavenward gaze as the earlier portrait (Figure 7).[22]

This conflation of the two figures, Mme de Staël and her heroine, is intriguing, and it clearly implies that Mme de Staël was not disadvantaged by her association with a woman whose genius fails. This may in part have something to do with the fact that the novel's mode of narration does not establish a direct identification between its author-narrator and its heroine. Moreover, before even considering its narrative mode, almost everything about the novel distin-

Figure 7. François Gérard, *Corinne at Cape Miseno* (1819). Musée des Beaux-Arts, Lyon. © Lyon MBA, photo by Alain Basset

guishes it from the artistic practices favored by Corinne. Her talents are almost all those of performance, and where they involve her literary skills, these are employed in the spoken rather than the written word. Even when she does write (for the last performance that she is too ill to carry out herself), her text is designed for performance, not reading.

Mme de Staël's heroine, then, is not a writer. In fact, it could be said that it is Corinne's reluctance, or refusal, to write that contributes in a major way to the rupture between her and Oswald, since she fails to answer his letters when he returns to Britain. In any case, her preferred literary medium is poetry, not prose, and the difference between the two is underscored in the novel itself where it is claimed that poetry is the only form in which the peoples of the South can give voice to their feelings, and that they lose all spontaneity when they move from the spoken to the written word. Novels are a genre almost un-known in Italy, and the language of *Corinne*—French—is very different from the Italian in which Corinne composes and performs and whose spirit she gives creative voice to. In short, *Corinne* is a novel written in French about a heroine whose genius is for performing improvised verse in Italian.

The mode of narration is impersonal, the narrator having neither face nor gender, and authorial comments are kept to a minimum. Moreover, *Corinne* is unusual for a novel of its time in having no preface, where the author might have introduced herself.[23] But despite the fact that Corinne differs from her creator in being a performer rather than a writer, she does nevertheless become a kind of surrogate author, regularly adopting an authorial tone and posture, thanks to the fact that most of the novel's commentary about the arts and cul-ture of Italy is delivered by its heroine as she introduces her lover to its major sites and cultural artifacts. The novel is about Italy as well as about Corinne, and she is presented as an authority on Italian culture. The effect of this is to make the few interventions from the author proper sound like those of her heroine, and, as the novel progresses toward its sad conclusion, the pathos of the hero-ine's decline is underscored in sentences such as the following, which differ al-most not at all from those uttered by Corinne herself as she comments on her plight:

> Believing she was suffering a fatal illness, Corinne wanted to bid Italy and especially Lord Nelvil, a last farewell which would recall the time when her genius shone in all its glory. It was a weakness which we must forgive her. Love and fame had always been mingled in her mind, and until that moment when her heart made the sacrifice of all earthly affections, she wanted the ungrateful man who had deserted her to feel once more that he had given the death blow to the woman who, of all those of his time, knew best how to love.[24]

The author's sympathies emerge in this appeal for the reader's understanding.

Only in the very last sentence of the entire novel does the author speak in her own—but still ungendered—voice in response to a series of questions about what became of Oswald, what the world thought of his past conduct, and whether, after all that he had lost in Corinne, he was happy in his humdrum existence with Lucile. Adopting the first person for the first and only time, she replies, "I do not know, and, on that matter, I want neither to blame nor to ab-solve him."[25] This final intervention, though it concerns Oswald and not Corinne, can be read as a sign that Corinne's plight has ultimately drawn its previously invisible author-narrator into a sympathetic understanding of her heroine. It is perhaps less that Corinne has been constructed in the image of her author, than that, as with the portraits of Mme de Staël, the author has come to resemble her heroine out of imaginative sympathy with her. Sympathetic un-derstanding was, of course, the prerogative of the novel as Mme de Staël had defined the genre, attributing this quality to the influence of women in society.

True to the female inspiration of the genre to which it belongs, the novel turns its attention to the phenomenon of genius, and comes into its own in its description of the nuances of the suffering soul of its genius heroine.

As far as Mme de Staël herself is concerned, readers were divided about the extent to which the genius that the novel credited her with was specifically female. Women writers such as Maria Edgeworth or George Sand may have taken inspiration or comfort from the combined example of Mme de Staël and her heroine, but in the laudatory essay that Sainte-Beuve wrote about her in 1835 he makes no reference to her sex when he remarks that "as art, as a poem, the novel of *Corinne*, would constitute an immortal monument in its own right," and adds that it revealed its author to be an "an artist to the utmost degree."[26] His willingness to take women writers seriously, as implied by the existence of the volume, *Portraits de femmes* (Portraits of women), in which this essay appears, indicates that he did not share the hostility of his contemporaries toward talented women who include Mme de Lafayette, Mme de Sévigné, Mme Roland, and Mme de Duras. He is more than willing to use the word "genius" about women, although in the case of Mme de Staël he describes her intellect and the tone of her writing as "masculine." He attributes to her what he claims is one of the defining characteristics of genius, which is to find itself paired with a rival (as instanced in the cases of Voltaire and Rousseau, Scott and Byron, or Goethe and Schiller), and suggests that Mme de Staël's genius rival is the indubitably male Chateaubriand.[27] This remark places her alongside the author of the *Génie du christianisme*, and implicitly acknowledges the fact that *Corinne*—female author and female protagonist notwithstanding—has its own truth to tell about the nature of genius.

By including the "other" of woman in its account, *Corinne* explores a truth about genius in general. The story of the failure of a woman genius serves the cause of *all* genius by ascribing its failures to some of its essential features. In doing so it also qualifies its author for the accolade of genius in her turn, but it would seem that it nonetheless fails to establish the possibility of a definitive gendering of genius as female. Subsequent depictions of genius in fiction almost always give the starring role to men, and reserve women for the role of helpmeet or destroyer. In Balzac's *Louis Lambert*, it is Lambert who is the genius figure, and Mme de Staël—specifically described as the author of *Corinne*—is given a walk-on part as the person who has the honor of recognizing the boy's talent, before disappearing from the story and leaving its male author to narrate the destruction of its hero's male genius.

CHAPTER 11

Balzac's *Louis Lambert*

Genius and the Feminine Mediator

that figure, who appears sinister to people who are unable to
recognize the strangeness of genius.

—Balzac, *La Rabouilleuse*

In an essay on artists—"Des artistes" (On artists)—written in 1830 during the
early days of his career as a realist novelist, Balzac makes the familiar observation that creative artists have no insight into the way that their intelligence operates. Their power may be due to "a deformity in the brain," genius may be "a
human illness as the pearl is an infirmity of the oyster," or it may simply derive
from "the exercise of a faculty common to all men," but whatever the case, the
artist operates "under the sway of certain circumstances whose combination is
a mystery. He is not master of himself." This is a vulnerability that, as with the
Romantic poet, makes genius dependent on a third party who will respect and
defend it against ignorance and hostility. Inspiration constitutes the artist as a
special kind of being, characterized here as a "perpetual antithesis, which exists
both in the majesty of his power and in the nullity of his life: he is always either
a god or a cadaver." This strange mode of being makes the artist subject to "social reproof on the part of sticklers" who have no inclination to help him out
with the practical and material support that his absorption in creative matters
makes him unable to provide for himself.[1]

The essay is a plea for the defense of art and its vulnerable creators, but
rather than develop the sort of social critique outlined in Vigny's *Stello*, Balzac
takes the opportunity to depict the artist as an intriguingly anomalous kind of
character, alternating between majesty and nullity under the effects of forces
that he does not control. Fortunately for some, women provide where society
does not: "if there is an activity worthy of human recognition, it is the devotion
of a few women who dedicate themselves to looking after these glorious beings,
these blind creatures who have the world at their disposal but not a crust to
eat."[2] There is much that the world itself is blind to: not just the special character
of artists, but also the essential role played by women in their survival, and

these are the topics that Balzac the novelist takes it upon himself to examine and portray.

He writes here as if he were observing his specimens from without. Their human strangeness is extreme, and the lack of any insight into their own nature means, by definition, that artistic genius can give no account of itself. If more is to be known about these creatures—and it sounds as though, for their own survival, Balzac saw this as a matter of urgency—then that knowledge will have to come from a sympathetic third-party observer. The scientific perspective on genius, like that of the "Germanic minds" devoted to a logical examination of the relation of insanity to genius, will not provide the right kind of information.[3] And although Balzac never puts it in exactly these terms, it would seem that true insight must have mixed origins, both inside and outside the object of its scrutiny.

Balzac is certainly more than an objective observer of genius since he also aspires to being the genius he declared himself to be just three years later when he thought of the principle of reappearing characters as the basis for the creation the *Comédie humaine*, and ran halfway across Paris to announce it to his sister and her husband. As a realist novelist, Balzac is historian and scientist, but he is also an artist. He both is and is not one of the number whom he also set out to portray in figures such as Louis Lambert, Balthazar Claës, or indeed the entire cast of the *Comédie humaine*, about whom Baudelaire famously observed, "each of them, . . . even the portresses, is endowed with genius."[4] This hybridity is what distinguishes the novelist both from the poets and from other commentators.

Abortive Genius

The genius of Balzac's portresses is, however, of a different order from the genius of the creative artist, and they are not the pretext for the kind of fictional case study that Balzac carried out in *Louis Lambert*. The need for sympathetic insight into the man of genius is particularly acute in the character of Lambert, whose exterior gives no hint of the qualities that lie within. Lambert is diminutive (only five foot two when fully grown), pale, slight, self-effacing, and, except when roused, physically weak. This is a far cry from the image of the "future genius" anticipated by his classmates, which, as the narrator records, they imagined as "a wizard, a lad capable of writing a prose composition or a translation while [they] were being called into class, and of learning his lessons by reading them through just once."[5]

Lambert's only known work, the precocious *Traité de la volonté* (Treatise on the will), is confiscated by one of the masters and its pages used as paper cornets for the sweets sold in the local *confiserie*. The novel ends with a picture of what looks like genius utterly destroyed as Lambert—his hair grown long as a woman's—is seen sitting in a darkened room, obsessively rubbing his legs against each other and announcing obscurely that *"[t]he angels are white!"* There is very little to show for the genius he possesses, and this makes him— albeit very ambiguously—a failed genius, or what Gretchen Besser, in her study of Balzac, calls an "abortive genius," a category he shares with Frenhofer, Baltha- zar Claës, and Gambara.[6] But if, at the end of his life, Lambert appears to be more "cadaver" than "god," he nonetheless exemplifies all Balzac's own ideas about genius, and is also its most complete and elaborate theorist. Once again, fiction's interest in its failure may reveal more about genius than success. And that failure is also accompanied—still with considerable ambiguity—by the fe- male presence that Balzac argued also deserved recognition as the essential helpmeet of genius.

He places his own text under the aegis of female influence, dedicating it to "La Dilecta," Mme de Berny, in whose château at Saché he wrote the first ver- sion of his novel. Many years later, in a letter to Mme Hanska, he described this early draft as having been "much caressed . . . , and made . . . perfect . . . under the protection of the angel who is now in heaven"—the angel being his early benefactress and mistress.[7] This female sponsorship is recalled as having been bestowed on a text that seems to have mattered a great deal to Balzac. He re- vised and expanded it significantly between 1832 (the date of its first version, which appeared under the title *Notice biographique sur Louis Lambert* [Bio- graphical note on Louis Lambert] in the *Nouveaux contes philosophiques* [New philosophical tales]) and 1835 (the date of the final version). Altogether during his lifetime it appeared in seven different editions.[8] One may assume, then, that there was something important that Balzac wanted to get right, and that some- thing included the issue of the genius to which he himself—albeit ambiva- lently—also laid claim.

It is customary to regard *Louis Lambert* as an autobiographical novel, par- ticularly in its evocation of the Collège Vendôme where Balzac was a pupil be- tween 1807 and 1813. But if the novel is autobiographical, it is difficult to know whether to see Balzac in the narrator or in Lambert, in the sympathetic ob- server of genius or in the oblivious genius himself. On the one hand, the narra- tor insists on his own inferiority to Lambert, and it is Lambert who conceives of the theories that so closely echo those of Balzac.[9] And on the other, the nar- rator—derisively dubbed *Le Poète* by his classmates—seems to adopt Balzac's identity when he alludes to having written the *Études philosophiques* (Philo- sophical studies) and specifically to having given the name of Pauline to the woman loved by the author of another (or possibly the same) *Traité de la volo- nté*. Any reader of Balzac will understand from this that the narrator is claiming authorship of *La Peau de chagrin* (The wild-ass's skin), the first version of which was written a year before the first version of *Louis Lambert*.

Critics have suggested that Balzac splits himself equally into the two figures, and in an unpublished note, Balzac comments on the significance of his uncharacteristic use of a first-person narrator in this novel: "In narrating this story in an unusual form, I shall perhaps be depriving it of the interest that it might otherwise possess if I employed the resources that art lends to novelists. I know what kind of chill the use of *I* and *me* confers a on a tale, but . . . here *the I is the only way to explain the facts*."[10] Balzac's sole concession to first-person narration suggests that the figure of genius is inseparable from the other of its observer-witness, as if genius cannot be represented in unmediated form. As mediator, however, the narrator takes his place, chronologically speaking, between two female figures, Mme de Staël, who precedes him, and Pauline, Lambert's fiancée, who succeeds him in this role. I shall return presently to the implications of these female mediators of genius.

A DOSE OF PHOSPHOROUS

Balzac endows Lambert with most of the features that characterize genius in the thinking of the time.[11] Lambert has the imagination ("an almost divine imagination"), the originality ("[t]he larger the genius, the starker are the oddities that constitute the different degrees of originality"), and the sensitivity ("exquisite delicacy") that the eighteenth century had bequeathed to the nineteenth.[12] He is incapable of complying with the rules and conventions of the world around him, whether those of the school curriculum, the strict regime governing life in the Collège Vendôme, or the demands of a society where everything is based on money and every enterprise required to produce immediate results.

As Balzac demonstrates in "Des artistes," and as the example of the poets has already shown, the man of genius appears increasingly in the guise of a social misfit. Lambert is the butt of mockery on the part of his fellow *collégiens*, as well as a target for the scorn of teachers who are incapable of discerning the true forms of genius behind an exterior that does not conform to the image of the precocious "wizard" who can dash off a Latin prose and memorize his lessons at a glance. Lambert's genius is repeatedly misrecognized. The teacher who confiscates his *Treatise* sees in it only "garbage for which [Lambert] neglects [his] assignments." It does not occur to him that "at the age of fifteen Louis could have the profundity of a man of genius" and that "in this work Lambert [had] set down the ideas of a full-grown man."[13] Without the retrospective consecration of adult achievement, precocity becomes just another of the many reasons why genius may be overlooked or disparaged—unless there is a witness capable of seeing it for what it is.

Like Stello, and like the *poètes malheureux* on whose example Vigny draws, Lambert is "ill with his genius," and like Corinne, he suffers from the heightened sensitivity it confers. The final image of Lambert in his darkened room has something of Delacroix's Tasso about it, and the consensus of the outside world is that Lambert has gone mad. If he is not incarcerated in La Salpêtrière, this is only because Esquirol, whom Lambert's uncle has him consult, diagnoses his condition as incurable and sends him home with the recommendation that he be kept in isolation and protected from disturbance. Balzac himself was interested in medical views of genius, and like many of his contemporaries he saw it as a hair's breadth away from insanity. Or as his fictional Dr. Bianchon says in *La Peau de chagrin*, that hair's breadth consists in "a dose of phosphorus more or less [which] makes the man of genius or the scoundrel, the intelligent man or the idiot, the virtuous man or the criminal."[14]

After reading Moreau de Tours's study of the effects of hashish, Balzac wrote to its author with his own thoughts about the risks of madness for creative writers. But he was equally aware that it was all too easy for people to confuse genius with insanity, and as he has Mme Claës say in *La Recherche de l'absolu* (The search for the absolute), "it is only for the common herd [that] genius resembles madness."[15] Similarly, in *Louis Lambert* it is another female character, Pauline, who casts doubt on the medical diagnosis of Lambert's insanity, and suggests rather that his condition is the culmination of his capacity for second sight. Balzac unambiguously endorses these alternative views in an earlier draft of the novel where he talks of the challenge posed by the thinking of "a great genius who, for common men, seems to have reached a state of madness, when for a number of others, he is advancing through the loftiest regions of thought and attempting an assault on a few unknown truths."[16]

Elsewhere in Balzac's œuvre this second sight is presented as the defining feature of genius, but unlike the other markers of genius ascribed to Lambert, it is one entirely of Balzac's invention. Or rather, it is an extreme form of the power of observation with which the eighteenth century had endowed genius, and which for Diderot was its one indispensable quality. Lambert's pallor and physical frailty are offset by the power of his gaze: he has piercing eyes, described at one point as being "charged with thought as a Leyden jar is charged with electricity," whose effect his teacher is disconcerted to discover when a reprimand to Lambert for "doing nothing" is rewarded with "a glance that was a bolt of lightning."[17]

Seeing and thinking are one; and the power of sight is an expression of the *Volonté* that lies behind it. This Will is activated in turn by an electrical substance, which, in Lambert's own words, allows it to be "majestically enthroned in a look so as to obliterate all obstacles at the command of genius." Vautrin exercises the same devastating ocular force on Mlle de Michonneau in *Le Père Goriot* when he discovers her betrayal, though its importance for Balzac lies less in the ability to deal with the occasional inconvenient obstacle, than in its inwardness, and it is in this inner, or second, sight that genius is manifest. As Lambert himself says, "the person on whom the exercise of inner sight has bestowed a kind of strength inevitably leads us to suppose that the same distance must exist between men of genius and other beings as separates the sighted from the blind."[18] Through the faculty of second sight, Lambert is able to withdraw from his physical body and travel unhampered and at lightning speed through the universe.

In his final phase, the transmission of the thoughts that result from second sight does not always take the form of verbal expression, and is reliant on Pauline's ability to follow Lambert's thinking as he completes in words an idea begun in the mind, or begins to articulate a proposition that he then continues mentally without speech. The highest level of inwardness, set out in one of the *Pensées* (Thoughts) recorded by Pauline, is that of *Speciality*, which is at once the product of second sight and itself the most powerful type of vision possible: "*Speciality*, species *sight, speculate, see everything, and in a single glance*; Speculum, *a mirror or means of assessing a thing by seeing it whole.*"[19] Sight, in other words, is all. It is the supreme faculty, and the source of the greatest knowledge. According to Lambert, the finest geniuses of humanity are those who have succeeded in moving beyond the lower level of "Abstraction" to emerge into the light of "Speciality." In the following *Pensée*, however, Lambert seems to row back slightly from this definition, and claims that men of genius are the products of a mixed regime whereby "Speciality" is combined with "Abstraction." This is the level of existence from which society with its arts and philosophy and its laws is born, but which does not include access to the Infinite.

All this is heady stuff, but it is entirely serious on Balzac's part, as the work of Henri Evans and Per Nykrog has demonstrated. Lambert speaks for Balzac, but in doing so, he may be insufficiently hybrid: the quality of sight that he exhibits to such an extreme degree removes him too far from the sphere of Abstraction. So, if he is a failed genius, this is not because of the admixture of any insanity, but because his genius is *too* pure: it exemplifies too perfectly its own defining feature of second sight for which Lambert is nonetheless the entirely reliable theoretical exponent.

"THE DEVOTION OF A FEW WOMEN"

This conundrum introduces an ambiguous twist into Balzac's portrait of genius, and the extreme purity of Lambert's gift might explain why it needs to be translated or mediated by other figures, notably, the narrator, Mme de Staël, and Pauline de Villenoix. The feminine character of this mediation is established before any of them enters Lambert's life when, in a kind of primal scene, his genius is—literally—sparked by the sight of the electricity leaping up from his mother's head as she combs her hair in front of her son who observes her from the cot beside her bed. The electricity that powers Lambert's genius is bestowed by a woman who "was one of those creatures destined to represent Woman in the perfection of her attributes," and who in the course of her short life expended all her energies in the form of maternal love.[20]

Women have vital role in Lambert's story through their ability to recognize and facilitate a genius too fragile to hold its own in the world, and whose very fragility is described in markedly feminine terms, as suggested already by Lambert's slight stature and the long hair of his last years. His mother is the inspiration for the theory of Will, which is the theory of the genius that Lambert himself embodies. Mme de Staël steps out the pages of literary history to launch the young Lambert on the path of genius by recognizing his gifts. And Pauline de Villenoix, the woman whom Lambert was due to marry, becomes the translator and amanuensis of his mature *Pensées*. Pauline is a more vigorous version of the female figures who provide genius with secret recognition in Vigny's *Stello*— coincidentally, perhaps, written in the same year as the first draft of Balzac's novel. These include Kitty Bell, whose love for Chatterton obliquely condones his genius, and Mme de Saint-Aignan, who has several of Chénier's poems by heart and keeps a portrait of him among her belongings until the day she dies.

In almost every case, women's devotion to genius is inspired by love. Balzac makes Mme de Staël an exception to this rule, but she nevertheless plays a crucial role in providing Lambert's gifts with the consecration of recognition. Confirming her own dictum whereby genius recognizes its own, she sees a rare quality in the ragged tanner's son whom she discovers reading Swedenborg in the grounds of the house where she happens to be staying during her exile from Paris. With a prescience of which she herself cannot be fully aware, she declares, "*He is a true seer.*"[21] Balzac refuses Mme de Staël any capacity for maternal feeling, and he attributes her decision to pay for Lambert's education to a desire to cast herself in the role of Pharaoh's daughter rescuing Moses from the bulrushes, and to a determination to deny her enemies, Napoleon and the recently reestablished Catholic Church, the chance of benefitting from the boy's exceptional talent. Balzac then allows her to forget about Lambert, the money she paid over for his studies being deemed too small a sum to warrant her remembering his existence. When Lambert later sets out to meet his benefactress, he arrives in Paris on the day she dies and they never meet again.

There is more than a touch of misogyny in Balzac's portrait of Mme de Staël, whom he characterizes as easily bored, jealous, egotistical, and self-dramatizing, and for good measure he throws in a gratuitous reference to her reputation for loquacity. But the intervention of the author of *Corinne* would seem to be a vital stage on the way of Lambert's genius. Her intervention is described at one point as "feminine caprice" but elsewhere more positively as "protection," anticipating the word used by Balzac for the role that Mme de Berny played in the creation of *Louis Lambert* itself. Except that in the case of the young Balzac, the protection of a benefactress was expressed not by means of cash and caprice, but of tenderly bestowed caresses.

Such affection is also the currency of the relation between the narrator and Lambert, which has many feminine qualities and recalls those associated with the brief appearance of Lambert's mother. Lambert himself sets the tone for this ambiguous gendering by exhibiting "an almost feminine delicacy of feeling which is instinctive in great men," and the narrator speculates that "perhaps their sublimity is simply this need for devotion that distinguishes women, but applied to great things." At any rate, Lambert's pale complexion is feminine, as is his soft voice; he has the graciousness of a woman in love; he is "as ethereal as a woman can be," and "ill with his genius as a young girl is ill with the love that she attracts and remains unaware of." If there is something unmistakably feminine in the amorous devotion of genius to its objects, it is mirrored in the narrator's own devotion to genius, based on shared understanding and a communion of souls. "[L]ike two lovers," the two friends develop the habit of thinking together and sharing their thoughts and dreams.[22] The character of these tender exchanges is in marked contrast to the all-male, quasi-monastic regime of the Collège Vendôme, with its two or three hundred boys and their severe and unfeeling masters.

The narrator claims that it is only in hindsight that he has come to understand the nature of the phenomena of which he was the intimate witness in his youth, but his relations with Lambert are a kind of blueprint for those of Pauline with Lambert. Lambert's time in Paris is made unhappy by the absence of anyone with whom he can share "his most exquisite pleasures." When he meets Pauline he envisages in her the possibility of a perfect communion with the "angel-woman" that he has long dreamed of, and it is in these terms that he writes to her on the eve of their projected marriage: "I can see us both joined together, walking in step with each other, living from the same thoughts; each always deep inside the heart of the other, comprehending the other and understanding the other the way an echo receives and repeats sounds across empty space."[23] His attempted self-castration, which puts paid to the marriage and is taken to indicate the onset of insanity, could be interpreted positively as a means of ensuring that he and Pauline commune in thought without the distraction of the flesh. This is certainly how Pauline herself appears to view their arrangement. Where others—including the medical experts—see only incurable insanity, she sees entirely lucid ideas in the thinking that she claims to inhabit. Her devotion to Lambert matches his devotion to the mysticism of *Speciality*, and it is thanks to her that Lambert's two sets of *Pensées* (whose title echoes those of Pascal) are preserved.

And yet his genius ultimately eludes her. In her own words, reported after Lambert's untimely death at the age of twenty-eight, God took his genius while she had (only) his heart. Along with Mme Lambert *mère*, Pauline seems to be the nearest thing to the ideal Woman in the novel, a model of the support required by a genius that is incapable of self-sufficiency. As such a model, she treads a fine line between her role as external mediator of genius, and the imitation of its own pattern of amorous devotion. Pauline's relation to Lambert may replicate that of the narrator, but the two seem to diverge at the end of the novel where the narrator implies that she has leaned too far in the direction of simply reproducing the thoughts of genius and failed to maintain her mediating role. If this is the case, one must ask whether her ability to enter Lambert's thought processes is a sign of her sensitivity or of her part in a *folie à deux*. The narrator evidently sees Lambert's condition as that of a great mind destroyed rather than that of a great mind at work. He recoils from it as from a "contagion" and cannot bring himself to pay another visit to his one-time friend. It is as if he needed to establish a distance—which in due course becomes temporal as well as spatial—in order to provide the account of genius, which, as Balzac put it in his unpublished note, will have enough *froideur* to tell "truth of the facts."

Genius itself is a fairly androgynous affair, its femininity matched by the spurting liquids of *Volonté*. Its mode of expression is a male *jaillissement*, whether this be of electricity, ideas or moral force. Its full realization would be an ejaculatory "unitary system, compact and melded in single jet," which Lambert is said to lack the strength to produce.[24] Whether this lack of masculinity is the reason for his failure is moot; but equally, femininity is ambiguously—dangerously, even—essential to its success. Genius requires benefaction, which here is portrayed as female, in the figures of Mme de Staël and La Dilecta. It relates to the objects of its enquiries with an amorous devotion that is exemplified in the ideal Woman. And, finally, it depends for its existence on a mediation that seems to borrow these same gendered forms. But the dynamic is precarious, as vulnerable to the greater or lesser doses of phosphorous with which an individual is endowed, as it is to the greater or lesser components of femininity. Too little, and genius suffers and fails. Too much, and genius collapses into its own destructive purity.

The ambivalence of this portrait of genius and the uncertainty about where its limits might lie are exceptional in the literature on the subject, which tends otherwise to proceed in a mode of assertion. Whether affirmed or denied, celebrated or analyzed, genius is a topic that rarely invites doubt. But in the nineteenth-century novel it is subject to a questioning where its apparent failure may be interpreted as a form of fulfillment, and where two views—sympathetic identification and quasi-scientific scrutiny—are combined in the hybrid and ambivalent mediation of the realist novelist himself.

CHAPTER 12

Creativity and Procreation in Zola's L'Œuvre

> Women carry inside them an organ that is subject to terrible
> spasms, over which they have no control, and which creates
> phantoms of every kind in their imaginations.
>
> —Diderot, *Sur les femmes*

When Zola sent a synopsis for the ten novels of his projected Rougon-Macquart cycle to his publisher, Albert Lacroix, in 1869, he included a plan for one that would describe "the erethism of the intelligence," "the modern sickness of the artist," and "the unhealthy conceptions of brains that develop into insanity." He was familiar with the work of Moreau de Tours from which he very probably borrowed this terminology, and the hereditary pathology that serves to link the various novels in the cycle has many echoes of the "morbid psychology" explored by Moreau in his book of that title. The hero of the novel that Zola eventually began in 1885 and published a year later under the title *L'Œuvre* (The masterpiece) was to illustrate the "singular effect of heredity transmitting genius to the son of illiterate parents," and in particular the "nervous influence of the mother." The mother in question is Gervaise, the heroine of *L'Assommoir*, whose "neurosis" manifests as alcoholism and is transmitted with a range of pathological consequences to her four children, Nana, Étienne, Jacques, and Claude Lantier, the central figure of *L'Œuvre*.[1]

Moreau's illustrative tree of nervous pathologies had already defined genius as a morbid phenomenon and linked it to a whole range of other phenomena, from the alcoholism that grew on the branch of the "Spontaneous phrenopathies," to the "Prostitution" at the tip of the "affective" branch of the hereditary nervous conditions, of which another was that of the "Utopists," who derived from the nearby "intellectual" offshoot. Nana (as prostitute) in *Nana* and Étienne (as "utopist") in *Germinal* would seem to have their origins in these morbid outgrowths of Moreau's tree.[2] Claude's son Jacques, who dies at the age of twelve with the "enormous head that marked him as the blemished offspring of genius" and swollen to the proportions of cretinism, exemplifies the "Imbecility" that is yet another variant of the same cluster of "Spontaneous phrenopathies." The Rougon-Macquart family tree (which Zola drew up several times) is closely, though far from slavishly, mapped onto Moreau's tree. It grows out of a similar "idiosyncratic hereditary nervous condition," one of whose principal expressions is the genius that Moreau discusses so fully in the body of his text.

In other words, Claude's defining feature in Zola's elaboration of his character is his genius. This is a "genius novel" just as much as an "artist novel," and Claude is as much the inheritor of Balzac's Louis Lambert as he is that of the Frenhofer of *Le Chef d'œuvre inconnu* (The unknown masterpiece) with whom he is much more commonly compared. In the family tree that opens *Une page d'amour* (One page of love), the note on Claude outlines the pathology of his genius before mentioning his occupation as a painter: "Heredity of neurosis that develops into genius. Painter." And Zola elaborates, "Moral and physical preponderance from the mother, inherited neurosis." In the preparatory notes for *L'Œuvre* he reminds himself not to forget "the original neurosis that develops into genius," and in the longer *Ébauche* (Draft), the pathology of Claude's genius returns as a central theme: "Genius is disequilibrium. Claude a genius."[3]

Sandoz, Zola's novelist alter ego and mouthpiece, gives voice to this view when he speaks of Claude as having been "ravaged by an excessive lesion in his genius," and in an echo of Bianchon's comments about phosphorous, Claude himself acknowledges "some maladjustment of the nerve centres, or . . . some hereditary flaw," which, because of "a gram or two of substance too much or too little," would make him a lunatic instead of a great man.[4] The language of the novel replicates the one used by the medical profession to describe genius as a pathological condition, with its *erethisms* of which Moreau made so much, its *lesions*, its *neuroses*, its *disequilibrium*, and the *unhealthy conceptions of the brain*. The hydrocephalus of poor Jacques is a further borrowing from this pathologizing repertoire.

Claude, then, is a genius before he is a painter. Given the views of the medical literature of the day—which also included Lombroso's *Man of Genius* and Francis Galton's *Hereditary Genius* (1869)—the genius had much more than the mere painter to offer the novelist whose template was hereditary pathology. The artist novel was certainly a major feature of nineteenth-century fiction, and novelists almost always portrayed their painters as mad, but the madness in these texts was rarely the specific insanity of genius. Balzac's Frenhofer is more "master" than "genius," the latter term being reserved for the young Poussin, "the genius adolescent."[5] And although the painter hero of the Goncourts' *Manette Salomon* (1867) eventually goes mad, he is never portrayed as a genius.

If the painter is a natural candidate for Zola's exploration of genius, this is not just because painters are made by nineteenth-century novelists to bear the burden of the madness that, according to the statistical record, writers suffered to the same degree. Zola was closely associated with many of the painters of his time, including his childhood friend Cézanne, who is usually taken to have been the model for Claude. In Zola's many writings about painting genius is a recurrent point of reference, although the term is used mostly to convey positive aesthetic value, rather than latent pathology: "Genius alone is sovereign in art," he wrote in 1881. This positive connotation of genius is repeated in an essay on "L'argent dans la littérature" (Money in literature), written in 1880, where Zola states categorically that "genius alone matters," and he criticizes the system of patronage under the ancien régime because it was ill suited to the workings of "[g]enius as we understand it nowadays, with its disruptive power."[6]

Genius may be a largely positive term for Zola the art critic who regards disruption as a virtue, but for Zola the novelist these "disruptions" are an ambivalent quantity that allows him to explore it *both* positively as central to the artistic enterprise *and* negatively as a sterile or destructive pathology. Like Mme de Staël and Balzac, he does so both from an objective external and from a sympathetically internal perspective. Although the collaboration with Édouard Toulouse was still a decade off, he anticipates the scientific outlook by placing rather more distance than do either of the two other novelists between the authorial viewpoint and the failed genius he examines. As a painter, Lantier offers less scope for identification on the part of the author than did Corinne or Lambert, but both author—especially as projected into the figure of Sandoz—and painter are bound together by the issue of artistic creativity that is the novel's central concern.

Creative Genius

What Zola valued in genius was its creativity, the sheer capacity to produce, and in *Le Roman expérimental* (The experimental novel) he defends the experimental method on the grounds that it ensures the freedom of the novelist's "creative genius."[7] The biological thinking of the time—enthusiastically embraced by Zola—encouraged the conflation of creation and procreation that is applied both to his conception of the individual productions of the artist and to the artist's ability to engender a collective future for his chosen medium. Works of art are produced by the individual artist, but his productions also contribute to the genealogical evolution of his own profession. Pathology has a part to play in both processes.

The literary tradition of doomed artists contributes to this representation of pathology, but so too did Zola's view of contemporary art as debilitated by a "nervous crisis" that results for painters in "a breakdown of the entire cerebral mechanism." The ambivalent character of genius in the domain of midcentury painting is summed up when Zola writes that Delacroix was "[t]he only genius of our time," but that he was "afflicted by acute neurosis." This affliction notwithstanding, the "disruptions" of genius are presented as the means whereby painting might emerge from its stalled development, and in the *Ébauche* for *L'Œuvre* Zola writes that "[a]ll this new art . . . requires a *genius to be fully realized*."[8] In the novel itself, the entire art world is described as awaiting "the man of genius" capable of creating the masterpieces that would inaugurate a new era in painting.

Zola's portrayal of the characteristics of this kind of genius are relatively familiar: audacity, force, the unbridled energy of youth, total devotion to art, indifference to public opinion or material reward, and so on. Claude quite clearly fits the bill. He has youth, his life revolves entirely around his art, his painting is bold and energetic to the point where it is described as having a "superb violence." The older painter Bongrand—whose opinions are portrayed as entirely reliable—is full of admiration for Claude's *Plein air* (Open air) and says that he would give ten years of his life to have painted it. This is enough to encourage Claude to believe that he does indeed have the genius he aspires to. But as it turns out, his genius is not enough to enable him to create the masterpiece that would renew a stagnant artistic tradition.

Sandoz, a further source of reliable opinion, comments after Claude's death that "he was not the man for his own artistic formula . . . he hadn't quite the genius necessary to establish it on a firm foundation and impose it on the world in the form of some definitive work." As Claude himself surmises, his genius is "incomplete." The judgment, which he hears spoken behind his back one day (and which Zola himself notes in his preparatory draft for the novel), both flatters and horrifies him, and leads him to see his genius as poised on a knife edge between triumph and catastrophe.[9] The difference between the two is infinitesimal but decisive: the mere few grams of hereditary substance whose presence or absence will determine whether their bearer becomes a great man or a lunatic.

It is actually never quite clear in the novel whether Claude's pathology is his genius as such, or its insufficiency. The regular output of the novelist Sandoz does not depend on genius, and it seems to offer the more reliable means of artistic production. The contemporary medical view of genius as inherently unstable is illustrated by Claude whose working habits are portrayed as inveterately erratic. The ecstasy of inspiration experienced at the sight of Christine's naked breast and the ensuing frenzy of creativity quickly turn into "fever," "crisis," and an attack of "crazed rage." The courageous brutality of his painting all too easily becomes a destructive violence, expressed not just in Claude's frequent outbursts of anger but in the attacks on his own canvases: he punches a hole in the last one he paints. The masterly outline produced by an initial upsurge of creativity is spoiled through the painter's inability to move beyond the first moment of inspiration: "he was unable to finish what he had started."[10] His youth also eventually tells against him. Like the other characters, he grows older over the course of the novel but remains a child, usurping his own son for Christine's maternal attentions and thereby, it is hinted, contributing to the neglect that leads to Jacques's death. The potential of which Sandoz was once in awe is never realized, and the genius that was supposed to launch a new era in painting is destroyed by an increasingly sterile repetition of the gestures of youth, inspiration, and energy. The creativity of whatever genius he has is repeatedly aborted.

Women: Living Flesh and the Muse

This biologizing of artistic creativity inevitably introduces the issue of its gendering, and women are given a variety of roles to play in this connection. Zola is far from unique in providing his painter with a female companion. Following a paradigm established by Balzac's *Chef d'œuvre inconnu*, the plot of the artist novel frequently turns on the rivalry between the painter's mistress and his art. This certainly applies to *L'Œuvre* where Christine's sense of Claude's painting as rival is particularly acute. But in another narrative strand that runs through the tradition of the artist novel, the emphasis is on the threat posed by women to the ideals of the artist. Balzac's *La Maison du chat-qui-pelote* (At the sign of the cat and racket) is perhaps the source for this. Dating from 1829, it describes how the painter Théodore is captivated by the beauty of a young woman who becomes his muse and inspires the masterpiece that earns him recognition for his talents. However, after marrying her, he is obliged to recognize the "cruel truth" that his muse is quite indifferent to his art, and that "his wife was insensible to poetry, she did not inhabit his sphere . . . ; she walked prosaically through the real world, whereas he had his head in the heavens."[11] Augustine's origins as the daughter of a shopkeeper define the female sphere as domestic and pecuniary in ways that recur in many later novels.

This female sphere is regularly portrayed as a threat to an art whose integrity seems to depend on preserving its implicit masculinity against female contamination. The Goncourt brothers offer an extreme example of this, not just in real life, but also in their novels. The would-be writer, Charles Demailly, in the novel of that name, is brought low by the domesticity and banality of his wife Marthe, whose true nature he fails to spot before he marries her. Charles forgets what he once knew, namely that a writer cannot be a husband, and that celibacy is necessary for thought.[12]

In *Manette Salomon*, it is the woman rather than the painter who gives her name to the novel, and who is the conduit through which bourgeois domesticity, commerce, and the demands of family are introduced into the world of art, which is their antithesis. Like Demailly, Coriolis in principle knows better than to marry, and he spells out the various pitfalls of marriage over the course of several paragraphs, the key one of which reads as follows:

> In his view, celibacy was the only state that left the artist his freedom, his strength, his brain, his consciousness. He maintained the idea about women and wives, that it was

through them that artists become vulnerable to weakness, to subservience to fashion, accommodation with gain and commerce, renunciation of aspiration, to the sad courage to abandon the disinterestedness of their vocation and lower themselves to hasty and botched industrial production, and to money which mothers oblige them to earn from the humiliation and the sweat of talent. And on the far side of marriage there also lay fatherhood which, in his eyes, damages the artist, distracts him from his spiritual productions, and binds him to an inferior type of creation, reducing him to a bourgeois pride in the ownership of fleshly being.[13]

The emotional, domestic, financial, and procreative demands imposed by women are disastrous for the creative artist, and the rest of the Goncourts' novel bears this out. Art is portrayed as a male preserve that must be defended against the predations of a femininity that can also attack the artist from within: Coriolis's moments of weakness and creative inertia are ascribed to the feminine streak in his personality.

These views are echoed in a variety of more or less misogynistic scenarios in Alphonse Daudet's collection of portraits, *Les Femmes d'artistes* (Artists' wives), published in 1878, just a few years before Zola started work on *L'Œuvre*. (Daudet was a friend of Zola's.) Claude too invokes the need for celibacy when, toward the end of the novel, he suspends sexual relations with Christine and announces that "genius must be chaste, it must make love only to its own works."[14] Celibacy is the artist's only defense against the femininity that is art's undoing. Except that—and this is where the situation starts to become interesting—painters are portrayed as being uniquely dependent on women as models for their art.

If the novels are to be believed, almost every painting in the nineteenth century depicted a woman, and even where the woman is not the central subject of the painting, she is presented as the indispensable component for its success. Frenhofer's *Belle noiseuse*, Coriolis's *Bain turc*, and Claude's *Plein air* are all transformed and reenergized when the artist stumbles on the one woman who can serve as the model for his painting. So, despite the ferociously antifeminine principle of celibacy, it turns out that painting—and sculpture too, for that matter—is crucially reliant on the contribution of a woman. In most cases this contribution is provided by their beauty: Gillette, Augustine, and Manette Salomon are all remarkable for their physical perfection. On this score, however, Christine is different. What she offers to Claude is the living element of human flesh, which can be transferred into the painting itself. Painting in Zola's procreative aesthetic aspires not to beauty, but to life.

The accidental exposure of Christine's breast as she sleeps reveals to Claude the figure that he had tried in vain to find for his painting, and she provokes in him the "thrill" of inspiration. For Christine, however, the painter's gaze is felt as an almost physical raid on her flesh, and this physicality is carried over into the painted canvas: "[S]he was as revolted . . . as if it were herself lying there, stripped to her virgin nakedness. What hurt her more than anything, was the vehemence, the uncouthness of the painting itself; it pained her as if she had been assaulted and beaten." Claude works on his canvas as if he is assaulting the body he is in the process of portraying: "he attacked the breasts, which as yet were barely sketched in." But this assault is driven by the painter's desire to create flesh of his own: "His excitement grew, for, chaste as he was, he had a passion for the physical flesh of women, an insane love of nudity desired but never possessed, and he was powerless to satisfy himself or to create as much of the flesh as he dreamed of enfolding in an ecstatic embrace."[15]

Claude's virginality and his avoidance of women recall Pygmalion, but his desire is less to create his own painterly mistress than to turn canvas into living flesh, which is his criterion of artistic success. When the passage he is painting falters, he scrapes the canvas clean and the result is tantamount to murder: "It was murder he was committing, total obliteration . . . , all that remained . . . was a naked woman's body with neither head nor breast, a mutilated trunk, a vague, corpse-like shape, the dead flesh of the beauty of his dreams."[16] The canvas is restored to life only when Christine finally agrees to pose and offers her naked body—"female flesh"—to Claude's art.

She reluctantly makes the same offer when Claude fails to make progress with his final canvas, but the reluctance here is of a slightly different order. She is no longer young and her figure has been distorted by childbirth. More particularly she has an acute sense that the women on Claude's canvases are now the only ones that he is really interested in, and this includes her younger self portrayed in the *Plein air* piece. When he comes across his earlier canvas one day, he exclaims, "Elle a noirci" (She's turned black), where *elle* seems to refer as much to the woman as to the canvas (*la toile*) or to the paint (*la peinture, la couleur*). "He was completely in love with her, the way he talked about her as if she were a real person, a person he felt sudden urges to see again from time to time and who made him forget everything else in his haste to keep their rendezvous."[17]

As Claude frantically works on his doomed canvas, Christine is sacrificed in his desire to create a living figure in the painting. She is described as consenting to the "defeat of her body" as Claude "kills" her with the poses he requires of her "while he added to the charms of the other. . . . And was it not torture to have to make the sacrifice of her own body to help to bring the other woman to life?" Painting becomes an ever greater aggression practiced on the living model: the looks Claude directs at Christine from the top of his ladder are described as "slash[ing] across her like knives from shoulder to knee," and her body is dismembered and portioned out to the three figures on the boat according to whether the scene requires a breast, a belly, a shoulder or a foot.[18]

It is through his frustration at not ultimately being able to "create flesh" and "breathe life" that Claude eventually punches a hole in his canvas, which immediately appears to him like a wound from which the lifeblood of his work seems to be flowing. When he has finally succeeded in "closing" the wound, what remains is the faint trace of a "scar" just below the woman's heart. Claude's desire to create a living entity is reflected in this confusion of real and painted women, flesh and canvas, until the central figure takes on an eerie life of her own and Claude hears galloping behind him "the pale ghost of his nude figure, still formless after endless recastings and pursuing him now with its aching desire to be born."[19] She finally takes revenge on her failed creator as she wakes Claude from sleep and calls him to a death that may look like a suicide, but which his friend Sandoz claims was a strangling for which he blames the alarming dominatrix in the painting.

All this has a slightly gothic ring to it, but Claude's failure to realize his masterpiece goes to the heart of Zola's own aesthetic to which living flesh is also the key. Both Sandoz (who remains reliable on these matters) and Claude (who admittedly is not) share the ambition to capture life itself in their work. Sandoz dreams of creating an "ark" that would contain all life forms, and be produced "in the mighty flow of universal life" rather than in accordance with any manual of philosophy. If this sounds rather short on specifics, it nevertheless echoes the core motif of the demands Zola himself makes elsewhere, namely that the work of art consist of "blood and nerves," and that the artist give himself body and soul to his work. Or, in the words he places in the mouth of the painter in the essay on Courbet, "I am an artist, and I give you my flesh and my blood, my heart and my thought." Zola's Courbet belongs to the family of "makers of flesh," and his is a painting in which "firm, supple flesh is powerfully alive." In a wonderful formulation, Zola's imaginary artist "will applaud when he hears flesh cry out" (lorsqu'il entendra le cri de la chair), and it is this cry that echoes through L'Œuvre.[20]

BELLIES AND BIRTHING

The focus of Claude's preoccupation with living flesh is the belly (le ventre). Although he makes his first appearance in the Rougon-Macquart cycle with a small part in Le Ventre de Paris and its depiction of food in Les Halles, he himself is not much interested in food, and often forgets to eat in the frenzy of painting. It is Sandoz who, like his creator Zola, is the gourmet, and fills the bellies of his friends with the meals that unite the group of artist friends every Thursday, and whose menus are carefully recorded in the novel. The bellies that interest Claude are the bellies of women, and he has a particular talent, as the dealer Malgras notes, for painting this feature of their bodies. In trying to explain his "love of beautiful bellies" Claude says, "That's the part that's always thrilled me more than all the rest, the belly. . . . It's so lovely to paint, like sunshine."[21] As he paints the central figure of his final canvas, his brushstrokes are described as "caressing" her belly. Claude's bellies are always female bellies, but the embrace he pursues in his painted figures is less the expression of an erotic desire than a fantasized appropriation of the capacity of women to produce living flesh from within their own bodies.

Sandoz makes his own case for inclusion of the sexual act in his own work when he says, "[E]verything must be expressed ... and especially the sexual act, the origin and unceasing realisation of the world itself." For Sandoz too, sex is not the enactment of erotic desire, but, in an audible reference to the title of Courbet's famous painting of 1866, the "Origin of the world." The goal of art is to portray "nature's process of perpetual creation—in short, life itself, all life from end to end."[22] Claude's preoccupation with the female belly reflects this procreative emphasis; and it is as if in his increasing obsession with the belly of the woman in the canvas, he were desperately trying to find the key to create living flesh of his own. The dictionary definition of *le ventre* encompasses the entire abdominal cavity, but it becomes increasingly synonymous in *L'Œuvre* with the uterus. When Claude hangs himself in front of his canvas, his eyes are fixed on the figure's genitals, to which he has added a mystic rose as if in homage to their procreative powers. His dying breath is interpreted as having been a final attempt to breathe his soul into the painted canvas.

But it fails. And if it fails it is because he never succeeds in bringing forth what he himself has in his own belly. In his early, optimistic phase, he describes his view of the artistic process as follows: "What was Art, after all, if not simply giving out what you have in your belly? Didn't it all boil down to sticking a female in front of you and painting her as you feel she is?"[23] To give what one has inside one's belly is to paint a woman the way one experiences her—that is, in Claude's case—with the thrill that the flesh of her own belly inspires in him. The male artist and his female model are both endowed with this procreative belly through which, perhaps, each gives birth to the other. The female character of flesh is no longer confined to the female model, but becomes what the painter himself aspires to. And this is all the more bizarre when one recalls that it is precisely the procreative function of women that conventionally posed the greatest threat to genius.

The notion of artistic creation as a kind of birth is inescapable in *L'Œuvre*, and this feminization of the creative process is particularly noteworthy if one considers that the engendering capacity of genius was traditionally conceived as male. When the Goncourts make the claim in *Charles Demailly* that "our children are the works we create," it is part of their attempt to keep art separate from the female sphere and the demands of real children. In Zola's reworking of this idea through his focus on the actual birthing process whereby these "children" come into the world, he redefines artistic creation in unambiguously female terms. Zola's list of key words in the *Ébauche* includes *The Work, The living Work, The Work of flesh*, and so on, but also *Creation, create, procreate*, and then variously *Childbirth, Giving birth, Parturition, Conception, Bring forth, Fecundity, the blood of Childbed*, and again *Create, Give birth*.[24] These were the words running through Zola's head as he wrote *L'Œuvre*, and their drift is clear: *Creative Power* (another topic in the list) is nurtured in the womb and realized through parturition.

Claude's inspiration for his final doomed canvas is directly compared to the experience of women in pregnancy: "as if some process of germination were at work within him and something was coming to life, with the accompanying exaltation and nausea familiar to women in pregnancy."[25] Despite these promising symptoms, the pregnancy never reaches term, and the failure of Claude's genius is a generalized abortion, whether described as the failure of genius to give birth to a work of art, or as his inability to give birth to his own genius. Zola's attention is on a stalled process of parturition, and he is not attempting a detailed analysis of the mechanisms of genius itself.

In a bizarrely mixed gendering of this procreative view of artistic production, Bongrand is described as devoting himself to the "mightiest effort, the blow that he had been longing to strike for years, one last great work brought forth [*enfantée*] in his desire to prove that his virility was still unimpaired," before he finally admits that "he would never give birth to any more living works of art."[26] To "give birth" to a living work of art would be the mark of his virility. As with the mechanics of genius (does it give birth or is it given birth to?), the logic of parturition seems to override distinctions of gender itself.

Even Sandoz, for all that he is presented as succeeding where Claude fails and as having a paternal role in relation to his contemporaries, describes himself as being involved in an endless and agonizing birthing process: "I deliver my own offspring with forceps, and even then the child always looks to me like a monster." The regular labor of creation through which he produces the offspring that invariably disappoint him can be read as having overtones of this universal—and universally painful—reproductive biology. In the *Ébauche* Zola too notes that he intends to portray his own experience of the "inner life of production, an endless and very painful birthing." The "damned of art" are those who "die without being able to create life . . . and from not being able to deliver what they have in their bellies." Sandoz is drawing on the same idiom when he describes Claude's final canvas as an abortion, albeit "a superb abortion."[27]

This reproductive blight extends well beyond the artistic sphere, and is everywhere in the novel. The only biological births in *L'Œuvre* produce sickly children who will ultimately prove not to be viable: in addition to Jacques, who doesn't live beyond childhood, the two children of Margaillon the architect are the victims of the scrofula and the tuberculosis that are their biological inheritance. Sandoz originally has a job recording births in the *Mairie* of the fifth *arrondissement* in Paris, but the grave in which Claude is buried at the end of the novel lies next to a vast cemetery for children, a "children's city of death" with rows and rows of tombstones recording lives cut short at the ages of two years, sixteen months, five months, and, in the case of one little Eugénie, three days.

L'Œuvre was written at a time when Zola and his wife Alexandrine were suffering from their own childlessness, but the phenomenon of failed parturition is pervasive in the novel and integral to its treatment of genius. If none of the characters succeeds, and no masterpiece is created, this is ultimately ascribed to something much larger than the failure of individual genius. Or rather, individual genius is portrayed as being dependent on broader historical and cultural developments, which are themselves marked by morbidity. Sandoz's comments at Claude's funeral are as much a funeral speech for the times as a eulogy for the man. "The century has been a failure," he claims. "We're living in a bad season, in a vitiated atmosphere, with the century coming to an end and everything in process of demolition; buildings torn down wholesale; every plot of land being dug and redug and every mortal thing stinking of death." The solution to the times lies, however, with the times, since they are, Sandoz continues, a period of transition: "We are not an end; we're a transition, the beginning of something new."[28] For the "deficient reproducers" that Sandoz describes his generation as being, salvation lies with a belief in the continuities of a life force that will eventually result in a purging of contemporary corruption in the form of a viable birth—as happens with the arrival of the "unknown child" at the end of *Le Docteur Pascal* who is the offspring of a male scientist and a female artist.

The failed machismo of individual genius is counterpointed against this gradual evolutionary process whose rhythm is determined by a transcendent and implicitly female life force that gives birth in its own good time. Individual failure is to be seen in the context of a larger evolutionary process, as Sandoz suggests in his euology: "Could anything be more frustrating than seeing his new notation of light, his passion for reality, . . . the evolution he started with such originality, delayed, trifled with by a lot of smart nobodies, leading to nothing, simply because the man for the situation has yet to be born? . . . But he will be, one day! Nothing's ever completely wasted, and there's simply *got* to be light!"[29] This belief in the ultimate triumph of a beneficent life force is evident elsewhere in Zola's fiction, most notably, perhaps, at the end of *Germinal*, the novel that immediately preceded *L'Œuvre*. But its interest here lies in the way that it affects the perception of genius, and of its gender associations in particular.

Artistic creativity is powerfully feminized by being envisaged in terms of parturition; and the achievements of revolution and rupture associated with individual and implicitly male genius are offset against the continuities of an implicitly female life force. The effect, however, is not to open up the possibility of female genius, and there is no sense in Zola's novel that the twentieth century, whose arrival is so eagerly awaited, will offer a stage for the women whose genius Kristeva celebrates in *Le Génie féminin* (Female genius) and two of whom were already alive, namely, Colette (b. 1873) and Melanie Klein (b. 1882). So too was Gertrude Stein (b. 1874), who later unashamedly proclaimed her own genius through the mouth of Alice B. Toklas. For Zola, women's art, insofar as it exists at all, is minor: their preferred medium is the modest water color or pastel, and its examples are the fan painting from which Christine's mother makes a living, or the flower illustrations that Clotilde paints in *Le Docteur Pascal.*

Like Mme de Staël's portrait of Corinne or Balzac's study of Louis Lambert, Zola's depiction of failed genius in Claude Lantier is a complex affair, poised ambivalently between contradictory perspectives. In the first instance, it allows Zola to create another version of hereditary pathology to add to his Rougon-Macquart family saga, and he does so by drawing freely on the medical literature of the day. To this extent, fiction is merely replicating the view of genius established by the medical profession, and the novelist apparently shares their superior diagnostic vantage point. But the parturient imaginary through which the failures of genius are also represented ends up marginalizing genius within a much larger process, while turning the anxiety about creativity into an experience shared by a whole generation. It is as if Zola were not quite sure whether he himself aspired to genius or no, and his response is to leave the decision to his own biology, which Édouard Toulouse would scrutinize in such detail ten years later. By then Zola was the father of the two (illegitimate) children he had with Jeanne Rozerot—though he doesn't let on to Toulouse about their existence—and had completed the twenty volumes of Rougon-Macquart cycle. When he died in 1902, genius was moving into the hands of a new breed of professionals, the psychologists of intelligence, and its bearers were no longer virile or parturient artists and writers, but children themselves.

PART V

Precocity and Child Prodigies

CHAPTER 13

Exemplarity and Performance in Literature for Children

> Genius is always young, and essentially so. It never grows old.
> —Derrida, *Genèses, généalogies, genres et génie*

Youth and precocity have long since been written into the notion of genius. Although (Pseudo-)Aristotle's exceptional men are adults with proven achievements, Plato endows Ion with an arrogance and a naivety that make it hard to imagine him being anything other than young. From the ancient world onward, artistic talent presupposed its early manifestation and in the written lives of the Greek poets their gifts were likely to be marked by distinctive "portents" in childhood. In their history of the image of the artist, Ernst Kris and Otto Kurz also note the tendency of the "artist stories" of the Renaissance to include examples of this topos: "Several biographies tell of how the master first gave evidence of his gifts by sketching the animals he herded as a shepherd. Then a connoisseur happened to pass by, recognized the extraordinary talent in these first artistic endeavors, and watched over the proper training of this young shepherd, who later emerged as this or that far-famed genius."[1] These scenarios may have had more to do with the mythological thinking associated with traditional conceptions of the artist than with any precise theory of genius, but, as we shall see in what follows, the topos of precocious talent has been remarkably persistent. However, from the start of the nineteenth century to the mid-twentieth century, child prodigies and the childhood of genius—though not necessarily the same thing—became the focus of new forms of attention that subjected them to particularly intense scrutiny in three major areas: children's literature, experimental psychology, and, in the middle of the twentieth century, the popular press.

The association between genius and childhood was already implicit in the image of innate genius in the eighteenth century, gearing it essentially to youth. As Peter Kivy notes, Longinus's rediscovered theory of genius defines it as a power of expression that grows, flourishes, and must perforce decline, and this endows genius with an organic trajectory that privileges youthful vigor over venerable old age.[2] Being a natural endowment, genius is independent of learning, and the man of genius needs no instruction. As Dubos writes, "What a man born with genius does best is what no one has shown him how to do." This leads naturally (nature being the issue here) to the assumption that genius manifests itself at an early age when its inborn and untutored character will give rise to its spontaneous expression: "Everything becomes palette and brush in the hands of a child endowed with the genius of painting. He reveals himself to others for what he is, when he himself does not yet know."[3]

The organicist thinking that emerges at this time (and that is so clearly articulated by the appositely named Young) contributes to making youth integral to the notion of genius, when youth is invited to turn the tables on the spurious authority of age embodied in the ancients. With the nineteenth century this attitude gains further credence as Romanticism pits a younger generation against its anachronistically classicizing elders. Both in fact and in fiction, its poets were, almost by definition, youthful: Chatterton's purity and idealism are those of tender years, and in his preface to the play, Vigny defines this moment as the time when genius emerges in any poet: "It is in his first youth that he feels his strength come into being, and embraces humanity and nature with immense love." Vigny goes on to suggest that the vulnerability and idealism of youth are the pretext used by society as reasons for rejecting the poet: "it is then that people become suspicious of him and repulse him."[4]

As we saw in chapter 5, Chateaubriand hailed Hugo as "a sublime *child*," and he was only twenty when he published his *Odes et ballades*. Louis Lambert's genius comes into its own during his adolescence, which it does not convincingly outlast. This equivalence of genius and youth—or even childhood—became a commonplace in the nineteenth-century imaginary, to the point where the genius, whatever his chronological age, was perceived as a perpetual child. Schopenhauer's account of genius accords a privileged place to childhood as its abiding characteristic: "every child is to a certain extent a genius, and every genius to a certain extent a child." Or again: "every genius is already a big child, since he looks out onto the world as into something strange and foreign . . . , and thus with purely objective interest." For Michelet too, genius had an affinity with childhood through the freshness of its vision, unclouded by received wisdom or excessive analysis. So much so, in fact, that the man of genius embodied the qualities of childhood in ways that real children never do: "Genius has the gift of childhood as no child ever has it." This is because "[g]enius retains native instinct in its greatness and its powerful drive, along with a God-given grace that unfortunately children lose—young and lively hope."[5] Childhood made sense of a way of thinking about genius when genius was seen not only as innate and original, but more specifically as having the ability to purge the world of the prejudices and presuppositions of convention and stereotype.

Baudelaire: Genius as Childhood Recovered at Will

This, albeit in a more nuanced form, is the claim made by Baudelaire when, in *Le Peintre de la vie moderne* (The painter of modern life), he writes that "genius is simply childhood *recovered at will*," or, as he puts it in *Les Paradis artificiels* (Artificial paradises), it is "childhood clearly formulated." Baudelaire provides a theoretical underpinning for the nineteenth-century tendency to equate poetic genius with youth. The genius shares with the child and the convalescent the ability to see the world afresh, to be alive to its shapes and its colors in the most apparently insignificant objects: "It is to this deep and joyful curiosity that one should ascribe the fixed stare and animal ecstasy of children in the face of something new, whatever it may be." But if genius is synonymous with childhood in this account, it is a childhood rediscovered and "reformulated" by the adult artist. Genius and childhood are not strictly interchangeable, since "[t]he nerves of the man of genius are strong, those of children are weak."[6] The nervous system of adult genius makes it possible to withstand the disruptive effects of inspiration that might destroy a child. Furthermore, genius requires the adult attributes of "virility" and analysis: the childhood voluntarily regained by genius is a "childhood now endowed for the purposes of expression with virile organs and an analytical mind, which allow it to order the sum of involuntarily amassed material."[7] Childhood constitutes a dual horizon for the artist of genius: it lies in the past but can be retrieved and reinvented in a future that requires the aid of adult strength and mature organizational control.

Baudelaire uses the term "genius" in connection with almost all of the painters, poets, and composers he admired (Delacroix, Poe, Wagner). In his essay on Wagner, he defines genius as "*will, desire, concentration, nervous intensity*," adding that it is an amplification of a response first experienced in childhood: "The child's small sorrow or delight, disproportionately magnified by an exquisite sensitivity, later becomes the principle of a work of art in the grown man, who may not even be aware of it." The sources of the artist's genius also lie in the reverie and imagination first experienced in childhood. The child can conjure up a whole world with his toys, where, as Baudelaire says in *Morale du joujou* (The morality of toys), they become "actors in the great drama of life." Battles can be fought with corks for soldiers, books for fortifications, and marbles for ammunition, and these are enough to fill the child's imagined world with casualties, hostages, prisoners, peace treaties, and even taxes. This ability to "satisfy the imagination" is the prototype for artistic creation, and toys are "the child's first initiation into art, or rather, its first realization." So much so, in fact, that the satisfactions they bring can never be equaled by the "perfected realizations" of the adult artist.[8] In sum, although Baudelaire's artist-genius is not actually a child, childhood provides an experience of curiosity, of vision, of emotional intensity, and perhaps above all of creative imagination, out of which his art will develop and to which he also needs to return.

Precocity, then, is a recurrent feature of the ways in which genius was conceptualized from the beginning of the eighteenth century onward: its innateness, its individual character, its natural expressiveness, its originality, and its energies all predisposed genius to early manifestation. Genius and childhood consequently became increasingly interchangeable concepts, and accounts of the early years of genius along with stories about "the childhood of famous men" helped to create the figure of the child prodigy through which the idea of genius was reshaped for the edification of all children.

FAMOUS CHILDREN AND CHILDREN'S LITERATURE

When Balzac has le Père Haugoult announce to his class the imminent arrival of "the most extraordinary new boy" in *Louis Lambert*, he paints the portrait of the child prodigy as the nineteenth century fondly created and imagined it: "already a poet, beloved by Mme de Staël, [and] a future genius." Having recently read Nougaret's recently published *Enfans célèbres* (Famous children), the narrator is only too ready to be persuaded by the portrait of the new arrival, and he excitedly recalls Nougaret's examples of the young Montcalm, Pico della Mirandola, Pascal, and all the other "precocious brains, famous anomalies in the history of the human mind" to whose names he assumes Lambert's would soon be added.[9]

The full title of Nougaret's compendium of famous children runs over several lines and spells out the attributes of these juvenile paragons: *Famous children among ancient and modern peoples, renowned for their precocious talents; for the astonishing progress made in their studies, in science and in poetry; for their witty, naïve and innocent responses; for their presence of mind and their mischief; for their heroism, their wisdom, the virtues they draw out, and even for their serious failings.* Nougaret does not distinguish between famous children and the childhoods of famous men (and a few women). Candiac de Montcalm was a prodigy of learning, who had mastered Latin by the age of four, and, while his coevals were stammering their first prayers, he had already assimilated the works of a multitude of historians, orators, epistolarians, grammarians, and philosophers, and was soon conversing with academicians about geometry, languages, history, and geography, for which he displayed a particular aptitude. However, the boy died at the age of seven, and his fame therefore rested on the manner in which he conducted himself in childhood.

Pascal's childhood was like that of Bossuet portrayed in the same volume, who, "while still a child, offered happy signs of what he would one day become." Nougaret devotes one of his longest entries to the story of the young Pascal's curiosity about a resonating glass accidentally struck at the dinner table, and the persistence that led the boy to discover the first thirty-three of Euclid's propositions for himself "through the sole penetration of his genius."[10] But whether the children were famous for what they were as children, or whether their childhoods were described for what they intimated of the adult genius, they were equally exemplary.

The book was one of the first instances of the nineteenth-century literature of exemplarity that portrayed child prodigies for the benefit of child readers in a new climate of "solicitousness toward children."[11] These tales were part of the more general emergence of literature for children that saw the publication of illustrated alphabets in the 1820s, and that took off in the 1850s with Mme de Ségur's books for children and the creation of *La Bibliothèque rose* (The pink library) by the publisher Hachette. The genre of "famous children" or "childhoods of famous men" serves to promote the notion of the child prodigy in the nineteenth century, and to give a particular and very popular form to the equation between childhood and genius.

Nougaret's *Les Enfans célèbres* was published one year before Pierre Blanchard's scarcely less wordily titled *Modèles des enfans, traits d'humanité, de piété filiale, d'amour fraternel, et progrès extraordinaires de la part d'enfans de six à douze ans* (Models of childhood, acts of humanity, filial piety, brotherly love, and extraordinary progress on the part of children aged between six and twelve—an amusing and moral volume), and over a decade after Anne-François Joachim Fréville's *Vie des enfans célèbres, ou les modèles du jeune âge* (Lives of famous children or models of tender years), dating from 1797. The child prodigy is presented as a model for other children on the grounds of his precocity and the speed at which he develops his talents, which in most accounts are inseparable from the emphasis on his moral qualities advertised by Blanchard's title. Many other books followed in the same vein, and like recipe books and dictionaries, they often recycle the same material, recounting the same episodes in the lives of the same children, and always with the moral improvement of their readers in mind.

This use of children as models of behavior for their child readers goes back as far as 1688 and Adrien Baillet's *Des enfans devenus célèbres par leurs études ou par leurs écrits* (Children made famous by their studies or their writings), which establishes the principle of "inciting Children to the Study of Letters and to the Love of Science through examples of every type," as the publisher's preface has it.[12] Baillet was the librarian of the advocate general, François-Chrétien de Lamoignon, and his book was explicitly directed at his employer's son, whose age and inclinations determined its contents. His prodigies are prodigies of learning, and it is their studiousness that is presented as the key to their precocious attainments.

Baillet's volume contains some eighty portraits with examples from the ancient world (the majority) to the present day, and includes future staples such as

Pico della Mirandola and Pascal along with classical figures such as the Greek comic poet, Eupolis, who had written seventeen comedies by the age of seventeen, Pliny the Younger, who wrote a tragedy at the age of sixteen, and Alexander, whose military feats were the result of conceptions that would have been impossible without the studies to which he had devoted himself since childhood. The precocity of these achievements is constantly emphasized through references to the age of the young protagonists, supporting Baillet's claim that children are never too young to study, and that it is in childhood that the habits of a lifetime can best be formed. The diligence that was later contrasted with the spontaneous nature of genius is portrayed here as one of its key virtues.

Providing children with the example of other children is mentioned by several of the nineteenth-century authors as a way of encouraging in them what Nougaret terms a "noble emulation." The "gallery of *Models*" assembled by Blanchard in his *Modèles des enfans* is based on the widely held belief that children are imitators. Speaking over the heads of his young readers to the adults who are advised to read and discuss the book with their charges, he continues with his advice: "[T]ake advantage of this natural disposition; present them with wise beings of their own size, heroes of their own age; they will soon want to be like them; they will, so to speak, repeat their actions. If you wish, it will just be a kind of game to start with; but this imitation, or better still, this emulation will accustom their young hearts to good actions and give them a taste for such things."

Virtuous action is Blanchard's main goal, and there are as many anonymous and presumably fictional examples of this—"*L'écolier généreux*" (The generous schoolboy), for instance—as there are historically attested ones, such as the "Amitié de Caton pour son Frère" (Cato's friendship toward his brother), and the ubiquitous "Pascal, enfant." Blanchard's narrative is interrupted by occasional exchanges with his postulated young readers whose reactions show them to be responsive to the models of behavior the book proposes for them. If there is precocity here, it is implied in the exercise of virtue, rather than in the learning celebrated by Baillet. Nougaret, however, lays claim to both aspirations, and he mentions his desire to "inspire [children] with love of the virtues" as well as to "redouble their zeal and application to their studies."[13]

Mme Touchard, in the preface to *L'Enfance des grands hommes* (The childhoods of great men) dating from 1821, adds patriotism to the aims of this literature. By familiarizing children with the names of great men, she hopes to encourage her readers to extend their affection from the nation's great individuals to the nation itself. But emulation is as much part of the design as affection. The "great captains" and the "good writers" (they include Turenne and Condé, as well as Pascal and Racine), on whom national prestige depends, are portrayed at the age of the adolescent readers to whom the book is addressed and who are implicitly destined for the same careers. The emulation here is professional: the great soldiers and writers of the future are to be created by reading about the best examples from the past.

EDIFYING VIRTUE

There are, however, limits to emulation. Eugénie Foa warns her young readers against excessive ambition, and, assuming that they are too young to be impressed by an aristocracy based on the "wealth of fine names," she urges upon them the thrill that derives from the "aristocracy of talents."[14] For Jules Caboche-Demerville, whose *Panthéon de la jeunesse: vies des enfants célèbres de tous les temps et de tous les pays* (A pantheon of youth: lives of famous children from all times and all places) appeared in 1842, one year before Mme Foa's *Contes historiques pour la jeunesse* (Historical tales for young people), there is a risk that these books about famous children will create a desire for fame itself, rather than for its cause: "[I]n writing the lives of famous children, and in offering them to be admired by children like themselves, the author did not, thank Goodness, intend to create in the hearts of his young readers a love of precocious celebrity. . . . [H]e places happiness above all wealth and he does not believe that celebrity is happiness."

His own volume is designed to encourage "the simple, innocent and hidden virtues of the family," and the stories are intended as an antidote to the celebrity culture of French society under the bourgeois monarchy: "We live under a type of government that excites and licenses every kind of ambition; we live in a century where everyone is carried away by an immoderate desire for wealth and luxury." Fame is associated with a desire for material gain that has disrupted the social order: "celebrity frequently brings riches, and everybody has been overtaken by a love of celebrity: from the humblest shopkeeper to the orator or the most famous poet, everybody is seeking to have his name proclaimed far and wide by the thousand voices of publicity." The ultimate—explicitly Christian—goal of Caboche-Demerville is to instill in his readers the moral qualities and the simple virtues of his young heroes by reminding them that in addition to the famous examples he describes, there are other "children [who] have distinguished themselves through acts of courage, devotion, probity, bravery and charity," and whose modest example demonstrates that "consideration and fortune never fail to reward those who wish to conquer them through work and study."[15]

The discrepancy between the fame of the examples and the outcome desired by the authors for their readers becomes even clearer in the case of girls. Although the majority of the prodigies portrayed in these books are boys, there is explicit consideration of a female readership. The second part of each of Caboche-Demerville's two volumes is devoted to "famous girls" from

Sainte-Geneviève to Louise Labbé (*sic*), Joan of Arc, Jacqueline Pascal, and Charlotte Corday. Adrien Baillet also has a general chapter justifying the benefits of study for girls, and Mme Touchard includes two examples of famous girls: Jacqueline Pascal—who becomes almost as important as her brother in this literature—and Anne Dacier, who later translated Homer into French. Pierre Blanchard produced a sequel to *Modèles des enfans* devoted entirely to girls, and Mme Foa includes three girls in her *Contes historiques pour la jeunesse*, as does Victor Delcroix in *Les Jeunes enfants illustres* (Illustrious young children, 1862).

Louise Colet in her *Enfances célèbres* (Famous childhoods, 1854) and Mlle Émilie Carpentier in *Les Enfants célèbres* (Famous children, 1869) both present the childhood of a famous man from the perspective of his sister. Correggio is a character in Mlle Carpentier's story of "La Sœur d'Antonio" (Antonio's sister), and in Louise Colet's book, Filippo Lippi and Blaise Pascal are both upstaged in the narrative by their sisters. The many female authors of these collections have had an understandable interest in the development and place of girls, but their inclusion is used largely to redirect any desire for unseemly celebrity toward filial piety and sisterly devotion. Mme Touchard specifically mentions that the girls in her collection represent "models of virtue, learning and candor," and she states that she has avoided portraying any "heroines" because she did not want to "turn our young misses into amazons."[16] Instead, she says, "it is taste that we have sought to inspire," taste having been specifically mentioned by Virey in his entry to the *Dictionnaire des sciences médicales* as an essentially female quality, which he contrasts with the masculine characteristics of genius.

Blanchard makes a similar distinction in the introduction to his volume of *Modèles des jeunes personnes* (Models of young persons), for and about girls, when he comments that "[t]hese are not heroines that we offer as models, but tender and submissive girls, charitable persons, virtuous wives, and mothers who sacrifice everything to their duty." This is because "[g]entle and habitual virtues . . . are those that befit the gentler sex, and the only ones through which they contribute happiness to society."[17] The authors' concern with the education of girls emphasizes the role of the literature of edification in inculcating private virtue through the exhibition of public example. Both precocity and celebrity would have been unbecoming in the fairer sex, and they are not in and of themselves the primary goals for boys. The emphasis in these little cameos is on the effort that the anticipated readers are implicitly incited to make, and this too is in equally implicit contrast to the spontaneity of the expression of the prodigy's genius. The young reader needs to be encouraged to study and to work by means of the example of those for whom these activities were, as it were, in their nature, and for whom even the perseverance, of which genius provides so many examples, is an innate proclivity.

The young Pascal (a very different figure from Lélut's victim of hallucinations) cannot help re-creating Euclid's propositions, despite his father's banning

Figure 8. The young Pascal studying geometry. Illustration from Louise Colet, *Enfances célèbres* (1854).

of mathematical books (Figure 8). In Victor Delcroix's *Les jeunes enfants illustres*, the young Mozart will not be kept away from his harpsichord, and his father has to lock the instrument and hide the key in order to get the boy to go outside and play like other children. In Mlle Carpentier's story of the young Linnaeus reduced to mending shoes to make money, his devotion to botany is such that "[t]hanks to the indefatigable perseverance associated with true genius, he triumphed over fate, and, after many struggles, saw a brilliant future opening up before him." The speed of these events contributes powerfully to the sense of the inevitability of genius's triumph over adversity. It may not be possible to emulate genius itself, but tenacity is a virtue that all children are invited to exercise, and the child prodigy is used as a means of instilling qualities other than those of genius in its young admirers.

Sentiment and Spectacle

By the midcentury, the tone of this literature has become much more sentimental and much less overtly edificatory. Louise Colet (who published the *Enfances célèbres* as a money spinner in the year her relationship with Flaubert came to an end) cites as the motive for her account of various famous childhoods, the wish to "awaken in young minds a desire to become acquainted with the work or the noble actions of those glorious lives." Curiosity about the origins of the lives of great men and women replaces emulation as the basis of the reader's anticipated interest: "we want to get to know the father and the mother of the predestined child; it gives us pleasure to be initiated into the scenes of his youth, to see him loved by a sister or a brother."[18] There are more illustrations to accompany the printed text than in the earlier publications, the stories are longer, and they include imagined dialogues and (possibly) imaginary characters: it is hard to be sure whether Correggio's sister Angela in Mme Carpentier's portrait of the young painter or Buonavita the bandit who kidnaps Louise Colet's Filippo Lippi really existed.

The narrators often introduce their juvenile heroes quasi-anonymously. The young Correggio as portrayed by Émilie Carpentier appears as little Antonio who lives in village incidentally named Correggio. Molière is introduced in a story titled "Le petit tapissier" (The little upholsterer) as Jean, the son of M. Poquelin, upholsterer to the king. And in Louise Colet's account of Mozart hearing Allegri's *Miserere*, he is described simply as "[a] solitary child, aged twelve or fourteen, of slender build, with an intelligent face and a high forehead whose large pale-blue eyes sparkled beneath his powdered hair [and who] seemed to be paying no attention to the fresco. . . . His head was raised and tilted right back, his eyes in ecstasies, his mouth smiling and half open as if to savor the sounds that rose . . . , everything about the boy expressed the liveliest and most excited attention."[19] It is not until seven pages later that we read, "This prodigious child was Mozart." Of course, the reader knows all along who the prodigy "really" is, not least because in the case of Louise Colet's stories, each of them is preceded by a little "notice" summarizing the life and achievements of the figure in question.

As future genius, the child is always "predestined," to use Colet's own word, and his illusory anonymity is just another way of expressing the inevitability of the realization of his gifts. Mlle Carpentier's young Poquelin accidentally spoils a piece of cloth in his desire to get back to reading his favorite dramatist, Corneille, and Colet's Filippo Lippi neglects the sheep he should be tending because his mind is on the Madonnas and the angels that he dreams of painting. He draws a picture of the family cat on his plate with the jam from his bread, and the cow in the byre acquires a twin in the form of the creature portrayed by the young Filippo on the wall beside her. These child prodigies cannot help themselves because their talent is an imperative that determines their every action. As Louise Colet says of the young Rameau, "every instinct propelled him toward music," and the boy confirms this when he announces that "my *vocation* calls me and I must obey."[20]

Genius will out, being spontaneously expressed and driven by an unstoppable vocation toward its realization in the adult work of genius. The tease of pseudo-anonymity is part of the two-way equation whereby the child prodigy predicts the adult genius, and the adult retrospectively confirms the burgeoning talents of the child. The reader is so far removed from the child protagonist that his relation to the young prodigy can only be one of curiosity and admiration. Any idea of emulation now seems irrelevant and genius has become a spectacle that confirms its own promise.

PERFORMANCE

These tales frequently stage obstructive or hostile adults who stand in the way of the prodigy's path with the result that the child is repeatedly called upon to perform his genius in order to convince doubters or opponents. Fortunately, the hardest of hearts will always melt at the sight of the talent of the future genius whose gifts leave the adults overwhelmed by admiration. The pope is charmed by the young Mozart in Victor Delcroix's repetition of the story of the boy's "theft" from the Vatican of Allegri's *Miserere*, whose music he writes down after hearing it only once. Far from punishing the "thief" as everyone expects, the Holy Father sees the boy's feat as proof of a God-given gift, for which he predicts a great future: "My son, God has placed genius in you: you will be greater than Allegri."[21] The adult Mozart duly confirms the prediction by creating his greatest piece of music (this is Delcroix's view) in the form of the God-fearing *Requiem*, composed on his deathbed. In Louise Colet's dramatized account of Filippo Lippi, the cruel bandit who has taken Filippo and his sister prisoner and threatens to make their parents destitute relents when he sees the portrait of one of the other brigands that the young Filippo has drawn. With such incontrovertible proof of the boy's talent, the bandit releases the children and also insists that the parents free Filippo from having to mind the family sheep and allow him to become the great painter he is clearly destined to be. The boy's talent has simultaneously saved his family from destitution and opened the way to his future as Fra Lippo Lippi.

The spectacle of the prodigy's precocity repeatedly astounds the adults: "Such precocious talent had never before been seen," writes Delcroix of the six-year-old Mozart. But however self-evident the prodigy's talent, it has nonetheless to be performed for the benefit of the adults whose admiration and emotional response duly provide confirmation of the child's future destiny. When Louise Colet has Jacqueline Pascal read her poems before an audience of ladies from the court, the queen refuses to believe that they could have been written by so young a child or without the help of an adult. Undaunted, Jacqueline, who is characterized as being as gifted in poetry as her brother is in science, immediately retreats to a quiet corner at the prompting of one of the other ladies and "improvises" a poem, "À Mademoiselle de Montpensier, *Fait sur-le-champ à son commandement*" (To Mlle de Montpensier, Composed on the spot at her command), followed by another in response to a further request from one Mme d'Hautefort.[22] The doubts about Jacqueline's authorship provide the pretext for a convincing demonstration of her exceptional talents, through which all suspicions are rapidly dispelled,

The self-evidence of genius that is denied by the wider world to the poets of the nineteenth century is abundantly—if sometimes belatedly—accorded to the child prodigies in these narratives for and about children. Equally, the childhoods depicted in the literature for children have little of the kind that Baudelaire's poet sought to recover at will and to relive with the maturity of poetic virility. The goals of emulation and emotion resurrect responses to genius more typical of the previous century, but when associated with the child prodigy as innocent performer of his or her gifts, they serve primarily to instill the socially consecrated attributes of studiousness, virtue, and perseverance in children who will grow up to become good citizens rather than any kind of exception. Genius is used by these authors to inculcate something other than itself, while passing on the legacy of its image as precocious talent.

CHAPTER 14

Alfred Binet and the Measurement of Intelligence

> Without the use of scales for measuring intelligence we can give no better answer as to the essential difference between a genius and a fool than is to be found in legend and fiction.
>
> —Lewis M. Terman, *The Measurement of Intelligence*

Children's literature was not the only means whereby the figure of the child prodigy was constructed, and at the turn of the century the new discipline of experimental psychology had its own part to play. If the precocity of the child prodigy is to have any basis, it will be vastly helped by the existence of a reliable scale for measuring the achievements of an average child, against which exceptional ability can then be gauged. The assessment of the talents that astonish the admiring adults in the lives of famous children is an impressionistic affair, but in the twentieth century the IQ test and developmental norms established by the new discipline of experimental psychology made it possible to calculate the degree of precocity that would supposedly identify any genius in the making.

Alfred Binet's "measuring scale of intelligence," which he devised and successively refined between 1905 and 1911 (the year he died), was picked up and developed by a group of American psychologists working under Lewis Terman at Stanford University. Terman had always been interested in genius, and his dissertation of 1906 was titled "Genius and Stupidity: A Study of Some of the Intellectual Processes of Seven Bright and Seven Stupid Boys," but it was Binet's scale that provided him with the basis for his subsequent work.[1] Terman and his associates used their adapted version of the test—the so-called Stanford-Binet Test—as the principal tool of investigation in their four-volume longitudinal study, Genetic Studies of Genius, which tracked the development of a group of intellectually gifted boys and girls into adulthood. It was also used in a quite extraordinary project to retrospectively calculate the level of intelligence in 301 geniuses of the past.[2] From all this it looked as though the discipline of developmental psychology could provide the tools for measuring genius as superior intelligence, and predict the geniuses of the future by identifying talented children. The modern version of the test explicitly ranks any score of 145 or more in terms of degrees of genius, namely,

> 145–154: genius (e.g., professors)
> 155–164: genius (e.g., Nobel Prize winners)
> 165–179: high genius
> 180–200: highest genius
> >200: unmeasurable genius

On this showing, anyone reading these pages is likely to be near or even within the category of "genius."

For the experimental psychologist, genius is defined as the top end of a single scale of intelligence whose nether regions are incrementally represented by debility, imbecility, and idiocy, to use the terms current at the turn of the century. The notions of creativity, originality, inspiration are replaced by the umbrella concept of intelligence, which already had currency in the work of Séailles and Toulouse. Rather than some kind of break or disruption, or even some kind of antithetical "other" such as *esprit*, intelligence is conceived in terms of progressive gradations that separate the two extremes of stupidity and genius, and as a mental attribute that develops incrementally through time with the growth of the child.

Hippolyte Taine's *De l'intelligence* (On intelligence, 1870) had already argued for a measurable concept of intelligence to replace the vaguer notion of "understanding or intellect," and his approach helped to establish the new discipline of experimental psychology. This discipline is "a factual science," and in Taine's account, intelligence is no longer a "deep and mysterious essence, which is sustained and concealed beneath the flux of transient phenomena," but a "flux and a bundle of sensations and impulses" or "a bundle of nervous vibrations" amenable to scientific scrutiny. More particularly, factual science will document the phenomena it observes on the basis of their genesis and development: "our main task is to discover what these entities are, how they emerge, and in what manner and under what conditions they combine."[3]

Science also places the human mind on a continuum that connects man to "the lower animals," where the difference between the animal and the human mind is merely a matter of degree, similar, in Taine's formulation, to the difference between the "well-endowed" races such as the Greeks and the Aryans and the "poorly endowed" ones such as the Australians and the Papuans. This difference in turn resembles that between "a genius" and "a numbskull."[4] These (historically dated) examples all confirm the concept of graded intelligence, which is replicated in the development of the human child. Intelligence, in other words, is a developmental affair, whether in the gradations that relate slow wits to genius or in the progress of the child from infancy to adulthood. And it is the task of experimental psychology to devise these incremental scales.

Scientific interest in child development became established as an academic discipline toward the end of the nineteenth century.[5] In France, Bernard Perez, author of a number of studies of children from birth to the age of seven, describes himself in the preface to *L'Enfant de trois à sept ans* (The child from the age of three to seven, 1886) as being one of the first to take a scientific interest in "infant psychology," which was otherwise documented only by novelists in whom he sees "psychologists minus the qualifications," and who thereby contributed to "the advancement of the science of children."[6] Writing in 1903, Alfred Binet described psychology as undergoing "a decisive evolution" thanks to the new possibilities that now existed for undertaking "rigorous experimental study of the higher forms of mental activity."[7] In 1894 he founded the *Année psychologique*, one of the first scientific journals devoted to the discipline, and he was the second director of the Laboratory of Physiological Psychology at the Sorbonne, founded in 1889.

In 1909, reflecting on a lifetime's work in this field, which he summarizes in *Les Idées modernes sur les enfants* (Modern ideas concerning children), Binet makes a powerful case for the value of this discipline—for which he adopts the recent coinage *pédologie*—on the grounds that it is qualified to identify intelligence in ways that, despite their pretensions, neither pedagogy nor medicine can match. It was a young discipline, which Binet says had been in existence for just three decades, predominantly in America and Germany, and hitherto only "a little" in France.[8] However, thanks to his invention of a "measuring scale of intelligence" Binet put France at the forefront of developmental psychology, and in the words of the American introduction to the 1916 translation of *Les Idées modernes sur les enfants*, Binet's measuring scale was a "magnum opus" whose rapid acceptance worldwide was "little less than marvelous."[9] It established a language in which genius could be quantified, and precocity plotted against scientifically established developmental norms.

INTELLIGENCE AND MENTAL RETARDATION

The measurement of genius was, however, very far from being Binet's aim. His scale was devised in response to a request from a commission set up by the French minister of public instruction in 1904 to explore strategies for educating retarded children. The special education that the commission proposed for such children required effective procedures to identify those capable of benefitting from it. In other words, the aim was to identify *débiles* (the mentally retarded) rather than prodigies, and indeed to use a scientific diagnosis of lower intelligence to differentiate between these *débiles*, and the weaker *imbéciles* and *idiots*. "There is nothing of greater interest," wrote Binet, "than discovering the psychology of dunces."[10] The tests by which these "dunces" could be identified were the result of the examination undertaken by Binet and his medically qualified associate, Théodore Simon, of more than two hundred children in various schools in Paris. This allowed them to establish a set of norms for age-specific achievements against which individual children could then be assessed.

Taking a broad view of intelligence, defined by Binet as "the faculty of knowledge, which is directed toward the outside world, and which labors to reconstruct it as a whole," they established a number of criteria that would make it possible to track the development of this faculty in children. They noted for example that it is at the age of five (and not four) that a child can compare two boxes of different weights and identify the heavier one; or that she can copy a square, and repeat a phrase of ten syllables (but not more). At eight he can name four colors and count backward from twenty, at twelve she can give definitions of abstract words, and at fifteen he can repeat seven figures, find three rhymes for a given word, and interpret—as opposed to merely describe—a scene in an engraving. The aim of the scale was to "determine whether a given subject has the intelligence of his age, or whether he is behind or ahead, and by how many months or years," and it was calibrated so as to produce an equal distribution of children who were ahead of the norm for their age as of children who were behind.[11]

Of these, almost all were no more than one year ahead or behind, and out of a sample of 203 schoolchildren only 2 were two years in advance of their peers. Two years difference in the other direction constituted, in Binet's words, "an extremely serious presumption of retardation." It was these children who were to benefit from the special education provided for them, and benefit they did, as many of them were able to make up for a whole year's retardation within a single year. Binet believed very strongly in the "educability of intelligence," and the purpose of the test was to match the aptitude of the child to the type of education on offer.[12] Or rather, the other way round, since Binet was highly critical of the existing school curriculum, which, in his view, failed to take into account the characteristics of the intelligence of children at different ages. In his view, developmental psychology was not primarily a means of identifying prodigies, so much as the basis for improving the education system, which he regarded as being in crisis.

Binet's horizons are collective and broadly utopian, and his ideal is a society where every individual—not just the exceptional prodigy—is able to realize his or her individual aptitudes, whether these be intellectual or manual, creative or methodical. Educating the weakest students is to the advantage of the rest of the populace because the number of "useless" citizens will be thereby reduced, along with the risk of the nuisance they might otherwise cause. The diagnosis of intelligence made possible by developmental psychology could help to create a future where society would be better organized, and where "each individual would work in accordance with his recognized aptitude, so that not one iota of his psychic strength was lost to society." Binet acknowledges that this would be "a utopian ideal" and that "[i]t is still a long way off."[13]

Unlike his North American successors, Binet makes only brief mention of children at the top end of the scale, whom he describes as *surnormaux* (supernormal, above average), but they too have their part to play in this utopian order, and he envisages the provision of special education to ensure the greatest social profit from their talents. Just as pity is irrelevant as a response to the feebleminded, so there is no sentiment here, no adult admiration for genius in the making. The talents of these *surnormaux*—now more commonly known as *surdoués* (gifted)—should be harnessed for the benefit of social progress to which they make a unique contribution: "[I]t is by means of the élite, and not through the efforts of the average population, that humanity invents and progresses; society therefore has an interest in ensuring that the elite receives the culture that it needs. A child of superior intelligence is a force not to be lost."[14] The developmental model of individual intelligence has implications for society at large and provides a means to integrate both extremes of intelligence into a continuous social whole.

Measurement and calculation were essential to the successful execution of Binet's "mental tests," although he is careful to insist that they cannot be mechanically administered, and that the computing of intelligence does not work like a weighing machine in a railway station, which spits out the result the instant anyone steps onto the scales.[15] He compares the test to a scientific tool like a microscope whose use requires professional expertise, and there is a considerable degree of humanity in his understanding of children. He is interested not just in levels of intelligence, but in its different types (subjective vs. objective) illustrated in his own two daughters, whom he describes in his 1903 study, *L'Étude expérimentale de l'intelligence* (The experimental study of intelligence). He is also very aware of the social and other factors that impinge on the intellectual performance of children. Measurement is nonetheless the key to understanding the mechanism and to translating it into a meaningful scale. Which takes us back to the 1890s and Binet's encounter with two mathematical prodigies, Jacques Inaudi and Pericles Diamandi, whose cases he wrote up in *Psychologie des grands calculateurs et joueurs d'échecs* (The psychology of remarkable calculators and chess players) in 1894.

CALCULATING PRODIGIES

In 1880, the thirteen-year-old Jacques Inaudi, an illiterate Italian immigrant with an unusual gift for rapid calculations involving very large numbers, was presented to the Société d'Anthropologie (Anthropological society) by the neurologist Paul Broca, renowned for his discovery of Broca's area in the brain and who had been a child prodigy himself. Inaudi was the most recent addition to what Binet calls the "natural family" of calculating prodigies who excited considerable public and scientific interest over the course of the nineteenth century. There were examples from all parts of Europe and the United States, and they included Zerah Colburn (b. 1804), George Parker Bidder (b. 1806), Zacharias Dase (b. 1824), Vito Magiamele (b. 1827), Henri Mondeux (b. 1826), and, contemporaneously with Inaudi, Pericles Diamandi. Inaudi attracted almost as much scientific interest as he did public curiosity through his performances in various cafés and music halls, through which he earned a reputation—in the words of the astronomer, Camille Flammarion—as "[t]he most extraordinary Calculator of modern times."[16] Mathematical genius had long since been celebrated in the figure of Newton, Chênedollé had recorded the achievements of Maupertuis in *Le Génie de l'homme*, and the premature death of the number theorist Évariste Galois at the age of twenty in 1832 (the date of *Stello* and Balzac's first draft of *Louis Lambert*) added a certain Romantic luster to genius in this domain.

In February 1892 Inaudi, currently performing at the Folies Bergères, was summoned to a session of the Académie des Sciences, which was sufficiently impressed to set up a committee to examine his gifts. The committee included the mathematician Poincaré and the neurological specialist Charcot, the brief of the latter being to investigate the young man from the perspective of "physiological psychology." (Poincaré, himself later regarded as a mathematical genius, became the object of an extensive examination by Édouard Toulouse in his follow-up to the Zola study, published in 1910 as *Enquête médico-psychologique sur la supériorité intellectuelle, II: Henri Poincaré*.) Charcot appointed his young assistant Alfred Binet to help him carry out the examination, which took place over the course of some fifteen sessions between 1892 and 1893, just three years before Zola submitted his own talent to the analyses of Édouard Toulouse's laboratory.

In the introduction to his account of calculating prodigies, Binet observes that there was nothing hereditary to explain the phenomenon, whose main feature was its unprecedented and precocious character: the age of three for the future mathematician Gauss, six for Colburn, ten for Mangiamele and Bidder. Inaudi's talent for calculation had emerged at the age of six. Many of the calculators came from a poor background and had no formal education. Inaudi, typically, had spent part of his childhood minding sheep and did not learn to read or write until the age of twenty. A number of these children also had some kind of handicap or deformity: Inaudi had a strangely shaped head (which intrigued both Broca and Charcot), Zerah Colburn had an extra finger on each hand, another calculator, Prolongeau, mentioned by Binet, was born without arms or legs, and several were considered to be retarded.[17]

These "calculating boys," as they were also known (and they are indeed all boys), display a number of characteristics that recall the prodigies portrayed in the tales of famous children being written in the same period, notably the poverty of the background of many of them and the spontaneity of their talent. In other words, the calculating prodigy looked like a genius in the making, and soon became an object of adult fascination. Many of them—especially the poorer ones—were put on show, performing for money: Inaudi's family had been quick to set him to lucrative use in various cafés in the south of France.[18] He later acquired more professional managers, and in fact spent the rest of his life performing in vaudeville and circuses. An article in the *Brooklyn Daily Eagle* on 15 October 1901 profiled "the math man" as follows:

> Inaudi and his manager were the very pink of politeness when an *Eagle* man saw them later in their dressing room. More tests in mathematics followed and with them every suspicion of possible treachery vanished.
>
> "What were you before making use of your ability at figures?" the reporter asked.
>
> "Monsieur Inaudi was a shepherd," his manager replied for him, "a shepherd, with hees sheep, in France. One day, years, ago, he came to Marseilles. A strangaire there learned what he could do in mathematiques. He heard him and took him to Paree. Since then he has been before scienteests, doctairs and all—and all say, "Monsieur Inaudi ees a man with two brains.""[19]

The talent of the precocious child is performed for the benefit of adults, but here it is the prelude to a life of celebrity and remunerated exhibition rather than artistic or scientific genius. As we shall see in due course, the child prodigy thereby sowed the seeds of his future imposture.

The scientist has a different view of his subject than does the public, and responds with analysis rather than applause. While Charcot documented the shape of Inaudi's strangely formed head, Binet set about pinpointing the mental attributes behind his extraordinary performances. He subjected Inaudi to a series of experiments where he measured the time it took him to memorize numbers of different size, for example, a minute and a half for thirty-six digits, four minutes for fifty-seven digits, five and a half minutes for seventy-five digits, and so on. These measurements were meticulously recorded by specially trained assistants, the accuracy of their numerical proficiency being essential for getting the measure of Inaudi's own numerical skills.

Binet's persistence in pursuing the analysis of Inaudi's talents revealed ultimately that the prodigy's gift lay with his memory rather than with any exceptional ability for calculation as such. The speed with which Inaudi retained eight-figure numbers was one hundred times greater than the average, although his capacity to retain letters, words, and quotations was distinctly below the norm. He could astonish his vaudeville audiences by instantly naming the day of the week for any given date of birth, and by recalling every one of the numbers chalked up on the blackboard behind him over the course of an evening, but when tested against a group of four cashiers from the Bon Marché department store, his skills in basic calculation (addition, subtraction, and the multiplication of small numbers) turned out to be neither greater nor faster than theirs. Binet's results are set out in tables that note the speed of the different

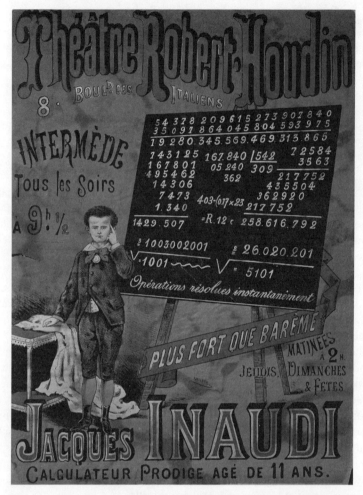

Figure 9. Poster advertising an appearance of Jacques Inaudi (1867–1939) at the Theatre Robert Houdin, Paris, 1878 (color litho), French School (19th century)/Musée de la Ville de Paris, Musée Carnavalet, Paris, France/Archives Charmet/The Bridgeman Art Library.

calculations down to the last half second. Number was clearly an effective method for demystifying Inaudi's own apparently exceptional way numbers.

The interest of Binet and Charcot in Inaudi lay in the data that his case provided about the operation of memory, and his precocity was not the primary focus of the study. Despite the fact that much was made of the writing down of large numbers on the blackboard in Inaudi's performances—and many of the posters and photographs of him show him in front of a blackboard covered in chalked up numbers—he proved to be a rare example of the phenomenon of auditory memory (Figure 9). He retained large numbers, which he manipulated in his calculations by means of multiple repetitions: a member of the audience would call out the figures, which were repeated first by Inaudi's manager, who appeared with him on stage, and then, while the number was being written down, by Inaudi himself. When Binet prevented Inaudi from speaking the numbers out loud by obliging him to sing a single vowel instead, his calculations were two or three times slower. Diamandi, by contrast, was an instance of the more conventional form of visual memory, as were the chess players discussed in the second part of Binet's book.

Binet compares Inaudi with figures like Ampère, the physicist and mathematician, Gauss, the German mathematician, and George Parker Bidder, who became a distinguished engineer, noting that their precocious gift for calculation waned as their intellectual interest in mathematical concepts grew. He distinguishes between the serious mathematician and the mere calculator on the basis that, while both may exhibit the same exceptional skill in mental calculation when young, for those with true mathematical genius this is a temporary "accident in their lives: they are destined to rise much higher."[20] Inaudi never moved beyond his initial interest in calculation, and while he demonstrated considerable sexual appetite, he gave no sign of any adult intellectual appetites. He was not even interested in exploring alternative strategies for calculation, preferring to keep his own, sometimes quite cumbersome methods, and he never showed any curiosity about geometry or algebra, even though algebra would have simplified some of his operations.

Despite his phenomenal memory for numbers, he not only had none for words but was very prone to forgetfulness in practical matters. He was happy to leave others to arrange his affairs for him, and his life was organized for instant gratification: he liked to get up late, and would spend his afternoons playing cards or billiards. His intelligence, in Binet's assessment, was "mediocre." The difference between those who grow up to become serious mathematicians and the mere calculators is that the calculators never grow out of being the prodigies they were in childhood, and that "they are in a sense children who never grow any older."[21] Child prodigies are likely to remain children for life, and their prodigious talents are quite precisely circumscribed.

It was not Binet's aim to expose Inaudi as a fraud, but the effect of his analysis was to identify the quite specific mental features that were responsible for his apparent talent. For Binet, what is noteworthy is not the performance that draws the crowds in the cafés and the music halls, but the fact that the prodigies practice their skill on a regular basis. If, like Inaudi, they are reluctant to acquire any further education, they nonetheless offer an instructive example for educators, suggesting that certain subjects—like mathematics or foreign languages—benefit from regular bouts of intensive practice. Binet is far more interested in educational methods than he is in the genius with which he credits Ampère and

Gauss but which he is content simply to assert and to leave undescribed. The genius enacted on the Folies Bergères stage is translated into measurable mental attributes and the prodigy's example used to justify diligence as the surest path to educational success.

Nonetheless, these attributes are increasingly perceived, both in the laboratory and in popular representation, as superior forms of quantification and mechanical ability, so that Binet's studies of calculators and chess players pave the way for a twentieth-century image of genius represented in figures such as Einstein, or chess masters such as Boris Spassky, who will occupy a prominent place in the public imaginary in the modern world.

CHAPTER 15

Minou Drouet

The Prodigy under Suspicion

> Everyone is born with genius, but most people only keep it a few
> minutes.
>
> —Edgard Varèse

Between September and December 1955 France was gripped by the so-called
Minou Drouet affair, Minou being a previously unknown eight-year-old child
poet who captured public interest. The publisher René Julliard had distributed
a selection of her letters and poems in the form of a little pamphlet sent to critics, writers, and friends "to put down a marker" and provide advance publicity
for the first commercial edition of Minou's poetry, *Arbre, mon ami* (Tree, my
friend), which was scheduled to appear in January 1956, whereafter it sold
forty-five thousand copies. In the meantime, and in the absence of any book
publication, the affair took off and developed into a full-scale controversy as the
authenticity of Minou's talent was called into question.

The controversy was pursued largely in the press, with the women's magazine *Elle* and the daily newspaper *Le Figaro* playing key roles on either side of
the ensuing debates about the nature of genius and its precocious manifestation. Public interest in Minou was sustained by journalists who sought to provide the necessary evidence, and articles about her were almost invariably
accompanied by photographs—most often, several. *Paris Match* had been
launched in 1949 and produced two lavishly illustrated reports on an undoubtedly photogenic Minou, where the child was, as it were, exhibited for public
inspection (Figure 10). It was thanks to this middle-brow press that the child
prodigy became what Maurice Blanchot described as an "object of collective
curiosity," and, ultimately, the target of suspicion.[1]

PRECOCITY OR IMPOSTURE?

As the controversy developed, fueled by contributions from Pasteur Vallery-
Radot of the Académie française, the major literary journalists of the day, and

Figure 10. Minou Drouet photographed for *Paris Match*, no. 346 (1955). Photograph by Phillippe Le Tellier. © Paris Match Archive/Getty Images

figures as various and as well-known as Jean Cocteau, André Breton, and the singer-songwriter Léo Ferré, Minou Drouet became the focus for many of the uncertainties and contradictions associated with the notion of genius in the twentieth century. In due course, she roused both Sartre and Barthes to major critiques of the concept of genius, whether construed as imposture (Sartre) or the embodiment of contemporary bourgeois myth (Barthes), that seemed to sound its death knell.

Minou was not the first precocious author of the modern period. Rimbaud's "Les Poètes de sept ans" (Poets aged seven, written when he was sixteen) is prescient of the age at which Minou Drouet began her own literary career, and although the idiom of Rimbaud's poem is very different from hers, his youthful example was a recurrent point of reference in the debates. So too was that of Raymond Radiguet, who had published his first poems and a novel at the age of seventeen, and died when he was only twenty. *Le Diable au corps* (The devil in the flesh, 1923) was promoted as "the first book by a novelist aged seventeen," and its author's literary precocity was compounded by the sexual precocity portrayed in his novel, which tells the allegedly autobiographical story of an adulterous affair between a teenage boy and a young married woman whose husband is a soldier at the front in the First World War. Radiguet had been energetically championed by Jean Cocteau, who himself had published his first collection of poetry at the age of nineteen and went on to cultivate what he called "the hieroglyphs of childhood" with *Les Enfants terribles* in 1929.[2] However, when it came to Minou Drouet, Cocteau famously contributed to the debate with his devastating *boutade*, "All children below the age of nine possess genius, except Minou Drouet."[3]

Closer to the example of Minou Drouet was Sabine Sicaud, whose *Poèmes d'enfant* (A child's poems) was published in 1926, when she was only thirteen, with a preface by Anna de Noailles, who hailed "the poems of a child prodigy" as "always a success and always poetic." Two years later—at the age of fifty-two—Noailles published a selection of her own *Poèmes d'enfance* (Childhood poems) with four photograph illustrations of her younger self and a long preface in which she recalled her early years and her first attempts at writing. Sabine Sicaud died of acute osteomyelitis at the age of fifteen, but in 1958, no doubt inspired by the success of Minou Drouet, her poems were given a new lease of life when they appeared complete under the title *Les Poèmes de Sabine Sicaud* (The poems of Sabine Sicaud) with an additional preface describing her short life and celebrating her "poetic genius."[4] In her memoir published in 1993, *Ma vérité* (My truth), Minou Drouet mentions other examples of child prodigies among her contemporaries, including Roberto Benzi, born in 1937, whose musical talents were portrayed in two films that appeared in 1950 and 1953, respectively, the first of which, appropriately titled *Prélude à la gloire* (The prelude to fame), won a prize at Cannes.[5]

The year before the Minou Drouet affair Françoise Sagan had provided a further instance of Radiguet's provocative mix of sexual and literary precocity with her first novel, *Bonjour tristesse*, published in March 1954 (also by Julliard) when she was still only eighteen. In September 1955, just as the affair was taking off, Nabokov introduced the nymphet into the currency of high literary culture when Olympia Press published *Lolita* in Paris (Lolita herself is twelve but has no literary ambitions). Rather more innocent and more youthful examples of precocity still lingered in French cultural memory, and in 1949 Claude-Edmonde Magny, an intellectually sophisticated critic known for her work on the modern novel, edited and illustrated a *de luxe* volume under the title *Les Enfants célèbres* (Famous children) that is oddly redolent of the nineteenth-century tradition of children's literature. It includes lists of child prodigies organized by the nature of their gifts (poetry, painting, science, mathematics, music, etc.) and by their national origin, with brief thumbnail sketches of their achievements.[6]

A degree of anxiety about imposture was also in the air. Pascal Pia, one of the leading literary critics of the time, had recently had his fingers burned over the supposed discovery of a lost manuscript by Rimbaud, *La Chasse spirituelle* (The spiritual pursuit), in a case that strengthened the association between precocity and fraud. The manuscript, whose real existence had in any case always been in doubt, turned up under mysterious circumstances in the offices of the journal *Combat*. It was authenticated by Pia, who published extracts from it in

May 1949, whereupon its status as a forgery was revealed by the perpetrators of the scam. They were a pair of young actors whose stage performance of Rimbaud's *Une saison en enfer* (A season in hell) had received bad reviews from the press, and the hoax was a pastiche designed to prove that their understanding of Rimbaud's work was much greater than the critics had given them credit for. They described the hoax as "a joke," but the result was a furor in which literary criticism itself was felt to be on trial.[7]

Introducing suspicion from a slightly different angle, the mention of Radiguet in association with Minou Drouet led another commentator to claim that Radiguet's worth had been exaggerated by the publicity his novel had received—thanks in large part to Cocteau's contribution—and that his reputation was not fully deserved. An article in the daily newspaper *L'Aurore* recalled the case of "little Beauchâteau," a ten-year-old poet from the seventeenth century whose work turned out to have been written by his father, a case that *Elle* returned to in a roll call of child prodigies over the ages designed to provide a benchmark against which to assess the Minou phenomenon.[8]

The implications of these examples make the child prodigy distinctly suspect: either the child simply does not live up to the claims made on his behalf or he is prone to manipulative exploitation by self-interested adults. In her memoir, published in 1993, Minou Drouet herself recorded that René Julliard was considered to be "a champion of literary publicity," and had a reputation as "*Monsieur jeunes auteurs*," having also signed up Françoise Sagan and the twenty-one-year-old Françoise Mallet-Joris within a very short space of time.[9] She even suggests that Julliard had orchestrated or at least instigated the "*affaire* Minou Drouet," and that it made him the money that paid for the shiny new Cadillac that she noticed one day in the courtyard below his apartment.

Regardless of any opportunism on the part of adults, there was also a fear that the child prodigy might simply not mature into the adult genius. However fondly genius was imagined as precocity, precocity might be just that, and the precocious child fail to become the future genius. The journalist Georges Altmann, writing in *Franc-Tireur* on 17 November, did not doubt that Minou Drouet was the author of her own poetry, but nevertheless felt that the phenomenon of the child poet had served to debase the notion of genius:

> It is enough nowadays for a young girl or a boy to show signs of a certain skill and a certain lack of modesty in the confidence of the public for a peculiar fuss and excitement to break out. . . . The age of geniuses by the dozen is turning into the age of bluffers and is falsifying every value! Nowadays literature is being concocted, like dwarves or bearded women in a fairground, on the basis of the unusual appearance of its authors. The time has come to reverse the tide and to restore to art its dignity, and to the word genius its Goethean, Hugolean, Racinian or Shakespearean meaning, which does not deceive.[10]

The child prodigy is little more than a circus freak and seems bound either to deceive or to disappoint. But with reminders in the press of the precocity of many of the great geniuses of the past—including Goethe and Hugo, whose precocious achievements were recorded among the examples of "child prodigies in History" listed by *Elle* in the number of 12 December—how was one to tell the difference?

THE MAKING OF A PRODIGY

Minou's story made good copy for journalists of both camps. Although her precocious talent for poetry was the key feature of her identity, she had spent the first years of her life unable to speak at all and was written off as seriously retarded. Her biological mother was unmarried and her paternity unknown, and when Minou was adopted at the age of nearly two, she was virtually blind and largely unresponsive. She remained in this state, and the only form of communication she appeared to be capable of was barking in dialogue with the local dogs. However, her condition was dramatically transformed when, at the age of six, she heard some music by Bach on the radio. In Minou's own words, she was "metamorphosed" by something akin to a miracle.[11]

She was raised in La-Guerche-de-Bretagne, a village in Brittany of some four thousand inhabitants, by her unmarried adoptive mother and her grandmother, and everything about her speaks of the obscure and unpropitious origins familiar from many of the nineteenth-century tales of "famous children." After the "miracle" of the Bach episode she began to speak and made dramatic progress on all fronts. It was initially her musical talents that seemed to mark her out, and through family acquaintances she came to the attention of Lucette Descaves, who taught piano at the Paris Conservatoire and with whom she went on to have lessons. As the affair took off, Minou was reported in exaggerated terms by the women's magazine *Marie-France* to be "Lucette Descaves's most brilliant pupil," although the view of the pianist herself was that "Minou is an interesting, undoubtedly talented child, but *she is not a prodigy*."[12] These reservations notwithstanding, Pascal Pia confidently predicted that she would become best known for her musical talents.

Precocious brilliance is most convincing when it comes in the measurable form of musical or mathematical performance. But, although she played and sang in public, Minou Drouet's success was due to her way with words. In addition to writing poetry, she was also a prolific letter writer and it would seem that the impression she made on Lucette Descaves was principally through her letters. It was thanks to this correspondence that Minou came to the attention of Julliard. Lucette Descaves had shown Minou's letters to Pasteur Vallery-Radot (grandson of Louis Pasteur), who was impressed, and he in turn passed them on to the publisher after meeting him at a dinner party. Unlike music (Roberto

Benzi had perfect pitch) or mathematics, literary expression does not lend itself to precise measurement and quantification, and the evaluation of Minou's talent was subject to the vagaries of literary judgment.

This inevitably produced its own anxieties: In dismissing Minou's poems, was a future Rimbaud being overlooked? Or in praising their quality, was the critic making a fool of himself? Vallery-Radot, who declared Minou to be "quite simply a genius," was adamant in his expression of the first of these views: "Would people have had the right to keep Rimbaud's talent hidden? . . . I am convinced that time will consecrate the genius of this child as it consecrated Rimbaud." André Rousseaux, writing in *Le Figaro* of 5 November, suggests that there is a generalized nervousness about genius that made people reluctant to give Minou her due: "[I]f we are dealing with a child of eight, the aversion to genius is unmasked. Everyone rushes in as if to look at an educated monkey or a five-legged monster. And then people take their revenge on genius by regarding the child as a monster."[13]

The author of an article in *Marie-France* recognizes the difficulty of distinguishing between the youthful genius of a Mozart or a Pascal, which is a promise of greater things to come, and mere precocity, which offers nothing more than the "illusion of genius" and vanishes with adolescence. The journalist Madeleine Chapsal, writing in *L'Express,* acknowledges the embarrassment of the uncertainty: "We are now caught in the trap created by our own investigations, and obliged to admit that we are unable to reach a conclusion," though she recognizes that, whatever the conclusion, Minou herself will be its principal victim.[14] In December *Elle* called upon fourteen writers, from Jean Giono and Marcel Pagnol to Jean Paulhan, Jean Cocteau, and Jean-Paul Sartre—as well as the nine-year-old daughter of the poet Jacques Prévert—to exercise that judgment. By then, however, the problem had taken on a different aspect. The debate was no longer about whether Minou Drouet was a genius in the making or a mere child prodigy. Instead the question was whether Minou Drouet was really the author of these poems. Could it be her mother? Putting the question in these terms made the phenomenon much easier to deal with.

Testing for Genius and Compulsory Performance

André Breton, writing in the daily newspaper *Paris Presse* on 20 December, had no doubt that the poems had genuine literary value: "I should like to say that this has been a boost to true poetry which has even been *royally served.*" In his opinion, the quality of Minou Drouet's poetry was such that it could not have been written by an eight-year-old child. Recalling the episode of the fake Rimbaud manuscript and the lessons it taught about the need to consider the internal evidence of the text itself, he asserted that the poems contained a *"certain timbre of lived experience [which] a life that is still to be lived can under no cir-*

cumstances affect."[15] Minou, in other words, was simply too young to be the author of the sentiments that her poems expressed, and Breton backed up this view by citing the "magisterial research" of the great French psychologist Piaget, notably *La Représentation du monde chez l'enfant* (The child's conception of the world, 1926) and *Le Jugement moral chez l'enfant* (The moral judgment of the child, 1932). Piaget had spent a year working at a school founded by Alfred Binet and directed by Binet's associate Théodore Simon, and it was while marking intelligence tests based on Binet's model that he began to evolve his own theories of cognitive development in children. The scientifically based implication of Breton's remark was that the real author of Minou's poems could only have been Minou's adoptive mother, though for him she was more of a "Sybil" than the fraudster that so many of the anti-Minou partisans accused her of being.

The test of Minou's genius thus became an enquiry into the authorship of her work. But who had the expertise to judge? A self-styled *psychotechnicienne* wrote to the letters page of *Le Figaro* diagnosing serious mental and emotional problems in the child, and recommending medical treatment. She also blamed Mme Drouet for not protecting Minou from the "hoo-hah" that she had attracted. André Parinaud, who was himself a journalist (and at the time codirector of the literary review *La Parisienne*), consulted an expert in para-psychology, but otherwise those who carried out the various "tests" to which Minou was subjected were two or three graphologists and a large number of journalists. The graphologists came up with contradictory assessments, one claiming that Minou's poems were unquestionably written in her mother's hand, and another that the two handwritings expressed quite different characters: creative and imaginative in the case of Minou, repressed and conventional in the case of her mother.[16] Both graphological verdicts, contradictory though they were, supplied grist to the mill of a psychological enquiry into the mother as opposed to the child, and there was much in Mme Drouet's circumstances and character to provide material that would reward such scrutiny.

The gender dimension of Minou's supposed genius is rarely raised directly in connection with her. One commentator told her to go back to her dolls, but in general the case for or against Minou's genius does not seem to have been affected by considerations of her sex. Comparisons with Rimbaud never mention their sexual difference, although according to Lewis Terman's 1930 enquiry into gifted children, it was only girls who were endowed with "exceptional literary ability in childhood," boys having abandoned their former literary interests because they now have "so many other interesting things to do."[17] It is noteworthy that of all the publications that took an interest in the Minou Drouet case, at least two were women's magazines—*Elle* and *Marie-France*—and *Elle*'s seven-page feature on Minou played a large part in launching the controversy in the first place. The gendering of the affair shows up most visibly in the portrait of Mme Drouet that emerges from the various accounts of the Minou phenomenon, and it contributes to making her the villain of the piece.

Her honorific "Madame" turned out to conceal the reality of her unmarried status, and she was not the widow she gave herself out to be. Nor was the story she originally told about Minou's origins, whereby her parents had both been drowned at sea, true. These discrepancies—understandable though they were as attempts to protect Minou, who had not been aware of her adopted status— led to further allegations. At one stage Mme Drouet was suspected of being the real mother of Minou after giving birth to her illegitimately, an accusation she countered with the offer to submit herself to medical examination. She was also accused of ill-treating Minou, and a rumor started by a neighbor claimed that she had been seen beating the girl with a wet towel. Journalists who met Mme Drouet found her prone to exaggerate Minou's talents, reporting her sayings with a barrage of sentences that began "Minou said. . . ." On one occasion she was caught out attributing to Minou a remark that she herself had made about the statue of a saint looking as though it was covered in Ambre-Solaire sun oil.

Perhaps the most incriminating of all the accusations made against Mme Drouet was the discovery that she had had literary ambitions of her own when younger. A long poem in alexandrines written during the 1920s had failed to win a prize in the *Jeux floraux* (she may well have lost out to Sabine Sicaud, who was awarded the prize in 1925), and a story about a blind child had been turned down more recently by the publisher to which she had submitted it. Like Minou herself, she had also suffered from visual impairment and insisted that the origins of the story were entirely autobiographical.[18] All this was used variously as evidence of Mme Drouet's potential guilt in passing off her own work as that of Minou. If there was imposture, it was, to use the more precise French word, *supercherie*, active deception or fraud, and Mme Drouet was the culprit, a bad mother who abused her child for the gratification of her own frustrated literary ambitions.

Even in the more benevolent accounts, Mme Drouet was portrayed as the moving spirit behind Minou's productivity. She was known as something of a clairvoyant and cartomancer, and apart from the aura of general dubiousness that this gave her, it led to the charge on the part of the writer and journalist Louis Pauwels that she had, as it were, taken possession of Minou. Describing Mme Drouet as "an unmarried provincial woman, full of complexes, repressed ambition and unhealthy nonsense," Pauwels suggested that she failed to distinguish between herself and her adopted child, and manipulated Minou in order to fulfill her own poetic yearnings.[19] In this view, the deception was unconscious and the issue was not so much imposture as something resembling witchcraft. André Breton's description of Mme Drouet as a Sybil is in much the same vein.

Most of the accounts of the Minou Drouet affair end up—quite plausibly— pointing the finger at the girl's adoptive mother. Parinaud himself, after his careful and exhaustive documentation of the affair, concludes that Minou's poetry was the product of a kind of *folie à deux*, or what he calls "a special 'psyche' characterizing the relations between the child and her mother" and which took the form of an unconscious "collaboration" between the two. In her memoirs, Minou Drouet provides her own insights into her mother and is quite aware of their mutual indebtedness. She reports that her mother had never recovered from an unhappy affair with a married man, and that Minou's success was a lonely woman's attempt at revenge on the lover who had rejected her.[20] Minou's talents also offered her adoptive mother a way of escaping from the restrictions of a life that had failed to satisfy her intelligence and education. In fact, it was these attributes, exercised in the form of private lessons for local children at which the mute and retarded infant was invariably a silent presence, that had given Minou the literary education on which she was later able to draw for her own compositions. The main reproach Minou directs at her adoptive mother concerned the way in which she allowed her to be exploited as a celebrity in the years following the affair.

Even if it seems likely that, in the words of Jean-Max Tixier, the editor of Minou Drouet's memoirs, there was something "suspect" in the relation between Minou and Mme Drouet, the point is not to get to the bottom of Mme Drouet's psyche or to arrive at some verifiable "truth" about the relations between mother and child. For the urge to get to the bottom of things is itself symptomatic of the frantic desire for explanations that accompanied the anxieties provoked by Minou's talents. After the weekly magazine *France Observateur* first raised doubts about the authenticity of the poems by asserting that "[i]t is impossible to believe that a more expert hand had not guided the fingers of the seven-and-a-half-year old child," the literary journalist Robert Kemp called for a full investigation.[21] Thereafter every journalist took it upon himself or herself to subject Minou to a series of more or less covert "tests" in an attempt to establish authorship of the poems.

Michèle Perrein, who wrote the original feature in *Elle*, thought that Minou recited her poetry as if she were rattling off a lesson learned by heart, and she found it suspicious that Minou was indifferent to the poetic sight of the sun setting over the sea and preferred to play with a friend's poodle. Minou is shown up as not knowing the meaning of some of the words she uses in her poems, fails to recognize one of her own poems, and makes contradictory claims about whether she knows the work of Lamartine. In response to these suspicions, René Julliard and his wife invited Minou to stay—without her mother—for five days, during which time she was kept under constant observation and encouraged to write letters and poems to provide proof of her talents. In an attempt to clear her name and to put an end to the endless scrutiny, Minou later subjected herself voluntarily to a similar test under the auspices of the Société des auteurs, compositeurs et éditeurs de musique (Society of authors, composers and music publishers), the organization responsible for overseeing the payment of rights to authors and composers.[22] But the investigations had their own unstoppable momentum, and in a particularly gruesome episode, which she recounts in *Ma vérité*, the BBC shut her into a studio with pencil and paper, and set her a topic to write about as the camera rolled for the benefit of a panel of experts.

The effect of all these tests was to turn the child prodigy into a performer, and it does nothing so much as call to mind Beckett's *Waiting for Godot*, premiered in Paris in January 1953, where Pozzo boasts of Lucky's talent for "thinking" and, with Vladimir and Estragon as audience, brutally instructs him to think with the command: "Think, pig." Minou was instructed to "create" in a very similar way. If Minou has genius, it needs to be authenticated; but authentication can only take the form of a performance, and, as was the case with Louise Colet's story of Jacqueline Pascal composing her poems for the queen and the ladies at court, performance must always come as a response to demand.

In sum, the child prodigy becomes the child performer, and although Minou continued to write, her poetry soon took second place to her career as a celebrity. She appeared in a variety of venues, modeled children's clothes for an upmarket label, and even starred in a film titled *Clara et les méchants* (Clara and the wicked men). *Ma vérité* includes photographs of her being received in the Vatican by the pope (in 1957) and having her hand kissed by Maurice Chevalier, whose rendition of "Thank Heavens for Little Girls" helped to make Vincente Minnelli's 1958 film adaptation of Colette's *Gigi* the box-office success that it became. In a sense she joined the dwarves and the bearded ladies mentioned by Georges Altmann (in fact on one occasion she appeared at the Cirque d'hiver with a large python), and she ended up looking less like the young Goethe than Shirley Temple—or even Jacques Inaudi, who had recently died at the age of eighty-three after a long career on the stage.

All this may appear to confirm the vacuity of the child prodigy, but if we are tracing the fortunes of the notion of genius, its mutation into the performances of the child prodigy must also track the language and the vehicles in which that mutation occurs. Although Proust had defended genius against its theorists,[23] and although some commentators, like Altmann, harked back to an era of great literary geniuses, there is little sign of active interest in genius on the part of "serious" literature in the twentieth century, and it was a journalism associated with middle-brow culture and "collective curiosity" that picked up the notion. In defending—or even in suspecting—Minou Drouet, that culture was ignoring or indeed implicitly protesting against the difficulty of a high literary culture that, as Barthes would very soon indicate, had long since dispensed with any notion of genius.

PART VI

Genius in Theory

CHAPTER 16

Cultural Critique and the End of Genius

Barthes, Sartre

> With a little tear for Minou Drouet, and a little frisson for poetry, we are rid of Literature!
>
> —Barthes, *Mythologies*

The child and the brain have remained the main focus of thinking—both positive and negative—about genius. IQ testing keeps children in the foreground, and a fifth edition of the Stanford-Binet Intelligence Scale was introduced in 2003. The "gifted child," or the French *enfant surdoué*, is the object of various types of enquiry and concern in the West and beyond. There was a serious proposal in the early years of the Soviet Union to create institutions that would nurture budding geniuses while accommodating their "individualistic, unsociable tendencies and frequent ailments." There was also a plan for an Institute of Genius, which decreed "the compulsory dissection of brains of all outstanding people without exception, and, if necessary, also a post-mortem on the corpse, which will then be kept in the anatomical theatre for subsequent study." Both proposals for the institute came to nothing, but the growth of neuroscience over the course of the twentieth century continued the search for the seat of genius in the cerebral cortex. Einstein's brain—preserved in the University Medical Center at Princeton—has been the object of exactly the sort of study that the Institute of Genius would have promoted, and has helped to sustain the promise of a neuroanatomical explanation of genius. In 1999 his parietal lobe was discovered to be 15 percent wider than normal, and neuroglia—with which he was supposedly more generously endowed than the average—have become popularly known as the "genius cells" of the brain.[1]

But physiology and precocity have also been the basis for a wholesale discrediting of notion of genius. It is with a certain regret that Robert Musil observes that genius has effectively been destroyed by scientific explanations that allow footballers, boxers, and even racehorses to be described as geniuses. Having had ambitions to become a "great man" in the world of science, Musil's protagonist, Ulrich, finds that "when as a result of his varied exertions he perhaps could have felt within reach of his goal, the horse had beaten him to it"—and was nodding at him from the finishing line. Writing at roughly the same time (the 1920s), Isaac Babel disparagingly recalls the *Wunderkind* factory in his native Odessa, where "Jewish dwarfs in lace collars and patent leather shoes" were turned into musical virtuosi for the simple reason that *Wunderkinder* offered their ambitious parents a path out of poverty. And in the 1924 *Manifeste du surréalisme* (Surrealist manifesto) André Breton may have celebrated childhood for its uninhibited exercise of the imagination, but he is adamant that the psychic mechanism that generated the work of the great poets of the past had nothing to do with "*what, through misplaced confidence, people call genius*" and was actually a form of Surrealist automatic writing *avant la lettre*. He therefore advises those who aspire to the secrets of Surrealist magic art to begin by jettisoning any genius or talent that they may think they possess.[2]

Genius was clearly losing its cachet in certain quarters and this continued. In France in the 1950s, contemporaneously with the Minou Drouet affair, it became the object of a powerful cultural critique under the aegis of literary theory, when Sartre and Barthes—more or less simultaneously—portrayed it as an anachronistic legacy from the previous century, and denounced it as a one of the myths that lay at the heart of bourgeois ideology. Two of Barthes's texts in *Mythologies* specifically target genius—one devoted to Einstein's brain, and the other to Minou Drouet. The mix of disciplines that fed the eclectic methodology behind these texts—first published between 1954 and 1956 as a regular column in the recently founded literary journal *Les Lettres nouvelles*—included sociology, semiology, which Barthes had encountered through his acquaintance with A.-J. Greimas, and the structural anthropology of Lévi-Strauss.[3] The book publication of the texts was rounded off by a long theoretical essay, "Le mythe aujourd'hui" (Myth today), which retrospectively provided a structuralist underpinning for the rest. Barthes's theoretically informed approach defined literature in ways that made genius both an irrelevance and an active misrepresentation.

Much the same goes for Sartre, whose autobiography, *Les Mots*, begun in 1953 (and finally published in 1964), targets genius and the child prodigy as central components of his farewell to literature. Autobiography in the form of Sartre's first-person narrative essay is the vehicle for an outright debunking of genius, which, like Barthes's *Mythologies*, treats it as the product of bourgeois ideology.[4] Theory—whether structuralist or existentialist in inspiration—was a mode of thinking in which genius seemed to have no place, and from which it is summarily ousted in terms that nonetheless provide it with a new, if negative, definition.

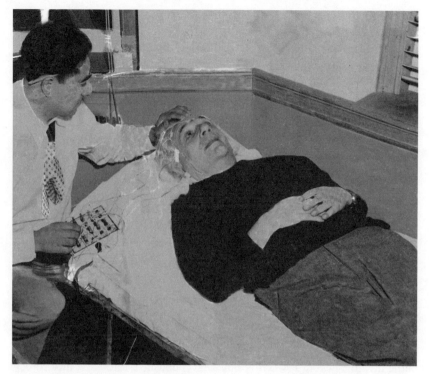

Figure 11. Albert Einstein thinks about relativity. AP photo/handout.

BARTHES: THE MYTHOLOGY OF GENIUS

Barthes's account of Einstein's brain (first published in *Les Lettres nouvelles* in June 1955) presents it as a "mythical object," whose aura derives from the fact that it is viewed as a piece of mechanical perfection designed to "produce thought." Einstein's brain had been removed within hours of his death on 18 April 1955, underscoring the sense that his exceptional mathematical abilities must have had a physiological basis. Taking his cue from two illustrated articles that appeared in *Paris Match* on 23 and 30 April, Barthes describes a photograph of Einstein while still alive, "his head bristling with electric wires." These are connected to devices designed to register the results as Einstein, rather like Lucky in Beckett's play or Minou Drouet in front of the BBC TV cameras, responds to an instruction to "think about relativity" (Figure 11).[5]

The thought itself, despite its supposedly material basis in the brain, is then represented as the famous equation $E = mc^2$. This, says Barthes, is nothing less than a magical formula, which supports the old idea that "total knowledge can only be discovered all at once, like a lock which suddenly opens after a thousand unsuccessful attempts." Certainly, the image of Einstein in front of a blackboard covered in mathematical formulas does nothing so much as recall the illustrations of the young Pascal in children's stories, or of Inaudi in the music hall. Einstein's brain, viewed as the presumed origin of all these calculations, has been molded into a kind of fetish by a culture that made it the vehicle for a myth that requires him to be at once "magician and machine," while simultaneously transcending this contradiction so as to satisfy the bourgeois desire for "a euphoric security." Barthes uses his own analytical techniques to uncover in turn what lies behind the celebrated brain matter and to show how the electrodes attached to it serve as much to construct a myth as to reveal any neurological basis for genius. Genius—even of the most mathematical and physiological kind—has become part of a bourgeois mythology. And its mythic appeal continues: in 2012, over three hundred slides made from Einstein's brain were digitized and made available by Apple as an iPad app that "will allow researchers and novices to peer into the eccentric Nobel winner's brain as if they were looking through a microscope."[6]

It is, however, the myth of the child prodigy that is the object of Barthes's most devastating critique of genius. Writing in January 1956 as the Minou Drouet affair was beginning to wane, Barthes devoted one of the longest and most complex of his "little mythologies of the month" to "La Littérature selon Minou Drouet" (Literature according to Minou Drouet). A number of these "little mythologies" in Les Lettres nouvelles (published, through a nice coincidence, by Julliard) had already explored the place of children in bourgeois ideology, but the association of poetry and childhood embodied in the figure of Minou provokes Barthes to undertake a particularly thoroughgoing analysis of the ideological investment in the figure of the child prodigy.

Whereas most of the participants in the Minou Drouet affair had taken sides on the question of her genius and the authenticity of her poetry, Barthes places himself above the fray. He begins by commenting on the forensic nature of the treatment meted out to Minou, which included "the usual police techniques (minus torture—if that!): investigation, sequestration, graphology, psycho-techniques and the internal analysis of documents." To mobilize this degree of "quasi-judicial apparatus" in the attempt to resolve the "poetic enigma" posed by Minou suggests to Barthes that, as with Einstein's brain, there is more at stake than the terms of the enquiry might at first sight imply. The mix of precocity and poetry is particularly potent, because the image of the child poet answers an unspoken need at the heart of bourgeois culture, namely its reverence for "irresponsibility" of which "the genius, the child and the poet are the sublimated figures."[7]

The thrust of Barthes's argument in Mythologies is that bourgeois culture conceals the ideological nature of its own value systems by passing them off as natural. The supposed naturalness of genius—whether in the form of the

human organ that is the brain, the child, or the spontaneity of poetic creation—
is therefore a prime candidate for demythologizing examination. The child poet
provides her adult readers not with poems, so much as with "*signs* of poetry,"
which satisfy certain cultural requirements placed upon poetry to be innocent
and natural: "to believe in the poetic 'genius' of childhood is to believe in a sort
of literary parthenogenesis, and once again to posit literature as something
god-given." The fact that poetry, like all literature, is culturally and historically
determined is ignored by those who want only its signs. Minou's readers, says
Barthes, remain blind to the fact that the "twee preciosity" produced by "the
Drouet family" (he hedges his bets on the question of the poems' authorship) is
historically dated and harks back to the minor poets who were writing around
1914. It has nothing to do with the literature of the 1950s, which Barthes describes as a confrontation with "an *elsewhere* that is foreign to the very language
that seeks it."[8] In other words, Minou's genius provides French society with a
seductive excuse not to read, or even acknowledge, the poetry of its own time.

Equally, the child herself, considered as an entirely natural—albeit exceptional—phenomenon, provides that same society with the excuse not to see its
own values projected onto her. For, as Barthes points out, childhood is not so
much the antithesis of adult culture, as the moment when social beings are
formed through a "constant osmosis" with the adult world. The child prodigy
masks an underlying view of genius as nothing more than an accelerated passage toward adulthood: the child deploys adult skills, and achieves at the age of
eight what others manage only at the age of twenty-five. For all its apparent
spontaneity, genius is a measurable quantity and the product of an essentially
capitalist thinking devoted to "saving time, reducing the human span to a nu-
merative question of precious moments."[9]

In Barthes's account, Minou is the invention—or, more precisely, the sacrifi-
cial victim—of a society bent on seeing in poetry, genius, and childhood not
the disruption that these phenomena potentially contain, but a reassuring
image of itself as part of the natural order. The implication is that genius could
in principle be conceived in terms other than those in which it appears through
the lens of Barthes's critique of bourgeois ideology, and, though he does not
pursue this line of thinking, he seems to be hinting at the possibility that genius
could potentially be regarded a beneficial disorder.

SARTRE: PRODIGIOUS FRAUD

For Sartre genius has no redeeming features, and his autobiographical essay is
the pretext for a wholesale denunciation of the concept through the figure of
the child prodigy that he portrays himself as having been. By the mid-1950s
Sartre had long since ceased to believe in his own genius and his writing was
fueled less by inspiration than by a cocktail of corydrane (a mix of aspirin and

amphetamines that was subsequently banned), caffeine, alcohol, tobacco, and sleeping pills.[10]

Sartre was one of Barthes's *maîtres à penser* in his early years, and *Mythologies* is often regarded as Barthes's attempt to introduce a more Marxist slant to Sartrean cultural analysis. But in this instance, it is Sartre who follows Barthes, since the Minou Drouet piece was written while Sartre was working on *Les Mots*. He began the autobiography, which eventually became his farewell to literature, under the provisional title of *Jean sans terre* in 1953, and added further to it in 1955 and 1956, just at the time when the Minou Drouet affair was at its height and to which he contributed with an acerbic comment in *Elle*, where he stated, "People are crazy. These texts have absolutely no literary value. If you remove a certain amount of contrived naivety, you'll see what's left."[11]

In citing Cocteau's *boutade* about Minou Drouet and applying it to himself in *Les Mots*, Sartre explicitly compares his younger poetry-writing self to her: "All children are geniuses except Minou Drouet, as Cocteau said in 1955. In 1912 they were all geniuses except me." His self-portrait as child prodigy could equally well—and, of course, just as uncharitably—be applied to her: "I come out with childish sayings, people remember them and repeat them back to me: I learn to produce more. . . . I know how to say things that are 'old beyond my years,' without altering them. These things are poems; the recipe is simple: you just have to put your trust in the Devil, in chance, or in the void, borrow complete sentences from the adults, place them end to end and repeat them without understanding them. In a word, I utter genuine oracles and everyone interprets them as they please."[12] But the comparison with Minou can be extended considerably further than the performance of such "contrived naivety."

To begin with, there is the superficial resemblance of their visual impairment: Minou was partially sighted and Sartre had a walleye.[13] More substantively, both were fatherless, both only children brought up by a teacher: Mme Drouet in Minou's case, Karl Schweitzer in Poulou's. Neither of them attended school in their early years—though both had what proved for each of them to be a brief and unsuccessful experience of primary education in the classroom—and both were taught at home. Both lived almost exclusively among adults, and both were encouraged to engage in charmingly misspelled correspondence with other adults: Poulou with his favorite author, Courteline, and, in an exchange of letters and poems, with Karl himself; Minou with Pasteur Vallery-Radot, Lucette Descaves, Mme Drouet, and others. Both responded to adult encouragement to write, and both were suspected of fraud: Sartre's grandmother, Louise, repeatedly accuses the boy of "showing off" and Minou is scrutinized by a series of skeptical journalists, beginning with Michèle Perrein from *Elle* whose *dossier* on Minou opens with the headline "Child Prodigy or Prodigious Fraud?"

Minou and Poulou both take up their pens at the same age (eight), and Poulou's early writing years coincide with the date (around 1914) to which Barthes suggests the style of Minou's poems belongs. The reasons for the fatherlessness of both children were not the same, but in both cases it allowed another adult (Mme Drouet and Karl, respectively) to unwittingly demonstrate the truth of Sartre's claim that the child—and it's especially true of the child prodigy—is "the monster that [adults] fashion out of their regrets."[14] Both children provide support for the further truth that what is required of this monster is a performance that meets the adult expectations laid upon it. In Sartre's case, the performance was private, acted out within the four walls of the family home in the Rue Le Goff; in Minou's case it took place on a very public stage, where the stakes required constantly repeated proof of the claims that were made on her behalf.

These parallels are nice, but the autobiographical accounts given by the two protagonists of their experiences are very different, and the story told in Minou Drouet's *Ma vérité* bears little resemblance to the one told by Sartre in *Les Mots*. As her title suggests, Minou Drouet's autobiography asserts her right to present her own, first-person record of the *affaire* in which she had figured as the object of the doubts and convictions of others. Sartre, on the other hand, narrates his autobiography from a perspective that implicitly endorses Barthes's view of the child prodigy as a construct answering the needs of the bourgeois culture that creates and celebrates it. For Barthes, Minou Drouet is "the child martyr to the adult yearning for poetic luxury," and Sartre makes a similar point, with himself as chief example, when he writes, "[W]hether they are listening to my chatter or to the Art of Fugue, adults have the same conniving smile of sly enjoyment; it reveals what I am at bottom: a piece of cultural goods. I am saturated with culture and I radiate it back to the family, the way that ponds in the evening give off the heat of the day."[15]

Though their analyses of the child prodigy are similar, Barthes and Sartre write from somewhat different positions. Barthes is doubly removed from the pretext of his critique (Minou, Einstein's brain), commenting on the commentators, and never writing in the first person. Sartre's purpose, on the other hand, is to implicate *himself* in the phenomenon that he is denouncing and to portray his own complicity in becoming the prodigy that others required him to be. Critique in *Les Mots* takes the form of autocritique, and while Barthes is seeking to redefine apparently natural phenomena as the vehicles for a covertly cultural meaning, Sartre focuses on his own imposture—the word appears frequently in the text. In both cases, however, the indictment of bourgeois culture—whether encouraging imposture (Sartre) or constructing an illusory nature (Barthes)—is based on the fact that it denies history and seeks refuge in anachronism.

Genius is presented by Sartre as a myth inherited from "an outmoded conception of culture," which the child prodigy is tasked with reflecting back to the adults who still subscribe to it. The currency of exchange that sustains this culture specifically includes a number of received ideas about genius that date back to a nineteenth-century past, and these are rehearsed to great comic effect in Sartre's account of his childhood: "[The priest of the religion] would whisper to me [that] genius is merely loaned: it must be earned through great suffering, through modestly but resolutely endured ordeals; you end up hearing voices and you write under dictation."[16] This picture leads the young Sartre to anticipate years of obscurity before his lonely genius is discovered in accordance with a narrative that he retrospectively locates as belonging to the era of Louis-Philippe.

In the view inherited from Schopenhauer or Michelet and transmitted by Karl Schweitzer, the genius and the child appear as interchangeable: "all children are inspired, and they have nothing to envy the poets for poets are quite simply children." The prescriptive nature of these images becomes apparent at various points when Poulou inadvertently fails to comply with them. He incurs adult disapproval when he misjudges his responses to a questionnaire about his tastes. Mme Picard's pursed lips and her reprimand for his lack of sincerity make clear that "what was wanted was the child prodigy and I had provided the infant sublime." And when Poulou's literary talent takes the form of adventure stories about explorers in the Amazon, he seriously disappoints his grandfather, whose conception of the child prodigy called instead for "a chronicle of our family with piquant observations and adorable naivety."[17] As a consequence Karl withdraws the accolade of "genius."

In Sartre's narrative, the "child prodigy" is cumulatively revealed to be indistinguishable from the "prodigious fraud," and not, as *Elle* had suggested, its indisputable obverse. The manner in which Sartre establishes this equation is, as I have suggested, frequently comic. But an equally telling element of Sartre's critique of genius comes in his account of the existential damage that is done in its name. Minou Drouet's *Ma vérité* recounts a much simpler story than Sartre's about her experience of being what Barthes calls a "propitiatory victim," but Sartre's narrative tells of something much more insidious as he finds himself unable to pinpoint the "elusive and mobile boundary that separates spiritual possession from ham acting."[18] Perhaps he wasn't just an impostor, but he cannot tell for sure.

In the same equivocal vein, the comic summary of the contents of *L'Enfance des hommes illustres*, a fictional synthesis of the children's literary genre that harks back to the previous century, ends on a much more disquieting note. When he imagines himself into the book and joins the child prodigies it portrays, little Jean-Paul finds himself alongside Jean-Jacques and Jean-Sébastien as the most recent incarnation of "the great man in thrall to childhood." He realizes that he is being seen by the young readers of the future, to whom his life appears in reverse, beginning with his death, while, as he puts it, "I never stopped giving out messages that I was unable to decipher myself." There is nothing comic when Sartre adds, "I shuddered, numbed by my own death, which was the true sense of all my gestures, dispossessed of myself." In sum, as a future genius he is condemned to live his life as if he were already dead: "I became my own obituary."[19]

This experience nonetheless fails to cure the young Sartre of the belief in his genius, which continues to be a source of existential inauthenticity. At the end of *Les Mots* he castigates his younger adult self for the way in which his obliviously persistent belief in the bourgeois culture he thought he had purged, allowed him to exempt himself from the existential conditions he ascribed to others. The genius implicitly inhabits a different world from that of his fellow humans, as Sartre acknowledges to Simone de Beauvoir in the conversations she recorded in 1974: "I regarded myself—in all modesty, if I may say so—as a genius. I talked to my friends the way a genius talks to his friends. In all simplicity, but on the inside, it was a genius talking."[20] The exemption he unconsciously granted himself was based on nothing other than his own conviction for which the mere fact of writing was the sole supporting evidence. The admission is damning testimony to the morally corrupting effects of the myth, and in bidding farewell to literature Sartre is also taking his leave of genius, which is henceforth dispatched by the various forms of his cultural critique to a past where it seems henceforth to belong.

CHAPTER 17

The Return of Genius

Mad Poets

All minds interested by the substance of art and its limits, have
come up against the question of the relation between genius and
madness.

—Pierre Jean Jouve, *Folie et génie*

The issue of genius seems to frame the time of theory in France—roughly the
second half of the century—and it rarely features in the middle years. The analyses of Barthes and Sartre might suggest that genius is inimical to theory, but it
is also through theory that genius is rehabilitated as a viable object of thought.
As we shall see, however, it makes this return in the company of psychotics,
women, and impostors, as if to prove that it is the most unlikely companions
who will endow it with the greatest conceptual energy. Each of these associations calls for separate examination, but, broadly speaking, they all draw on the
same language of French theory—that mix of literary criticism and philosophy
that, in the case of Barthes and Sartre, was so powerfully deployed against genius when it took the form of the child prodigy.

But it is theory with a biographical bias—or rather, theory that relies on case
studies of a more or less extensive kind. In the early years of theory Pierre Jean
Jouve (a poet-essayist, more than a theorist in the late twentieth-century style)
and Maurice Blanchot examine the case of Hölderlin, with supporting illustration from other examples. In theory's later years Julia Kristeva cites three instances of women geniuses—Hannah Arendt, Melanie Klein, and Colette—in
her trilogy of biographies published under the umbrella title of *Le Génie féminin*.
And Derrida reconsiders genius in the light of Hélène Cixous and her memories of her erstwhile American boyfriend, Gregor. The spirit of enquiry for all of
these discussions remains that of the essay rather than scientific analysis. While
the scientific study of genius continues across the Western world in the form of
neuroscientific exploration of the brain, the analysis of intelligence, and research into the relation between creativity and mental illness, what is striking
about the terms in which genius is rehabilitated in French theory (a term I shall

use as shorthand) is the avoidance of the language of causal explanation, and the refusal of a superior insight.[1]

A significant component of the discursive mix of these biographically informed essays is psychoanalysis, which seems in these discussions to encourage a resolutely nonhierarchical relation between genius and its commentators. Indeed, despite his willingness to examine the psychosexual history of Leonardo da Vinci or the daydreaming of the creative writer, Freud himself was surprisingly diffident about pronouncing on the topic of genius, as a remark in *Moses and Monotheism* illustrates: "We know that genius is incomprehensible and unaccountable and it should therefore not be called upon as an explanation until every other solution has failed." A footnote at this point adds, "The same consideration holds good for the remarkable case of William Shakespeare of Stratford."[2]

THE MADNESS OF HÖLDERLIN

Freud's self-chosen domain was in any case that of neurosis, not psychosis, but it is in conjunction with full-blown psychosis that genius commands greatest attention in the latter half of the twentieth century, most notably in the figure of Hölderlin, who becomes the object of theoretical attention in the early 1950s. French interest in Hölderlin had begun innocuously enough with a doctoral thesis, the first part of which was published in 1921 under the title *La Jeunesse d'Hölderlin jusqu'au roman d'Hypérion* (Hölderlin's youth up until the novel Hyperion). Its author, Joseph Claverie, was killed during the First World War before he could complete his original project, which was to examine the complete life and works. Another thesis, devoted to Hölderlin's *Hyperion*, was published in 1924 by Marie Crayssac. Neither study dealt with the period of Hölderlin's madness, whose onset in 1801 was roughly contemporary with the publication of Pinel's *Traité médico-philosophique sur l'aliénation mentale* and might have offered its author a further example of the "mania" he attributes to "poets extatized by their productions."[3]

In 1930 the poet Pierre Jean Jouve placed Hölderlin's madness at the center of the German poet's œuvre with a volume titled *Poèmes de la folie de Hölderlin* (The poems of Hölderlin's madness). It consisted of a selection of Hölderlin's poems translated by Jouve in collaboration with Pierre Klossowksi: seven under the heading "Poems from Several Periods," thirty-one "Fragments," and some thirty representing the "Poetry of the Last Years." The translation incorporates Hölderlin's own bizarre datings (e.g., 9 March 1940 or 24 May 1758) and signature (Scardanelli). The preface by the philosopher Bernard Groethuysen treats Hölderlin's life and poetic project as a single continuous development, and makes no exception for the period of his madness. The volume concludes with a brief biographical chronology and extracts from contemporary eyewitness accounts describing Hölderlin's condition in his last years. Jouve's was the first published translation of Hölderlin's poetry in French, and it established Hölderlin's madness as an integral part of his work, rather than an anomaly or a decline.[4]

In 1951 Jouve returned to Hölderlin in one of a series of three radio broadcasts titled *Folie et genie* (Madness and genius), where he reused much of the material from the 1930 chronology along with some of the same documents and poems. (The talks were published posthumously in book form in 1983.) By the early 1950s Hölderlin had become much more visible in France than he had been twenty-five years previously. Stefan Zweig's *Der Kampf mit dem Dämon* (The struggle with the demon), devoted to Hölderlin, Kleist, and Nietzsche, was translated almost immediately into French after its German publication in 1925, whereas there was no English translation until 2012. Other studies of Hölderlin appeared during the 1930s, and in 1938 the first French anthology of writings by Heidegger contained the text of a lecture on "Hölderlin and the Essence of Poetry." Maurice Blanchot published a long article in 1946, "Hölderlin et la parole sacrée" (Hölderlin and the sacred word), which was later included in *La Part du feu* (The work of fire, 1949). In another article on Hölderlin, which appeared the following year in *L'Observateur*, Blanchot sets out to answer his opening question, "Why is Hölderlin such a presence amongst us today?," and a footnote refers to a recent study of the poet by a French academic from the Collège de France.[5] In sum, for the listeners of Jouve's radio talks in 1951 Hölderlin would not have been an unfamiliar figure, and the insanity of his later years had become a widely recognized fact that any conception of his genius had therefore to reckon with.

Jouve's earlier Hölderlin volume did not make much of the notion of genius, and the title of the *Radiodiffusion* broadcasts certainly places "madness" ahead of "genius." But genius comes to the fore when Jouve considers Hölderlin alongside the examples of Tasso and Nerval, as Tasso had been viewed as an exemplary instance of melancholy genius from the Romantic period onward. In 1951, a few months before Jouve's radio broadcasts, Blanchot had published a further essay on Hölderlin, "La folie par excellence" (Madness par excellence*)*, where he acknowledged "the fine book in which Pierre Jean Jouve and Pierre Klossowski translated some of Hölderlin's *Poems of Madness*." In his talk on Hölderlin, Jouve in turn quotes at length from Blanchot's discussion, which he clearly saw as endorsing his own perspective. Two years later, Blanchot's essay appeared as the preface to a new French translation of Karl Jaspers's 1922 study of the relation between madness and creativity, which examines the cases of Strindberg, van Gogh, Swedenborg, and Hölderlin.[6] This was 1953, the year when Sartre was beginning to draft the first version of what would later become *Les Mots*, and just one year before Minou Drouet began writing the poems that brought her to public attention. But Hölderlin, and the discussion his case provoked, engendered a conception of genius that had nothing to do with child prodigies, and a very different view of poetry from the one associated with Minou Drouet.

GENIUS AS ENIGMA: PIERRE JEAN JOUVE

In the essay on Hölderlin, Jouve begins by stressing the importance of the period of madness in considering the poetry: "Hölderlin undoubtedly provides one of the most crucial cases of madness in poetry, not just because for the ten years of his lucid activity he was one of the greatest poets in Germany, but because, after seven years of crisis and periodic confinement, he outlived his own form for thirty-six years of insanity, still writing mysteriously admirable things."[7] Mystery and admiration set the tone for the discussion of the relation between genius and madness in a spirit that owes much to psychoanalysis. The approach is quite unlike that of nineteenth-century medical science, which claimed to be able to explain the etiology of genius, whether as hallucination, lesion, hyperesthesia, or measurable deviation from clinically established norms. Jouve rejects the principles of scientific explanation and declares that "[w]e know almost nothing about man. Science acts on the world, but it has scarcely any purchase on man. The mystery accompanying human initiative remains deep, and often impenetrable."[8]

The science that described Zola as a racehorse and a racehorse as a genius is irrelevant to Jouve's project. If, as he suggests, we know nothing of genius, the same is also true of madness in its various forms. And although he provides a brief diagnostic label for each of the examples he discusses (melancholia and paranoia for Tasso, manic-depressive illness for Nerval, *dementia praecox*— now more commonly known as schizophrenia—for Hölderlin), Jouve insists that the relation between genius and madness should be considered as an enigma that calls for "wonderment" rather than pathologizing explanation.

He is not interested in the cases, such as that of Nietzsche, where insanity destroyed genius. And he is as dismissive of the view that mental illness fosters genius as he is of the view that genius is a kind of mental deficit. His focus is rather on the mystery of those cases where, as with Nerval, the artist, despite his insanity, has "not only retained his gifts, but increased them without altering his style, applying them meticulously to subject matter that terrified him." This harks back to the phenomenon noted by (Pseudo-)Aristotle, whereby Maracus the Syracusan produced his best poetry when he was mad, and it is exactly the point that the poetry of Hölderlin's madness illustrates. Jouve finds support for his approach in Blanchot's essay, which is equally adamant in asserting the necessity of considering the conjunction of insanity and poetry as an enigma: "Should one not get closer to the enigma, and search out the point where it is possible to see it without making it vanish, where it can be grasped in its purity, in the purity of its enigma, in all the clarity that it both opposes and offers to the person confronting it with the desire to examine it without disturbing it and to be examined by it in turn?"[9] This remark is approvingly quoted by Jouve and it exemplifies a very different relation between commentator and phenomenon to the one illustrated by the professional confidence with which Lélut or Moreau de Tours had described the pathologies they identified in Socrates, Pascal, or their own real-life clinical cases.

Jouve's sense of the nature of the poet's psyche in general is derived largely from Freud's notion of the unconscious, reinforced by his own experience as a poet and as an unusually sensitive individual with depressive tendencies. In his essay on Nerval he describes madness as an extreme eruption of the unconscious—"that peremptory eruption of the unconscious organized to form a world, a world of system or the dispersal of broken things"—and many of his other writings ascribe a central role to the unconscious in poetry where there is no question of the poet being considered clinically insane. In the prefatory essay to the collection of his own poems, *Sueur de sang* (The sweat of blood), "The Unconscious, Spirituality and Catastrophe," published in 1933, Jouve makes much of the new image of man that has emerged from psychoanalysis. Human nature has been redefined by the unconscious, which Jouve glosses as "the erotic drive and the death drive, bound together." These twin impulses mean that, like any human being, the poet finds himself constantly threatened by catastrophe, but this is a situation that can be turned to advantage since "what the poet does with the death instinct is the reverse of what catastrophe seeks to do." Continuing this line of thinking in his autobiographical reflections, *En miroir* (Mirrored), published the year after the radio talks, Jouve describes the unconscious as anonymous, vast, indifferent to time and "truly formless," but, he insists, it is nonetheless "a great generator of form."[10] Likewise, madness, though it can lead to catastrophe, is not a pathology but, as an extreme version of the unconscious and its conflicting tensions, also contains the potential for poetry.

The unconscious may be fundamental to Jouve's conception of poetry, but it never becomes an excuse to turn the poet or poetry into the object of a psychoanalytical interpretation. Jouve does not write from a position of knowledge, and there can be no systematic definition of poetry. The poem's truth requires it to be regarded as a mystery, where, moreover, the unconscious is better hidden than flaunted.[11] This is despite the fact that Jouve was well acquainted with psychoanalytic theory and with the work of Freud. His second wife, Blanche Reverchon-Jouve, whom he married in 1925, was an early pioneer of psychoanalysis in France. She had trained as a psychiatrist and subsequently became a practicing psychoanalyst. In 1923 she published the first French translation of Freud's *Three Essays on the Theory of Sexuality* with Bernard Groethuysen (who wrote the preface to Jouve's *Poèmes de la folie de Hölderlin*), and she was one of the first members of the Société psychanalytique de Paris, founded in 1926.

In 1933 Blanche and Jouve jointly authored a case study of one of her patients, which was published in the *Nouvelle Revue Française* under the title "Moments d'une psychanalyse" (Moments from a psychoanalysis), and is regarded as a milestone in the development of psychoanalysis in France. In the late 1930s Blanche analyzed the English Surrealist poet David Gascoyne who shared Jouve's interest in Hölderlin and published his own *Hölderlin's Madness* in 1938.[12] Jouve's meeting with Blanche led him in 1928 to renounce all his writing prior to 1925 and to embark on what he called his "vita nuova." Although Blanche advised Jouve against undergoing analysis himself, his new life was lived under the aegis of psychoanalysis. Neither analyst nor patient, Jouve shared the perspectives of both.

He never lays his own claim to genius, and though he took the term *Génie* as the title of a volume of poems published in 1948, it makes no obvious reference to genius of any kind and he did not include it in his collected poetry.[13] Nor is Jouve seeking to claim genius for poets who have previously been denied it, as Lamartine and Hugo had done. The tripartite biographical study *Folie et génie* allows him to take three figures whose genius is uncontested, in order to explore the collision or struggle (he uses both terms) of genius with madness in the case of exceptionally unbalanced minds which nonetheless produced exceptional poetry.

Even before its encounter with madness, genius is divided against itself as a struggle between creative and destructive forces, "the genius that brings forth [*enfante*] and the genius that destroys." Madness exacerbates the conflict since it is the antithesis of genius: "there is nothing more contrary to a commanding genius than madness which is always mechanical." And yet, in the three cases described by Jouve, the dual struggle—between the creative and destructive tendencies of genius, and between genius and madness—results in something strange and admirable: "at the same time as the illness starts, there appears in the work a change that is not foreign to the initial aim, but that contributes something unique and exceptional, and reveals depths never previously glimpsed." This is Blanchot, quoted by Jouve from "La Folie par excellence" in support of his own argument.[14] Neither genius nor madness is worth examining in isolation, and for both Blanchot and Jouve the extraordinary realization of the poet's individual poetic trajectory is produced by the inextricable conjunction of the two.

Blanchot: The Essence of Poetry

While Blanchot's concern is not primarily with genius, he acknowledges that the exceptional achievement of Hölderlin is possible only in "profound artistic geniuses." He shares Jouve's view that insanity is not itself creative, and argues that while schizophrenia is not the source of Hölderlin's poetry it is also not its antithesis. Among "creative personalities"—and only there—schizophrenia may become the condition for the "depths" to open up, but the resulting poetry cannot simply be attributed to the illness: "the experiments and the figures, the forms and the language have their roots in the mind. They seem to be related to the truth of that mind and categorically cannot be conceived except in relation to it, and yet, without the schizophrenia they would not have been possible." The schizophrenic poet has all the recognized features of other schizophrenics, but Hölderlin's response is a struggle whose aim is to "give form to the extreme," a form endowed with "the vigor, the order, and the sovereignty of poetic power to its highest degree."[15]

The individual may be subject to a radical division of his being and destroyed by psychosis, yet in the case of Hölderlin this created the channel through which his own poetic language was realized to an extent that would not otherwise have been possible. Like Jouve, Blanchot insists on the "absolutely mysterious" character of Hölderlin's madness, which allowed what he calls "poetic exigency" to reach its acme. He argues more generally that scientific explanations on the basis of causalities do not offer any kind of understanding for the issues he is addressing, and he gives Jaspers—himself a psychiatrist—credit for refusing to capitulate before the incomprehensible and for "seeking to understand it as irreducible." As Jouve approvingly acknowledges, Blanchot's stated goal is to grasp Hölderlin's madness "in the purity of its enigma."[16]

The psychoanalytic perspective is less valuable here for the knowledge that it supplies than for the relation that it enables between doctor and patient, analyst and analysand, which is something other than diagnosis or explanation. Blanchot had had some experience of psychiatry as part of his medical studies at the Hospital of Sainte-Anne in the early 1930s, where he specialized in neurology and psychiatry. This is no doubt relevant to his interest in Jaspers's "comparative psychiatric study," but it is in an article titled "Freud" in 1956 that Blanchot explores the analytic relationship as practiced in Freudian psychoanalysis, and reradicalized by Lacan in the context of the breakaway group Société française de la psychanalyse in 1953. The significance of the psychoanalytical relationship established by Freud was that it provided an alternative to the one where "a man . . . throws his weight around in front of another . . . who is assumed to be irrational." In the Freudian model, the analyst positions himself in the place of the patient, and the relation is determined by the power of the one to speak and of the other to listen. Although the analyst may be tempted to believe that he possesses knowledge to which the patient does not have access, Lacan's return to the Freudian model demonstrates that "the essential factor in analysis is the relation with the *other*, in the forms made possible by the development of language."[17]

Blanchot's concerns are not those of a practicing analyst (in the early 1950s he was a novelist and a literary critic), but the model of the psychoanalytic relation and the centrality of language in Lacan's account of that relation are significant for any consideration of the examples of genius and insanity. Jouve argues for an approach to the question of the relation between madness and genius that preserves "the light of art." Similarly, for Blanchot the case of Hölderlin is ultimately far more instructive about the workings of the language of poetry than about the specific nature of either insanity or genius. The destruction of Hölderlin through insanity may have been the consequence of having "desired something great too strongly," but the result of this destruction was "something like the truth and the affirmation of the essence of poetry." Hölderlin's insanity was not a punishment for Promethean poetic ambition (as it is in Stefan Zweig's Romantic account), and in Blanchot's view, what Hölderlin sought—and achieved—was a destiny for poetry itself, a destiny and a truth that he "he gave himself the task of fulfilling" even in his madness.[18]

The essays by Jouve and Blanchot accomplish precisely what Barthes saw as lacking in the debates about Minou Drouet: a reflection on genius that relates it to issues about the nature of poetry itself. Moreover, they do so in a way that turns genius into a question that is addressed *to* the would-be observer as much as one that is formulated *by* him. All this makes the essay the appropriate genre for a discourse that may go by the name of theory, but that has no pretensions to offering theoretical answers or to constructing theoretical systems. Hölderlin's schizophrenia restores genius for consideration in conjunction with poetry and in the process once again transforms the language in which genius is examined.

CHAPTER 18

Julia Kristeva and Female Genius

>When [women] possess genius, I believe that it makes a more
original impression than in us.

—Diderot, *Sur les femmes*

In the four decades that followed these portraits of Hölderlin, French theory
showed little interest in the issue of genius. But at the very end of the century
the notion makes a dramatic and unexpected return in female guise with Julia
Kristeva's three biographical studies of Hannah Arendt (1999), Melanie Klein
(2000), and Colette (2002). Published under the collective title *Le Génie féminin*,
these biographies make no explicit connection with either Jouve or Blanchot,
though three lines from Jouve's translation of one of Shakespeare's sonnets provide an epigraph for the Melanie Klein volume. Nor is Kristeva concerned with
insanity and its possible relations to genius. Her perspective is, nonetheless,
predominantly psychoanalytic: each of the books describes Kristeva as a "psychoanalyst," as well as a professor at the University of Paris VII and *docteur ès
lettres*. Collectively, the trilogy offers a psychoanalytically grounded account of
gender and femininity as part of its reflection on genius. Genius takes a new,
explicitly gendered form and it does so thanks to the mix of literary criticism,
feminist theory, and psychoanalysis that is characteristic of the later years of
"French theory."

There is a certain boldness in Kristeva's approach, which, against the grain of
previous tradition, treats female genius as a given rather than defensively pleading the cause. Her generic title is a defiant assertion that women can be geniuses
too, her three subjects being offered as ostensive proof for her claim. There is
also a certain defiance in the very recourse to the notion of genius, which in the
context of French theory, Kristeva acknowledges as a "provocative hyperbole."[1]
Hannah Arendt herself said in *The Human Condition* (1958) that the term
smacks of idolatry and that twentieth-century artists had preferred to empha-
size craftsmanship or competence as the necessary conditions for artistic production.[2] But, as we shall see, it is Arendt who supplies Kristeva with some of
the key arguments that she uses to justify genius. Indeed, the word "justification" is much closer to the spirit of Kristeva's project than any other. Like Jouve
and Blanchot, Kristeva eschews explanation and treats genius as an object of

celebration—or, to use her own word, "admiration." And like them, she approaches her subject through biographical example rather than theoretical abstraction. What Hölderlin, Nerval, and Tasso were for Jouve, Arendt, Klein, and Colette are for Kristeva, albeit on a much larger scale, since each of her biographies runs to several hundred pages.

Exemplary Singularities

What is new about Kristeva's justification of genius is the case she makes for its necessity, a necessity that arises from the social, cultural, and existential conditions of the modern world. "Genius" has a specific application in our age, says Kristeva, and is now a "therapeutic term" that saves us from "dying of uniformity." Whereas Barthes and Sartre condemned genius for its complicity with contemporary cultural values, Kristeva regards it as a necessary corrective to them: "the term 'genius' seems to me to designate those paradoxical occurrences, singular experiences and surprising extremes that arise, despite everything, in our increasingly standardized universe." Norms are everywhere, and individual character is now an exception of which the singularity of genius is an extreme but vital instance, opening up human existence to the possibility of meaning in ways that are capable of transforming the lives of *all* those who encounter it. The examples proposed by Kristeva are precious because they suggest "that our existence is indefinitely renewable by means of the extraordinary."[3] Genius is restored to exemplarity and its extraordinary character offered for emulation.

The singularity that Kristeva identifies as the central feature of genius is not innate so much as achieved, and the work of genius is the means whereby its exemplar realizes herself as a subject. To read the life of a genius as these biographies present it is to track "the forming of a subject," and to be invited to "attempt an analogous surpassing of oneself." It is to discover the possibility of becoming a *qui* rather than a *quod*, a "who" rather than a "what," a "someone" rather than an "anyone." This distinction (if not the precise terms) is central to Hannah Arendt's thinking—of which Kristeva's argument can be seen as a continuation—even though neither Arendt, nor Klein, nor Colette had any interest of her own in the issue of genius. Genius in Kristeva's version is an extreme form of the constitution of subjectivity as *qui* that she urges everyone to aspire to. It is such *ecceitas* (a term she takes from Duns Scotus) that provides the necessary antidote to the modern "maladies of the soul," conditions that Kristeva explored a few years earlier in a work of that title and for which she is proposing genius as a cure.[4] Genius in this argument both goes against the grain of social norms and once again constitutes a model of psychic health.

The singularity of genius is exemplified in the manner in which the genius-subject constitutes her own subjectivity through her life and her work. But it is also written into the intellectual practices she adopts: narrative rather than theory, relation rather than autonomy, example rather than system. None of Kristeva's geniuses is a theorist, though each—Arendt and Klein in particular—is a major thinker. However, "far from being a 'professional thinker,' Hannah Arendt enacts her thinking in the midst of her life." Her criterion for evaluating the human condition is narrative rather than theoretical, and this narrative is pragmatic rather than poetic. "Arendt rehabilitates the *praxis* of narrative," and the goal of human life is to transform mere biological *zôè* into meaningful, narratable *bios*.[5]

Equally pragmatic, Melanie Klein left it to her followers to draft the theory that bears her name. In Kristeva's account Melanie Klein was primarily a clinician and worked by intuition: "a courageous clinician and in no sense a '*maître à penser*'." Her work takes the form of case studies (of Dick or Richard, for example), and narrative is once again the medium of her thought whose novelty is, however, nothing less than "a *psychoanalysis of the capacity to think*."[6] The same absence of abstract thought characterizes the work of Colette who stands out from her novelist contemporaries Proust and Gide for her indifference to theoretical discussions of the novel, whether her own or any other. In pursuing genius through the medium of biography, Kristeva is responding not only to the singularity that each genius-subject represents, but also to their own preference for pragmatism and narrative over theory.

Relationality

The second feature common to each of Kristeva's female geniuses is the preference for *relation* in their thinking, a preference that follows as a kind of logic from their refusal of abstraction. For Arendt there is no "solitary Ego," and the transcendence of the individual subject is achieved by "acting and speaking *with others*."[7] The fullest elaboration of relation and its importance in human existence is to be found in Melanie Klein's notion of object relations. The human subject comes into being through its relations to objects (the good breast, the bad breast) and to others, but in particular through its complex negotiations with the mother figure. In Kristeva's estimation, it is the mark of Melanie Klein's genius not only to have had this insight, but also to have achieved her own, real-life negotiation of this relation. Genius is its outcome, and in her accounts of Colette and of Melanie Klein, Kristeva makes the maternal relation a key feature of their individual development.

As in the case of Hannah Arendt, Melanie Klein's own thinking provides Kristeva with the basis for her identification of this dimension of genius, and her reading of Colette is explicitly Kleinian in this regard: "Wonderfully illuminated by the perspicacity of Melanie Klein, Colette's genius carves out . . . a path that breaks through her own guilt to a more archaic oedipal relation with an

all-powerful mother, and transforms the angry stance, . . . and even the infan-
tile psychoses, into a *reparation*." The breakthrough (*dépassement*) develops
into a form of female sexuality that Kristeva regards as a further achievement in
its own right: "In a general intuition, Colette senses that by appropriating her
mother, and creating the mythical figure of Sido, it will become possible for her
to definitively transmute perversion [*père-version*] into '*mère-version*,' to recon-
cile herself to her slightly humiliated femininity, and finally to settle into the
selfless sensuality of a writing that will henceforth be her destiny." On the basis
of this "intuition"—expressed through Kristeva's punning on the auditory overtones of "perversion" as pronounced in French to suggest a maternal alternative—Colette pursues a path that both reveals and fulfils a female sexuality,
which for most women remains unrealized, but whose pursuit is a manifestation of Colette's genius: "it is the journey to the end of the night of her passions,
which she stamps with her true genius."[8]

In Kristeva's eyes this genius is most manifest in Colette's physical relation to
the material world. Her achievement is to have devised a form of writing that is
multiply relational, an "interpenetration of language and world, style and the
body." The material world is palpable in her writing, and the relation between
words and living things exists equally as one between Colette's own life and her
work. This is not just a matter of Kristeva's choice of critical approach (the-life-
and-work), but is presented as an exceptional feat, which in and of itself demonstrates the genius of Colette. If life and work are indistinguishable, they are
so to an unusual degree in the case of Colette because hers is a life "entirely re-
made in and through writing."[9]

Kristeva is more lavish in her use of the term *genius* for Colette than she is
for either of her other two genius-subjects, and this seems to stem from Colette's multiple and entirely untheorized exemplification of relation. In fact, relation proves to be contagious, and Kristeva repeatedly writes her own relation
to Colette's work into her narrative as she recalls first reading the novels in
Bulgaria with the aid of a French dictionary, compares Colette's arrival in the
capital from the provinces to her own experience of arriving in Paris as a for-
eigner, or acknowledges her initiation into gardening through Colette's horti-
cultural lexis.

MATERNITY

Kristeva's discussion of genius is guided first and foremost by her own admiration, expressed in her choice of subjects and by her own elaborations of their
thinking. But, as has already become clear, her treatment of those subjects reveals certain recurrent motifs, which collectively suggest a definition—if not a
full-blown theory—of female genius. Following on from the collective title of
the biographical trilogy, the issue is directly addressed in the first volume,

which opens with an introductory essay titled "Female Genius." This introduction sets out the case, which the concluding essay of the third volume completes by outlining a response to the question posed in its title, "Does Female Genius Exist?"

Kristeva starts out from the ungendered and uncontentious core notion of genius as exceptional, but she goes on to make the quite specific claim that this exceptionality is proven by the necessity of reading the work of genius as being rooted in the biographical experience of its creator: "Let us call 'geniuses' those whose lives we are compelled to narrate because they are inseparable from their inventions." Genius is characterized by its representation in the form of the biography it elicits; and biography is the response to the admirer's sense that behind the invention of genius there is a "someone" whose example is an invitation to "be someone" in turn. The exceptionality of genius is "the most complex and the most seductive" form of the singularity on which survival in an automatized world henceforth depends.[10] This seduction and the resulting admiration constitute a further form of the relationality that Kristeva associates with genius.

So far, so gender-neutral. But the modern era has tipped the balance toward female genius by creating unprecedented conditions that make genius available to women. The twentieth century required a female work force and produced the means of controlling the fertility that had previously excluded women—whether in reality or because of prejudice—from the activities in which they might excel. Added to this, twentieth-century feminism granted women the chance to assert their own difference, whether in language, sexuality, or politics. But Kristeva takes the argument a stage further by claiming that motherhood, which previously debarred women from genius, is now its essential feature. Victor Hugo may have declared that "[t]here is something maternal in genius," but for him this maternal quality was little more than a variant of the predominantly *fraternal* capacity of genius to welcome others into its abode.[11] For Kristeva, by contrast, motherhood lies at the very core of female genius and, as the cases of Klein and Colette have already indicated, is manifest in a variety of forms.

The first of these is Hannah Arendt's privileging of birth as the model for the absolute beginning that ensures the uniqueness of every individual. Unlike Melanie Klein and Colette, Hannah Arendt was not herself a mother, but she makes the inaugural force of natality (this is her term) the fundamental condition for becoming a "someone." In Kristeva's view it is the mark of Arendt's genius—especially as a woman, and even more especially a Jewish woman in the shadow of the Holocaust—to have conceived of freedom in these terms. Melanie Klein was a mother several times over, and became a psychoanalyst as a means of emerging from a particularly difficult relationship with her own mother. According to Kristeva, this dual experience of motherhood is integral to Klein's reflection on the infant's relation to the mother and the basis for her groundbreaking conception of object relations. More importantly for Kristeva, the Kleinian approach allows for a gendering of the child's development to provide an account of the specific experience of girls who are notably absent from Freud's male-oriented Oedipus theory.

Each of Kristeva's women geniuses had to break a mold established by a powerful male precursor—Freud in the case of Melanie Klein, Heidegger in the case of Arendt, and a rather more anodyne Willy in the case of Colette. To this extent they subscribe to a common pattern of genius, and although Kristeva describes Arendt and Melanie Klein as "insubordinate" and as "dissidents in the worlds into which they were born, prey to the hostility of prescriptive coteries, but also capable of fighting mercilessly to develop and defend their original ideas," much the same might be said about any male counterpart.[12] But when Melanie Klein breaks with Freud as the "father" of psychoanalysis to become its "mother," she does so by demonstrating the extreme complexity of the relation between mothers and daughters, a complexity that makes the daughter's necessary break with her mother a far more difficult and demanding negotiation than is the boy's necessary break with either mother or father.

Motherhood lies at the heart of Melanie Klein's object relations, but it is also the model for the psychoanalytic relation between analyst and analysand as described by Kristeva in her own development of Kleinian thinking. Maternity offers women their first encounter with a unique other: for women, "[t]he child is the first other," and motherhood becomes an apprenticeship in the recognition of the singularity of another being. The psychoanalyst shares this "maternal vocation," and psychoanalysis is portrayed by Kristeva as a "[c]ontinuous creation of alterity," in which the analyst is simultaneously "reborn and allows the analysand to be reborn." Which returns us to Arendt's topic of natality, but with the addition of the double-gendering that follows from the bisexual identity of women, argued for by Kristeva on the basis both of Kleinian theory and of Colette's notion of a "mental hermaphroditism." The regendering of psychoanalysis also applies to the male analyst whose role requires him to acknowledge "the feminine and even the maternal that he carries within himself."[13] The task of the maternal analyst—whether male or female—is to facilitate the emergence of the singularity of which the genius is the supreme example.

All this comes very close to suggesting not just that female genius is possible, but that genius can now *only* be female. For better or for worse, says Kristeva, the twenty-first century will be female—and if it is not to be for worse, this will be because of the distinctive qualities of female genius. Female genius as it emerges in Kristeva's three examples is peculiarly well suited to the conditions of the third millennium, which—this still according to Kristeva—will be "that of individual possibilities, or it will not be."[14] In their different ways, in their different domains, and by means of their different strategies, Hannah Arendt, Melanie Klein, and Colette each exemplify the singularity that is the hallmark of genius and that will be the key to survival in the future that Kristeva envisages for contemporary civilization.

There is, however, a paradox in Kristeva's version of genius, since she also indicates that while preparing the way for the future, her three female geniuses belong to a past that no longer exists. The era of "geniuses" and their accompanying systems is over, she says, and has been succeeded by one that now takes the form of "chance and personal risk, and intersecting networks of exchange." Colette (b. 1873), Melanie Klein (b. 1882), and Hannah Arendt (b. 1906) all belong to a time when the twentieth-century conditions for female genius were not yet in place, and they demonstrated their own genius through the manner in which they broke out of the circumstances in which their respective worlds sought to constrain them. The examples of *ecceitas* that they offer are their legacy to a changed world in which genius has, as it were, become democratized as the capacity of each individual subject to invent her own sexuality: "this is where his or her genius lies, and it is quite simply his or her creativity."[15] Or, in a slightly different but equally democratic formulation, genius shares with all singularity the character of its incommensurability. If genius remains special, it is no longer because it is restricted to a small number of exceptional figures, but because its specialness is something to which each and every person can—and, as Kristeva insists, must—aspire.

It might seem something of an anticlimax to discover that the conclusion to Kristeva's argument is that if women can be geniuses, then anyone can. But this misses the contention that it is women geniuses who have made it possible for the rest of us to seek to develop our own creative singularity. Put another way, we owe the best chance of achieving singularity to the discourse in which women have excelled and which calls for particularly feminine qualities in its practitioners, namely, psychoanalysis. Kristeva's account of female genius is essentially psychoanalytic, and this is due to something more than the accident of her own disciplinary preferences. Psychoanalysis may favor women practitioners, but its importance in Kristeva's argument derives from her view that it has the capacity to provide a better understanding of our contemporary world than any other form of thought. In combining Melanie Klein's psychoanalysis with Hannah Arendt's political philosophy and her own literary-critical reading of Colette's texts, Kristeva has woven three discursive strands together to consider afresh the topic of genius. The result is a mutually reinforcing justification of genius and of the implicitly gendered psychoanalytic language in which it is rehabilitated.

CHAPTER 19

Derrida, Cixous, and the Impostor

> After all, a little charlatanism is always permitted to genius, and in
> fact is not ill-suited to it.
>
> —Baudelaire, "La Genèse d'un poème"

Genèses, généalogies, genres et le génie (Geneses, genealogies, genres and genius), one of Derrida's last books, is the text of a lecture given in 2003 to mark
the gift made by Hélène Cixous of her archive to the Bibliothèque nationale de
France. One year after the publication of the third volume of Kristeva's *Le Génie
féminin*, genius and gender are once again associated in relation to an individual figure—in this case, the writer Hélène Cixous. As Derrida's compound title
indicates, genius is not the sole topic of his discussion, but the occasion is the
pretext for a thoroughgoing reevaluation of the notion as exemplified by Cixous herself and, in particular, as implied by the narrative of her past affair with
an American boyfriend and self-proclaimed genius recalled in her recent *Manhattan* (2002).

Genius, named last in Derrida's title, is the topic on which his book begins,
and it is addressed in the form of a series of questions:

> What is a genius?
> What of genius?
> What of this common noun which claims to name what is least com-
>   mon in the world?[1]

The questions continue, and one in particular returns at regular intervals,
directed at genius itself: "Genius, who are you?" (*Génie, qui es-tu?*), which is
also punningly read as a recognition of the impossibility of any answer: "génie
qui es tu"—"genius who are silenced." Genius, says Derrida, does not lend itself
to discussion in the form of statements that assert "Genius is...." Questions
addressed *to* genius—even in the likely absence of any reply—are preferable to
statements *about* genius. The issue of statements *by* genius is another matter,
and I shall return to it presently.

Rethinking Terms

The refusal of constative assertion is due in part to the nature of genius itself, but also to the fact that there is something bothersome about the very notion: "The name 'genius,' as we know only too well, is an embarrassment. . . . And has been for a long time." But rather than repudiate it outright, as Barthes or Sartre had done, Derrida is selective in his refusal of the aspects of genius that might otherwise make it inadmissible as a concept. He rejects only what he calls "an obscurantist abdication before genes, . . . a concession to the genetics of *ingenium* or, worse still . . . a creationist innatism." Whether it be the "biologizing naturalism" of the genetic view, or the "theology of ecstatic inspiration" that underwrites "the intoxication . . . of writing under dictation," these received notions of genius get in the way of Derrida's questions because, as Sartre and Barthes had already pointed out, they merely encourage "mute adoration before the ineffable."[2] The ineffable is very different from the silence of the genius apostrophized by Derrida in an enquiry that reconsiders a number of the assumptions previously associated with genius and ends up giving the concept a new lease of life.

The aim is to "demonstrate in what ways the concept of *genius*, if indeed it is a concept, must be removed both from its common meaning and from its place, however obvious and plausible, in the homogeneous, homogenetic, genetic, generational and generic series." The genealogies engendered by the early etymological sense of genius are now antithetical to any validity the concept may have in the future. Derrida's genius is neither genetic nor genealogical, and its gender is not necessarily male. Past conceptions of genius have treated it in the singular and attributed it to men: "The geniuses of a woman . . . have never been recognized in the feminine." The gender of genius is ungrammatically feminized in Derrida's French when he rewrites it as "*une* génie" and ascribes it to Cixous: "More than one genius [*une génie*] in one."[3]

As this formulation indicates, genius is also viewed as manifold, and not as a single identifying characteristic of the kind that made it possible to talk about *le génie de la langue française*. This national linguistic genius is another component of the inherited conceptual baggage that comes in for reassessment as Derrida pits Cixous's distinctive literary idiom against the genius of the French language in the form of an encounter between two different kinds of linguistic genius. The "genius of the language" conventionally refers to "its grammatical, lexical or semantic riches, the infinite potentiality of its specific resources," and, as Rivarol argued, its riches are writ large in the works of the writers of genius like Pascal or Boileau who pay homage to it by displaying its essential characteristics. The genius of Cixous's language does not subscribe to such continuities. Its relation to French is ambivalent, "both a responsible inheritor and yet a violent, unpredictable, eruptive, heteronomous, severing," and its effect is to open the eyes of the French language to an unconscious and previously unacknowledged genius contained within it.[4]

The notion of genius as innate endowment also comes under scrutiny when Derrida claims that "[a] genius that was a natural gift would not be a genius." To describe genius as a gift would be to assimilate it into an economy of exchange, whereby gifts are annulled through the presupposition of some form of return—whether reciprocation in kind, gratitude, or simple recognition. If the work of genius is given and received by a donor and a recipient who each know what is given, then, by being translated into terms of contract and symbolic value, it too ceases to be a gift. The gift of genius, as Derrida conceives it, is given without knowledge of its content: "Genius gives without knowing." And by the same token, "those who receive from it (whether individual or institutional subjects) do not and must not know what they are receiving, which is always something more, always something other, and older and more unpredictably new, more monstrously unheard of and inexhaustible, more inappropriable than anything we can consciously picture it as being."[5] Derrida's is an even more radical reading of the originality of genius than that of Kant for whom genius entailed the ignorance on the part of genius itself as to its own procedures, but not the ignorance of the beholders on whom its recognition depended.

This rethinking of genius as a gift is part of Derrida's rethinking of its originality, though he does not use the word. The novelty so often celebrated in genius, its capacity to dispense with convention and break the mold, is taken to the extreme of an absolute singularity that is articulated as event rather than as entity. The events created by the singularity of genius are without precedent and resist replication: "the quality of genius consists precisely in bringing about, in giving rise to, giving *tout court*, giving birth to the work as event, by breaking paradoxically with all genealogy, all genesis and all genres."[6] This makes genius the odd one out in the words listed in Derrida's title: not to be explained by reference to genealogies or geneses, genius is resistant to generic assimilation or gender assignment (*genre* having both these senses in French), and singular as distinct from their plurals. It is for this reason that it does not lend itself to constative definitions, for to say "genius is this or that" is to imply that genius is repeatable, that it can be the same thing in more than one instance, and so to negate its essential singularity.

Singularity was also the core feature of Kristeva's account of genius, but hers was the singularity achieved by human subjects as a necessary condition for living in the modern world. Derrida's singularity of genius as event has more to do with literature than with living: "the quality of genius in the happening of genius [*événements géniaux*] is bound up with Literature and its All-powerful-other." Literature here has a capital L, and the formula "All-powerful-other" is taken from Cixous, who declares repeatedly in *Manhattan*, "*I loved Literature above all else.*"[7] Once again, literature provides the horizon for the evaluation of genius, as it did for Barthes and Sartre (negatively) or for Jouve and Blanchot (positively), and indeed for Kristeva in the prominence given to Colette, as if each provided a necessary measure for the other in some implicit resistance to the categorical, quantitative definitions of genius that were being pursued elsewhere.

COUNTERFEIT GENIUS

It is, however, Literature with a capital L that allows the impostor to enter the frame. The young Hélène Cixous is sitting on one side of a desk in the Beinecke Library in Yale reading Homer, Shakespeare, and Joyce while a young American sits across from her reading Milton. Cixous is tracing the figure of Ulysses, a character she both fears and admires, but whose "tricks" she dislikes, through three national literatures. The literature to which each of the two readers is devoted becomes the bond between them, and Cixous soon falls for the young man whose fraudulent claim to be ill and dying lends a "supernatural theatricality" to this "false reality." Cixous's love of literature translates into a fear of betraying "a powerful-other," so that, despite her distaste for Ulysses's trickery, she falls for a man who calls himself Gregor (like the character in Kafka's *Metamorphosis*), whose first letter to her turns out to have been taken word for word from the *Letters to Milena*, whose imprecations against the world are actually a poem by Mandelstam, and whose supposedly mortal illness is borrowed directly from Kafka and a host of other tubercular writers. He claims to be writing a novel that has been accepted by Knopf and is set to change the course of American literature. He intimates that he is friends with the conductor Klemperer and an associate of the Nobel Prize–winning physicist Kusch. More theatrically—and, a skeptic might say, more suspiciously—he also sports an eye patch, symptomatically brings a faux crocodile suitcase to his assignation with Cixous in a hotel bedroom, and bears a scar down his chest that may not actually exist. In sum, "Gregor's identity as a dying man was just temporary and cobbled together, a fabulous montage of quotations and references borrowed from world literature, classical, and extremely modern literature."[8] However, Cixous is seduced by this ragbag of literary allusion and allows herself to believe that it is proof that Gregor is the genius he gives himself out to be.

Fake genius, however, is not as easily distinguished from the real thing, as Cixous's mother (or common sense) might have one believe. The six-thousand-franc phone bill that Gregor inveigles Cixous into running up at her mother's expense contributes to the conviction with which Mme Cixous accuses her daughter of sheer gullibility: "You cannot distinguish between a genius and a liar. Whereas I didn't even read the letters from the suspect genius." But nearly half a century on from the affair, Cixous is still not willing to concede the point, and instead persists in seeing a kind of genius in Gregor, even if it is not the one he himself laid claim to:

> He wanted to be Kafka and so to escape Gregor. . . . Or rather he would have liked a
> certain Kafka to be him, Gregor. He would have liked to be a great writer of fables
> and allegories I say and I have always thought that he almost was, I have always been
> able to think that he had genius I say and after the end of the affair I was still able to
> think that by some misfortune his genius was misplaced and he himself hadn't real-
> ized it while he wanted to be one at all costs he had taken himself for someone else
> entirely to the utter ruin of his own identities.

If Gregor is almost a genius, it is not *despite* his imposture, but *because* of it.
Imposture was the very substance of the genius that he never quite had: "If he
had written down the story he made up day after day in order to pass himself
off as a real writer, perhaps he would have been a real writer."[9] The story he
made up about himself might have been a work of genius, if it had been carried
off with greater conviction. However, "[t]he one thing Gregor lacked was his
own willingness to be taken in by it: What a mistake, but it was ineluctable, not
to have believed in himself (who, I don't know) in the presence of a self who was
of equal worth to another and to have become a thief of souls. A genius thief.
You can tell genius from *what* it steals. From the fact that it *steals*." The identity
of true genius is stolen from others. But it requires the right kind of credulity to
fly (the French word *voler* means both "to steal" and "to fly"), and Cixous recognizes her own part in creating the impostor in place of the genius: "this character would never have existed if I hadn't believed him to my core—cruel credulity." She sees in retrospect that her mistake was to have given credence to the
genius Gregor pretended to be rather than to the very fact of pretending: "I
loved him for his counterfeit genius he would like to have been loved for his
other genius, the genius for counterfeiting."[10] The genius of the impostor consists precisely in his imposture, and it is the presence of such imposture that
brings genius back on the agenda for consideration.

Counterfeiting Genius

There is something characteristically twentieth century about this conjunction
of genius and fraudulence. Or rather between genius and the possibility of
fraud. Sartre may have denounced genius as a form of imposture, but elsewhere
genius frequently appears as a kind of bravado where the would-be genius declares—in the first person—her or his claim to genius in a manner that suggests
a measure of provocation, and introduces a margin of potential fakery along
with the assertion of genius itself. There are some fine examples of this, all of
which, as it happens, come from figures who made France their adoptive home
or had close associations with it. The first, Gertrude Stein, complicates the first-
person attribution, since the assertion of her genius is ostensibly attributed to
Alice B. Toklas in *The Autobiography of Alice B. Toklas* (published in 1933),

whose author is nonetheless clearly identified on the cover page as Gertrude Stein herself. Early on in the text she has Alice B. announce:

> I may say that only three times in my life have I met a genius and each time a bell within me rang and I was not mistaken, and I may say in each case it was before there was any general recognition of the quality of genius in them. The three geniuses of whom I wish to speak are Gertrude Stein, Pablo Picasso and Alfred Whitehead. I have met many important people, I have met several great people but I have only known three first class geniuses and in each case on sight within me something rang.[11]

Unlike Cixous's Gregor, Gertrude Stein appears to be entirely convinced of her own genius, and she makes sure that Alice B. distinguishes it from mere greatness or importance.

However, the company she places herself in does not completely exclude a margin for potential imposture. Picasso is one of the most commonly cited examples of genius in the twentieth century, being the iconic artistic genius to complement the equally iconic mathematical genius of Einstein. But this image of creative genius brings with it the suspicion of charlatanism, which is what Braque implied when he declared that "Picasso used to be a great painter. Now he is just a genius," as if genius equated with a form of showmanship or posturing that had nothing to do with great art.[12] The genius in this view is someone who merely performs the role of genius, and the performance becomes a substitute for the reality.

A similar charge is provocatively invited by Salvador Dali in his *Diary of a Genius*, where, not content with the claim made in the book's title, Dali begins with the declaration—in the first person—that he is "the genius of the greatest spiritual order of our day, a true modern genius." He promises to show through his own example that "the daily life of a genius, his sleep, his digestion [that great nineteenth-century index of mental superiority], his ecstasies, his nails, his colds, his blood, his life and death are essentially different from those of the rest of mankind." This record allegedly makes his book "the first diary by a genius," who also, as it happens, had the "unique fortune" to be married to "the genius Gala."[13]

And yet it is also possible to see the impersonation of genius as an index of the very thing it seems merely to simulate. The imposture that Socrates accuses Ion of is based on a fraudulent claim to knowledge—about chariot racing or medicine or warfare—that the rhapsode passes off as his own, as well as on Ion's lack of knowledge about the workings of the poetry he recites or the inspiration on which it draws. Like Dali or Gertrude Stein, Ion is boastfully confident about his own talent: "I reckon I can talk on Homer better than anybody. [No one else] who has ever lived has had so many fine thoughts to deliver about Homer as I."[14] Nevertheless, the thrust of Socrates's accusation is concerned less with Ion's presumptuous assertion of his abilities than with the unjustified claim that, should the need ever arise, his knowledge of the way generals speak would be enough for him to actually become a general. Ion is a fraudulent general, not a fraudulent rhapsode.

But this is to talk as if these distinctions were clear, whereas what Cixous admires is the undecidability of the fraud perpetrated by Gregor, particularly on the matter of his scar—a scar of a rather different kind from the one that identifies Ulysses as the person he claims to be. On reflection, Cixous cannot say whether the scar on Gregor's chest really existed, whether it was a fake, or whether it simply was not there, and if the latter, whether Gregor had willed her to see something where there was nothing, or whether he wanted her to acknowledge that the scar was pure fabrication. So many undecidables, but their undecidability is the point: "If he devised the scenario, the Scar is a stroke of genius, genius as undecidability, undecidably genius: Should I have 'not seen it'? Or 'seen' it? Seen that it was 'fake.' . . . Perhaps he was holding it out to me with a begging hand to *be read*, like a confession?"[15] Poised on a knife edge between real and fake, the scar positions genius itself on an equally undecidable divide between genuine and fraudulent. And, in a further step, makes it synonymous with that very undecidability.

It is this undecidable character of genius that Derrida homes in on in his reading of Cixous's *Manhattan*, and it becomes the core of his rethinking of the concept. Gregor's status as "the ideal type of counterfeit and counterfeiting genius" points to "a vertiginous truth," the "essence of the truest genius: namely the ever present risk of an undecidable counterfeiting." He suggests that the discovery of Gregor's imposture might have been enough for Cixous to lose her faith in the "All-powerful-other" of the Literature out of which Gregor fabricated his phony identity, and thanks to which she allowed herself to be taken in. But, in Derrida's discussion, literature itself has the same undecidability as genius, for it is the very essence of literature to strip readers of the capacity to distinguish between reality and fiction. The undecidability extends still further than the relation between fiction and reality, for it concerns literature in general. It becomes the mark of literature in Derrida's argument to make the very distinction between literature and nonliterature one that it is within the power of literature itself to erode: "The All-powerful-other deprives us, under the name of literature, of the right or the power to decide between literature and non-literature, between fiction and documentary, and this is a situation without equivalent in the world and in the history of humanity."[16] Just as genius hovers between itself and its counterfeiting, so Literature is the hesitation both between fiction and nonfiction, and between itself and its not-self—literature and nonliterature.

Rethinking genius for both Cixous and Derrida goes via imposture. Or, as Derrida himself says, "counterfeit *and* counterfeiting genius is not worst placed to give us the pretext for thinking genius [lit. to give us genius to think]." At the start of the twenty-first century, the "untenable word" of genius is placed back on the agenda for renewed reflection: dismantled and reconstituted on the basis of the very feature—imposture—that had been most responsible for bringing the notion into disrepute.[17] A gift that neither donor nor recipient may be aware of, an event that may be registered but that has no identifiable content, an equivocation that simultaneously affirms its importance and casts its existence into doubt.

For theory, literature remains the horizon against which genius loses or acquires its worth. And where that worth is affirmed, it is in a mode that resists the quantifications that seemed so often to lead to the undoing of genius. All this suggests that genius fares best as the focus of open-ended enquiry—as Blanchot's "enigma," as the pretext for Jouve's "wonderment" or Kristeva's "admiration," or as a reflection, like that of Cixous or Derrida—which does everything except turn it into an object of knowledge. It is in this form that genius remains "good to think with."

Notes

INTRODUCTION

1. Jane Chance Nitzsche, *The Genius Figure in Antiquity and the Middle Ages* (New York: Columbia University Press, 1975), ix. I have benefited from the insights of Jonathan Morton in an unpublished paper titled "Ingenious Genius: Invention, Creation, Reproduction in the High Middle Ages" devoted to Bernardus Silvestris, Alain de Lille, and Jean de Meun's *Roman de la rose.*

2. Cicero, *De Oratore*, ed. H. Rackham, trans. E. W. Sutton, Loeb Classical Library (Cambridge, Mass.: Harvard University Press, 1967), 2:xxxv, 149–50. For the Italian Renaissance use of the word, I am indebted to an unpublished paper by Dilwyn Knox. See also H. Weinrich, "Ingenium," in *Historisches Wörterbuch des Philosophie*, ed. Joachim Ritter and Karlfried Gründer (Basel: Schwabe & Co., 1976), 4:360–63.

3. Peter Kivy, in his instructively titled book *The Possessor and the Possessed: Handel, Mozart, Beethoven, and the Idea of Musical Genius* (New Haven, Conn.: Yale University Press, 2001), takes the examples of Mozart and Beethoven to illustrate this distinction.

4. I borrow the notions of "overdetermination" and "underspecification" from Terence Cave, *Mignon's Afterlives: Crossing Cultures from Goethe to the Twenty-First Century* (Oxford: Oxford University Press, 2011): "Mignon is 'overdetermined': she has more characteristics and more potential storylines than one would expect in a relatively marginal narrative figure, and these features are clustered in ways that can easily seem discontinuous or even dissonant . . . , as if she were composed of more than one fictional character. At the same time, her story is underspecified: it leaves plenty of gaps for the reader, or for other writers, to fill. This special combination of overdetermination and underspecification seems to me to be what makes this literary instance (a character and story invented by Goethe) particularly prone to mutation, adaptation, imitation" (9). Despite the fact that Cave is examining a literary character, it seems to me that there are suggestive analogies between the construction of Mignon and the notion of genius.

5. Joseph Addison and Richard Steele, *Critical Essays from the Spectator*, ed. Donald F. Bond (Oxford: Clarendon, 1970), 250–53 (250). For the *Querelle des anciens et des modernes*, see Jean-Alexandre Perras, *L'Exception exemplaire: Une histoire de la notion de génie du XVIe au XVIIIe siècle* (Thèse de doctorat, Université Paris 8 Vincennes Saint-Denis & Université de Montréal, 2012), 215–52, and passim.

6. Longinus, *An Essay upon Sublime* (Oxford: Printed by L.L. for T. Leigh, 1698).

7. Jacques Chouillet, *L'Esthétique des lumières* (Paris: Presses universitaires de France, 1974), 146.

8. See Jonathan Bate, *The Genius of Shakespeare*, 2nd ed. (London: Picador, 2008).

9. Logan Pearsall Smith, *Four Words: Romantic, Originality, Creative, Genius*, Society for Pure English, Tract No. 17 (Oxford: Clarendon, 1924), 3–48 (footnote on 31).

10. Jochen Schmidt, *Geschichte des Genie-Gedankens in der deutschen Literatur, Philosophie und Politik 1750–1945*, 2 vols. (Darmstadt: Wissenschaftliche Buchgesellschaft, 1985).

11. Kineret S. Jaffe, "The Concept of Genius: Its Changing Role in Eighteenth-Century French Aesthetics," *Journal of the History of Ideas* 41, no. 4 (1980): 579–99, and Herbert Dieckmann, "Diderot's Conception of Genius," *Journal of the History of Ideas* 2, no. 2 (1941): 151–82. I should also mention Georges Matoré and A.-J. Greimas, "La naissance du 'génie' au XVIIIᵉ siècle: étude lexicologique," *Le Français moderne* 25 (1957): 256–72.

12. Penelope Murray, ed., *Genius: The History of an Idea* (Oxford: Basil Blackwell, 1989) and Christine Battersby, *Gender and Genius: Towards a Feminist Aesthetics* (London: Women's Press, 1994). Darrin McMahon's *Divine Fury: A History of Genius* (New York: Basic Books, 2013), which appeared just before my own book went to press, is, however, admirably comprehensive in its coverage.

13. Claude Lévi-Strauss, *Le Totémisme aujourd'hui* (Paris: Presses universitaires de France, 1962), 128.

14. There is only one study to my knowledge that provides a continuous history of the idea in France, but it covers the period from the sixteenth to the eighteenth century (partially overlapping with my own). It was coincidentally written at the same time as I have been writing mine, and gratifyingly confirms a sense not only that such a history is possible but that the time is ripe for it. See Perras, *L'Exception exemplaire*.

15. Étienne Bonnot de Condillac, *Essai sur l'origine des connaissances humaines* [1746], ed. Charles Porset, preface by Jacques Derrida, "L'archéologie du frivole" (Paris: Galilée, 1973), 152–53, my emphasis. All translations into English are mine unless otherwise indicated.

16. Edward Young, *Conjectures on Original Composition* [1759] (Leeds: Scolar Press, 1966), 12, emphasis original. Unless otherwise indicated all further emphases in quotes are those of the original.

17. Ibid., 36.

18. Aristotle, "Problem XXX,1," in *Problems: Books 32–38. Rhetorica ad Alexandrum*, trans. W. S. Hett and H. Rackham, rev. ed., Loeb Classical Library (Cambridge, Mass.: Harvard University Press, 1957), 953a. The scholarly consensus seems to be that even if Aristotle himself was not the author of the *Problemata*, they are sufficiently "Aristotelian" in character for attribution not to pose serious problems of interpretation. See, for example, Aristotle, *L'Homme de génie et la mélancolie: Problème XXX,1*, ed. Jackie Pigeaud (Paris: Rivages, 1991), "Présentation," 1–78 (54). Klibansky is of the same view. See Raymond Klibansky, Erwin Panofsky, and Fritz Saxl, *Saturn and Melancholy. Studies in the History of Natural Philosophy, Religion, and Art* (London: Nelson, 1964), 34.

19. See Marsilio Ficino, *Three Books on Life* [1489], ed. and trans. Carol V. Kaske and John R. Clark (Binghamton, N.Y.: Medieval & Renaissance Texts & Studies, 1989); Juan Huarte, *Examen de ingenios: The Examination of Mens Wits* [1594], translated out of the Spanish by M. Camillo Camilli, translated to English out of his Italian by Richard Carew,

facsimile reproduction ed. Carmen Rogers (Gainesville, Fla.: Scholars' Facsimiles & Reprints, 1959); and Cesare Lombroso, *The Man of Genius* [1877] (London: W. Scott, 1891).

20. Aristotle, "Problem XXX,1," 954a. Pigeaud describes the text as "une rêverie du mélange," "Présentation," 20.

21. Aristotle, "Problem XXX,1," 954a.

22. Smith, *Four Words*, 23–24; Immanuel Kant, *Critique of Judgment* [1790], trans. Werner S. Pluhar (Indianapolis: Hackett, 1987), §47. On inspiration, see also Timothy Clark, *The Theory of Inspiration: Composition as a Crisis of Subjectivity in Romantic and Post-Romantic Writing* (Manchester: Manchester University Press, 1997).

23. On this, see Penelope Murray, "Introduction," in *Plato on Poetry: Ion; Republic 376e-398b9; Republic 595-608b10*, ed. Penelope Murray (Cambridge: Cambridge University Press, 1997).

24. Plato, "Ion," in *Early Socratic Dialogues*, ed. and trans. Trevor J. Saunders (London: Penguin Books, 1987), 49–65 (538b).

25. Ibid., 533e, 534b, 534c.

26. Kant, *Critique*, §46.

27. Ibid., §46.

28. Ibid., §47.

29. Ibid., §47.

30. Ibid., §49.

Chapter 1 The Eighteenth Century: Mimesis and Effect

1. Strictly speaking the term "aesthetics" was coined by Alexander Gottlieb Baumgarten in his *Meditationes philosophicae de nonnullis ad poema pertinentibus* [Reflections on poetry] (Halle, 1735).

2. Jean D'Alembert, *Discours préliminaire de l'Encyclopédie*, ed. Michel Malherbe (Paris: Vrin, 2000), 84, translated as *Preliminary Discourse to the Encyclodpedia of Diderot* by Richard N. Schwab (Chicago: University of Chicago Press, 1995), http://quod.lib.umich.edu/d/did/did2222.0001.083?rgn=main;view=fulltext;q1=preliminary+discourse (accessed 11 December 2013).

3. Ibid., 117.

4. "Inventer" and "Invention," in *Dictionnaire de l'Académie française*, 4th ed. (Paris, 1762).

5. Condillac, *Essai sur l'origine*, 152; Claude-Adrien Helvétius, *De l'esprit* [1758], ed. François Châtelet (Verviers: Éditions Gérard & Cie., 1973), 375; Jean-Antoine-Nicolas de Caritat, Marquis de Condorcet, *Esquisse d'un tableau historique des progrès de l'esprit* [1793–94], ed. Jean-Pierre Schandeler and Pierre Crépel (Paris: Institut national d'études démographiques, 2004), 417.

6. Condillac, *Essai sur l'origine*, 152; Helvétius, *De l'esprit*, 377–82. For Diderot's response to Helvétius, see Denis Diderot, *Réfutation suivie de l'ouvrage d'Helvétius intitulé l'Homme*, in *Œuvres complètes*, vol. 24, ed. Roland Desné and Annette Lorenceau (Paris: Hermann, 2004), e.g., "Do not talk about chance; there is no happy or productive chance for narrow minds.... Do not talk to me either about sustained and powerful

attention; weak minds are incapable of this." Diderot, *Œuvres philosophiques*, ed. Paul Vernière (Paris: Garnier, Classiques Garnier, 1961), 584–85; Voltaire, "Génie," in *Œuvres complètes de Voltaire*, vol. 5. *Dictionnaire philosophique* (Paris: P. Dupont, 1824), 30–35 (33).

7. Condillac, *Dictionnaire des synonymes*, in *Œuvres philosophiques de Condillac*, ed. Georges Le Roy (Paris: Presses universitaires de France, 1951), 3:95; Luc de Clapiers Marquis de Vauvenargues, *Introduction à la connaissance de l'esprit humain* [1747], ed. Jean Dagen (Paris: Flammarion, 1981), 76 and 78. For further discussion of the different views of genius in the eighteenth century, see Annie Becq, *Genèse de l'esthétique française moderne: de la raison classique à l'imagination créatrice* (Paris: Albin Michel, 1994), livre III, 2ᵉ Partie, chap. 2, and Perras, *L'Exception exemplaire*, chaps. 8 and 9.

8. Charles Bonnet, *Essai analytique sur les facultés de l'âme* [1760], ed. Serge Nicolas (Paris: L'Harmattan, 2006), 239; Abbé Dubos, *Réflexions critiques sur la poésie et sur la peinture* [1719], 4th ed. [1740], ed. Dominique Désirat (Paris: École supérieure des Beaux-Arts, 1993), 2:2, 175; Vauvenargues, *Introduction à la connaissance*, 77; Diderot, "Sur le génie," in *Œuvres esthétiques*, ed. Paul Vernière (Paris: Garnier, Classiques Garnier, 1959), 19–20 (19).

9. "Article Génie," in Diderot, *Œuvres esthétiques*, 9–17 (9).

10. D'Alembert, *Discours préliminaire*, 102, 103.

11. Boileau, *L'Art poétique*, in *Œuvres complètes*, ed. Antoine Adam and Françoise Escal (Paris: Gallimard, Bibliothèque de la Pléiade, 1966), 157; Charles Perrault, "Le génie. Épistre à Monsieur de Fontenelle," in *Parallèle des anciens et des modernes en ce qui regarde les arts et les sciences*, ed. Hans Robert Jauss and Max Imdahl (Munich: Eidos Verlag, 1964), 172–74 (172).

12. M. H. Abrams, *The Mirror and the Lamp: Romantic Theory and the Critical Tradition* [1953] (London: Oxford University Press, 1971).

13. Peter Kivy's account of genius in the eighteenth and early nineteenth centuries takes composers as its focus, but his account of the presentation of genius in Handel, Mozart, and Beethoven is based on models of genius that are not restricted to the specific case of musicians. See Kivy, *Possessor and the Possessed*.

14. Batteux, *Les Beaux-Arts réduits à un même principe* [1746], ed. Jean-Rémy Mantion (Paris: Aux Amateurs des livres, 1989), 92; Charles Batteux, *Cours de Belles-Lettres* (1753), 10–11, quoted in the notes to *Les Beaux-Arts*, 109, my emphasis. The *Cours de Belles-Lettres* were an expanded version of the earlier *Beaux-Arts*, and adopt the same lines of argument.

15. Diderot, *Éloge de Richardson*, in *Œuvres esthétiques*, 29–48 (35, 40), my emphasis; Diderot, "Sur le génie," 19, 20.

16. For a history of the idea of originality in the eighteenth century, see Roland Mortier, *L'Originalité, une nouvelle catégorie esthétique au siècle des lumières* (Geneva: Droz, 1982).

17. Dubos, *Réflexions*, 1:26, 75; 1:27, 77.

18. Ibid., 1:77; Jean-François Marmontel, *Éléments de littérature* [1787], ed. Sophie Le Ménahèze (Paris: Desjonquères, 2005), 585–86.

19. Dubos, *Réflexions*, 1:24, 71.

20. "Article Génie," 9, 16.

21. Ibid., 13.

22. Dubos, *Réflexions*, 2:1, 171.

23. Ibid., 1:2, 9; 1:1, 3; 1:3, 9–10.

24. Diderot, *Éloge de Richardson*, 31, 44. On the novel of sensibility in France, see Philip Stewart, *L'Invention du sentiment: Roman et économie affective au dix-huitième siècle*, SVEC, 2010/02 (Oxford: Voltaire Foundation, 2010).

25. Marmontel, *Éléments*, 587.

26. "Article Génie," 17; Voltaire, "Génie," 33.

27. Condillac, *Essai sur l'origine*, 152–53.

28. Marmontel, *Éléments*, 585.

29. Dubos, *Réflexions*, 2:2, 177; Marmontel, *Éléments*, 585; "Article Génie," 12.

30. Denis Diderot, *Salon de 1765*, in Diderot, *Salons*, ed. Jean Seznec and Jean Ad-hémar (Oxford: Clarendon, 1957–67), 2:71.

31. Louis-Sébastien Mercier, *Le Génie, le goût et l'esprit: poëme, en quatre chants*, dédié à M. le Duc de **** (The Hague, 1756), 10. Despite the vehemence with which he defends genius in this poem, Mercier later denounces the whole notion as a prejudice concocted by men of letters. See his article "Génie" in *Néologie, ou vocabulaire des mots nouveaux, à renouveler, ou pris dans des acceptions nouvelles* (Paris: Moussard-Mardran, an IX, 1801), discussed by Perras, *L'Exception exemplaire*, 410–11.

32. Matoré and Greimas, "La naissance du 'génie,' " 262–63.

33. Diderot, *De la poésie dramatique*, in *Œuvres esthétiques*, 169–287 (226). The text was first published in 1758; "Pastiche," in *Encyclopédie ou dictionnaire raisonné des sciences, des arts et des métiers*, http://portail.atilf.fr/cgi-bin/getobject_?a.89:55./var/artfla /encyclopedie/textdata/image/ (accessed 21 February 2013).

34. Mercier, *Le Génie*, ii–iii, 11.

35. Batteux, *Les Beaux-Arts*, 83; 91.

36. Ibid., 87.

37. Dubos, *Réflexions*, 1:1, 1.

Chapter 2 Genius Obscured

1. Jean-Jacques Rousseau, *Dictionnaire de musique*, in *Écrits sur la musique, la langue et le théâtre. Œuvres complètes*, vol. 5, ed. Bernard Gagnebin, Marcel Raymond, and Samuel Baud-Bovy (Paris: Gallimard, Bibliothèque de la Pléiade, 1995), 837, 838. The polemical tone in this entry is no doubt due to Rousseau's partisan position on the question of French vs. Italian music: French music is for those devoid of genius. The epi-graph to this chapter is taken from the entry for "Scène."

2. Voltaire, *Dictionnaire philosophique*, 34–35; Diderot, *Réfutation*, in *Œuvres phi-losophiques*, 590–91.

3. Diderot, *Paradoxe sur le comédien*, in *Œuvres esthétiques*, 289–381 (310, 313).

4. Ibid., 358, my emphasis.

5. Ibid., 307, 378.

6. See Vernière's discussion of the matter in his edition of Diderot's *Œuvres esthé-tiques*, 5–8.

7. Diderot, *Salon de 1767*, in Diderot, *Salons*, 3:147; Diderot, *Le Neveu de Rameau*, ed. Jean-Claude Bonnet (Paris: Flammarion, 1983), 106. Bonnet's Introduction provides

a good account of the history of the text's protracted composition. English translation from Denis Diderot, *Rameau's Nephew; and, First Satire*, trans. Margaret Mauldon, ed. Nicholas Cronk (Oxford & New York: Oxford University Press, 2006), 63, translation modified. All further translations from this edition unless otherwise indicated.

8. Diderot, *Le Neveu*, 112/69; *Entretiens sur le Fils naturel*, in *Œuvres esthétiques*, 69–175 (115).

9. Diderot, *Le Neveu*, 111/68.

10. Ibid., 123/80.

11. Ibid., *Le Neveu*, 46/3; Diderot, *De la poésie dramatique*, 179–287 (218); *Le Neveu*, 55/12.

12. Diderot, *Le Neveu*, 75, my translation.

13. Ibid., 47/4. Herbert Dieckmann makes the point about individuality very clearly. See "Diderot's Conception," 151–52 and passim.

14. Diderot, *Le Neveu*, 50, my translation; 122/79, translation slightly adapted.

15. Ibid., 52/9.

16. Ibid., *Le Neveu*, 55/12.

17. Diderot, *Entretiens*, 98.

18. Condillac, *Essai sur l'origine*, 153.

Chapter 3 Language, Religion, Nation

1. Jean-François de La Harpe, "Introduction," in *Lycée, ou Cours de littérature ancienne et moderne* [1798–1804], 14 vols. (Paris: Depelafol, 1825), 1:10, 11. The original edition was published in 18 vols.

2. Ibid., 1:15, 14, 2.

3. Ibid., 1:20.

4. For Sainte-Beuve's treatment of genius in literary criticism, see my *Biography and the Question of Literature in France* (Oxford: Oxford University Press, 2007), chap. 6.

5. La Harpe, "Introduction," 1:ii.

6. Arthur Schopenhauer, *The World as Will and Representation* [1818], 2 vols., trans. E. F. J. Payne (New York: Dover, 1969). See also Schmidt, *Geschichte des Genie-Gedankens*.

7. See Samuel Taylor Coleridge, "On Poesy or Art," in *Biographia Literaria*, ed. J. Shawcross (Oxford: Oxford University Press, 1979), 2:253–63; William Hazlitt, "On Genius and Common Sense," in *Table Talk: The Selected Writings of William Hazlitt*, ed. Duncan Wu (London: Pickering & Chatto, 1998), 6:26–43, and "Whether Genius Is Conscious of Its Powers?," in *The Plain Speaker: The Selected Writings of William Hazlitt*, ed. Duncan Wu (London: Pickering & Chatto, 1998), 8:108–17; Ralph Waldo Emerson, "Self-Reliance" [1841], in *Selected Essays*, ed. Larzer Ziff (Harmondsworth: Penguin, 1982), 175–203.

8. Victor de Vautré, *Génie du whist méconnu jusqu'à présent, quoique joué avec une espèce de fureur par toute l'Europe, avec ses explications et des maximes certaines pour gagner* (Paris: Ledoyen, 1839); *Le Génie de la mode. Journal de l'élégance parisienne* (1862–84); M. Gustave Mercier-Lacombe, *Naissance et génie* (Paris: H. Souverain, 1839),

11; *Le Génie et ses droits*, vol. 6 of *Paris vivant par des hommes nouveaux* (Paris: G. de Gonet, 1858), 5–7.

    9. Voltaire, "Génie," 36.

    10. Bertrand d'Ayrolles, ed., *Dictionnaire classique de Géographie Ancienne, pour l'intelligence des auteurs anciens, Servant d'introduction à celui de la Géographie moderne de Laurent Echard, ou description abrégée des Monarchies, des Royaumes, ... depuis le commencement du monde, jusqu'à la décadence de l'Empire Romain dans lequel on donne une idée succinte du Genie, des Moeurs, de la Religion, ... des Peuples de la terre sous les différentes Dominations des Perses, des Assyriens, des Grecs & des Romains*, (Paris: Lacombe, libr., 1768); M. de L. M. de l'Académie de P. Luc, *Description historique de l'Italie, en forme de dictionnaire: contenant 1) la géographie tant ancienne que moderne, ... 2) l'esprit de leur gouvernement ... 3) le génie des habitants, les mœurs, ... 4) un détail circonstancié des monumens antiques, ... 5) la description des églises, palais et édifices publics, ... 6) un détail des peintures en mosaïques et tableaux répandus dans les églises et galeries ...*, 2 vols. (Avignon: Chambeau, 1790).

    11. Dominique Bouhours, *Les Entretiens d'Ariste et d'Eugène* [1671], ed. Ferdinand Brunot (Paris: A. Colin, 1962), 40, 32. For a history of the notion of the genius of the French language, see Gilles Siouffi, *Le Génie de la langue française: Études des structures imaginaires de la description linguistique à l'âge classique* (Paris: Champion, 2010).

    12. Quoted in Sylvain Menant's "Présentation" in Antoine comte de Rivarol, *Pensées diverses, suivi de Discours sur l'universalité de la langue française, Lettre sur le globe aérostatique*, ed. Sylvain Menant (Paris: Desjonquères, 1998), 20. Menant's introduction includes a useful account of earlier discussions of the French language.

    13. Rivarol, *Discours*, 105, 114.

    14. Ibid., 116, 123, 125, 124.

    15. Quoted from Chênedollé's memoir of Rivarol by Sainte-Beuve in his essay on Chênedollé in Charles-Augustin Sainte-Beuve, *Chateaubriand et son groupe littéraire sous l'empire: Cours professé à Liège en 1848–1849*, ed. Maurice Allem (Paris: Garnier, 1949), 2:119–26 (127). Chênedollé was the author of a didactic poem titled *Le Génie de l'homme* (1807), which Rivarol had encouraged him to write and to which I shall return in the next chapter. See *Œuvres complètes de Chênedollé*, rev. ed. (Paris: Firmin-Didot, 1864). Sainte-Beuve also wrote a preface for this edition.

    16. Preface to the first edition. François René Chateaubriand, *Essai sur les révolutions; Génie du christianisme*, ed. Maurice Regard (Paris: Gallimard, Bibliothèque de la Pléiade, 1978), 1281–83 (1282).

    17. *Essai historique, politique et moral sur les révolutions anciennes et modernes considérées dans leurs rapports avec la révolution française*, in *Génie du christianisme*, 41–42.

    18. Chateaubriand, *Génie du christianisme*, 469–70.

    19. Ibid., 529, 769, 629, 632, 633.

    20. Ibid., 833.

    21. Ibid., 635.

    22. Ibid., 805, 825.

    23. Madame de Staël, *De la littérature considérée dans ses rapports avec les institutions sociales* [1799], ed. Axel Blaeschke (Paris: Garnier, Classiques Garnier, 1998), 17, 146, 152.

24. Preface to Madame de Staël, *De l'Allemagne* [1813], ed. Simone Balayé (Paris: Flammarion, 1968), 1:39. The book was officially published only in 1813. On this episode, see Angelica Goodden, *Madame de Staël: The Dangerous Exile* (Oxford: Oxford University Press, 2008), 192–93. The ten-year exile had required Mme de Staël's exclusion from a certain radius around Paris, rather than from France itself. In practice, she spent much of the time at her estate at Coppet on the shores of Lake Geneva in Switzerland.

25. As Simone Balayé says in her discussion of Mme de Staël's views on genius, her lifelong concern with the topic never took the form of a theory. See Simone Balayé, "Le génie et la gloire dans l'œuvre de M.me de Staël," *Rivista di letterature moderne et comparate* 20, nos. 3–4 (1967): 202–14.

26. Staël, *De l'Allemagne*, 1:181 and 371. For the other references see, for example, 1:203 and 233.

27. The beneficial effects of Christianity on civilization and culture were already a theme in Staël, *De la littérature*.

28. Staël, *De l'Allemagne*, 1:162, 46, 131, 46, 191.

29. Ibid., 1:197.

30. Ibid., 2:50.

31. "Désormais il faut avoir l'esprit européen," quoted by Émile Faguet, "Madame de Staël," *Revue des deux mondes* 83 (1887): 357–94 (394).

32. Staël, *De l'Allemagne*, 1:99, 2:72.

Chapter 4 Individual versus Collective Genius

1. Chênedollé, *Le Génie de l'homme*, 136.

2. Édouard Alletz, *Génie du dix-neuvième siècle, ou Esquisse des progrès de l'esprit humain depuis 1800 jusqu'à nos jours* (Paris: Paulin, 1842–43), xi.

3. Ibid., l. [this shd be the letter 'l'. does it work better as a capital? L??]

4. Jules Michelet, *Le Peuple* [1846] 5th ed., ed. Paul Viallaneix (Paris: Flammarion, 1974), 236.

5. Ibid., 184, 190.

6. Alfred de Vigny, *Chatterton*, ed. Pierre-Louis Rey (Paris: Gallimard, folio-théâtre, 2001), 1:v (71).

7. Charles Nodier, "Notice historique," in M. (Nicolas-Joseph-Laurent) Gilbert, *Œuvres de Gilbert* [1817], ed. Charles Nodier, rev. ed. (Paris: Garnier, 1921), 1–14 (5).

8. John Keats, "Sonnet to Chatterton" (1815); William Wordsworth, "Resolution and Independence" (1807); Chateaubriand, *Génie du christianisme*, 1153n15. On the suicide of Escousse and Lebras, see Paul Bénichou, *Les Mages romantiques* (Paris: Gallimard, 1988), 169. On the issue of suffering poets, see also Jean-Luc Steinmetz, "Du poète malheureux au poète maudit (réflexion sur la constitution d'un mythe)," *Œuvres & critiques* 7, no. 1 (1982): 75–86, and Pascal Brissette, *La Malédiction littéraire: du poète crotté au génie malheureux* (Montreal: Presses de l'Université de Montréal, 2005).

9. Alfred de Vigny, *Stello*, in *Œuvres complètes*, ed. Alphonse Bouvet (Paris: Gallimard, Bibliothèque de la Pléiade, 1993), 2:623, 625. *Stello* was first published in three separate installments in the *Revue des deux mondes* between October 1831 and April 1832.

10. Chatterton's remark about his heart on a shop counter comes from act 3, scene 1 of the stage version. Vigny, *Chatterton*, 101; Vigny, *Stello*, 547. Chatterton's story is told in "L'Histoire de Kitty Bell" in *Stello*.

11. Vigny, *Chatterton*, 44.

CHAPTER 5 THE ROMANTIC POET AND THE BROTHERHOOD OF GENIUS

1. Alfred de Vigny, "Moïse," in *Poèmes antiques et modernes, Œuvres complètes*, vol. 1, ed. François Germain and André Jarry (Paris: Gallimard, Bibliothèque de la Pléiade, 1986).

2. Alfred de Vigny, "Lettres à une puritaine," *Revue de Paris* 4, quoted in Paul Bénichou, *Le Sacre de l'écrivain, 1750–1830: Essai sur l'avènement d'un pouvoir spirituel laïque dans la France moderne* (Paris: J. Corti, 1973), 370.

3. "Vox clamabat in deserto," "Nos canimus surdis," Victor Hugo, *Odes et ballades*, in *Œuvres complètes: Poésie I*, ed. Claude Gély (Paris: Laffont, 1985).

4. Victor Hugo, "Sur un poète apparu en 1820," *Littérature et philosophie mêlées*, in *Œuvres complètes: Critique*, ed. Jean-Pierre Reynaud (Paris: R. Laffont, 2002), 82–84 (83, 84).

5. Hugo, "Préface," in *Odes et ballades*, 58.

6. Ibid., 62.

7. Lamartine, "Ferrare." The poem was inspired by a visit to Tasso's prison, Tasso being the patron saint of the suffering poet in the period. It was included in the 1849 edition of the *Meditations*. The line from Hugo is in "À M. de Chateaubriand," in *Odes et ballades*, iii, 2; Hugo, "Préface," 59, 56.

8. Lamartine, "Première préface des Méditations (1849)," in Alphonse de Lamartine, *Méditations*, ed. Fernand Letessier (Paris: Garnier frères, 1968), 297–319 (310 and 304–5); Hugo, "Préface," 59; Lamartine, "Ode," in *Méditations*, x.

9. Hugo, *Odes et ballades*, iv, 9 and iv, 6.

10. Lamartine, "Première préface," 303.

11. Hugo, "Preface," 62. See Aurélie Loiseleur, *L'Harmonie selon Lamartine: utopie d'un lieu commun* (Paris: Honoré Champion, 2005), 66ff., for a discussion of the importance and frequency of the *génie/harmonie* rhyme in Lamartine's poetry.

12. Hugo, *Les Orientales* in *Œuvres complètes: Poésie I*, xxxiv.

13. On the notion of an entry into literature, see José-Luis Diaz, *L'Écrivain imaginaire: scénographies auctoriales à l'époque romantique* (Paris: Honoré Champion, 2007).

14. Lamartine, "Commentaires," in *Méditations*, 328.

15. Ibid., 359. "Bonaparte" appeared in the *Nouvelles meditations*, whose first edition was published in 1823.

16. Lamartine, "Commentaires," 343, 358.

17. Ibid., 340.

18. Victor Hugo, *Victor Hugo raconté par un témoin de sa vie*, in *L'œuvre complète de Victor Hugo* (Paris: Jean de Bonnot, 1979), 42:187. The episode is recounted in chap. 4 of Graham Robb, *Victor Hugo* [1997] (London: Picador, 1998).

19. Hugo, "Sur un poète apparu en 1820," 82. He had already dedicated "La lyre et la harpe" to Lamartine (who is represented by the harp) in 1822.

20. Sainte-Beuve, "Victor Hugo. *Odes et ballades*," reprinted in Charles-Augustin Sainte-Beuve, *Premiers lundis*, 3 vols. (Paris: Calmann-Lévy, 1883–86), 1:164–88 (164–65, 178).

21. Hugo, "À mon ami S.B.," in *Odes et ballades*, iv, 17.

22. Hugo, *Victor Hugo raconté*, 212, 213, 215.

23. Hugo, "Préface," 54; Hugo, *Victor Hugo raconté*, 216.

24. My emphases.

25. Sainte-Beuve, "Victor Hugo," 166, 170.

26. John Keats, *Endymion* (1818). Keats, like Shelley, also favored the form of the ode.

27. Hugo, *Odes et ballades*, iv, 17, my emphasis.

28. Honoré de Balzac, *Pensées, Sujets, Fragmens*, ed. Jacques Crépet (Paris: A. Blaizot, 1910), 18, quoted in Gretchen R. Besser, *Balzac's Concept of Genius: The Theme of Superiority in the "Comédie Humaine"* (Geneva: Droz, 1969), 25.

CHAPTER 6 VICTOR HUGO, WILLIAM SHAKESPEARE, AND THE DYNASTY OF GENIUS

1. Victor Hugo, *William Shakespeare*, in *Œuvres complètes: Critique*, 237–462 (310).

2. Bénichou, *Les Mages romantiques*, 492–93.

3. Hugo, *William Shakespeare*, 390.

4. Ibid., 257, 340. English translation here from Victor Hugo, *William Shakespeare*, trans. Melville B. Anderson [1887] (Honolulu, Hawaii: University Press of the Pacific, 2001), 191.

5. Hugo, *William Shakespeare*, 246.

6. Ibid., 289, 349, 373, 288, 372–73. Longer quotation from Anderson translation (slightly adapted), 262.

7. Ibid., 375, 354.

8. Ibid., 278, 267, 274, 303.

9. Ibid., 271, 274, 282.

10. Ibid., 377 (my emphasis), 381.

11. Hugo, "Du génie," in *Œuvres complètes: Critique*, 560–63 (561).

12. Hugo, *William Shakespeare*, 316.

13. Ibid., 289.

14. Henri Meschonnic, *Hugo, la poésie contre le maintien de l'ordre* (Paris: Maisonneuve & Larose, 2002), 56. Meschonnic has a rewarding discussion of the historical function that Hugo ascribes to genius.

15. Hugo, *William Shakespeare*, 283, 406, 399.

16. Ibid., 431, 433, 397.

17. Ibid., 43; Michelet, *Le Peuple*, 57.

18. Hugo, *William Shakespeare*, 288. On the reception of Shakespeare's genius by the French, see Bate, *Genius of Shakespeare*, chap. 6.

19. Quoted in Robb, *Victor Hugo*, 245 and 378. Dickens's remark appears in a letter to the Countess of Blessington dated January 1847. Robb also provides an excellent account of Hugo's political evolution.

CHAPTER 7 GENIUS UNDER OBSERVATION—LÉLUT

1. On this history, see Jan Goldstein's indispensable study, *Console and Classify: The French Psychiatric Profession in the Nineteenth Century* (Cambridge: Cambridge University Press, 1987); Juan Rigoli, *Lire le délire, aliénisme, rhétorique et littérature en France au XIX siècle* (Paris: Fayard, 2001); Ian R. Dowbiggin, *Inheriting Madness: Professionalization and Psychiatric Knowledge in Nineteenth-Century France* (Berkeley: University of California Press, 1991); and Elizabeth A. Williams, *The Physical and the Moral. Anthropology, Physiology, and Philosophical Medicine in France, 1750–1850* (Cambridge: Cambridge University Press, 1994). Goldstein also discusses the issue of terminology (6), as does Rigoli, 16.

2. Mme de Staël, *Essai sur les fictions* [1796], in *Œuvres de jeunesse*, ed. Simone Balayé and John Isbell (Paris: Desjonquères, 1997), 131–56 (131); and Staël, *De l'Allemagne*, 1:259.

3. Vigny, *Chatterton*, 42; Baudelaire, "La reine des facultés," *Salon de 1859*, in *Curiosités esthétiques, L'Art romantique et Autres œuvres critiques de Baudelaire*, ed. Henri Lemaitre (Paris: Editions Garnier, 1986), 320–24.

4. Unsigned "Avertissement" to "Série de fragments sur l'aliénation mentale," *Journal général de médecine* 62 (1818): 145, quoted in Goldstein, *Console and Classify*, 106. Esquirol's encomium comes from his *Des passions* (1805), 7, also quoted by Goldstein, 80.

5. Julien-Joseph Virey, "Génie," in *Dictionnaire des sciences médicales: par une société de médecins et de chirurgiens*, 60 vols., ed. M. M. Alard et al. (Paris: Panckoucke, 1812–22), 18:87.

6. Joseph-Henri Réveillé-Parise, *Physiologie et hygiène des hommes livrés aux travaux de l'esprit, ou Recherches sur le physique et le moral, les habitudes, les maladies et le régime des gens de lettres, artistes, savants, hommes d'état, jurisconsultes, administrateurs*, rev. ed., ed. Dr. Ed. Carrière (Paris: J.-B. Baillière et fils, 1881), 61. First published in 1834, the book subsequently went through several further editions.

7. Lombroso, *Man of Genius*, 1; on the history of the link between melancholy and genius, see Klibansky, Panofsky, and Saxl, *Saturn and Melancholy*, and Jean Clair, ed., *Mélancolie: génie et folie en occident* (Paris: Réunion des musées nationaux, 2005).

8. Dubos, *Réflexions*, 2:175; Diderot, "Sur le génie," 19; Samuel Auguste André David Tissot, *De la santé des gens de lettres* (Lausanne: F. Grasset, 1775), 31. The first edition appeared in 1758. On the pathologizing of writers, see Anne C. Vila, "Somaticizing the Thinker: Biography, Pathography, and the Medicalization of *gens de lettres* in Eighteenth-Century France," in *Littérature et médecine: approches et perspectives (XVIᵉ–XIXᵉ siècle)*, ed. Andrea Carlino and Alexandre Wenger (Geneva: Droz, 2007), 89–111; Louis-Francisque Lélut, *Le Génie, la raison et la folie: le démon de Socrate. Application de la science psychologique à l'histoire* (Paris: Librairie J.-B. Baillière et fils, n.d.), 332.

9. On the role given to observation by the emergent profession, see Rigoli, *Lire le délire*, 51ff.

10. Pinel, letter dated 11 nivôse Year XIV, quoted by Goldstein, *Console and Classify*, 66, my emphasis; Jacques-Joseph Moreau de Tours, *Psychologie morbide: dans ses rap-*

ports avec la philosophie de l'histoire, ou de l'influence des névropathes sur le dynamisme intellectuel (Paris: V. Masson, 1859), passim. See Lélut, *Le Génie, la raison et la folie* (this was a revised and enlarged edition of *Du démon de Socrate, spécimen d'une application de la science psychologique à celle de l'histoire* [Paris: Trinquart, 1836] and *L'Amulette de Pascal pour servir à l'histoire des hallucinations* [Paris: Baillière, 1846], first published as *De l'amulette de Pascal, étude sur les rapports de la santé de ce grand homme à son génie* [Paris: impr. de Bourgogne et Martinet, 1845]). All references are to the second edition of each study; Lélut, *L'Amulette de Pascal*, 35.

11. Lélut, *Le Génie, la raison et la folie*, 48.

12. John Dryden, *Absalom and Achitophel* (1681), pt. 1, lines 163–64; Schopenhauer, *World as Will*, 1;190.. On the literary representation of the sick artist, see Françoise Grauby, *Le Corps de l'artiste: discours médical et représentations littéraires de l'artiste au XIXᵉ siècle* (Lyon: Presses universitaires de Lyon, 2001).

13. Philippe Pinel, *Traité médico-philosophique sur l'aliénation mentale, ou La manie* (Paris: Richard, Caille et Ravier, 1800), 110–11; English translation: *A Treatise on Insanity*, trans. D. D. Davis, M.D. (London: Cadell and Davies, 1806), 113–14. The translator is described as being "physician to the Sheffield Royal Infirmary" and is the author of an enthusiastic and well-informed preface that is suggestive of the degree of interest outside France in Pinel's ideas.

14. On this see Jackie Pigeaud, "Lélut et le démon de Socrate," in *Poétiques du corps: aux origines de la médecine* (Paris: Les Belles lettres, 2008), 621–56 (622).

15. Pinel, *Traité*, 70, my translation; Vila, "Somaticizing the Thinker," 98; Condillac, *Essai sur l'origine*, 146.

16. Lélut, *Le Génie, la raison et la folie*, 332.

17. Lélut, *L'Amulette de Pascal*, 4, 2–3, 21.

18. Ibid., 44.

19. Ibid., 82.

20. Ibid., 109.

21. On this, see Goldstein, *Console and Classify*, 53–54, 260, and 92.

22. Lélut, *Le Génie, la raison et la folie*, 29.

23. This remark is made in the earlier edition, *Du démon de Socrate*, 18.

24. Lélut, *Le Génie, la raison et la folie*, 174.

25. Lélut, *L'Amulette de Pascal*, xiii.

26. Lélut, *Le Génie, la raison et la folie*, 8, 16, 91.

27. Ibid., 155.

28. Ibid., 152.

29. Ibid., 251, 157–58. There is nothing unusual in Lélut's surprise, as can be seen from a modern study of Pascal in which the author, while not endorsing Lélut's diagnosis of hallucinations, sees evidence of clinical depression caused by separation in infancy and marasmus following unsuccessful weaning. See John R. Cole, *Pascal: The Man and His Two Loves* (New York: New York University Press, 1995).

30. Lélut, *L'Amulette de Pascal*, 147. Lélut was not alone in using this term for the phenomenon previously known as melancholy. Esquirol introduced the term *lypémanie* for the same condition in 1820, though it proved to be less durable than *hypocondrie*. On the classical education of medical men of Lélut's generation, see Rigoli, *Lire le délire*, 133ff.

CHAPTER 8 GENIUS, NEUROSIS, AND FAMILY TREES: MOREAU DE TOURS

1. Moreau, *Psychologie morbide*, 8.
2. Ibid., 33, 99, 109.
3. Ibid., 530.
4. Ibid., 465, 217, 464.
5. Ibid., 39, 37, 384, 386, 422, 423.
6. Ibid., 493.
7. Ibid., 494.
8. Ibid., 39, 18.
9. Ibid., 448, 390, 391, 244–45.
10. Ibid., 388, 390.
11. Ibid., 495, 426.
12. Pinel, *Traité*, 78, quoted in Rigoli, *Lire le délire*, 98; Émile Deschanel, *Physiologie des écrivains et des artistes: ou, Essai de critique naturelle* (Paris: Librairie de L. Hachette et cie, 1864), 148; Moreau, *Psychologie morbide*, 495.
13. Lélut, *Le Génie, la raison et la folie*, 205, 196.
14. Jacques-Joseph Moreau de Tours, *Du hachisch et de l'aliénation mentale: études psychologiques* (Paris: Librairie de Fortin, Masson et cie, 1845), 29–30, 4.
15. Ibid., 32–33; Moreau, *Psychologie morbide*, 230.
16. Moreau, *Psychologie morbide*, 459 (my emphasis), 458.
17. Ibid., 458, 457, 459, 460.
18. Ibid., 503.
19. Ibid., 503.
20. On the development of the profession, see Dowbiggin, *Inheriting Madness*.

CHAPTER 9 GENIUS RESTORED TO HEALTH

1. Pierre Flourens, *De la raison, du génie, et de la folie* (Paris: Garnier frères, 1861), 116.
2. Deschanel, *Physiologie des écrivains*, 150.
3. Gabriel Séailles, *Essai sur le génie dans l'art* [1883], 3rd ed. (Paris: F. Alcan, 1902), 174, 72. Séailles refers in particular to Maudsley's *The Physiology of Mind* (1876).
4. Séailles, *Essai sur le génie dans l'art*, 123.
5. Ibid., 254, 247.
6. Deschanel, *Physiologie des écrivains*, 6. Toulouse's study of Poincaré appeared as *Enquête médico-psychologique sur la supériorité intellectuelle: Henri Poincaré* (Paris: Flammarion, 1910).
7. Édouard Toulouse, *Emile Zola: Enquête intellectuelle médico-psychologique sur les rapports de la supériorité avec la névropathie* (Paris: Flammarion, 1896), xiv, 280.
8. Ibid., 1.
9. Deschanel, *Physiologie des écrivains*, 150.

10. Maurice de Fleury, *Introduction à la médecine de l'esprit* (Paris: Félix Alcan, 1897), 140, 123–24.

11. Réveillé-Parise, *Physiologie et hygiène des hommes livrés aux travaux de l'esprit* (ed. Carrière), 98, 126.

12. Zola's biographer, Henri Mitterand, points out that Toulouse accepted Zola's information about his family background on trust, without checking facts that turned out later to be erroneous, and that discretion about Zola's sex life extends to complete silence about his relationship with Jeanne Rozerot and his two illegitimate children. See Henri Mitterand, *Zola*, vol. 3, *L'Honneur 1893–1902* (Paris: Fayard, 2002), 233.

13. Toulouse, *Emile Zola*, 179, 153.

14. Ibid., 179.

15. Ibid., vi–vii.

16. Fleury, *Introduction à la médecine de l'esprit*, 147.

17. Ibid., 111.

18. Ibid., 137.

Chapter 10 A Novel of Female Genius: Mme de Staël's *Corinne*

1. Rousseau, *Lettre à Mr. d'Alembert sur les spectacles*, ed. M. Fuchs (Lille: Librairie Giard, 1948), 138–39n, quoted in English translation by Christine Battersby in *Gender and Genius*, 50. Battersby provides an energetic discussion of the gendering of genius.

2. Diderot, *Sur les femmes*, in *Œuvres*, ed. André Billy (Paris: Gallimard, Bibliothèque de la Pléiade, 1951), 958, quoted by Yvon Belaval, *L'Esthétique sans paradoxe de Diderot* (Paris: Gallimard, 1950), 152–53.

3. Julien-Joseph Virey, *De l'influence des femmes sur le goût dans la littérature et les beaux-arts, pendant le XVIIᵉ et le XVIIIᵉ siècles* (Paris: Deterville, 1810), 12–16, mentioned in Anne C. Vila, "The Scholar's Body: Health, Sexuality and the Ambiguous Pleasures of Thinking in Eighteenth-Century France," in *The Eighteenth-Century Body: Art, History, Literature, Medicine*, ed. Angelica Goodden (Oxford: Peter Lang, 2002), 115–33 (121).

4. Staël, *Essai sur les fictions*, 146; Staël, *De la littérature*, 149, 223.

5. Staël, *Essai sur les fictions*, 138, 141, 149.

6. Balzac, "Avant-propos," in *La Comédie humaine*, ed. Pierre-Georges Castex et al. (Paris: Gallimard, Bibliothèque de la Pléiade, 1976), 7–20 (8). On the masculine bias of the realist novel, see Naomi Schor, *Breaking the Chain: Women, Theory, and French Realist Fiction* (New York: Columbia University Press, 1985).

7. Reported by Balzac's sister, Laure Surville, *Balzac, sa vie et ses œuvres d'après sa correspondance* (Paris: Librairie Nouvelle, 1858), 95.

8. Staël, *De la littérature*, 139–40. On this, see Goodden, *Madame de Staël*, 85. Goodden makes it clear that Mme de Staël had little time for issues that would now be described as feminist, and invariably preferred the intellectual and social company of men to that of women.

9. Madame de Staël, *Corinne ou l'Italie* [1807], ed. Simone Balayé (Paris: Gallimard, folio classique, 1985), 51. Translation taken from Mme de Staël, *Corinne, or, Italy,*

trans. and ed. Sylvia Raphael, introduction by John Isbell (Oxford: Oxford University Press, 2008), 23. All further translations are from this edition unless otherwise indicated. Modified translations are indicated by an asterisk.

10. Staël, *Corinne*, 57/27, 582/401.

11. Ibid., 68/34.

12. Ibid., 84–85/46. Simone Balayé is the only person to have specifically addressed the issue of *gloire* in connection with Mme de Staël's portrayal of genius. See Balayé, "Le génie et la gloire," 202–14.

13. Staël, *Corinne*, 431/293, 579/399, 98/55–56.

14. Ibid., 54/24*, 55/25*.

15. Ibid., 430/291.

16. Ibid., 177/111, 55/25*.

17. Ibid., 125/76.

18. Ibid., 584/402, 216/140, 217/140.

19. Ibid., 419/284*.

20. Ibid., 410/277–78*, 516/354.

21. Madelyn Gutwirth, *Madame de Staël, Novelist: The Emergence of the Artist as Woman* (Urbana: University of Illinois Press, 1978), 299 and 259, and Goodden, *Madame de Staël*, 64 and 299; on Mme de Staël as genius, see Claudine Herrmann, "Corinne, femme de génie," *Cahiers staëliens* 35 (1984): 60–76 (60).

22. Completed in 1822, it now hangs in the Musée des Beaux-Arts in Lyon and is reproduced on the cover of the Gallimard "folio" edition of *Corinne*, as if to encourage the confusion between novelist and heroine.

23. See Béatrice Didier, *Corinne ou l'Italie de Madame de Staël* (Paris: Gallimard, 1999), 83.

24. Staël, *Corinne*, 579–80/399.

25. Ibid., 587/404.

26. Charles-Augustin Sainte-Beuve, "Madame de Staël" [1835], in *Portraits de femmes* [1844], ed. Gérald Antoine (Paris: Gallimard, folio classique, 1998), 125–216 (131).

27. He might also have mentioned Napoleon, an emblematic genius figure for the nineteenth century, who, if not directly a rival, was her tormentor, condemning her to exile, but finally conceded, after her death and during his own exile on Saint Helena, that "she would last." See Goodden, *Madame de Staël*, 4.

CHAPTER 11 BALZAC'S *LOUIS LAMBERT*: GENIUS AND THE FEMININE MEDIATOR

1. Balzac, "Des artistes," in *Œuvres diverses, L'œuvre de Balzac*, ed. Albert Béguin (Paris: Formes et reflets, 1952), 14:960–77 (964, 967).

2. Ibid., 967.

3. Quoted in Michel Lichtlé's notes to the Pléiade edition of the novel, in Balzac, *La Comédie humaine*, vol. 11, *Études philosophiques, Études analytiques*, ed. Pierre-Georges Castex (Paris: Gallimard, Bibliothèque de la Pléiade, 1980), 1600.

4. Baudelaire, *Théophile Gautier*, in *Curiosités esthétiques*, 659–88 (679).

5. Balzac, *Louis Lambert, Les Proscrits, Jésus-Christ en Flandre*, eds Raymond Abellio and Samuel S. de Sacy (Paris: Gallimard, folio classique, 1980), 43.

6. Ibid., 160; Besser, *Balzac's Concept of Genius*, 78.

7. Balzac, *Lettres à l'étrangère* (Paris: Calmann-Lévy, 1906), 15 April 1842, 30.

8. On this, see Lichtlé's introduction.

9. See Henri Evans, *Louis Lambert et la philosophie de Balzac* (Paris: J. Corti, 1951), and Per Nykrog, *La Pensée de Balzac dans la Comédie humaine: esquisse de quelques concepts-clé* (Copenhagen: Muksgaard, 1965).

10. Quoted from the manuscript of an early version of the novel in Lichtlé's notes to the Pléiade edition, 1502, my emphasis. See also Tim Farrant, *Balzac's Shorter Fiction: Genesis and Genre* (Oxford: Oxford University Press, 2002), 154.

11. For a discussion of this and for an account of genius in Balzac's entire œuvre, see Besser, *Balzac's Concept of Genius*.

12. Balzac, *Louis Lambert*, 56, 151–52, 51.

13. Ibid., 75, 71, 76.

14. Balzac, *La Peau de chagrin*, in *La Comédie humaine*, ed. Pierre-Georges Castex (Paris: Gallimard, Bibliothèque de la Pléiade, 1979), 10:104.

15. Balzac, *La Recherche de l'absolu*, ed. Raymond Abellio and S. de Sacy (Paris: Gallimard, folio, 1976), 174. The novel was written in 1834, in the period when Balzac was revising *Louis Lambert* for publication in the *Études philosophiques*. On Balzac's correspondence with Moreau de Tours, see Besser, *Balzac's Concept of Genius*, 79, and Goldstein, *Console and Classify*, 266.

16. This variant is quoted by Lichtlé, 1599.

17. Balzac, *Louis Lambert*, 58.

18. Ibid., 88, 65.

19. Ibid., 168.

20. Ibid., 79.

21. Ibid., 34.

22. Ibid., 33, 59, 62.

23. Ibid., 106, 67, 147.

24. Ibid., 95.

CHAPTER 12 CREATIVITY AND PROCREATION IN ZOLA'S *L'ŒUVRE*

1. Henri Mitterand, "Étude," editor's introduction to *L'Œuvre*, Émile Zola, *Les Rougon-Macquart*, vol. 4, ed. Armand Lanoux (Paris: Gallimard, Bibliotheque de la Pléiade, 1966), 1337–1406, 1347; Émile Zola, *L'Œuvre*, ed. Henri Mitterand (Paris: Gallimard, folio classique, 1983), 253. On Zola's familiarity with the work of Moreau de Tours, see Mitterand, *Zola*, 3:229. Both Zola and Moreau had been influenced by Prosper Lucas. See Mitterand, *Zola*, vol. 1, *Sous le regard d'Olympia (1840–1871)* (Paris: Fayard, 1999), 719ff.

2. Nana is the central figure in the novel of that title (1880), Étienne of *Germinal* (1885) the novel that immediately preceded *L'Œuvre*, and Jacques of *La Bête humaine* (1890). *L'Assommoir* appeared in 1877.

3. Mitterand, "Notice," 1364. The note from *Une page d'amour* is quoted in the "Notice," 1350. The remark from the *Ébauche* is quoted in Patrick Brady, *"L'Œuvre" de Émile Zola, roman sur les arts* (Geneva: Droz, 1967), 387. Brady's study contains the *Ébauche* in an appendix.

4. Zola, *L'Œuvre*, 402, 281. Translation from Émile Zola, *The Masterpiece*, trans. Thomas Walton and Roger Pearson, ed. Roger Pearson (Oxford: Oxford University Press, 2008), 357, 240. All further translations are from this volume, unless otherwise indicated. Modified translations are indicated by an asterisk.

5. Balzac, *Le Chef-d'œuvre inconnu*, in *La Comédie humaine*, 10:414. On the depiction of insanity in artists, see Max Milner, "Le peintre fou," *Romantisme* 66 (1989): 5–21.

6. Zola, "Après une promenade au Salon" (*Le Figaro*, 23 May 1881), in Zola, *Mon salon, Manet, Écrits sur l'art*, ed. Antoinette Ehrard (Paris: Flammarion, 1970), 353–58 (358); "L'argent dans la littérature," in *Le Roman expérimental*, ed. Aimé Guedj (Paris: Flammarion, 1971), 175–210 (208, 180). Much has been written about the possible models for Claude, and I do not intend to rehearse it here. See Mitterand's "Notice," 1341ff.; Gaëtan Picon, "Zola's Painters," *Yale French Studies* 42 (1969): 126–42; and Robert J. Niess, *Zola, Cézanne, and Manet: A Study of L'Œuvre* (Ann Arbor: University of Michigan Press, 1968).

7. Zola, *Le Roman expérimental*, 66.

8. Zola, *Mon salon*, 136; *Ébauche*, 300/38—301/39, reproduced in Brady, *"L'Œuvre" de Émile Zola*, 438.

9. Zola, *L'Œuvre*, 403–4/358.

10. Zola, *L'Œuvre*, 269/229.

11. Balzac, *La Maison du chat-qui-pelote*, in *La Comédie humaine*, 1:74.

12. Edmond and Jules de Goncourt, *Charles Demailly* [1896] (Paris: Ernest Flammarion, Eugène Fasquelle, n.d.), 191.

13. Edmond and Jules de Goncourt, *Manette Salomon* [1867] (Paris: Ernest Flammarion, Eugène Fasquelle, n.d.), 154–55.

14. Zola, *L'Œuvre*, 390/346.

15. Ibid., 117/84*, 71–72/42.

16. Ibid., 79/48–49*.

17. Ibid., 290/249*.

18. Ibid., 279/ 239*, 280/239*, 276/235.

19. Ibid., 283/242, 286/243.

20. Ibid., 66/36*; Zola, "Le Moment artistique," in *Mon salon*, 59; Zola, "Proudhon et Courbet," *Mes haines, causeries littéraires et artistiques*, in *Écrits sur l'art*, ed. Jean-Pierre Leduc-Adine (Paris: Gallimard, 1991), 41–54 (47, 44, 50); Zola, "M. H. Taine, artiste," in *Écrits sur l'art*, 63–83 (68).

21. Zola, *L'Œuvre*, 277/236*.

22. Ibid., 222/184*.

23. Ibid., 64/35*.

24. Goncourt, *Charles Demailly*, 191; *Ébauche*, 317/55–318, quoted in Brady, *"L'Œuvre" de Émile Zola*, 442–43.

25. Zola, *L'Œuvre*, 248/209.

26. Ibid., 327–28, /285–86*.

27. Zola, *Ébauche*, 429; Zola, *L'Œuvre*, 301/259*, 240–41, 296.

28. Zola, *L'Œuvre*, 404–5/359.

29. Ibid., 403–4/358.

Chapter 13 Exemplarity and Performance in Literature for Children

1. See Mary Lefkowitz, *The Lives of the Greek Poets*, 2nd ed. (Baltimore: Johns Hopkins University Press, 2012), 129; Ernst Kris and Otto Kurz, *Legend, Myth and Magic in the Image of the Artist: A Historical Experiment* [1934], trans. Alastair Laing and Lottie M. Newman (New Haven, Conn.: Yale University Press, 1979), 8.

2. Kivy, *Possessor and the Possessed*, 17.

3. Dubos, *Réflexions*, 2:177, 178.

4. Vigny, "Dernière nuit de travail," in *Chatterton*, 37–52, 44.

5. Schopenhauer, *World as Will*, 2:395–96; Michelet, *Le Peuple*, 185.

6. Baudelaire, *Le Peintre de la vie moderne*, in *Curiosités esthétiques*, 453–502 (462); "Un Mangeur d'opium," in *Les Paradis artificiels*, *Œuvres complètes*, ed. Claude Pichois. (Paris: Gallimard, Bibliothèque de la Pléiade, 1975), 2:442–517 (498)

7. Baudelaire, *Le Peintre de la vie moderne*, 462.

8. Baudelaire, *Richard Wagner et Tannhäuser à Paris*, in *Curiosités esthétiques*, 689–728 (719); *Paradis artificiels*, 498; *Morale du joujou*, in *Curiosités esthétiques*, 201–7 (203–4).

9. Balzac, *Louis Lambert*, 41–43, 45,

10. Pierre-Jean-Baptiste Nougaret, *Les Enfans célèbres chez les peuples anciens et modernes . . .* (Paris: Cretté, 1810), 180, 174.

11. V. de Laprade, *L'Éducation homicide: plaidoyer pour l'enfance* (Paris: Didier, 1868), 19, quoted by Rosemary Lloyd, *The Land of Lost Content: Children and Childhood in Nineteenth-Century French Literature* (Oxford: Clarendon, 1992), 7. Lloyd provides a good account of the rise of children's literature in France, 21ff.

12. Adrien Baillet, *Des enfans devenus célèbres par leurs études ou par leurs écrits: traité historique* (Paris: Antoine Dezallier, 1688), n.p.

13. Nougaret, *Enfans célèbres*, i, ii; Pierre Blanchard, *Modèles des enfans, traits d'humanité, de piété filiale, d'amour fraternel, et progrès extraordinaires de la part d'enfans de six à douze ans* [1810], 10th ed. (Paris: Pierre Blanchard, 1823), xi.

14. Mme Eugénie Foa, *Contes historiques pour la jeunesse* (Paris: Desforges, 1843), 229.

15. Jules Caboche-Demerville, *Panthéon de la jeunesse: vies des enfants célèbres de tous les temps et de tous les pays*, 2 vols. (Paris: Panthéon de la jeunesse, 1842–43), 1:i, iv, ii, i–ii.

16. Mme Touchard, *L'Enfance des grands hommes: étrennes dédiées à l'adolescence* (Paris: F. Didot, 1821), ix.

17. Pierre Blanchard, *Modèles des jeunes personnes, ou Traits remarquables, actions vertueuses, exemples de bonne conduite* (Paris: Pierre Blanchard, 1811), viii.

18. Louise Colet, *Enfances célèbres* (Paris: L. Hachette, 1854), i–ii. Colet had failed to find a publisher willing to take her feminist epic, *Poème de la femme*. See Francine du Plessix Gray, *Rage and Fire: A Life of Louise Colet: Pioneer Feminist, Literary Star, Flaubert's Muse* (New York: Simon & Schuster, 1994), 204.

19. Colet, *Enfances célèbres*, 378.

20. Ibid., 263, 269–70.

21. Victor Delcroix, *Les jeunes enfants illustres* (Rouen: Mégard et compagnie, 1862), 366.

22. Ibid., 359; Colet, *Enfances célèbres*, 193.

CHAPTER 14 ALFRED BINET AND THE MEASUREMENT OF INTELLIGENCE

1. See preface by Lloyd M. Dunn to the reprint edition of Alfred Binet and Théodore Simon, *The Development of Intelligence in Children*, trans. Lewis M. Terman (Nashville: Lloyd M. Dunn, 1980), vii.

2. Catherine Morris Cox et al., *The Early Mental Traits of Three Hundred Geniuses* (1926). This occupies the second volume of Lewis M. Terman et al., *Genetic Studies of Genius*, 4 vols. (Stanford, Calif.: Stanford University Press, 1926–47).

3. Hippolyte Taine, *De l'intelligence* [1870], rev. ed. (Paris: Hachette, 1883), 1:1, 2, 7.

4. Ibid., 1:373, 394.

5. On this, see Sally Shuttleworth, *The Mind of the Child: Child Development in Literature, Science, and Medicine, 1840–1900* (Oxford: Oxford University Press, 2010).

6. Bernard Perez, *L'Enfant de trois à sept ans* (Paris: Alcan, 1886), x.

7. Alfred Binet, *L'Étude expérimentale de l'intelligence* (Paris: Schleicher frères, 1903), 1, 8.

8. Alfred Binet, *Les Idées modernes sur les enfants* (Paris: Ernest Flammarion, 1909), 1.

9. Henry H. Goddard, "Introduction," in Binet and Simon, *Development of Intelligence in Children*, 5–8 (6).

10. Binet, *Les Idées modernes*, 125, 9. On the background to the project, see Serge Nicolas's preface to Alfred Binet and Théodore Simon, *L'Élaboration du premier test d'intelligence (1904–1905), Œuvres choisies*, ed. Serge Nicolas (Paris: L'Harmattan, 2004).

11. Binet, *Les Idées modernes*, 117, 125.

12. Ibid., 135, 140.

13. Alfred Binet and Théodore Simon, "Le développement de l'intelligence chez les enfants," *L'Année psychologique* 17 (1907): 1–94 (83).

14. Binet, *Les Idées modernes*, 109.

15. Binet uses this simile twice, once in "Le développement de l'intelligence" (60) and again in *Les Idées modernes* (136).

16. Alfred Binet and Camille Flammarion, *Notice sur Jacques Inaudi, le plus extraordinaire calculateur des temps modernes* (Rennes: Impr. artistique, 1925).

17. For all this, see Alfred Binet, *Psychologie des grands calculateurs et joueurs d'échecs* [1894], ed. Christophe Bourian and Serge Nicolas (Paris: L'Harmattan, 2004), 180–92.

18. Paracelse, "Le calculateur Inaudi," *Revue hebdomadaire*, 19 July 1892, 303–8.

19. http://afflictor.com/2011/04/03/old-print-article-man-with-two-brains-brooklyn-daily-eagle-1901/ (accessed 6 March 2013).

20. Binet, *Psychologie des grands calculateurs*, 8.

21. Ibid., 192.

Chapter 15 Minou Drouet: The Prodigy under Suspicion

1. *Paris Match*, 26 November 1955 (no. 346) and 14 January 1956 (no. 353); Maurice Blanchot, "La grande tromperie," *La Nouvelle Revue Française* 54 (June 1957): 1061–73, repr. in Maurice Blanchot, *La Condition critique: articles 1945–1998*, ed. Christophe Bident (Paris: Gallimard, 2010), 241–53 (247). Translated as "The Great Hoax" by Anne Smock, in *The Blanchot Reader*, ed. Michael Holland (Oxford: Basil Blackwell, 1995), 157–66 (161).

2. Jean Cocteau, *Les Enfants terribles* [1929] (Paris: Le Livre de poche, 1966), 57. On the literature of adolescence, see Justin O'Brien, *The Novel of Adolescence in France: The Study of a Literary Theme* (New York: Columbia University Press, 1937). O'Brien is careful to distinguish between childhood and adolescence. He identifies the years 1890–1930 as those of the "novel of adolescence," and he limits the category to novels in which the characters remain adolescents—thus excluding Proust.

3. "À propos de l'affaire Minou Drouet," *Elle*, no. 520 (12 December 1955): 32–33 (32).

4. Sabine Sicaud, *Poèmes d'enfant*, preface by Mme la Comtesse de Noailles (Poitiers: Les Cahiers de France, 1926), 5–7 (5, 6); Sabine Sicaud, *Les Poèmes de Sabine Sicaud*, ed. François Millepierres (Paris: Stock, 1958), 9.

5. *Prélude à la gloire* (1949) and *L'Appel du destin* (1952), both directed by Georges Lacombe.

6. Claude-Edmonde Magny, ed., *Les Enfants célèbres* (Paris: L. Mazenod, 1949).

7. The *Chasse spirituelle* episode is recounted in full by Bruce Morrissette, *The Great Rimbaud Forgery: The Affair of La Chasse spirituelle* (St. Louis, Mo.: Washington University, Committee on Publications, 1956).

8. The case is included in the list of child prodigies in history assembled in the issue of *Elle* dated 12 December 1955 (no. 520). The comment in *L'Aurore* is quoted in André Parinaud, *L'Affaire Minou Drouet: petite contribution à une histoire de la Presse* (Paris: Julliard, 1956), 67. Parinaud provides a detailed and largely nonpartisan account of the *affaire*, and includes extracts from a number of relevant documents that appeared at the time.

9. Minou Drouet, *Ma vérité*, ed. Jean-Max Tixier (Paris: Edition °1, LGP, 1993), 74. Françoise Mallet-Joris published her first novel, *Le Rempart des Béguines*, with Julliard in 1951.

10. Cited in Parinaud, *L'Affaire Minou Drouet*, 68.

11. Drouet, *Ma vérité*, 22.

12. The literary critic Robert Kemp made a similar claim in *Les Nouvelles littéraires* on 20 October. On this issue, see Parinaud, *L'Affaire Minou Drouet*, 22 and 60.

13. Quoted in Parinaud, *L'Affaire Minou Drouet*, 20, 22, 24.

14. Quoted in ibid., 61, 59.

15. Quoted in ibid., 140, 141.

16. See the article in *L'Express*, "Minou Drouet demande la confiance," 16 November 1955, 6–7.

17. Michel de Saint-Pierre, "Minou Drouet, à vos poupées!," quoted by Michèle Perrein in her article "L'affaire Minou Drouet: enfant prodige ou imposture prodigieuse,"

Elle, no. 516 (14 November 1955): 40–43 and 100–101 (40); for the gendering of literary precocity, see vol 3. of Terman et al., *Genetic Studies of Genius*, 458.

18. The detail and distortions of all of this are set out by Parinaud, *L'Affaire Minou Drouet*, 114–22.

19. Ibid., 133.

20. Ibid., 236; Drouet, *Ma vérité*, 17.

21. Parinaud, *L'Affaire Minou Drouet*, 16.

22. Drouet, *Ma vérité*, 76.

23. Proust's views on genius are discussed by Richard Terdiman in *Present Past: Modernity and the Memory Crisis* (Ithaca, N.Y.: Cornell University Press, 1993), 171ff.

CHAPTER 16 CULTURAL CRITIQUE AND THE END OF GENIUS: BARTHES, SARTRE

1. On the Soviet proposals for research into genius, see Irina Sirotkina, *Diagnosing Literary Genius: A Cultural History of Psychiatry in Russia, 1880–1930* (Baltimore: Johns Hopkins University Press, 2002), 162–63. For a recent discussion of the approach to gifted children in France, see Wilfried Lignier, *La petite noblesse de l'intelligence: une sociologie des enfants surdoués* (Paris: La Découverte, 2012). The term "surdoué" became established during the 1970s and is regarded as politically contentious by some who prefer the term "précoce." On Einstein's brain, see Sandra F. Witelson, Debra L. Kigar, and Thomas Harvey, "The Exceptional Brain of Albert Einstein," *Lancet* 353 (1999): 2149–53.

2. Robert Musil, *The Man without Qualities*, trans. Sophie Wilkins and Burton Pike (London: Picador, 1997), 42; Isaac Babel, "Awakening," in *Red Cavalry and Other Stories*, trans. David McDuff, ed. Efraim Sicher (London: Penguin, 2005), 59–60. "Awakening" dates from 1930; André Breton, *Manifestes du surréalisme* [1962] (Paris: Gallimard, idées, 1972), 38, 42.

3. On this, see Marie Gil's biography, *Roland Barthes: au lieu de la vie* (Paris: Flammarion, 2012), chap. 4.

4. "Narrative essay" is the term used by Jacques Lecarme, "Sartre palimpseste," in *Pourquoi et comment Sartre a écrit "Les mots": genèse d'une autobiographie*, ed. Michel Contat (Paris: Presses universitaires de France, 1996), 183–248 (193).

5. Roland Barthes, *Mythologies*, in *Œuvres complètes*, ed. Éric Marty (Paris: Éditions du Seuil, 1993), 1:561–722 (618); translation from Roland Barthes, *Mythologies*, trans. Annette Lavers and Siân Reynolds, rev. ed. (London: Vintage, 2009), 77.

6. Barthes, *Mythologies*, 618/78, 619/79. For the iPad app, see http://www.wired.com/wiredscience/2012/09/einstein-brain-app/ (accessed 28 September 2012).

7. Barthes, *Mythologies*, 657. The other pieces in *Mythologies* that deal with children are "Romans et enfants," "Jouets," and "Bichon chez les nègres."

8. Barthes, *Mythologies*, 658, 661

9. Ibid., 658, 659.

10. See Annie Cohen-Solal, *Sartre* (Paris: Gallimard, 1985), 484–85.

11. "À propos de l'affaire Minou Drouet," 32.

12. Jean-Paul Sartre, *Les Mots* [1964] (Paris: Gallimard, folio, 1974), 120, 28–29.

13. Minou was successfully operated in 1955 to correct bilateral diplopia. See Drouet, *Ma vérité*, 53–55.

14. Sartre, *Les Mots*, 72.

15. Ibid., 36. Barthes's comment is on p. 661 of *Mythologies*.

16. Sartre, *Les Mots*, 208, 55–56.

17. Ibid., 59, 94, 124.

18. Ibid., 62. Barthes's phrase comes from *Mythologies*, 661.

19. Sartre, *Les Mots*, 170, 172, 174. On Sartre's childhood reading, see Philippe Lejeune, "Les souvenirs de lectures d'enfance de Sartre," in *Lectures de Sartre*, ed. Claude Burgelin (Lyon: Presses universitaires de Lyon, 1986), 51–87.

20. Simone de Beauvoir, *La Cérémonie des adieux; suivi de Entretiens avec Jean-Paul Sartre, août-septembre 1974* [1981] (Paris: Gallimard, folio, 1987), 229.

CHAPTER 17 THE RETURN OF GENIUS: MAD POETS

1. For recent research, see the bibliography in Andrew Robinson, *Genius: A Very Short Introduction* (Oxford: Oxford University Press, 2011), most of which dates since 2000. For the neuroscientific approach, see Nancy C. Andreasen, *The Creating Brain: The Neuroscience of Genius* (New York: Dana Press, 2005).

2. Sigmund Freud, *Moses and Monotheism*, trans. Katherine Jones, 2nd ed. (London: Hogarth Press, 1940), 105.

3. The poems from Hölderlin's period of madness were published in German for the first time only in 1910, the year after Wilhelm Lange-Eichbaum's *Hölderlin: Eine Pathographie* (Stuttgart: F. Enke, 1909). For Pinel's remark, see chapter 7 above.

4. Pierre-Jean Jouve, *Poèmes de la folie de Hölderlin*, trans. Pierre Jean Jouve and Pierre Klossowski, introduction by Bernard Groethuysen (Paris: J.-O. Fourcade, 1930). Three of the poems in the volume and the "Première visite de Waiblinger à Hölderlin" appeared in the literary review *Bifur*, no. 3 (September 1929): 119–25. Two other translations of Hölderlin appeared in the same year, *Hypérion ou l'Hermite en Grèce*, by Joseph Delage, and *La Mort d'Empédocle* by André Babelon.

5. Martin Heidegger, "Hölderlin et l'essence de la poésie," in *Qu'est-ce que la métaphysique?*, trans. Henry Corbin (Paris: NRF/Gallimard, 1951), 231–52; Maurice Blanchot, "Hölderlin," *L'Observateur*, no. 17 (3 August 1950): 19. The reference is to Ernest Tonnelat, *L'œuvre poétique et la pensée religieuse de Hölderlin* (1950). A biography by Pierre Bertaux, *Hölderlin, Essai de biographie intérieure* (1936) had portrayed Hölderlin's insanity as a cover for political radicalism.

6. Maurice Blanchot, "La Folie par excellence," *Critique* 45 (February 1951): 99–118. Jouve's lectures were broadcast in June and July 1951. All references to Blanchot's essay are to the preface in Karl Jaspers, *Strindberg et Van Gogh, Swedenborg, Hölderlin: Étude psychiatrique comparative*, trans. Hélène Naef [1953] (Paris: Éditions de Minuit, 1990). Blanchot's comment appears on p. 28. In 1970 Blanchot appended a note to the essay, reevaluating the term "folie" as requiring "an interrogative position," so that the very assertion "Hölderlin was mad" has to be followed immediately by the question "but was he?"; ibid., 30.

7. Pierre Jean Jouve, *Folie et génie* (Paris: Fata Morgana, 1983), 51.

8. Ibid., 25.

9. Quoted in ibid., 47, 56.

10. Ibid., 39; Pierre Jean Jouve, *Sueur de sang*, in *Œuvre*, ed. Jean Starobinski (Paris: Mercure de France, 1987), 1:199, 196; Pierre Jean Jouve, *En Miroir*, in *Œuvre*, 2:1051–1191 (1123). On Jouve's depressive tendencies, see Béatrice Bonhomme, *Pierre Jean Jouve: la quête intérieure: biographie* (Croissy-Beaubourg: Aden, 2008).

11. Pierre Jean Jouve, *Apologie du poète (suivi de) Six lectures* [1947] (Fontfroide-le-Haut: Fata Morgana, 1987), 39–40.

12. David Gascoyne, *Hölderlin's Madness* (London: J. M. Dent & Sons, 1938). The book is remarkably similar to Jouve's volume, consisting of an introductory essay followed by English versions of many of the Hölderlin poems translated by Jouve, with the addition of a few poems of his own. Gascoyne also translated some of Jouve's poetry: Pierre Jean Jouve, *Despair Has Wings: Selected Poems of Pierre Jean Jouve*, trans. David Gascoyne, ed. with an introductory essay by Roger Scott (London: Enitharmon Press, 2007). "Moments d'une psychanalyse" was first published in the *NRF* in March 1933, no. 234. It is included in vol. 2 of the *Œuvre*. See the editorial note in vol. 2, 1553.

13. Margaret Callander says of this collection that it "seems to lack the usual coherence of Jouve's poetry." Margaret Callander, *The Poetry of Pierre Jean Jouve* (Manchester: Manchester University Press, 1965), 262. The title of the collection may be an allusion to the last poem in Rimbaud's *Illuminations* from which the epigraph to my own book is taken.

14. Jouve, *Folie et génie*, 25, 26, 57–58, quoting from Blanchot, "La Folie par excellence," 17.

15. Blanchot, "La Folie par excellence," 18, 19, 17.

16. Ibid., 13, 12, 11.

17. Maurice Blanchot, "Freud," *Nouvelle Revue Française*, no. 45 (September 1956): 484–96. The article was later published as "La parole analytique" in *L'Entretien infini* (Paris: Gallimard, 1969), 343–54 (343, 351). On Blanchot's medical training, see Christophe Bident, *Maurice Blanchot: partenaire invisible* (Paris: Champ Vallon, 1998), 49.

18. Jouve, *Folie et génie*, 27; Blanchot, "La Folie par excellence," 23.

Chapter 18 Julia Kristeva and Female Genius

1. Julia Kristeva, *Le Génie féminin: la vie, la folie, les mots, 3. Colette* [2002] (Paris: Gallimard, folio essais, 2008), 539.

2. Hannah Arendt, *The Human Condition* [1958], rev. ed., introduced by Margaret Canovan (Chicago: University of Chicago Press, 1998), 210–11.

3. Julia Kristeva, *Le Génie féminin: la vie, la folie, les mots, 1. Hannah Arendt* [1999] (Paris: Gallimard, folio essais, 2003), 8.

4. Kristeva, *Colette*, 9, 540. See Julia Kristeva, *Les nouvelles maladies de l'âme* (Paris: Fayard, 1993).

5. Kristeva, *Arendt*, 26, 76.

6. Julia Kristeva, *Le Génie féminin: la vie, la folie, les mots, 2. Melanie Klein* [2000] (Paris: Gallimard, folio essais, 2006), 22, 69.

7. Kristeva, *Arendt*, 277–78, my emphasis.

8. Kristeva, *Colette*, 178, 30.

9. Ibid., 15, 42.
10. Kristeva, *Arendt*, 9; Kristeva, *Colette*, 540.
11. Hugo, *William Shakespeare*, 377. See chapter 6 above.
12. Kristeva, *Klein*, 24–25.
13. Ibid., 252, 253, 254. The reference to mental hermaphroditism is in Kristeva, *Colette*, 564.
14. Kristeva, *Colette*, 566.
15. Kristeva, *Klein*, 395; Kristeva, *Colette*, 543, 566.

Chapter 19 Derrida, Cixous, and the Impostor

1. Jacques Derrida, *Genèses, généalogies, genres et le génie: Les secrets de l'archive* (Paris: Galilée, 2003), 9.
2. Ibid., 11, 12.
3. Ibid., 14, 13.
4. Ibid., 32.
5. Ibid., 87, 88. This situation is analyzed extensively by Derrida in his *Donner le temps, I. La Fausse monnaie* (Paris: Galilée, 1998).
6. Derrida, *Genèses, généalogies, genres et le génie*, 55.
7. Ibid., 57–58; Hélène Cixous, *Manhattan: lettres de la préhistoire* (Paris: Galilée, 2002), 77 and passim.
8. Cixous, *Manhattan*, 84, 85.
9. Ibid., 196, 215.
10. Ibid., 217, 222, 231 (Cixous omits punctuation here in the original French).
11. Gertrude Stein, *The Autobiography of Alice B. Toklas* [1933] (London: Arrow Books, 1960), 9. On Stein and the idea of genius, see Barbara Will, *Gertrude Stein, Modernism, and the Problem of "Genius"* (Edinburgh: Edinburgh University Press, 2000).
12. Alex Danchev, *Georges Braque: A Life* (New York: Arcade, 2005), 226.
13. Salvador Dali, *Journal d'un génie*, ed. Michel Déon (Paris: La Table Ronde, 1964), 13. English translation from *Diary of a Genius*, trans. Richard Howard, ed. Michel Déon (London: Picador, 1976), 11.
14. Plato, "Ion," 530c–d.
15. Cixous, *Manhattan*, 232.
16. Derrida, *Genèses, généalogies, genres et le génie*, 81, 67–68.
17. Ibid., 83, 11.

Bibliography

Abrams, M. H. *The Mirror and the Lamp: Romantic Theory and the Critical Tradition* [1953]. London: Oxford University Press, 1971.

Addison, Joseph, and Richard Steele. *Critical Essays from the Spectator*. Edited by Donald F. Bond. Oxford: Clarendon, 1970.

Agamben, Giorgio. "Genius." In *Profanations* [2005], translated by Jeff Fort, 9–18. New York: Zone Books, 2007.

Alletz, Édouard. *Génie du dix-neuvième siècle, ou Esquisse des progrès de l'esprit humain depuis 1800 jusqu'à nos jours*. Paris: Paulin, 1842–43.

Andreasen, Nancy C. *The Creating Brain: The Neuroscience of Genius*. New York: Dana Press, 2005.

Arendt, Hannah. *The Human Condition* [1958]. Revised edition. Introduced by Margaret Canovan. Chicago: University of Chicago Press, 1998.

Ariès, Philippe. *Centuries of Childhood: A Social History of Family Life*. Translated by Robert Baldick. New York: Random House, 1962.

———. *L'Enfance et la vie familiale sous l'Ancien Régime*. Paris: Plon, 1960.

Aristotle. *L'Homme de génie et la mélancolie: Problème XXX,1*. Edited by Jackie Pigeaud Rivages Poche/Petite Bibliothèque. Paris: Rivages, 1991.

———. *Problems: Books 32–38. Rhetorica ad Alexandrum*. Translated by W. S. Hett and H. Rackham. Revised edition. Loeb Classical Library. Cambridge, Mass.: Harvard University Press, 1957.

Ayrolles, Bertrand d', ed. *Dictionnaire classique de Géographie Ancienne, pour l'intelligence des auteurs anciens, Servant d'introduction à celui de la Géographie moderne de Laurent Echard, ou description abrégée des Monarchies, des Royaumes, . . . depuis le commencement du monde, jusqu'à la décadence de l'Empire Romain dans lequel on donne une idée succinte du Genie, des Moeurs, de la Religion, . . . des Peuples de la terre sous les différentes Dominations des Perses, des Assyriens, des Grecs & des Romains*. Paris: Lacombe, libr., 1768.

Babel, Isaac. *Red Cavalry and Other Stories*. Translated by David McDuff. Edited by Efraim Sicher. London: Penguin, 2005.

Baillet, Adrien. *Des enfans devenus célèbres par leurs études ou par leurs écrits: traité historique*. Paris: Antoine Dezallier, 1688.

Balayé, Simone. "Le génie et la gloire dans l'œuvre de M.me de Staël." *Rivista di letteratura moderne et comparate* 20, nos. 3–4 (1967): 202–14.

Balzac, Honoré de. *La Comédie humaine*, vol. 1. Edited by Pierre-Georges Castex et al. Paris: Gallimard, Bibliothèque de la Pléiade, 1976.

———. *La Comédie humaine*, vol. 11: *Études philosophiques, Études analytiques*. Edited by Pierre-Georges Castex. Paris: Gallimard, Bibliothèque de la Pléiade, 1980.

—. "Des artistes." In *Œuvres diverses, L'œuvre de Balzac*, vol. 14, edited by Albert Béguin, 960–77. Paris: Formes et reflets, 1952.

—. *Lettres à l'étrangère*. Paris: Calmann-Lévy, 1906.

—. *Louis Lambert, Les Proscrits, Jésus-Christ en Flandre*. Edited by Raymond Abellio and Samuel S. de Sacy. Paris: Gallimard, folio classique, 1980.

—. *La Peau de chagrin*. In *La Comédie humaine*, vol. 10, edited by Pierre-Georges Castex, 57–294. Paris: Gallimard, Bibliothèque de la Pléiade, 1979.

—. *La Recherche de l'absolu*. Edited by Raymond Abellio and S. de Sacy. Paris: Gallimard, folio, 1976.

Barthes, Roland. *Mythologies*. Translated by Annette Lavers and Siân Reynolds. Revised edition. London: Vintage, 2009.

—. *Œuvres complètes*. 3 vols. Edited by Éric Marty. Paris: Éditions du Seuil, 1993.

Bate, Jonathan. *The Genius of Shakespeare*. 2nd edition. London: Picador, 2008.

Battersby, Christine. *Gender and Genius: Towards a Feminist Aesthetics*. London: Women's Press, 1994.

Batteux, Charles. *Les Beaux-arts réduits à un même principe* [1746]. Edited by Jean-Rémy Mantion. Paris: Aux Amateurs des livres, 1989.

Baudelaire, Charles. *Curiosités esthétiques, L'Art romantique et Autres œuvres critiques de Baudelaire*. Edited by Henri Lemaitre. Paris: Editions Garnier, 1986.

—. *Œuvres complètes*. 2 vols. Edited by Claude Pichois. Paris: Gallimard, Bibliothèque de la Pléiade, 1975.

Baumgarten, Alexander Gottlieb. *Meditationes philosophicae de nonnullis ad poema pertinentibus* [Reflections on poetry]. Halle, 1735.

Beauvoir, Simone de. *La Cérémonie des adieux; suivi de Entretiens avec Jean-Paul Sartre, août-septembre 1974* [1981]. Paris: Gallimard, folio, 1987.

Becker, George. *The Mad Genius Controversy: A Study in the Sociology of Deviance*. Beverly Hills, Calif.: Sage, 1978.

Becq, Annie. *Genèse de l'esthétique française moderne: de la raison classique à l'imagination créatrice*. Paris: Droz, 1994.

Belaval, Yvon. *L'Esthétique sans paradoxe de Diderot*. Paris: Gallimard, 1950.

Bénichou, Paul. *Les Mages romantiques*. Paris: Gallimard, 1988.

—. *Le Sacre de l'écrivain, 1750–1830: Essai sur l'avènement d'un pouvoir spirituel laïque dans la France moderne*. Paris: J. Corti, 1973.

Besser, Gretchen R. *Balzac's Concept of Genius: The Theme of Superiority in the "Comédie Humaine."* Geneva: Droz, 1969.

Bident, Christophe. *Maurice Blanchot: partenaire invisible*. Paris: Champ Vallon, 1998.

Binet, Alfred. *L'Étude expérimentale de l'intelligence*. Paris: Schleicher frères, 1903.

—. *Les Idées modernes sur les enfants*. Paris: Ernest Flammarion, 1909.

—. *Psychologie de la création littéraire: œuvres choisies I*. Preface by Serge Nicolas. Edited by Christophe Mouchiroud and Todd I. Lubart. Paris: L'Harmattan, 2006.

—. *Psychologie des grands calculateurs et joueurs d'échecs* [1894]. Edited by Christophe Bourian and Serge Nicolas. Paris: L'Harmattan, 2004.

Binet, Alfred, and Camille Flammarion. *Notice sur Jacques Inaudi, le plus extraordinaire calculateur des temps modernes*. Rennes: Impr. artistique, 1925.

Binet, Alfred, and Théodore Simon. "Le développement de l'intelligence chez les enfants." *L'Année psychologique* 17 (1907): 1–94. Translated as *The Development of Intelligence in Children* by Lewis M. Terman. Nashville: Lloyd M. Dunn, 1980.

——. *L'Élaboration du premier test d'intelligence (1904–1905), Œuvres choisies*. Edited with a preface by Serge Nicolas. Paris: L'Harmattan, 2004.

Blanchard, Pierre. *Modèles des enfans, traits d'humanité, de piété filiale, d'amour fraternel, et progrès extraordinaires de la part d'enfans de six à douze ans* [1810]. 10th edition. Paris: Pierre Blanchard, 1823.

——. *Modèles des jeunes personnes, ou Traits remarquables, actions vertueuses, exemples de bonne conduite*. Paris: Pierre Blanchard, 1811.

Blanchot, Maurice. *La Condition critique: articles 1945–1998*. Edited by Christophe Bident. Paris: Gallimard, 2010.

——. *L'Entretien infini*. Paris: Gallimard, 1969.

——. "La Folie par excellence." *Critique* 45 (February 1951): 99–118.

——. "La Folie par excellence." Preface to Karl Jaspers, *Strindberg et Van Gogh. Swedenborg-Hölderlin* [1953], translated by Helene Naef, 7–32. Paris: Éditions de Minuit, 1990.

——. "Freud." *Nouvelle Revue Française*, no. 45 (September 1956): 484–96.

——. "The Great Hoax." In *The Blanchot Reader*, translated by Anne Smock, edited by Michael Holland, 157–66. Oxford: Basil Blackwell, 1995.

——. "Hölderlin." *L'Observateur*, no. 17 (3 August 1950): 19.

Boileau. *L'Art poétique*. In *Œuvres complètes*, edited by Antoine Adam and Françoise Escal, 157–85. Paris: Gallimard, Bibliothèque de la Pléiade, 1966.

Bonhomme, Béatrice. *Pierre Jean Jouve: la quête intérieure: biographie*. Croissy-Beaubourg: Aden, 2008.

Bonnet, Charles. *Essai analytique sur les facultés de l'âme* [1760]. Edited by Serge Nicolas. Paris: L'Harmattan, 2006.

Borel, Jacques. *Médecine et psychiatrie balzaciennes: la science dans le roman*. Paris: J. Corti, 1971.

Bouhours, Dominique. *Les Entretiens d'Ariste et d'Eugène* [1671]. Edited by Ferdinand Brunot. Paris: A. Colin, 1962.

Bowie, Theodore. *The Painter in French Fiction: A Critical Essay*. Chapel Hill: University of North Carolina, 1950.

Brady, Patrick. *"L'Œuvre" de Émile Zola, roman sur les arts*. Geneva: Droz, 1967.

Breton, André. *Manifestes du surréalisme* [1962]. Paris: Gallimard, idées, 1972.

Brissette, Pascal. *La Malédiction littéraire: du poète crotté au génie malheureux*. Montreal: Presses de l'Université de Montréal, 2005.

Caboche-Demerville, Jules. *Panthéon de la jeunesse: vies des enfants célèbres de tous les temps et de tous les pays*. 2 vols. Paris: Panthéon de la jeunesse, 1842–43.

Callander, Margaret. *The Poetry of Pierre Jean Jouve*. Manchester: Manchester University Press, 1965.

Carpentier, Mlle Émilie. *Les Enfants célèbres* [1869]. Paris: A. Rigaud, 1872.

Cave, Terence. *Mignon's Afterlives: Crossing Cultures from Goethe to the Twenty-First Century*. Oxford: Oxford University Press, 2011.

Chateaubriand, François René. *Essai sur les révolutions; Génie du christianisme*. Edited by Maurice Regard. Paris: Gallimard, Bibliothèque de la Pléiade, 1978.

Chênedollé, Charles de. *Le Génie de l'homme* [1807]. In *Œuvres complètes de Chênedollé*, revised edition, xix–205. Preface by Sainte-Beuve. Paris: Firmin-Didot, 1864.

Chouillet, Jacques. *La Formation des idées esthétiques de Diderot*. Paris: Librairie Armand Colin, 1973.

———. *L'Esthétique des lumières*. Paris: Presses universitaires de France, 1974.

Cicero. *De Oratore*. Edited by H. Rackham. Translated by E. W. Sutton. Loeb Classical Library. Cambridge, Mass.: Harvard University Press, 1967.

Cixous, Hélène. *Manhattan: lettres de la préhistoire*. Paris: Galilée, 2002.

Clair, Jean, ed. *Mélancolie: génie et folie en occident*. Paris: Réunion des musées nationaux, 2005.

Clark, Timothy. *The Theory of Inspiration: Composition as a Crisis of Subjectivity in Romantic and Post-Romantic Writing*. Manchester: Manchester University Press, 1997.

Cocteau, Jean. *Les Enfants terribles* [1929]. Paris: Le Livre de poche, 1966.

Cohen-Solal, Annie. *Sartre*. Paris: Gallimard, 1985.

Cole, John R. *Pascal: The Man and His Two Loves*. New York: New York University Press, 1995.

Coleridge, Samuel Taylor. "On Poesy or Art." In *Biographia Literaria*, vol. 2, edited by J. Shawcross, 253–63. Oxford: Oxford University Press, 1979.

Colet, Louise. *Enfances célèbres*. Paris: L. Hachette, 1854.

Condillac, Étienne Bonnot de. *Dictionnaire des synonymes*. In *Œuvres philosophiques de Condillac*, vol. 3, edited by Georges Le Roy. Paris: Presses universitaires de France, 1951.

———. *Essai sur l'origine des connaissances humaines* [1746]. Edited by Charles Porset. Preface by Jacques Derrida, "L'archéologie du frivole," 13–95. Paris: Galilée, 1973.

Condorcet, Jean-Antoine-Nicolas de Caritat, Marquis de. *Esquisse d'un tableau historique des progrès de l'esprit*. Edited by Jean-Pierre Schandeler and Pierre Crépel. Paris: Institut national d'études démographiques, 2004.

Contat, Michel, ed. *Pourquoi et comment Sartre a écrit "Les Mots": genèse d'une autobiographie*. Paris: Presses universitaires de France, 1996.

Cox, Catherine Morris, Lela O. Gillan, Ruth Haines Livesay, and Lewis M. Terman. *The Early Mental Traits of Three Hundred Geniuses. Genetic Studies of Genius*. Vol. 2. Stanford, Calif.: Stanford University Press, 1926.

Currie, Robert. *Genius: An Ideology in Literature*. London: Chatto & Windus, 1974.

D'Alembert, Jean le Rond. *Discours préliminaire de l'Encyclopédie*. Edited by Michel Malherbe. Paris: Vrin, 2000. Translated as *Preliminary Discourse to the Encyclopedia of Diderot* by Richard N. Schwab. Chicago: University of Chicago Press, 1995.

Dalí, Salvador. Salvador Dali, *Journal d'un génie*. Edited by Michel Déon. Paris: La Table Ronde, 1964. Translated as *Diary of a Genius* by Richard Howard. Edited by Michel Déon. London: Picador, 1976.

Danchev, Alex. *Georges Braque: A Life*. New York: Arcade, 2005.

Daudet, Alphonse. *Les Femmes d'artistes*. Edited by Martine Reid. Arles: Actes sud, 1997.

Delcroix, Victor. *Les jeunes enfants illustres*. Rouen: Mégard et compagnie, 1862.

Derrida, Jacques. *Donner le temps, I. La Fausse monnaie*. Paris: Galilée, 1998.

———. *Genèses, généalogies, genres et le génie: les secrets de l'archive*. Paris: Galilée, 2003.

———. "L'archéologie du frivole." In Condillac, *Essai sur l'origine des connaissances humaines*, 13–95.

Deschanel, Émile Auguste Étienne Martin. *Physiologie des écrivains et des artistes: ou, Essai de critique naturelle*. Paris: Librairie de L. Hachette et cie, 1864.

Diaz, José-Luis. "L''artiste' romantique en perspective." *Romantisme* 54, no. 4 (1986): 5–23.

———. *L'Écrivain imaginaire: scénographies auctoriales à l'époque romantique*. Paris: Honoré Champion, 2007.

Diderot, Denis. *Le Neveu de Rameau*. Edited by Jean-Claude Bonnet. Paris: Flammarion, 1983. Translated as *Rameau's Nephew; and, First Satire* by Margaret Mauldon. Edited by Nicholas Cronk. Oxford: Oxford University Press, 2006.

———. *Œuvres esthétiques*. Edited by Paul Vernière. Paris: Garnier, Classiques Garnier, 1959.

———. *Œuvres philosophiques*. Edited by Paul Vernière. Paris: Garnier, Classiques Garnier, 1961.

———. *Réfutation suivie de l'ouvrage d'Helvétius intitulé l'Homme*. In *Œuvres complètes*, vol. 24, edited by Roland Desné and Annette Lorenceau, 421–767. Paris: Hermann, 2004.

———. *Salons*. 4 vols. Edited by Jean Seznec and Jean Adhémar. Oxford: Clarendon, 1957–67.

Diderot, Denis, et al. *Encyclopédie ou dictionnaire raisonné des sciences, des arts et des métiers* [1751–72]. ARTFL Project, University of Chicago. http://portail.atilf.fr/encyclopedie/index.htm.

Didier, Béatrice. *Corinne ou l'Italie de Madame de Staël*. Paris: Gallimard, 1999.

Dieckmann, Herbert. "Diderot's Conception of Genius." *Journal of the History of Ideas* 2, no. 2 (1941): 151–82.

Dowbiggin, Ian R. *Inheriting Madness: Professionalization and Psychiatric Knowledge in Nineteenth-Century France*. Berkeley: University of California Press, 1991.

Drouet, Minou. *Ma vérité*. Edited by Jean-Max Tixier. Paris: Edition °1, LGP, 1993.

———. *Poèmes et extraits de lettres*. Paris: René Julliard, 1955.

Dubos, Abbé. *Réflexions critiques sur la poésie et sur la peinture* [1719]. 4th edition [1740]. Edited by Dominique Désirat. Paris: École supérieure des Beaux-Arts, 1993.

Duchet, Michèle, and Michel Launay, eds. *Entretiens sur "Le Neveu de Rameau."* Introduced by Jean Fabre. Paris: Nizet, 1967.

Duff, William. *Critical Observations on the Writing of the Most Celebrated Writers and Original Geniuses in Poetry*. New York: Garland, 1971.

———. *An Essay on Original Genius and Its Various Modes of Exertion in Philosophy and the Fine Arts: Particularly in Poetry* [1767]. Edited by John Mahoney. Gainesville, Fla.: Scholars' Facsimiles & Reprints, 1964.

Emerson, Ralph Waldo. "Self-Reliance" [1841]. In *Selected Essays*, edited by Larzer Ziff, 175–203. Harmondsworth: Penguin, 1982.

Esquirol, Étienne. *Des Maladies mentales considérées sous les rapports médical, hygiénique et médico-légal*. 2 vols. Paris: J. B. Baillière; Ch. Savy, 1838.

Evans, Henri. *Louis Lambert et la philosophie de Balzac*. Paris: J. Corti, 1951.

Faguet, Émile. "Madame de Staël." *Revue des deux mondes* 83 (1887): 357–94.

Farrant, Tim. *Balzac's Shorter Fiction: Genesis and Genre*. Oxford: Oxford University Press, 2002.

Fellows, Otis E. "The Theme of Genius in Diderot's *Neveu de Rameau*." In *Diderot Studies 2*, edited by Otis E. Fellows and Norman L. Torrey, 168–99. Geneva: Droz, 1952.

Ficino, Marsilio. *Book of Life* [1489]. Edited and translated by Charles Boer. Dallas, Tex.: Spring, 1980.

Ficot, Françoise. "Le Fou, le sage, le philosophe, le poète." In *Entretiens sur "Le Neveu de Rameau,"* edited by Michèle Duchet and Michel Launay, 199–206. Paris: Nizet, 1967.

Fizaine, Jean-Claude. "Génie et folie dans *Louis Lambert, Gambara* et *Massimilia Doni.*" *Revue des sciences humaines* 175 (1979): 61–75.

Fleury, Maurice de. *Introduction à la médecine de l'esprit.* Paris: Félix Alcan, 1897.

Flourens, Pierre. *De la raison, du génie, et de la folie.* Paris: Garnier frères, 1861.

Foa, Mme Eugénie. *Contes historiques pour la jeunesse.* Paris: Desforges, 1843.

Foucault, Michel. *Histoire de la folie à l'âge classique* [1972]. Paris: Gallimard, Collection Tel, 1976.

Freud, Sigmund. *Moses and Monotheism.* Translated by Katherine Jones. 2nd edition. London: Hogarth Press, 1940.

Fréville, Anne-François Joachim. *Vie des enfans célèbres, ou les modèles du jeune âge.* Paris, 1797.

Fulton, Josephine, and Mensa. *Mensa Book of Total Genius.* London: Carlton, 1999.

Fumaroli, Marc. *Trois institutions littéraires.* Paris: Gallimard, folio/ histoire, 1994.

Galton, Francis. *Hereditary Genius: An Inquiry into Its Laws and Consequences* [1869]. 2nd edition. London: Macmillan, 1914.

Garber, Marjorie. *Academic Instincts.* Princeton, NJ: Princeton University Press, 2001.

Gascoyne, David. *Hölderlin's Madness.* London: J. M. Dent & Sons, 1938.

Gerard, Alexander. *An Essay on Genius* [1774]. Edited by Bernhard Fabian. Theorie und Geschichte der Literatur und der schönen Künste. Texte und Abhandlungen, no. 3. Munich: Wilhelm Fink, 1966.

Gil, Marie. *Roland Barthes: au lieu de la vie.* Paris: Flammarion, 2012.

Gilbert, M. (Nicolas-Joseph-Laurent) [sic]. *Œuvres de Gilbert* [1817]. Edited by Charles Nodier. Revised edition. Paris: Garnier, 1921.

Gill, Miranda. *Eccentricity and the Cultural Imagination in Nineteenth-Century Paris.* Oxford: Oxford University Press, 2009.

Goldschläger, Alain, Yzabelle Martineau, and Clive Thomson, eds. *Règles du genre et inventions du génie: actes du colloque international ayant eu lieu du 18–19 septembre 1998 à l'Université de Western Ontario, London, Ontario.* London, Ont.: Mestango Press, 1999.

Goldstein, Jan. *Console and Classify: The French Psychiatric Profession in the Nineteenth Century.* Cambridge: Cambridge University Press, 1987.

Goncourt, Edmond, and Jules de. *Charles Demailly* [1896]. Paris: Ernest Flammarion, Eugène Fasquelle, n.d.

———. *Manette Salomon* [1867]. Paris: Ernest Flammarion, Eugène Fasquelle, n.d.

Goodden, Angelica. *Madame de Staël: The Dangerous Exile.* Oxford: Oxford University Press, 2008.

Grappin, Pierre. *La Théorie du génie dans le préclassicisme allemande.* Paris: Presses universitaires de France, 1952.

Grauby, Françoise. *Le Corps de l'artiste: discours médical et représentations littéraires de l'artiste au XIXᵉ siècle.* Lyon: Presses universitaires de Lyon, 2001.

Gray, Francine du Plessix. *Rage and Fire: A Life of Louise Colet: Pioneer Feminist, Literary Star, Flaubert's Muse.* New York: Simon & Schuster, 1994.

Gutwirth, Madelyn. *Madame de Staël, Novelist: The Emergence of the Artist as Woman.* Urbana: University of Illinois Press, 1978.

Guyer, Paul. "Exemplary Originality: Genius, Universality, and Individuality." In *Values of Beauty: Historical Essays in Aesthetics*, 242–62. Cambridge: Cambridge University Press, 2005.

Haroche-Bouzinac, Geneviève. *Louise Élisabeth Vigée Le Brun, histoire d'un regard*. Paris: Flammarion, 2011.

Hazlitt, William. *The Selected Writings of William Hazlitt*. Vols. 4 and 6. Edited by Duncan Wu. London: Pickering & Chatto, 1998.

Heidegger, Martin. "Hölderlin et l'essence de la poésie." In *Qu'est-ce que la métaphysique?*, translated by Henry Corbin, 233–52. Paris: NRF/Gallimard, 1951.

Heinich, Nathalie. *L'Élite artiste: excellence et singularité en régime démocratique*. Paris: Gallimard, 2005.

———. "La faute, l'erreur, l'échec: les formes du ratage artistique." *Sociologie de l'art* 7 (1994) : 11–24.

Helvétius, Claude-Adrien. *De l'esprit* [1758]. Edited by François Châtelet. Verviers: Éditions Gérard & Cie., 1973.

Herrmann, Claudine. "Corinne, femme de génie." *Cahiers staëliens* 35 (1984): 60–76.

Hobson, Marian. *The Object of Art: The Theory of Illusion in Eighteenth-Century France*. Cambridge: Cambridge University Press, 1982.

Huarte, Juan. *Examen de ingenios: The examination of mens wits* [1594]. Translated out of the Spanish by M. Camillo Camilli. Translated to English out of his Italian by Richard Carew. A facsimile reproduction with an introduction by Carmen Rogers. Gainesville, Fla.: Scholars' Facsimiles & Reprints, 1959.

Hugo, Victor. *Odes et ballades*. In *L'Œuvres complètes: Poésie I*, edited by Claude Gély, 51–407. Paris: Laffont, 1985.

———. *Œuvres complètes: Critique*. Edited by Jean-Pierre Reynaud. Paris: R. Laffont, 2002.

———. *Victor Hugo raconté par un témoin de sa vie*, in *L'Œuvre complète de Victor Hugo*. Vol. 42. Paris: Jean de Bonnot, 1979.

Jaffe, Kineret S. "The Concept of Genius: Its Changing Role in Eighteenth-Century French Aesthetics." *Journal of the History of Ideas* 41, no. 4 (1980): 579–99.

James, Tony. *Dream, Creativity, and Madness in Nineteenth-Century France*. Oxford: Clarendon, 1995.

Jaspers, Karl. *Strindberg et Van Gogh, Swedenborg, Hölderlin: Étude psychiatrique comparative*. Translated by Hélène Naef [1953]. Introduction by Maurice Blanchot. Paris: Éditions de Minuit, 1990.

Jeanneret, Michel. "La folie est un rêve: Nerval et le docteur Moreau de Tours." *Romantisme* 27 (1980): 59–75.

Jefferson, Ann. *Biography and the Question of Literature in France*. Oxford: Oxford University Press, 2007.

———. "Genius and Its Others." *Paragraph* 32 (2010): 182–96.

———. "The Geography of Genius in Eighteenth-Century France." In *Enlightenment Cosmopolitanism*, edited by David Adams and Galin Tihanov, 46–57. Oxford: Legenda, MHRA, 2011.

Joly, Henri. *Psychologie des grands hommes*. 2nd edition. Paris: Hachette, 1891.

Jones, Howard Mumford. "The Doctrine of Romantic Genius." In *Revolution & Romanticism*, 261–95. Cambridge, Mass.: Belknap, 1974.

Jouve, Pierre Jean. *Apologie du poète (suivi de) Six lectures* [1947]. Fontfroide-le-Haut: Fata Morgana, 1987.

———. *Despair Has Wings: Selected Poems of Pierre Jean Jouve.* Translated by David Gascoyne. Edited with an introductory essay by Roger Scott. London: Enitharmon Press, 2007.

———. *Folie et Génie.* Paris: Fata Morgana, 1983.

———. *Génie* [1948]. Paris: Fata Morgana, 1983.

———. *Œuvre.* 2 vols. Edited by Jean Starobinski. Paris: Mercure de France, 1987.

———. *Poèmes de la folie de Hölderlin.* Translated by Pierre Jean Jouve and Pierre Klossowski. Introduction by Bernard Groethuysen. Paris: J.-O. Fourcade, 1930.

Kant, Immanuel. *Critique of Judgment* [1790]. Translated, with an introduction, by Werner S. Pluhar. Foreword by Mary J. Gregor. Indianapolis: Hackett, 1987.

Kivy, Peter. *The Possessor and the Possessed: Handel, Mozart, Beethoven, and the Idea of Musical Genius.* New Haven, Conn.: Yale University Press, 2001.

Klibansky, Raymond, Erwin Panofsky, and Fritz Saxl. *Saturn and Melancholy. Studies in the History of Natural Philosophy, Religion, and Art.* London: Nelson, 1964.

Kopp, Robert, and Dominique de Roux, eds. *Pierre Jean Jouve.* Paris: Éditions de L'Herne, 1972.

Kris, Ernst, and Otto Kurz. *Legend, Myth and Magic in the Image of the Artist: A Historical Experiment* [1934]. Translated by Alastair Laing and Lottie M. Newman. New Haven, Conn.: Yale University Press, 1979.

Kristeva, Julia. *Le Génie féminin: la vie, la folie, les mots, 1. Hannah Arendt* [1999]. Paris: Gallimard, folio essais, 2003.

———. *Le Génie féminin: la vie, la folie, les mots, 2. Melanie Klein* [2000]. Paris: Gallimard, folio essais, 2006.

———. *Le Génie féminin: la vie, la folie, les mots, 3. Colette* [2002]. Paris: Gallimard, folio essais, 2008.

———. *Les nouvelles maladies de l'âme.* Paris: Fayard, 1993.

La Harpe, Jean-François de. *Lycée, ou Cours de littérature ancienne et moderne* [1798–1804]. 14 vols. Paris: Depelafol, 1825.

Lamartine, Alphonse de. *Méditations.* Edited by Fernand Letessier. Paris: Garnier frères, 1968.

Lange-Eichbaum, Wilhelm. *Hölderlin: Eine Pathographie.* Stuttgart: F. Enke, 1909.

———. *The Problem of Genius* [1930–31]. Translated by Eden and Cedar Paul. London: K. Paul, Trench, Trübner, 1931.

Lauvrière, Émile. *Edgar Poe, sa vie et son œuvre: étude de psychologie pathologique.* Paris: Félix Alcan, 1904.

Lecarme, Jacques. "Sartre palimpseste." In *Pourquoi et comment Sartre a écrit "Les mots": genèse d'une autobiographie,* edited by Michel Contat, 183–248. Paris: Presses universitaires de France, 1996.

Le Génie de la mode. Journal de l'élégance parisienne. 1862–84.

Le Génie et ses droits. Vol. 6, *Paris vivant par des hommes nouveaux.* Paris: G. de Gonet, 1858.

Lefkowitz, Mary. *The Lives of the Greek Poets.* 2nd edition. Baltimore: Johns Hopkins University Press, 2012.

Lejeune, Philippe. "Les souvenirs de lectures d'enfance de Sartre." In *Lectures de Sartre,* edited by Claude Burgelin, 51–87. Lyon: Presses universitaires de Lyon, 1986.

Lélut, Louis-Francisque. *L'Amulette de Pascal pour servir à l'histoire des hallucinations.* Paris: Baillière, 1846. First published as *De l'amulette de Pascal, étude sur les rapports de la santé de ce grand homme à son génie.* Paris: impr. de Bourgogne et Martinet, 1845.

———. *Du démon de Socrate, spécimen d'une application de la science psychologique à celle de l'histoire.* Paris: Trinquart, 1836.

———. *Le Génie, la raison et la folie: le démon de Socrate. Application de la Science psychologique à l'histoire.* 2nd enlarged edition of *Du démon de Socrate.* Paris: Librairie J.-B. Baillière et fils, n.d. [1855].

Lévi-Strauss, Claude. *Le Totémisme aujourd'hui.* Paris: Presses universitaires de France, 1962. Translated as *Totemism* by Rodney Needham. London: Merlin Press, 1991.

Lignier, Wilfried. *La petite noblesse de l'intelligence: une sociologie des enfants surdoués.* Paris: La Découverte, 2012.

Lloyd, Rosemary. *The Land of Lost Content: Children and Childhood in Nineteenth-Century French Literature.* Oxford: Clarendon, 1992.

Loiseleur, Aurélie. *L'Harmonie selon Lamartine: utopie d'un lieu commun.* Paris: Honoré Champion, 2005.

Lombroso, Cesare. *The Man of Genius* [1877]. London: W. Scott, 1891.

Longinus. *An Essay upon Sublime.* Oxford: Printed by L.L. for T. Leigh, 1698.

Luc, M. de L. M. de l'Académie de P. *Description historique de l'Italie, en forme de dictionnaire: contenant 1) la géographie tant ancienne que moderne, . . . 2) l'esprit de leur gouvernement . . . 3) le génie des habitants, les mœurs, . . . 4) un détail circonstancié des monumens antiques, . . . 5) la description des églises, palais et édifices publics, . . . 6) un détail des peintures en mosaïques et tableaux répandus dans les églises et galeries . . . .* 2 vols. Avignon: Chambeau, 1790.

Magny, Claude-Edmonde, ed. *Les Enfants célèbres.* Paris: L. Mazenod, 1949.

Mall, James. "Le Neveu de Rameau and the Idea of Genius." *Eighteenth-Century Studies* 11, no. 1 (1977): 26–39.

Marcus, Laura. *Auto/biographical Discourses: Theory, Criticism.* Manchester: Manchester University Press, 1994.

Marmontel, Jean-François. *Éléments de littérature* [1787]. Edited by Sophie Le Ménahèze. Paris: Desjonquères, 2005.

Mason, John Hope. *The Value of Creativity: The Origins and Emergence of a Modern Belief.* Aldershot: Ashgate, 2003.

Masson, Michel. *Les Enfants célèbres, ou Histoire des enfants de tous les siècles et de tous les pays, qui se sont immortalisés par le malheur, la piété, le courage, le génie, le savoir, et les talents.* Paris: Au Bureau central des dictionnaires, 1837.

Matoré, Georges, and A.-J. Greimas. "La naissance du 'génie' au XVIIIᵉ siècle: étude lexicologique." *Le Français moderne* 25 (1957): 256–72.

McMahon, Darrin M. *Divine Fury: A History of Genius.* New York: Basic Books, 2013.

Méra, Brigitte. *Balzac et la figure mythique dans les Études philosophiques.* Paris: L'Harmattan, 2004.

Mercier, Louis-Sébastien. *Le Génie, le goût et l'esprit: poëme, en quatre chants. dédié à M. le Duc de ****.* The Hague, 1756.

Mercier-Lacombe, M. Gustave. *Naissance et génie.* Paris: H. Souverain, 1839.

Meschonnic, Henri. *Hugo, la poésie contre le maintien de l'ordre.* Paris: Maisonneuve & Larose, 2002.

Michelet, Jules. *Le Peuple* [1846]. 5th edition [1877]. Edited by Paul Viallaneix. Paris: Flammarion, 1974.

Milner, Max. "Le peintre fou." *Romantisme* 66 (1989): 5–21.

Mitterand, Henri. "Étude." In *L'Œuvre, Émile Zola, Les Rougon-Macquart*, vol. 4, edited by Armand Lanoux, 1337–1406. Paris: Gallimard, Bibliotheque de la Pléiade.

———. *Zola*. Vol. 1, *Sous le regard d'Olympia (1840–1871)*. Paris: Fayard, 1999.

———. *Zola*. Vol. 3, *L'Honneur 1893–1902*. Paris: Fayard, 2002.

Moi, Toril. "A Woman's Desire to Be Known: Expressivity and Silence in *Corinne*." In *Untrodden Regions of the Mind: Romanticism and Psychoanalysis*, edited by Ghislaine McDayter, 143–75. Lewisburg, Pa.: Bucknell University Press.

Moreau (de Tours), Jacques-Joseph. *Du hachisch et de l'aliénation mentale: études psychologiques*. Paris: Librairie de Fortin, Masson et cie, 1845.

———. *Psychologie morbide: dans ses rapports avec la philosophie de l'histoire, ou de l'influence des névropathies sur le dynamisme intellectuel*. Paris: V. Masson, 1859.

Morrissette, Bruce. *The Great Rimbaud Forgery: The Affair of La Chasse spirituelle*. St. Louis, Mo.: Washington University, Committee on Publications, 1956.

Mortier, Roland. *L'Originalité, une nouvelle catégorie esthétique au siècle des lumières*. Geneva: Droz, 1982.

Murray, Bradley. "The Notion of Genius in Kant's *Critique of Judgment*." *British Journal of Aesthetics* 47, no. 2 (2007): 199–214.

Murray, Penelope, ed. *Genius: The History of an Idea*. Oxford: Basil Blackwell, 1989.

———, ed. *Plato on Poetry: Ion; Republic 376e-398b9; Republic 595–608b10*. Cambridge: Cambridge University Press, 1997.

Musil, Robert. *The Man without Qualities* [1930–43]. Translated by Sophie Wilkins and Burton Pike. London: Picador, 1997.

Nahm, Milton C. *Genius and Creativity: An Essay in the History of Ideas*. New York: Harper Torch Books, 1965.

Newton, Joy. "Cézanne's Literary Incarnations." *French Studies* 61 (2007): 36–46.

Niess, Robert J. *Zola, Cézanne, and Manet: A Study of L'Œuvre*. Ann Arbor: University of Michigan Press, 1968.

Nitzsche, Jane Chance. *The Genius Figure in Antiquity and the Middle Ages*. New York: Columbia University Press, 1975.

Noailles, Anna de. *Poèmes d'enfance*. Paris: Bernard Grasset, 1928.

Nougaret, Pierre-Jean-Baptiste. *Les Enfans célèbres chez les peuples anciens et modernes. . . .* Paris: Cretté, 1810.

Nykrog, Per. *La Pensée de Balzac dans la Comédie humaine: esquisse de quelques concepts-clé*. Copenhagen: Muksgaard, 1965.

O'Brien, Justin. *The Novel of Adolescence in France: The Study of a Literary Theme*. New York: Columbia University Press, 1937.

Paracelse. "Le calculateur Inaudi." *Revue hebdomadaire*, 19 July 1892, 303–8.

Parinaud, André. *L'Affaire Minou Drouet: petite contribution à une histoire de la presse*. Paris: Julliard, 1956.

Perez, Bernard. *L'Enfant de trois à sept ans*. Paris: Alcan, 1886.

Perras, Jean-Alexandre. *L'Exception exemplaire: une histoire de la notion de génie du XVIe au XVIIIe siècle*. Thèse de doctorat, Université Paris 8 Vincennes Saint-Denis & Université de Montréal, 2012.

Perrault, Charles. *Parallèle des anciens et des modernes en ce qui regarde les arts et les sciences.* Edited by Hans Robert Jauss and Max Imdahl. Munich: Eidos Verlag, 1964.

Perrein, Michèle. "L'Affaire Minou Drouet: le public et le document vécu." *Arts* 16–22 (1955): 1, 6.

Picon, Gaëtan. "Zola's Painters." *Yale French Studies* 42 (1969): 126–42.

Pigeaud, Jackie. "Le génie et la folie: étude sur la *Psychologie morbide* . . . de J. Moreau de Tours." In *Littérature, médecine et société*, vol. 6, edited by Jackie Pigeaud, 1–28. Nantes: Université de Nantes, 1984. Reprinted in *Poétiques du corps*, 657–81.

———. "Lélut et le démon de Socrate." In *Littérature, Médecine et Société (La possession)*, 7–51. Nantes: Université de Nantes, 1988. Reprinted in *Poétiques du corps*, 621–56.

———. *Poétiques du corps: aux origines de la médecine.* Paris: Les Belles lettres, 2008.

Pinel, Philippe. *Traité médico-philosophique sur l'aliénation mentale, ou La manie.* Paris: Richard, Caille et Ravier, 1800. Translated as *A Treatise on Insanity* by D. D. Davis, M.D. London: Cadell and Davies, 1806.

Plato. "Ion." In *Early Socratic Dialogues*, edited and translated by Trevor J. Saunders, 49–65. London: Penguin, 1987.

Poirier, Richard. "The Question of Genius." *Raritan* 5, no. 4 (*1986*): 77–104.

Porter, Roy. "Madness and Genius." In *A Social History of Madness: Stories of the Insane*, 60–81. London: Weidenfeld & Nicolson, 1987.

Radiguet, Raymond. *Le Diable au corps.* Paris: B. Grasset, 1923.

Rémond, Antoine, and Paul Voivenel. *Le Génie littéraire.* Paris: F. Alcan, 1912.

Réveillé-Parise, Joseph-Henri. *Physiologie et hygiène des hommes livrés aux travaux de l'esprit, ou Recherches sur le physique et le moral, les habitudes, les maladies et le régime des gens de lettres, artistes, savants, hommes d'état, jurisconsultes, administrateurs, etc.* 2 vols. Paris: G.-A. Dentu, 1834.

———. *Physiologie et hygiène des hommes livrés aux travaux de l'esprit, ou Recherches sur le physique et le moral, les habitudes, les maladies et le régime des gens de lettres, artistes, savants, hommes d'état, jurisconsultes, administrateurs, etc.* Edited and revised by Dr. Ed. Carrière. Revised edition of 1834 publication. Paris: J.-B. Baillière et fils, 1881.

Rigoli, Juan. *Lire le délire, aliénisme, rhétorique et littérature en France au XIX siècle.* Paris: Fayard, 2001.

Rivarol, Antoine, comte de. *Pensées diverses, suivi de Discours sur l'universalité de la langue française, Lettre sur le globe aérostatique.* Edited by Sylvain Menant. Paris: Desjonquères, 1998.

———. *De l'universalité de la langue française.* Edited by Th. Suran. Paris: H. Didier, 1930.

Robb, Graham. *Victor Hugo* [1997]. London: Picador, 1998.

Robinson, Andrew. *Genius: A Very Short Introduction.* Oxford: Oxford University Press, 2011.

Rousseau, Jean-Jacques. *Dictionnaire de musique.* In *Écrits sur la musique, la langue et le théâtre. Œuvres complètes*, vol. 5, edited by Bernard Gagnebin, Marcel Raymond, and Samuel Baud-Bovy, 605–1191. Paris: Gallimard, Bibliothèque de la Pléiade, 1995.

———. *Lettre à Mr. d'Alembert sur les spectacles.* Edited by M. Fuchs. Lille: Librairie Giard, 1948.

Sacquin, Michèle, et al. *Le Printemps des génies: les enfants prodiges.* Paris: Bibliothèque nationale, 1993.

Sainte-Beuve, Charles-Augustin. *Chateaubriand et son groupe littéraire sous l'empire: cours professé à Liège en 1848–1849.* 2 vols. Edited by Maurice Allem. Paris: Garnier, 1949.

———. "Madame de Staël" [1835]. In *Portraits de femmes* [1844], edited by Gérald Antoine, 125–216. Paris: Gallimard, folio classique, 1998.

———. *Premiers lundis.* 3 vols. Paris: Calmann-Lévy, 1883–86.

Saisselin, Remy G. *The Rule of Reason and the Ruses of the Heart: A Philosophical Dictionary of Classical French Criticism, Critics and Aesthetic Issues.* Cleveland: Case Western Reserve University, 1970.

Sartre, Jean-Paul. *Les Mots* [1964]. Paris: Gallimard, folio, 1974.

Schaffer, Simon. "Genius in Romantic Natural Philosophy." In *Romanticism and the Sciences,* edited by N. Jardine and A. R. Cunningham, 82–98. Cambridge: Cambridge University Press, 1990.

Schmidt, Jochen. *Geschichte des Genie-Gedankens in der deutschen Literatur, Philosophie und Politik 1750–1945* [1985]. 2 vols. Revised edition. Heidelberg: Universitätsverlag Winter, 2004.

Schmidt-Dengler, Wendelin. *Genius: Zur Wirkungsgeschichte antiker Mythologeme in der Goethezeit.* Munich: Beck, 1978.

Schopenhauer, Arthur. *The World as Will and Representation* [1818]. 2 vols. Translated by E.F.J. Payne. New York: Dover, 1969.

Schor, Naomi. *Breaking the Chain: Women, Theory, and French Realist Fiction.* New York: Columbia University Press, 1985.

Schroder, Maurice. *Icarus: The Image of the Artist in French Romanticism.* Cambridge, Mass.: Harvard University Press, 1961.

Séailles, Gabriel. *Essai sur le génie dans l'art* [1883]. 3rd edition. Paris: F. Alcan, 1902.

———. *Le Génie dans l'art: anthologie des écrits esthétiques et critiques de Gabriel Séailles.* Edited by Sarah Linford and Michela Passini. Paris: Éditions Kimé, coll. "Esthétiques," 2011.

Shaftesbury, Anthony Ashley Cooper, Third Earl. *Characteristics of Men, Manners, Opinions, Times.* Edited by Lawrence E. Klein. Cambridge: Cambridge University Press, 1999.

Shuttleworth, Sally. *The Mind of the Child: Child Development in Literature, Science, and Medicine, 1840–1900.* Oxford: Oxford University Press, 2010.

Sicaud, Sabine. *Poèmes d'enfant.* Preface by Mme la Comtesse de Noailles. Poitiers: Les Cahiers de France, 1926.

———. *Les Poèmes de Sabine Sicaud.* Edited by François Millepierres. Paris: Stock, 1958.

Siouffi, Gilles. *Le Génie de la langue française: études des structures imaginaires de la description linguistique à l'âge classique.* Paris: Champion, 2010.

Sirotkina, Irina. *Diagnosing Literary Genius: A Cultural History of Psychiatry in Russia, 1880–1930.* Baltimore: Johns Hopkins University Press, 2002.

Smith, Logan Pearsall. *Four Words: Romantic, Originality, Creative, Genius.* Society for Pure English, Tract No. 17. Oxford: Clarendon, 1924.

Smith, Paul. "Literature and Art." *French Studies* 61 (2007): 1–13.

Staël, Madame de. *De l'Allemagne* [1813]. 2 vols. Edited by Simone Balayé. Paris: Flammarion, 1968.

————. *Corinne ou l'Italie* [1807]. Edited by Simone Balayé. Paris: Gallimard, folio classique, 1985. Translated as *Corinne, or, Italy* by Sylvia Raphael. Edited by Sylvia Raphael. Introduction by John Isbell. Oxford: Oxford University Press, 2008.

————. *Essai sur les fictions* [1796]. In *Œuvres de jeunesse*, edited by Simone Balayé and John Isbell, 131–56. Paris: Desjonquères, 1997.

————. *De la littérature considérée dans ses rapports avec les institutions sociales* [1799]. Edited by Axel Blaeschke. Paris: Garnier, Classiques Garnier, 1998.

Starobinski, Jean. "Diderot et la parole des autres." *Critique* 296 (1972): 3–22.

————. *La Relation critique: l'œil vivant II*. Paris: Gallimard, 1970.

Stein, Gertrude. *The Autobiography of Alice B. Toklas* [1933]. London: Arrow Books, 1960.

Steinmetz, Jean-Luc. "Du poète malheureux au poète maudit (réflexion sur la constitution d'un mythe)." *Œuvres & critiques* 7, no. 1 (1982): 75–86.

Stewart, Philip. *L'Invention du sentiment: roman et économie affective au dix-huitième siècle*. SVEC, 2010/02. Oxford: Voltaire Foundation, 2010.

Sully, James. "Genius and Precocity." *Nineteenth Century: A Monthly Review* 19, no. 112 (1886): 827–48.

Suran, Th. "Préface." In Rivarol, *De l'universalité de la langue française*, 12–161.

Surville, Laure. *Balzac, sa vie et ses œuvres d'après sa correspondance*. Paris: Librairie Nouvelle, 1858.

Taine, Hippolyte. *De l'intelligence* [1870]. Revised edition. 2 vols. Paris: Hachette, 1883.

Terdiman, Richard. *Present Past: Modernity and the Memory Crisis*. Ithaca, N.Y.: Cornell University Press, 1993.

Terman, Lewis M., et al. *Genetic Studies of Genius*. 4 vols. Stanford, Calif.: Stanford University Press, 1925–47.

Tissot, Samuel Auguste André David. *De la santé des gens de lettres*. Lausanne: F. Grasset, 1775.

Tonnelat, Ernest. *L'œuvre poétique et la pensée religieuse de Hölderlin*. Paris: M. Didier, 1950.

Touchard, Mme. *L'Enfance des grands hommes: étrennes dédiées à l'adolescence*. Paris: F. Didot, 1821.

Toulouse, Édouard. *Emile Zola: Enquête médico-psychologique sur les rapports de la supériorité intellectuelle avec la névropathie*. Paris: Flammarion, 1896.

————. *Enquête médico-psychologique sur la supériorité intellectuelle, II: Henri Poincaré*. Paris: Flammarion, 1910.

Tritter, J.-L. *Le Langage philosophique dans les œuvres de Balzac*. Paris: Nizet, 1976.

Vautré, Victor de. *Génie du whist méconnu jusqu'à présent, quoique joué avec une espèce de fureur par toute l'Europe, avec ses explications et des maximes certaines pour gagner*. Paris: Ledoyen, 1839.

Vauvenargues, Luc de Clapiers Marquis de. *Introduction à la connaissance de l'esprit humain* [1747]. Edited by Jean Dagen. Paris: Flammarion, 1981.

Vigny, Alfred de. *Chatterton*. Edited by Pierre-Louis Rey. Paris: Gallimard, folio-théâtre, 2001.

————. *Poèmes antiques et modernes, Œuvres complètes*. Vol. 1. Edited by François Germain and André Jarry. Paris: Gallimard, Bibliothèque de la Pléiade, 1986.

————. *Stello*. In *Œuvres complètes*, vol. 2, edited by Alphonse Bouvet. Paris: Gallimard, Bibliothèque de la Pléiade, 1993.

Vila, Anne C. "The Scholar's Body: Health, Sexuality and the Ambiguous Pleasures of Thinking in Eighteenth-Century France." In *The Eighteenth-Century Body: Art, History, Literature, Medicine*, edited by Angelica Goodden, 115–33. Oxford: Peter Lang, 2002.

———. "Somaticizing the Thinker: Biography, Pathography, and the Medicalization of *gens de lettres* in Eighteenth-Century France." In *Littérature et médecine: approches et perspectives (XVIᵉ-XIXᵉ siècle)*, edited by Andrea Carlino and Alexandre Wenger, 89–111. Geneva: Droz, 2007.

Virey, Julien-Joseph. "Génie." In *Dictionnaire des sciences médicales: par une société de médecins et de chirurgiens*, 60 vols., edited by M. M. Alard et al., vol. 18, 84. Paris: Panckoucke, 1812–22.

———. *De l'influence des femmes sur le goût dans la littérature et les beaux-arts, pendant le XVIIᵉ et le XVIIIᵉ siècles*. Paris: Deterville, 1810.

Voltaire. "Génie." In *Œuvres complètes de Voltaire*, vol. 5, *Dictionnaire philosophique*, 30–35. Paris: P. Dupont, 1824.

———. "Génie, Génies." In *Dictionnaire philosophique* [1764], *Œuvres de Voltaire*, vol. 30, edited by M. Beuchot, 31–40. Paris: Firmin Didot frères, 1929.

Weinrich, H. "Ingenium." in *Historisches Wörterbuch des Philosophie*, vol. 4, edited by Joachim Ritter and Karlfried Gründer, 360–63. Basel: Schwabe & Co., 1976.

Wiley, Margaret Lee. "Genius: A Problem in Definition." *University of Texas Studies in English* 16 (1936): 77–83.

Will, Barbara. *Gertrude Stein, Modernism, and the Problem of "Genius."* Edinburgh: Edinburgh University Press, 2000.

Willard, Nedd. *Le Génie et la folie au 18ᵉ s.* Paris: Presses universitaires de France, 1963.

Williams, Elizabeth A. *The Physical and the Moral. Anthropology, Physiology, and Philosophical Medicine in France, 1750–1850*. Cambridge: Cambridge University Press, 1994.

Witelson, Sandra F., Debra L. Kigar, and Thomas Harvey. "The Exceptional Brain of Albert Einstein." *Lancet* 353 (1999): 2149–53.

Wittkower, Rudolf. "Genius: Individualism in Art and Artists." In *Dictionary of the History of Ideas: Studies of Selected Pivotal Ideas*, 5 vols., edited by Philip P. Wiener, vol. 2, 297–312. New York: Charles Scribner's Sons, 1973.

———. "Imitation, Eclecticism and Genius." In *Aspects of the Eighteenth Century*, edited by Earl R. Wasserman, 143–61. Baltimore: Johns Hopkins University Press, 1965.

Wolf, Herman. *Versuch einer Geschichte des Geniebegriffs in der Deutschen Ästhetik des 18. Jahrhunderts. 1. Bd.: Von Gottsched bis auf Lessing*. Beiträge Zur Philosophie, 9. Heidelberg: C. Winter, 1923.

Woodmansee, Martha. *The Author, Art and the Market: Rereading the History of Aesthetics*. New York: Columbia University Press, 1994.

Young, Edward. *Conjectures on Original Composition* [1759]. Leeds: Scolar Press, 1966.

Zilsel, Edgar. *Le Génie. Histoire d'une notion, de l'antiquité à la renaissance* [1926]. Translated by Michel Thévenaz. Preface by Nathalie Heinich. Paris: Minuit, 1993.

Zola, Émile. *Écrits sur l'art*. Edited by Jean-Pierre Leduc-Adine. Paris: Gallimard, 1991.

———. *Mon Salon, Manet, Écrits sur l'art*. Edited by Antoinette Ehrard. Paris: Flammarion, 1970.

———. *L'Œuvre* . Edited by Henri Mitterand. Paris: Gallimard, folio classique, 1983. Translated as *The Masterpiece* by Thomas Walton and Roger Pearson. Edited by Roger Pearson. Oxford: Oxford University Press, 2008.

———. *Le Roman expérimental*. Edited by Aimé Guedj. Paris: Flammarion, 1971.

———. *Les Rougon-Macquart*. Bibliothèque de la Pléiade, 5 vols. Edited by Armand Lanoux and Henri Mitterand. Paris: Gallimard, 1960–75.

Zumthor, Paul, and Hubert Sommer. "À propos du mot 'génie.'" *Zeitschrit für romanische Philologie* 66 (1950): 170–201.

Index